DOPEWORLD

Adventures in Drug Lands

NIKO VOROBYOV

HODDER &
STOUGHTON

First published in Great Britain in 2019 by Hodder & Stoughton
An Hachette UK company

1

A CIP catalogue record for this title is available from the British Library

Hardback ISBN 9781529378016
Trade Paperback ISBN 9781529378023
eBook ISBN 9781529378047

Typeset in Adobe Caslon by Hewer Text UK Ltd, Edinburgh
Printed and bound in Great Britain by Clays Ltd, Elcograf S.p.A.

Hodder & Stoughton policy is to use papers that are natural, renewable
and recyclable products and made from wood grown in sustainable
forests. The logging and manufacturing processes are expected to conform
to the environmental regulations of the country of origin.

Hodder & Stoughton Ltd
Carmelite House
50 Victoria Embankment
London EC4Y 0DZ

www.hodder.co.uk

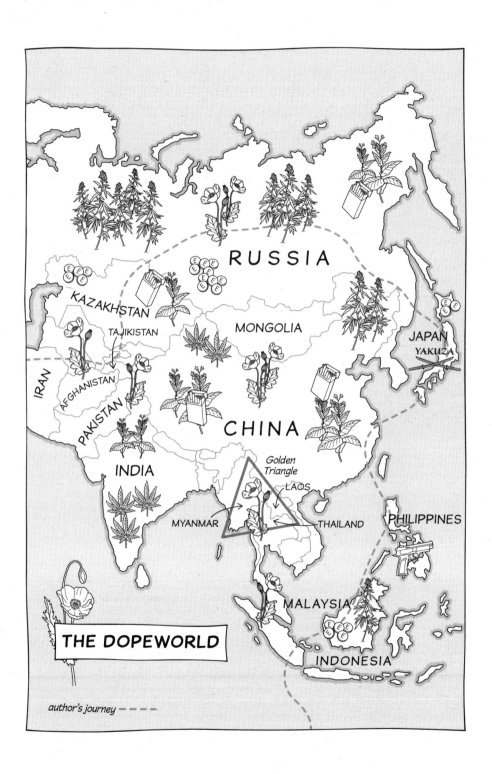

RUSSIA

KAZAKHSTAN

TAJIKISTAN

IRAN

AFGHANISTAN

PAKISTAN

INDIA

MONGOLIA

CHINA

JAPAN
YAKUZA

Golden
Triangle

LAOS

MYANMAR

THAILAND

PHILIPPINES

MALAYSIA

INDONESIA

THE DOPEWORLD

author's journey - - - - -

For my family and everyone else I've let down.

Contents

dopeworld *(noun):* the global social, economic and criminal underworld relating to the production, sale, and use of illegal substances.

Prelude

The police had already taken away the body, but the blood and brains were still fresh on the sidewalk. We'd been eating at a restaurant just a few blocks away when my partner looked up from his phone and said someone's been shot down the street. We got up and raced towards the sirens. The man whose cerebrum was now all over the floor had been the owner of a nearby scrap-metal shop. As the cops cleared the crime scene, a bystander lit two candles in memory of the victim, the tiny flames reflecting in a puddle of sticky red ooze. Just another night in Manila.

While we didn't know if this was a drug-related homicide, the MO was the same as thousands of other killings that had taken place across the archipelago since Duterte came to power. Witnesses saw two men fire two shots before fleeing on motorbikes into the urban jungle, their safe getaway guaranteed by the rush-hour traffic.

I'd come to the Philippines to investigate the drug war being waged by President Rodrigo Duterte, who'd vowed to cleanse the country of drugs by any means necessary. The story of the Filipino Drug War resonates with me, because, under another set of circumstances, I could have been the one lying there with a bullet lodged in my skull. I used to be a drug dealer, until one day I stupidly took my stuff on the London Tube and got busted by the Met's canine squad, which earned me a free year-long stay at Her Majesty's

Prison in Isis (South London, not Syria). With an uninspired menu, rude staff, slow room service and guests unable to leave their rooms twenty-three hours a day, suffice it to say that this place wouldn't get a good rating on TripAdvisor.

This isn't another true-crime story. I've always been more of a geek than a gangster, so if you picked this up expecting the millionth book about the Krays, my condolences. This is a true-crime, gonzo, social, historical-memoir meets fucked-up travel book.

A warning: some of you may find this uncomfortable. But remember, you're reading the perspective of a drug dealer. Since I've been known to be wrong about many things (especially the police presence on the Central line), I've travelled the world to hear perspectives other than my own: if I only talked to people who thought like me, this would be a very boring read.

We will explore our curious relationship with those plants, pills and powders that play with our minds, how and why we've tried to stamp them out of existence, and what the consequences of that may be. How come a gram of coke can land you in handcuffs, but you can buy beer and cigs at any corner shop? Why are so many kids dying, and why are our prisons filling up? Why does every society have an underclass whose chief source of employment seems to be black-market pharmaceuticals? Why do gangsters apparently control entire neighbourhoods, and in some cases, entire countries? And what, if anything, is going to change?

Welcome to dopeworld.

Part 1

Rise and Fall

(but mostly Fall)

From Russia With Drugs

I was born in St Petersburg, Russia, or Leningrad as we called it in the good old days. I come from a family with a long academic tradition: my dad's a professor, his dad's a professor, and my mum teaches economics. Just then the Soviet Union was becoming one big shit-sandwich, so we emigrated first to Italy, then to America, where I learnt English from the *Teenage Mutant Ninja Turtles*, and finally to Bath, a small boring town in the British countryside that doubles as a film-set whenever the BBC want to do a costume drama.

Because we moved around a lot, I was always the new kid in school. I was a nerd with a weird accent who loved watching films; I had no hand/leg/eye co-ordination, which made me shit at most sports; and my eyesight was fucked so I wore thick prescription glasses. As you can imagine, none of that endeared me much to the school's social hierarchy. All I wanted was to be normal and accepted for who I was, but every time someone made fun of my accent (even though I spoke perfect English – thanks, TMNT!) or I was excluded from a social activity, it reinforced my view that I'd never really be accepted by anyone. Over time this became a sort of self-fulfilling prophecy. I actually got so much shit for how I talked that I can't bear to hear the sound of my own voice, even today.

Until, one day, I decided the next motherfucker to chat shit to me, I'm gonna knock him dead. This kid on the playground, Mickey

Foreskin, was always a pain in the ass. I don't remember why they called him Mickey Foreskin and I'm not sure I want to find out, but he was definitely an ugly motherfucker. So one fateful lunchtime I was just out and about, minding my own business and eating my Petits Filous, when Mickey literally jumped from behind some bushes and started crooning 'Nikolai, the Russian Spy!' in a sneering imitation of my accent.

I came in like Bruce Lee; fists, knees and elbows flying. He tried to get away but I got him up against the fence and kept pounding. And pounding. And pounding. And then I stopped. Silence.

'Get the fuck outta here.'

Limping and crying like a little bitch, I pushed him away and looked around. I was so caught up in the moment that I hadn't noticed the whole playground staring at me, their mouths wide open in shock. All of a sudden, I heard someone chanting: '*Niko! Niko!*'

It got louder.

'*NIKO! NIKO!*'

Everyone joined in. I lifted my arms in triumph.

After that little incident, I was suspended for a week, but something in me clicked. Beating the shit out of that kid felt good. For the next few weeks everyone respected me. Both my parents were academics, but I didn't wanna go down that same road. It seemed a little too 'nice', a little too 'safe'. I didn't want to work nine to five as a corporate slave, writing reports I don't give a shit about to make someone else rich, then marry and have 2.4 children and settle down in a nice quiet house in the leafy suburbs. That's what everyone else does. I didn't want to be everyone else. I wanted to be that guy your mama warned you about.

Plus, what's the point of being old and rich? You don't wanna be that creepy old guy making it rain at the strip club when he can't get it up, or dive off the Great Barrier Reef when you've barely got enough lungs to make it up the stairs. Before you know it, you'll be on your deathbed, wondering how life passed you by. Better make hay while the sun shines.

But I was too much of a pussy to rob anyone and, besides, I'd feel bad about it afterwards. So I started selling pirate DVDs, a racket that earned me a couple of extra pounds until everyone discovered the Internet. That's when I settled on drugs.

2

A Brief History of Molly

We were all gathered in the woods. It was 14 February 2009. Valentine's Day. I've never had a good Valentine's Day. Three at night and it's going full swing. Trance music echoed through the trees and giant sheets with psychedelic patterns hung off the branches with trippy designs that seemed to move along with the beats. A few unsavoury characters stood around muttering 'hash, pills, MDMA' to all the girls in fluorescent body paint and the dreadlocked Italians in tank tops who went past. A few people pitched tents or sat around bonfires, the flickering flames radiating through the shadows of the forest.

Given that I'd spent a few hours sitting by the bonfire I started to smell like a chimney sweep, but it had been a profitable evening and I had a couple hundred quid in my pocket. I was selling my wares, minding my own business, when three guys in hoodies came up and asked to look at the goods.

'Sure, it's thirty-five on the g or twenty for half.'

'Why don't you just give it to us?'

'What?'

'Blud, if I wanted to rob you, I would have done it already,' said the tallest one, trying to lure me into a false sense of confidence.

'You must be having a laugh,' I said and pushed one of them out the way.

'Oi, why you makin' moves on my friend like that!'

Something hit me hard on the side of the head, then all three jumped me, repeatedly kicking me and stamping on my face. Sparks flew round my head like a cartoon as I felt the warm, metallic taste of blood gently filling my mouth.

'Hey, he's got a blade!' one of them said, and pulled out a Rambo knife from my jacket; ironically, the very one I'd brought to defend myself.

Oh shit, I thought, *please don't kill me.*

He stuck me six times: three times in the left leg, twice in the arm and once (lightly) in the side. They weren't trying to finish me off, only to make sure I wouldn't get back up again (although I'm well aware that if they'd hit my femoral artery it would have been a different story). They took all my Molly and cash but I managed to cling on to my gold chain and phone.

It's funny now, but at the time I hadn't even realised I'd been stabbed and went back to the party. The sensation of being stabbed isn't as painful as you might think. First of all, your adrenalin's going, and that can take a man through a lot. Second, when the knife went into my leg it severed my nerves, so I could literally feel no pain. My leg felt a bit funny and numb, but I thought that was just cos I fell over in a weird way when they were kicking me. I felt a bit cold as well, but I didn't realise it was from massive blood loss; just thought . . . you know . . . it was night-time, so it was cold. I only clocked what had happened after the sun came up and it was time to go home.

As we were making our way back to the train station, I heard an icky sound coming from my shoe . . . *squish, squish, squish.* I looked down and saw that the whole left side of my body was red and that blood had poured all the way down my leg, filling the shoe to the brim. I must have spent the previous three to four hours blissfully unaware I was bleeding all over the place. That's when I realised I should probably go to hospital. But for some reason I decided to call a taxi, which ended up costing me £5, when I really should have called an ambulance, which would have been free. When I got to the hospital, the nurse was amazed I was still conscious after losing such copious amounts of blood.

The first coke I ever sold, I bought one gram off some grubby crack-head on the street and mixed it with some crushed-up paracetamol to make it into two (note to aspiring drug dealers: do *not* do this – everyone will hate you). Realising this was a sure-fire way to get my ass kicked, I soon switched to selling drugs the 'legit' way; by going to raves and shotting MDMA.

I'd walk around, offering baggies of foul-tasting powders and aromatic greenery. The mark-up was huge: I'd buy an ounce (around 28 grams) for about £300 and split it into grams and half-grams, which went for £35 to £40. There was a rave every weekend and for a few hours walking round the party I could easily quadruple my investment. Drugs are an easy, low-risk source of tax-free profit. You can scream how it's wrong all you want, but name another business where you can quadruple your investment over a weekend. Go on, name one.

Molly (MDMA, 3,4-Methylenedioxymethamphetamine) was originally synthesised by German scientists looking for a weight-loss drug in the 1910s, but it wasn't till the 1960s that it came to the attention of one Alexander Shulgin, who realised they'd found something special.

Alexander Shulgin, or Sasha to his friends, was a crazy-haired, mad scientist who carried out experiments in the shed at the back of his garden in San Francisco, usually on himself, like a psychedelic Doc Brown. Soon after he put that foul-tasting powder in his mouth, Sasha was in for a wild ride. Molly gets your heart racing, makes you wanna dance, and floods your brain with serotonin and dopamine, filling you with happiness and euphoria. It's called the Love Drug because you feel such empathy and compassion for everyone around you, even complete strangers; it makes you wanna touch and hold them. On the flipside, ecstasy makes your penis shrivel up like an old carrot, so any relationships you enter into as a result will be strictly platonic (the scientific name for this is 'pilly willy'). It also makes you grind your teeth and burst into a silly gurn. Shulgin started sharing the love with his circle of friends, some of whom were psychiatrists, who used it to help their patients open up.

A little while after Shulgin's discoveries, house music was taking off in Chicago and Detroit's gay and black communities, before making its way to dance capitals Goa and Ibiza. People realised the only way to make this shit sound good was by taking heavy doses of mind-altering chemicals. Word got round the dance scene from Shulgin's psychiatrist mates and, before long, DJs were playing sets of trance music before crowds of loved-up party animals. The rave was born.

The first time I did MDMA is a night I'll never forget. Everyone kept banging on about how they were doing Molly and I figured that, if I was selling it, I might as well see what the fuss was about. So I went into the toilets, laid out a card over the box of toilet roll, and poured out half a gram (I didn't know how much you're supposed to take), then racked it all up into a line and snorted it (I didn't know you're not supposed to do that either) . . . Fuck!!!! The pain shot right up to my eyes. I stumbled out the cubicle and stared at myself in the mirror, looking like I'd just been pepper-sprayed at a football match. After about half an hour of standing by the tap and drinking water to wash the foul taste from my throat, I went back to the bar and ordered another beer. That's when it kicked in.

And oh my God . . . holy shit, there's a reason they call it ecstasy. Time slowed down and I felt this wave of joy come over me, like nothing was wrong with the world and I just felt love; love for myself and my fellow man . . . love for our species! The surface of the bar felt silky smooth rather than the grubby wooden board with spilled pints it was in reality. A girl from my school came up to me, and I had no idea what she said but it was great. When I went outside, it felt like I was gently floating, not walking, over the ground, and I floated all the way to my mate's club, where there was a private party, but he let me in and I started wandering around, shaking hands and saying hi to everyone while they were all, like, 'Who the fuck is that guy??' After fifteen minutes I went back outside and called everyone in my phone-book, chatting shit about what I thought was life, the universe and everything, but really I was off my nut, so who knows. I just felt so close to everyone around me, like they were all my friends and would happily listen to me talking twaddle for hours. But by now it was getting late, so I walked/floated all the way home, where, still buzzing, I went on Facebook and stayed up listening to the same five songs I had downloaded off LimeWire.

Raves had problems, sure – noise, litter – but for the most part it was just kids waving glowsticks and having a good time. But as the rave scene grew in the eighties and nineties, so did the tabloids' panic. MDMA was already banned because its ingredients fell under the Misuse of Drugs Act, but now you had a bunch of teen-agers in a field, doing god-knows-what, while the breweries weren't making any money. The turning point came during the weeklong rave in Castlemorton in 1992. The police didn't have enough manpower to arrest everyone, pictures went round of them looking like plonkers and this was followed shortly by the 1994 Criminal Justice Act, which gave police authority to shut down parties characterised by 'repetitive beats' (thus distinguishing them from those other parties, where everyone sat around gurning their teeth to Pavarotti). Now of course EDM's become part of mainstream clubbing, leaving behind the drug culture for good, clean, wholesome booze.

But the scene didn't die. Once I found this rave on Facebook – the Gathering of Celestial Souls or something like that. The way it's usually organised is you only get the address by ringing a number on the night – that way, by the time the Feds have managed to clock on, the party is well underway and they don't have the resources or manpower to stop it. This time though some idiot posted the address on Facebook and by the time we got there it was shut down, with cop cars surrounding the warehouse. There was now a crowd forming of two hundred or so disappointed partygoers with nowhere to go, and someone suggested a nearby park. After some negotiations with local bus drivers we all managed to find the place, only to find Old Bill had beaten us yet again. This time though there were only two squad cars with an officer each and a 'POLICE LINE: DO NOT CROSS' tape sealing off the park. They were outnumbered a hundred-to-one, so we figured if we all just rushed them there was nothing they could do. So we all turned to face the coppers and started counting down. I got ready. 'FIVE . . . FOUR . . . THREE . . . TWO . . . ONE!'

I jumped the barricades and sprinted down the road to the park. As I was running I could hear my footsteps . . . *only* my footsteps. I looked back and a horrible feeling hit me: I was the only one running. Everyone else was just standing there behind the checkpoint laughing their asses off while the two plodders looked on with a mixture of contempt and disbelief. I couldn't exactly turn back as in my jacket pocket I had a dozen or so wraps of some sticky Mary Jane ready for sale, so I had no choice but to keep on going, narrowly dodging another patrol car which arrived as backup. I ran through the park and into some bushes through to a narrow country lane and some fields and managed to run all the way out of town, eventually making my way back to civilisation by getting on the M4. By then someone had turned up their car stereo to the max and there was a full-fledged improvised street party going on, so I started shifting my gear. This went on for about an hour or two until the three Feds who remained at the scene called in the cavalry and about four vans full of goons showed up, all spoiling for a fight. Knowing it was time to make a quick exit, I started quickly walking away along with the rest of the crowd. The five-o however had other ideas, and I could hear voices and whistles behind me. Time to pick up the pace, I thought. My power-walk burst into a run.

'Stop!' I heard them shout, 'you're not gonna get away!'

But I still had a fair bit of green so I kept running, throwing my stash into some bushes as I went along but leaving one baggy as a sacrifice to give them a reason why I was running. Adrenalin gave me wings and I jumped a brick wall like it was nothing, and would have got away from those fat bastards too if it wasn't for one of their vans going round the corner. I hit the windshield on the way down and rolled onto the street. Six Feds jumped into the street and hauled me into the van where a certain policeman started going through my phone in an attempt to prove I was a 'filthy little drug dealer' (I was, but that's beside the point). I'm not 100 per cent certain in the five minutes we'd been acquainted he had time to go through formal procedure and get a warrant signed by a judge, so I can only assume that the policeman was one of those loose cannons, always getting in trouble with his superiors for refusing to play things by the book.

Fortunately since they had no real evidence on me apart from that one little baggy they had to let me go with a caution, after which I promptly went back to the bushes and picked up what was left of my stash.

When you're a dealer, you tend to gravitate naturally towards other dealers: your people introduce you to their people, and so on. Through some mutual acquaintances I met Shaa, a fresh-off-the-boat Sri Lankan refugee. He was surprisingly chill considering the crazy life he'd had. Fleeing the Tamil Tigers and civil war in his homeland, Shaa ended up on the south coast with a student visa, where he started rolling with a local crew selling weed. Things went haywire and there was a dispute about money, which led to one of them shooting him point-blank in the chest.

Shaa overstayed his visa but before he left (voluntarily, you racists), he introduced me to a higher tier of business, and the wholesale market – buying in nine-bars and kilos and breaking them up into ounces so you can sell them in bulk. Granted, I was still learning the ropes then and not very streetwise, so I fucked up by giving shit on credit to people I was never gonna hear back from. Rookie. Well, you live you learn.

Anyway, I was growing tired of this small-town shit. Nothing ever happens in Bath, and every time you'd leave the house you'd see someone you knew. It was time for me to move on to bigger things.

3

LDN

My parents had to coax me into applying for uni. Originally, I wanted to join the army, learn how to blow shit up, but my vision at the time was −6 in one eye and −6½ in the other, which isn't the best of selling points for a role with high-calibre weaponry. When it came to a degree, my first choice was actually film studies, but mother insisted I enrol in a 'real' course, because apparently the ability to quote Sean Connery lines on a whim ('ejectah sheat, you musht be joking!'), while impressive, is not highly prized by employers. So I went with history, since my train of thought literally was: *I've seen* Braveheart, *so maybe I already know what happens.*

I got into Queen Mary University of London, which was in the East End. Unlike Bath, Whitechapel was the perfect embodiment of a multicultural melting pot. A hundred years ago it had a reputation for being a squalid shithole, home to Russian and Polish Jews fleeing persecution in their motherland and Jack the Ripper, practising amateur surgery on some unlucky prostitutes. Eventually, the Jews made their money and left and the Bengalis moved in, turning Brick Lane synagogue into a mosque and the bagel shops into curry houses.

You wouldn't have thought it, but in the 1980s, Shoreditch was a proper white, working-class area and a stronghold of the neo-Nazi National Front. All the skinheads gathered there to launch attacks on Brick Lane. That's why the Asian gangs formed, to protect the community from these racist attacks. Since then, Brick Lane's been taken over by hipster pussies, so the one-time vigilantes have taken to brawling among themselves: the Bethnal Green boys hate the Brick Lane boys, and so on.

The story of Brick Lane is in some ways the story of London. A hundred years ago, Britain owned half the world; now, half the world is coming to us.

A lifetime ago, hard geezers like the Krays and the Richardson Gang ruled the underworld. But the 1980s changed everything. Old-school villains, who earned their bread and butter through armed robberies and extortion, saw that with CCTV those days were numbered. The hippies were right: the future lay in drugs. So they sat back and reinvested their money in coke, dope and ganja, leaving the hands-on work to a new generation.

In the 1980s, Maggie Thatcher saved the British economy, but it came at a price: the rich–poor divide grew as the welfare state was scaled back, while single-parent families and other low-income groups were herded together on the estates, leading to a lot of wayward youngsters running around causing mischief.

Meanwhile, immigration was changing the face of London. Black people, mainly from Africa and the Caribbean, suffered the most out of the growing poverty of the 1980s, being confined to ghettos in Brixton, Peckham and Hackney. The streets of South London in those days were ruled by the Yardies, career criminals from Jamaica. While in the UK they were seen as little more than a crew of ragtag crack dealers, back home, they were more akin to the Mafia.

In the 1980s, Jamaica was the mid-point for Colombian cocaine headed for Britain and Lester Lloyd Coke (yes, that was his real name) was the don of the Shower Posse, a gang who got their name because of how they sprayed their enemies with bullets. They were the enforcement arm of the Jamaican Labour Party (JLP), who used them to make sure voters ticked the right boxes on the ballot in their stronghold of Tivoli Gardens. In the 1960s, the JLP and its rival, the People's National Party (PNP), divided Kingston into 'garrison' slums such as Tivoli, where they could rig the vote. In 1976, Bob Marley tried to mediate between the warring factions and got shot for his efforts. He tried again, bringing the JLP and PNP leaders together onstage at the One Love concert in 1978, but the 1980 general election was the bloodiest yet, with over eight hundred people killed.

Coke became so powerful he once chased a man into a police station, had him brought outside, then beat him to death in a fit of road rage. Later, he murdered five people (including a pregnant woman) in a rampage through a Miami crackhouse. However, in 1989 the JLP lost the election and Coke lost his protection. Indicted for the crackhouse massacre, he then mysteriously burnt alive in his cell just as he was about to be extradited. It couldn't have happened to a nicer guy.

A big fuss was made about the Yardies setting off an explosion of gun crime, but the streets of Brixton never turned into the garrisons of Kingston. Still, with their Rasta heritage, the West Indians made easy targets for narcs looking to bump their arrest stats.*

'I find it quite interesting because around the seventies and eighties all the Yardies came in and they wanted that bad-boy gangster image,' my friend Paddy later told me. 'And, of course, that put a lot of fear into the local dealers cos people were turning up gutted in alleyways and all that. But now it's come full circle: because of all that effort they put in to look like bad-boy gangsters, now the black boys get pulled over just for being black. It's racial profiling because of what happened thirty years ago, so no one trusts them with drug

---

* Rastafarianism is a religion originally from Jamaica that believes the Ethiopian Emperor Haile Selassie was the second coming of Jesus. They also smoke a lot of weed.

stuff any more. It's much easier to get away with crime now if you're white.'

To someone who doesn't experience it, stop-and-search might seem like a minor inconvenience. But if you have to live with it every day, it starts to colour your view of the police and your place in society. It's unfair. Unfairness breeds suspicion, and suspicion breeds resentment.

In 1981, an officer in Brixton rushed to help a black boy who'd been stabbed. But no good deed goes unpunished and the bobby was quickly surrounded by a baying crowd convinced he'd attacked the boy. The rage against the police for the next two days left hundreds injured and property destroyed. A government inquiry into the Brixton riots found that the police's unchecked use of beatings and stop-and-search wound the Afro-Caribbean community into an angry mob.

Thirty years later, the Metropolitan Police shot Mark Duggan, an alleged gang member, on his way to a showdown. There was a lot of suspicion that Duggan, while no angel, had been killed unlawfully. An angry protest outside Tottenham police station escalated into a riot that enveloped nearly every other borough in the city, and then the country: Bristol, Nottingham, Birmingham, Manchester, Liverpool. With so many crazy kids, the Feds were actually running scared, while a couple of enterprising crooks took advantage of the chaos to rob businesses. While everyone quickly blamed bands of rampaging youths for the riots, in which five people died, the focus on opportunistic looters distracted from the specifically anti-police anger that prompted the unrest.

While South London territory belonged to the Yardies, another immigrant crime wave swept behind the Turkish cafés and kebab shops of North London. For years, the flow of heroin into Europe was tightly controlled by a secret alliance known as the *derin devlet*, or Deep State. During the Cold War, NATO launched Operation Gladio, which would organise resistance should those blasted commies take over the continent. In Turkey, where political turmoil was already sweeping the country, Operation Gladio hired thugs to liquidate undesirables, which sometimes meant murdering left-wing students en masse. Over the next few decades, this unholy union brought together police, gangsters, military and intelligence officers and the Grey Wolves, a far-right paramilitary group that once tried to assassinate the Pope. The Deep State mounted coups whenever they felt that the government was getting too Islamist or left-wing. This would have all remained under wraps were it not for a rather inconvenient car crash in the town of Susurluk in 1996, in which a police chief, a drug-dealing hitman for the Grey Wolves, the killer's girlfriend and a Kurdish warlord were pulled from the wreckage.

Since then, there haven't been more awkward car wrecks to give us further titillating insights into Turkey's puppet-masters, and since coming to power President Erdoğan has been obsessively purging the military of anyone who might dethrone him. However, while the original Turkish Mafia in London was mainly Cypriot (like Jamaica, Cyprus was a British colony), newer gangs like the Bombacilar ('Bombers') and the Tottenham Boys descended from the rugged hills of southeastern Anatolia where, long suppressed by Ankara's flag-waving nationalists, the Kurdistan Worker's Party (or PKK) has been waging a bloody struggle for independence since the 1980s. The Deep State fought a dirty war against the PKK, its death squads 'disappearing' thousands of Kurdish activists (or any man old enough to hold a rifle).

The PKK's struggle was allegedly funded by heroin. In the Turkish cafés and social clubs of Green Lanes, the Kurdish gangs acted as the militants' local smack-distribution fronts. Of course, living in a multicultural melting pot by definition means people have to mix together: in a disturbing display of inter-ethnic unity, ever since the beef erupted between the Bombacilar and the Tottenham

Boys, the two cliques began using black British gang members to subcontract one another's murders.

From Turkey the heroin moves through the Balkans, which has always been a passageway from East to West. A few decades ago, the region was in chaos. Marshal Tito, Yugoslavia's leader since the Second World War, had died, bringing nasty nationalistic differences to the fore, and sparking a three-way bloodbath between Serbs, Croats and Bosnians in 1991. Everyone in the Balkans hates each other, going back hundreds of years to Ottoman rule or depending on what side they fought on in WWII. In 1995, Serbian paramilitaries massacred 8,000 unarmed Bosnians at the town of Srebrenica.

To carry out ethnic cleansing, Serbian forces turned to militias like Arkan's Tigers led by gang lord Željko 'Arkan' Ražnatović. Wanted by Interpol for an epic, decades-long crime spree across Europe, Arkan was assassinated in a Belgrade hotel lobby in 2000, but the Mafia still deeply penetrated the security services long after his death. In 2003, Prime Minister Zoran Đinđić was shot dead by a sniper while walking into the Serbian government headquarters after announcing a crackdown on organised crime. The assassination was orchestrated by members of the Serbian secret police, the JSO, who were worried he'd interrupt their cosy relationship with Belgrade's cartels.

Things weren't looking so rosy in nearby Albania, either. For much of the twentieth century Albania was ruled by paranoid communist dictator Enver Hoxha, who dotted hundreds of thousands of bunkers across the countryside for fear of being invaded. While democracy arrived in the 1990s, it was still fragile, and in 1997 mass protests escalated into a full-on uprising after government officials were accused of running pyramid schemes. Many lost their life savings. Albania descended into anarchy as arms depots were looted, the weapons ending up in the hands of criminal gangs or the ethnic

Albanian rebels who made up the Kosovo Liberation Army (KLA) in Yugoslavia.

Supposedly to prevent another Srebrenica, NATO launched a furious bombing campaign, allowing the KLA to win independence from Yugoslavia in the late 1990s before embarking on some ethnic cleansing of their own – this time against the Serbs. As well as from NATO's devastating airpower, the KLA also got help from the Albanian godfathers running smack through Europe. The Kosovans were in a prime position to exploit this moneymaking opportunity since Yugoslavia lay right on the Balkan route, the main pathway by which heroin enters Europe from the Middle East. This wasn't lost on the other side, either: Serbian ultranationalists, eager to 'remove kebab', also got in on the action. But the narco-business is about as international as it gets, and so amid all the ethnic strife in the Balkans it was kind of heart-warming to see the Serbs, Bosnians, Albanians and of course the Bulgarians* put aside their differences to keep pumping smack into Europe's veins.

It's the Albanians these days who are the *en vogue* Scary Foreign Gangsters™, making all the pussy-whipped gangsters that came before (Russians, Italians, Jamaicans) look like fucking ballerinas. In the 1990s, one infamous gangster, in a row over drug traffic to Italy, cut the head off one of his rivals and paraded it through his home-town, before blowing up the headless corpse with dynamite. You know how in horror films, you think the killer is dead but he comes back for one last scare? Ain't none of that shit in Albania.

But that was Albania. In the 1990s. There's little reason to think Albanian gangsters would want to draw attention to themselves in this way *now*, at least not any more than any other common-or-garden crims.

---

* In the Cold War the Bulgarian secret service, inbetween assassinating dissidents with poison-tipped umbrellas, ran a lucrative sideline smuggling arms to African warzones and Turkish heroin into Europe. When the Cold War ended, these secret agents found work in 'private security enterprises'.

However, Albania is still a very poor country, a Third World in the middle of Europe whose economy depends on the ganja. The green-fingered inhabitants of one village, Lazarat, produced 4.5 billion euros' worth of herb a year – over half of Albania's GDP – defending their crop with mortars and Kalashnikovs.

Thousands of Albanians have fled to the UK as penniless immigrants or Kosovan refugees, and the papers are filled with how gangs with names like the 'Hellbanianz' are taking over Britain's underworld. Bloody immigrants, coming here and taking jobs off hard-working British criminals! The truth is, it's simplistic to think that if we didn't take in these people, we wouldn't have these problems, as if someone else wouldn't just step up to fill the demand. Before the Albanians it was the Yardies, and before the Yardies, the Krays. So the problem might lie elsewhere than the immigrants.

Beyond the occasional brothel, most Russian crime in London is about big money changing hands and nerve-wracked spies sipping polonium tea. The only other racket I was involved with was cigarette smuggling. In the winter of 2011, I touched down in Kiev and took the metro to the main train station. Scattered around the station were several kiosks, selling everything from bread and magazines to vodka and, most importantly, fags. I came up to one and asked the nice lady in the booth: 'A carton of Marlboro Lights, please.'

As she got up, I got a good view inside. There was plenty more where that came from.

'Say, how much for a couple more of those blocks?'

'How many more?'

'All of them.'

You see, thanks to the differences in taxes, a twenty-pack of Marlboro Lights costs £7 in London, but £1.50 in Russia or Ukraine. That's why big tobacco companies like British American Tobacco sell way more cigarettes to those countries than those cancer-loving

Slavs could ever hope to smoke, knowing they'll find their way into the hands of entrepreneurs like myself who'll do their best to ensure the goods make it to the European market.

I must have cleared out a good dozen or so kiosks before I could cram no more in my duffel bag and set off towards my hotel. Hookers mingled in the downstairs lobby hoping to catch a trick, and there was a free-entry strip bar on the eleventh floor (yes, more Eastern European stereotypes), so I enjoyed myself a bit with the ladies, splashing out some more hryvnia before heading back to my room.

The first time, I got waved through Ukrainian customs and boarded the plane to Heathrow, making my way afterwards to baggage collection through passport control. As I waited for my duffel bag full of smokes, I eyed the rest of the hall. I was tense. My stuff hadn't arrived yet and there was no customs officer in sight, but what if they were just waiting to spring a trap? Oh no, here comes my bag. I picked it up. Still no customs officers. Okaaaay. I made my way through the green corridor; Nothing to Declare. No one there either. I walked through the arrivals lounge as a huge smile formed across my face. I'd just smuggled 12,000 cigarettes into Great Britain.

I dropped the bag off to Aleksander, a stocky bull of a Belarusian in a leather jacket and a four-by-four, who rewarded me financially for my efforts.

'Where are you from?' he asked.

'Peter.'*

'Oh OK, I thought you were a Pole or a Jew or something.'

My accent; I've been here too damn long.

My last run wasn't so lucky. First off, they started to charge at the strip club. That was bullshit. Then I got stopped at the airport. Although they were cool with me engaging in flagrantly illegal activities outside their jurisdiction, they detained me and took a couple of packs of cigarettes that were outside the personal export limit

* St Petersburg.

(apparently such a thing exists), which didn't piss me off so much as the fact that they made me miss my flight. I would have been stranded in Kiev had it not been for a very nice stewardess who I'd never met before loaning me the cash for a last-minute flight, as the airport card machine wasn't working. Then, either because the Ukrainians were pissed off that I didn't try to pay a bribe, so informed their counterparts of my imminent arrival, or because MI5's counter-terrorism system flagged me as the one guy who kept buying return weekend flights to Kiev, or maybe because I was just unlucky, there was an army of customs officers waiting for me when I got back. I saw my bag going round and round the conveyor belt and hesitated, but picked it up anyway on the off-chance they might be idiots. I mean, I'm gonna lose my stuff anyway so might as well.

They weren't. The funny thing is that, apart from fags, the only thing in the bag was a can of Lynx. They were all jammed in pretty tight and laid in such a way that the weight of the cigarettes was pressing down on the deodorant for the whole two-hour flight, emptying the entire can over the contents of the bag. As soon as the bag was opened, an overwhelmingly masculine aroma filled the air. They didn't even let me have the one block I was entitled to. Dicks.

My first year in London ended with a massive setback – a group of dudes roped me in, pretended to be my friends and fleeced me out of a couple of grand. At one point, I heard a gun cocked over the phone. I got took like a shook fool. But, bit by bit, I built my connections up through uni, and by the second year my real friends started importing kilos of high-grade skunk straight outta Amsterdam, setting up shop all over London – north, east, south, west – and I became one of their most reliable distributors. We were paranoid about phone taps, and one of us had a clothing line so we came up with these codewords: 'shirts' meant an ounce, 'socks' meant something else, and so on. But there was a lot of to-and-fro and in-between dealing, so it got to the point where anyone listening in would be like, 'who are these dirty motherfuckers, always wearing each other's shirts . . . ?!'

I only got to know Dre *after* prison. I didn't know it at the time, his crew was one of my suppliers. That makes sense because they all studied at the same uni as me, but where it gets weirder is that while he was at uni he stayed in the same halls as me, in the *same room*, and his godfather is the dad of one of my mates who *also* went to Queen Mary but otherwise is completely unrelated. I mean, I know it's a small world, but I didn't know it's fun-size.

The West End might be better known for *Les Mis* and *The Lion King*, but there are some areas where even Mufasa dare not tread. Dre (or Andrzej) hailed from South Kilburn, another grimy estate near the notorious Stonebridge. Turns out he's something of an anomaly. The son of Polish dissidents, on the one hand he's quite cultured and sophisticated; he even plays the piano like an angel. On the other, he was in court every other week when he was eighteen. His crew, the Lo-Lifes, got their name from a New York gang who went around boosting polo shirts in the 1980s. But unlike their namesake, the Lo-Lifes weren't after Ralph Lauren or other designer brands, they were after making money.

'Our mentality was, if you're not in our circle you're gonna get it,' he says, passing me a spliff in the corner of his bedroom. 'Some people might say nah-nah-nah, but we decided who we did and didn't rob.'

The Lo-Lifes started out shaking down Chinese DVD sellers on Kilburn Road. But when Dre's mate, Gotti's cousin, came out of jail, they started making more serious moves.

'We'd ask someone who hung around with us but wasn't really our friend if they knew so-and-so was doing bits, and they'd say "Yeah, I'll hook you up." Then we'd go to the yard to pick up the food, and one of us had a strap or maybe two of us had a shank. Sometimes we even went barefaced, and if he calls his man, "Oi, your man robbed us", who cares? That's what people outside didn't get – anyone else could get it.'

Some of the robberies were mad reckless. After robbing one man outside his nan's house, Dre caught the Jubilee line with a handgun and half a key of chronic down his pants. But karma was taking its sweet time to catch up to them.

'Nah, no one came after us. People were shook. On one level, Gotti was so known in West London and people wanted to get him, but they were scared they'll meet him again and he'll just rob them again. He didn't give a fuck. One time, someone caught up to him, just walked up to him outside his yard and pulled a strap to his face. Gotti was like "Fuck it, go on then", then just walked back to his yard thinking he was gonna get shot. But the man never pulled the trigger.

'One time I stabbed a man five times on the road. I saw him a year and a half later, and he just saw me and walked quickly past. Unless you're a badman, if someone's stabbed you, you're not gonna wanna see them again. You're not gonna do anything.'

In April 2018, British newspapers screamed bloody murder as, for two short months, London's homicide rate had briefly overtaken New York's, that dystopic hellhole portrayed in films like *The Warriors*, *American Psycho* and *Home Alone 2*.

But it's not the 1980s any more. Even with guys like Dre running around, London ain't Detroit. Never mind that two months is too little time to make statistical inferences about anything – if we were comparing London to St Louis or Baltimore we might have a problem, but New York is one of the safest big cities in North America. For some reason we've got this tendency to view gangs in the UK in American terms, as if the grimiest row of cottages in the Cotswolds has anything on the urban warzones of South Central Los Angeles. No one here's cruising down the street popping off AKs. The guns we *do* have are usually stolen from some farm shed or smuggled in from abroad.

'I remember meeting some ex-IRA brer in Hackney who wanted to sell me an AK-47 for £800,' Dre recalled. 'It really didn't surprise me that they had so much weaponry floating around after the Troubles. But I told him nah, I'm not going to war – I just want a handgun.'

In the 1970s and 80s, the IRA got their weapons from supporters in America as well as Libya's Colonel Gaddafi. Though most of their firearms were meant to be decommissioned in 2005, many made their way into criminal hands. On 5 February 2016, six gunmen kitted out in SWAT-team gear stormed a boxing weigh-in at the Regency Hotel in Dublin, killing one man and wounding two others. The spectacular attack was directed at the powerful drug-dealing Kinahan clan by a rival crime family. Police later traced the three Kalashnikovs used in the shooting to a stockpile used by the IRA.

To be fair, it's not just the guns: we also have free healthcare and few American-style ghettos. Our newspapers might rage on about 'no-go zones', but the fact of the matter is that the mayor of any big American city will weep with envy over the crime stats of London's worst neighbourhoods. A few nasty, local beefs get wildly exaggerated to paint this picture of a 'Broken Britain', where grannies can't walk home at night without being set upon by bands of feral, hoodie-wearing hoodlums. A lot of this is blamed on black 'gangsta' culture and London's multicultural cesspool. But London's not even the UK's real gangs-and-knives capital – that honour goes to Glasgow, where you'd be hard-pressed to spot someone with a tan.

I stayed away from street shit. I didn't need it. Everyone at uni was popping pills, smoking weed or snorting powder. Queen Mary was one of the few campus unis in the capital, meaning first-years got to live in halls on-site. Everyone lived together, studied together and partied together, putting the market conveniently all in one place. For most of those kids it was their first time away from home and with a little cash from mummy and daddy and/or the government, they wanted to try out new things. I was more than willing to help.

My strategy was to show up at the party rocking the standard East European drug-dealer uniform of a tracksuit and leather jacket, with a plastic bag and a glass jar with a plethora of illicit substances. I'd stand just outside and spark up a joint, and within minutes everyone would have my number if they 'needed anything'.*

Uni times were great. Because I was doing a humanities degree, most of the time I could fuck around. I probably spent a third of the time drunk. Once, I went to the student bar and bought everyone there a drink, but because the bartenders were taking so long they all wandered off so I ended up consuming about a dozen beers, cocktails and Jägerbombs by myself. My Arab friend was drunk too and I had to stop him getting anti-Semitic, breaking into a Jewish cemetery to try and earn himself a place in hell by knocking over the tombstones. We found a house party, where I snorted a line of chilli pepper and played the knife game from *Aliens* before picking a fight with an Armenian kickboxer, which did not end well for me. We must have stolen a desk at some point, because another friend called me the next day and said he had a desk in his room that wasn't there before.

At the end of our third year, we were all about to graduate and party season was in full swing. It was my mate Crabman's birthday

* I hate it when people say drug dealers don't work for a living. Your baggies don't just weigh themselves and fly over to your people's houses, I don't care how stoned you are. Dealing for me was working a full-time job while trying to stay on top of my studies. I barely had any time left for myself and meeting new people, unless they were the type to call me at three o'clock in the morning asking if Uncle Charlie was in town. I also hate it when dealers say shit like, 'I made two grand today' . . . motherfucker, you didn't make two grand; *bankers* don't make two grand a day! Two grand might have passed through your hands but most of it is just gonna go towards buying more drugs, or how are you gonna have a sustainable business model? It's like they don't understand the concept of net profit. If you were making two grand a day you wouldn't still be living in the hood, you'd living in some posh country manor, not wandering Brixton with a couple of rocks shoved up your ass.

(we called him Crabman because he looked like Crabman from *My Name is Earl*) and he had a huge house, so we got a load of booze and invited everyone round. I hired a dominatrix to ride him half-naked through the living room like a pony while about two hundred people watched. It was a great turnout, and enough guests wanted to go on a chemical journey that we managed to recoup the stripper costs (and then some). And that's when I met Rita.

4

Busted

She came up to me as I frantically searched my pockets to appease a man in desperate need of white powder, and we hit it off. Short, brown and drop-dead gorgeous, you could lose yourself in those eyes. We'd seen each other before but never really talked. That was about to change. As the guy behind me railed nose candy, we exchanged numbers, and it got to the point where we chatted every day, or near enough. There was a lot to talk about; unlike me, she wanted to use her powers for good, campaigning and volunteering for various causes. I was in love.

Ah, love, the creator and destroyer of worlds. It's a powerful feeling, maybe the most powerful. Men have gone to war over love. At the same time, it's hard to tell what it really is. Like what's the difference between love, lust and obsession? A lot of people *think* they're in love, then change their mind afterwards: 'Oh, I wasn't in love, I was just young/naïve.' I guess love depends on what you feel in the moment, and the other person has to feel it too.

But that was something I'd never experienced, at least not mutual love. Now, I may have been a drug dealer* but I was also every girl's

---

* I got into drugs because I had low self-confidence. What I'd tell kids now is, it's like being a movie star. Those who make it, make it big. They make piles of money and everyone knows who they are. But it's far more likely you're gonna spend years washing dishes, waiting to land a cameo in a 30-second shampoo

worst nightmare – the creepy 'nice guy' who's too yellow-bellied to make a move but hangs around anyway because one day she's gonna realise her true feelings, or somesuch nonsense. Maybe it's because I got bullied at school, I don't know. But a little bird said she liked me and I thought this was my chance to break the cycle.

One night just before Christmas we were out in Canary Wharf and she was wearing her trademark red coat that she always wears. Rita Redcoat, we called her. After a few months of getting over my vaginaphobia, I figured I was now as ready as I'll ever be. If I don't ask her out now, I never will. It's do-or-die, motherfucker. So here went my first date proposal (at age twenty-three):

'Hey, Rita . . .'

'Yes?'

I fumbled a bit.

'I was wondering if you'd like to kind of . . . go out with me some-time, catch a show or something?'

'What, like on a date?'

' . . . Yeah . . .'

'Oh Niko, I'm sorry, you're a really sweet guy, but . . . I'm already seeing someone.'

I felt my heart plunge.

On 25 January I was still feeling kinda sucky about Rita, but life goes on. One of the many tactics used by the Metropolitan Police in their crusade against psychoactive substances is to deploy sniffer dogs at Tube stations to catch people with stuff on them. They don't have to do shit, just sit there, so it's an easy way to rack up arrest numbers and make it look like they're doing their job keeping the good citizens of London safe from drug-addled fiends. I always told people, 'Don't

---

commercial. Except in drugs the stakes are a lot higher and if you have low self-esteem, you're not so much getting away from bullies as diving headfirst into a lion's den dipped in barbecue sauce.

take drugs on the Tube, there are dogs on the Tube', but that night I was in a rush, so I thought, *fuck it*, and put a few wraps of Mandy in my back pocket. I got off at Tottenham Court Road station and made my way up the escalators. It was a long way up, and from the bottom it's impossible to see what's on the other side. And who do I find when I reach the top, but London's finest and their canine companions.

As I sat in a cell contemplating my options, a search warrant was executed at my house. As soon as my flatmate opened the door, they must have known they'd found the right spot since the aroma of skunk hit them like a four-tonne truck. I had maybe a kilo in my room, as well as an ounce each of cocaine and MDMA and around £6,000 in cash. About half an hour before they arrived, my flatmate and his guest had just ordered a pizza, so a very confused pizza man arrived to find a bunch of officers carrying away massive bags of evidence.

The next day I was released on bail (in this country you don't have to front any money; unless you're clearly an escape risk or a menace to society, you're free to go) and told to report to Blackfriars Crown Court on 15 March for my hearing. Since I chose to keep my parents out of the loop and the Feds confiscated all my money, I was given a shitty court-appointed lawyer who couldn't defend me if I was accused of sinking the Spanish Armada. In fact, his defence of me was so poor that the prosecutor (!!!) had to step in and have some words with the 'judge' – who actually had to have explained to him the difference between a caution and a conviction. It was a farce.

Since I'd most likely not see her again for a while, I arranged to link up with Rita, and she suggested we go to a cocktail bar in Covent Garden. She also said she'd had a rough week and could use a drink anyway, and since she didn't live in London any more, she asked if she could stay over at my place for the night. I said sure.

So we met up and went through all the obligatory jokes about prison food and how I'd toss more salad than a vegan jamboree. It was going well until I asked her what happened earlier in the week . . . she'd just split up with her boyfriend.

No. Fucking. Way.

I closed my eyes and imagined a plane crash on the runway.

5

CrIsis

It was 15 March 2013. I sat looking through the dark tinted windows on the armoured bus as the city of London went past. 'Thrift Shop' by Macklemore was playing on the radio, but most of my fellow passengers were more focused on banging as hard as they could on the reinforced glass to get the attention of women on the street, trying to grab at least one last look from a pretty face as they said goodbye to their freedom. The walls in my own personal little compartment bore the names of its previous occupants – 'Vitalij Ukraina' and 'Romka Dikij' ('Vitaly from Ukraine' and 'Crazy Roman') – clearly some *zemlyaki* had been here before me.

'What's this place like, lads?'

'Faakin' laavley! All the screws are ex-strippers, they let you out all day and they even got a swimming pool!'

After what seemed like a never-ending trek through rush-hour traffic listening to some frankly uninspired catcalls, we finally arrived at our destination. One by one we were herded off the bus into a waiting room to be briefed, have our pictures taken, be strip-searched and sat on a magical chair to check if we had filing tools stuck up our ass before being awarded our standard-issue uniform and trainers, or HMP Guccis as my mate Bobby liked to call them. We were now being detained at Her Majesty's Prison Isis in Thamesmead.

The reality of my situation dawned as soon as I heard that loud metallic bang as the guard locked the door behind me. I panicked and paced up and down, but there was nothing I could do to get out of my new, personal hell. To try and keep my mind busy, or more likely because a few of my screws had come loose, I sat down to work out the exact length of my sentence (913 days; 1,314,873 minutes; or 78,892,380 seconds) and began counting down. I stopped past a few thousand after realising this wouldn't make time go any faster.

Up till that point, jail was always something that happened to other people. One guy from school got addicted to crack and got busted selling fake ecstasy pills to an undercover officer in a pub parking lot. Another did some time for leading police on a miles-long car chase through the countryside after refusing to pull over, and on top of that got done for kidnapping charges cos he had a girl in the car and wouldn't let her out. But those weren't really dudes I hung out with.

That's the thing about crime – no one ever thinks they'll be the ones getting caught. And of course, most of them don't. After all, you don't frantically dial 999 every time you get a bag of weed. Plus, I was fairly insulated by being white, well-spoken and middle-class. Unlike those Bangladeshi street gangs roaming the projects just outside campus, I was a non-target in our government's war on drugs. Up till the day I actually got sent down, many people just wouldn't believe that a nice, university-educated guy like me could even go to prison. That's one way of looking at it; another is that convicted coke dealers tend to end up in prison. *This is it,* I thought, *my life is essentially over.*

Every day in prison, time stands still. Every morning you rise to the same thing. You wake up at 7.30 a.m. for breakfast and exercise, when you're let out in the yard where you can have a smoke, walk around in circles or do pull-ups or drips on the bars. I remember one time there were a couple of drops falling from the sky so not everyone was eager to come outside. One of the dudes though, to his credit, came out with me and said to them, 'What you man so scared of a little rain for? It'll help you grow if anything!' Now I know he meant well but ... help you grow? Maybe if this guy got enough sunlight and some nitrogen-rich soil, he would truly start to blossom.

After thirty minutes you get taken back to the wing, and at nine o'clock you have to either work or go to class, because for some of these guys it would be nice to have something other than Unofficial Home Removals Expert on their CV. Some days, instead of work or education there's 'association', when you could either go to the gym or hang around the wing, have a shower, use the phones, play pool or chat shit. The conversations quickly get boring: 'the food sucks'; 'when do you get out?'; 'so-and-so got rushed in the showers'.

It's not like you can come up to someone and say, 'Yo, what you sayin' tonight?' 'Not much mate; you?' 'Oh, I'm going out, man; we got a table at Ministry of Sound.' 'Nah bruv, I'm gonna take it easy; going fishing with my old man tomorrow!' The most exciting response you're gonna get is, 'Man, might be watching *Big Brother* tonight ...'

Things weren't all bad. Despite what you might have seen in the movies, *American History X*-style hijinks were kept to a minimum: the other dudes were as chaste as a group of old nuns at a Jonas Brothers concert. And even in my darkest hours, when I thought about ending it all, the toilet was right next to my bed, so if I ever needed a dump in the middle of the night, all I'd have to do is roll over.

My cellmate was Misha from Moscow. Misha was Kyrgqz of Uzbek descent, which in layman's terms means for some people he looked Chinese, although with his long, flowing hair he reminded me a lot of Soviet rock star and late 1980s, protest icon, Viktor Tsoi. A big hip-hop fan, he spoke English only with black American ghetto slang: nigga this, nigga that, tinged with a strong Russian accent. But no one seemed to get offended, probably owing to the fact he was so clearly not white and a foreigner.

Misha was doing five years for fraud conspiracy, and with some extra time added on for getting caught with a mobile phone. Conspiracy charges are a bitch. It becomes more serious if you're accused of 'organising' a crime: It's like, 'Oh, so you planned it?', to which you can only reply, 'No, because I casually just drive around with a ski mask and a sawn-off shotgun in my car in the off-chance I spot a cash-delivery van doing its rounds.' Anyway, his mate, a computer hacker from Ukraine, wrote a script for a virus, which he then sent off to various banks before siphoning off £3 million (around $4.5 million) from compromised accounts to ones controlled by him and another guy from Kazakhstan. Not bad for a twenty-year-old, right? Except one day, he forgot to turn on the encryption on his laptop. The judge called him a 'threat to national security' as he pronounced his sentence.

We plastered our wall with Page Three babes and glamour models (until I went to prison I always wondered who the remaining demo-graphic was for printed pornography), and got a guy in art class to paint us a huge Russian flag, which we stuck out of our window so errrbody knew where we at! We spent my twenty-fourth birthday together, on which I woke up to Misha serenading me with his Russian-accented jive.

My other cellmate was an award-winning rapper called Thomas who'd once performed with Mos Def. Thomas hailed from Montserrat, a British Caribbean island whose population, of mainly Afro-Irish descent, was evacuated in 1995 when a dormant volcano suddenly awoke. He got caught up in a major drugs sting, set up by someone who he thought was his boy but was actually an undercover, who convinced him to sort a few ounces of cocaine when funds were running low. We had a lot of things in common, including our love of movies, and many a night was spent watching or quoting 1980s classics.

Eventually, I managed to move into my own cell. No matter how cool your cellmates are, they get annoying after a while. Being on your own and not having a cellmate is fucking awesome. You can watch whatever you want on TV, you don't feel awkward when you have to take a dump, and you don't have to wait till the other guy's asleep when you need some 'alone time'.

Isis was a young offenders' institution: eighteens to twenty-fives, full of just dumb yutes, chavvy hoodlums and wannabe gangbangers trying to prove themselves. The jail was grossly underfunded, under-staffed and nothing was running properly, to the point where an emergency regime had to be implemented with half of the prison completely locked down every other day because they didn't have enough screws to watch everyone. Sometimes we'd spend up to twenty-three and a half hours a day locked in our cells, which effec-tively amounted to psychological torture. In other words, if you treat people like animals, don't be surprised when they act like fucking animals.

One of the first things they asked me when I got to pen was what ends I was from. Every hood was represented there. You had the street gangs like GAS and One Chance/OC, both based in Brixton, the SUK (Stick-Em-Up-Kids) from Battersea, Peckham Boys, Piff City and Asian Virus. They all had beef with each other and brought that shit from outside: 'You're from Brixton?? I'm from Peckham, fuck you!!!!' Gangs in London are defined by their area, meaning that anyone who comes from that area is seen as affiliated, whether they like it or not, to their local crew.

There were a few ethnic groups that stuck together, like the Travellers (think Brad Pitt in *Snatch*) and the Somalis, but even they split into street-based factions. One of the major beefs was between the Wood Green and the Camden Somalis. In Isis, one of the Somali camps, I forget which, seemed to be led by an angry dwarf with a serious Napoleon complex. There was a Somali kid who was in for robbing a petrol station after he lost his job. He was always polite to everyone, always said please and thank you. The Camden Somalis came up to him on his way out of mosque and asked him where he was from, and he innocently told them: 'Wood Green'. They kicked the shit out of him right in front of the imam.

But even if you keep your head down, you've still got to face your worst enemy: yourself. Spending day after day after day banged up in a cell with nothing but your own thoughts for company will play tricks on your mind. The isolation and paranoia from your people outside ... is my girlfriend cheating on me? Why isn't anyone replying to my letters? These thoughts go round and round your head in a loop, and if you're not strong enough, they can consume you.

Following the same routine, day-in day-out, you become almost like a robot. Your perception of time itself changes. Instead of letting it flow naturally, you break it down into units, counting down the weeks, days and months until your release, holding your breath for the next visit, next bit of news from the outside or next episode of whatever trash sitcom you're watching.

I felt worthless. Once you step onboard the crazy train, there's no stops till the end of the line. I started hating every little bit of myself. I hated how I couldn't pronounce my Ls properly. I hated my voice and the look of my face; I wanted to dig my nails into my skin, really dig in there, and claw my nose, cheeks and eyelids off piece by piece, *Poltergeist*-style, till there was nothing left but a bloody skull. I wanted to kill myself. This world is overpopulated anyway so I'd be doing everyone a favour. I was worthless. Life was worthless. I felt lower than a dung beetle. At least they make a valuable contribution to the ecosystem. What did I have to offer?

I wasn't the only one having those thoughts. During the year I was inside, prisoner suicides jumped 67 per cent. From 2013 to 2014, 125 men and women took their own lives. So it wasn't just me being a pussy; it genuinely was bad.

And then there was Rita. No matter how much I tried not thinking about her, she crept back into my mind. I'd got into my head the idea that maybe, just maybe, when I got out, she'd still be there and I'd have another chance. It was a stupid thing to hope for – pretty girls like her don't stay single for long – but when you're in a situation where you're facing an unknown future, when you don't know if anyone's going to employ you or how it will be with your family, you reach out for something, *anything* to hold on to. I couldn't move on; there was nothing to move on to. Ain't no girls in jail!! None you could wine and dine at a fancy Italian restaurant anyways. Massive, tattooed black guys and pasty-skinned white boys with gaps between their teeth and nicknames like Jamz and Deebo weren't exactly my idea of a good time. I was becoming obsessed.

The Travellers, by and large, were a thoroughly decent bunch and ran their own drug-smuggling operation. Yes, of course there's drugs in jail. You can't throw a bunch of lawbreakers together in one spot and expect them not to get high, are you fucking kidding me, son? There's a massive price difference on the inside – £50 for a gram of hash that weighs 0.7–0.8, if you're lucky – but that just makes it more profitable. You pay for your gear either by getting your people outside to send money to your dealer's prison account, or buying them shit from the canteen until your debt's repaid.

Drugs are usually smuggled in during visits. You get your girl to come in and hide it in her mouth as she gives you a kiss, passing it through as you trade saliva. If you're running a more sophisticated operation, get one of the screws on board.

'Usually it came to light because another prisoner would tell and say that's not fair because he's not sharing,' a former Isis governor later told me on the outside. 'My policy was I want a conviction, they should go to court – not to let them quietly resign like others do because it would be a scandal in the papers. So we'd do a sting where we searched them in the car park. If they see a police car or a dog, they might get scared and call in sick. We called it "squeaky squirrels" because it had to be done quietly, and we'd have to get the police to come and arrest them because the staff would touch everything and bungle up the crime scene.'

One day, some of the brothers managed to sneak in some MDMA and started handing it round among the prisoners. The wing was transformed. It was like a night in *Fabric*; every cell had guys with eyes like fucking saucers, jumping up and down on their beds, taking their shirts off and waving them in the air to the sound of Essential Ibiza Trance Classics. The screws saw it all go down but could do nothing; it was too short notice to set up a piss test and MDMA clears your system after three days. Weed stays in your system the longest – about four weeks. They'd make us wee into a test-tube every few months, but hardly anyone got caught because a prison joint is just a glorified cigarette; you'd have to be very unlucky or smoking like a chimney to have anything show up at all. Even so, whenever I smoked a zoot with my cellmates I was so scared of getting caught that every night for the next month I'd chug a small ocean of water to make sure my wizz stayed squeaky clean.

But spice doesn't show on most tinkle tests. You see, it's one of those 'legal highs' – chemicals that can be legally bought on the Internet marked as not fit for human consumption, but that, when taken, have much the same effect as the substances they're supposed to be replacing. I remember the Great Methedrone Craze of 2009, when someone realised that snorting a white powder innocuously labelled as 'Plant Food' gets you crazy high. Methedrone, also known as m-cat or 'meow-meow', ruined the livelihoods of coke dealers everywhere until lawmakers finally got wise and banned the stuff in April 2010. But with these designer drugs, all the chemists have to do is slightly tweak the molecules down at the lab *et voilà*, you've got a whole new compound. New chemicals can appear faster than the law can keep up, and that's dangerous because we've got a fairly good idea of what coke and heroin do to you, but when it comes to these new substances, we don't know jack.

I feel like, by not getting off my nut on spice and starting a riot, I missed an integral part of the British prison experience. Spice is (or was) a nastier, legal-ish version of cannabis. It's trippy, unsettling high can induce psychotic episodes, which obviously doesn't bode well for prison security. One time, when I was jamming with Thomas, he started breaking down his very weird trip.

'Smoking spice was like smoking a whole spliff in just one or two drags,' he said, while puffing on a normal doobie. 'It would send a nice, pins-and-needles feeling right through to your toes and back up again.'

So far, so good, but once, after Thomas got some bad news from the outside, he started smoking more and more until one day, he found himself in a cell with a bunch of other dudes passing round a spliff. Uh-oh. One of them had instrumentals downloaded to his Xbox and they were all sat around, smoking spice and rapping over the beat, when Thomas took one too many drags.

'So I was freestyling, and I was freestyling really well, and I thought, *Oh my God, this is the best shit I've ever done.* Then I started thinking about what I was saying and trying to pick it apart, and hook it to *this* and hook it to *that,* when all of a sudden I realised I was stood up, watching myself sat down rapping to the room and I was sat down watching myself in a stood-up position, and the moment I realised that I was back in my body I realised something was very wrong: I didn't know where I was and I needed to get out of there. Everyone was staring at me and they later told me I looked like a ghost or a zombie in that moment. I never smoked spice after that.'

On the outside, spice was cutting a swathe through the homeless population. People smoked up, passed out and found themselves the centrepiece of a *Daily Mail* article as the tabloids filled with reports of 'zombies' wandering Britain's streets. Of course, if weed was legal, no one would smoke that shit in the first place.

In 2016 Parliament passed a new law, the Psychoactive Substances Act, which basically meant that anything having a psychoactive effect (except those reliable tax-earners: alcohol, tobacco and pharmaceuticals) is banned, unless stated otherwise. It was meant to get a handle on the legal highs problem, but since 'psychoactive' simply means 'affecting your brain', that means everything from flowers to catnip is technically outlawed. While spice isn't sold openly any more, that's done nothing to solve the problems with the prisoners and homeless.

There was plenty of time to read. Being in a young offenders' institute, I was half-dreading a choice between *The Hungry Caterpillar* and *Horton Hears a Who!* but they actually had a decent selection. There was even a section with titles like *Diary of a Stripper*, and I noticed a few of them had pages missing when it came to the 'interesting' parts.

I began reading Howard Marks – because *everyone* read his book in jail – a Welsh ganja smuggler who did seven years in America's toughest penitentiary and came out a hero for the campaign for legalisation of cannabis. His story hit home. I might have thought I was a loser, a skid mark on the pants of society, but I still couldn't fully convince myself that what I'd done was wrong. Everybody I knew used drugs – or at least most of them drank alcohol, which is illegal in certain countries. Was I really much worse than a bartender? Could I even be compared to one? For all their self-righteous hooting and hollering, I sold coke to newspaper columnists. We're all part of the same hypocrisy. But *why?*

It seemed odd to me, being punished for something so . . . normal. It's just human nature, right? But maybe that's it. Maybe being a drug dealer clouded my perspective, and it was just a small band of us degenerates. That's what they call living in a bubble. Maybe I did deserve it, dirty drug dealer bastard.

Mostly, prison was just boring and depressing. For the first few weeks in jail, to escape the tedium and add some spice to my life I pretended to love crack so that I could join the Alcoholics and Narcotics Anonymous groups. Sitting in on the meetings was fun; you got some free orange juice and sat in a circle listening in to people's stories about how they drank, smoked and snorted their lives away. One crazy motherfucker told us how he licked a whole sheet of acid when he was twelve. OK, so it wasn't exactly a trip to Alton Towers, but anything beat being stuck in a cell and melting your brain to *The Jeremy Kyle Show*.

I also spent a lot of time filling out superfluous requests and applications, demanding the chaplaincy department officially recognise my religion as Jedi. I promised to only practise the 'Light Side of the Force, as preached by the wise master Yoda', as opposed to 'following the Dark Side, which would increase my risk of re-offending as a part of a diabolical scheme to take over the galaxy'.

Nevertheless, my request to Sister Susie was denied. I found her lack of faith disturbing. What was this, the 1970s? The National Offender Management Service (NOMS) couldn't be allowed to get away with such flagrant discrimination!!! So I wrote a letter to *Inside Time*, the national prison newspaper, noting that this was an 'example of the kind of intolerance and religious bigotry faced by members of our faith on a daily basis'.

The letter made national headlines. 'The farce is strong with this one!' screamed the *Daily Mail*. 'The force of law: Prisoner claims persecution for *Star Wars* faith', lamented the *Guardian*. Even a New York newspaper and a Canadian radio station got on the case.

But there was a disturbance in the Force. Sectarianism reared its ugly head when an infidel, Sith Lord (a certain Daniel Styles from HMP Peterborough) wrote in to *Inside Time* to offer his own side of the story.

'As a Sith Lord I have experienced, first-hand, oppression and bigotry from every Jedi I have come into contact with,' he wrote.

'Since the UK Census gave the Jedi cult recognised religion status, this country has been on a path towards "Jedification" without understanding what it is these violent, lightsabre wielding extremists actually stand for.

'The Dark Side will protect me. My anger makes me stronger. Come over to the Dark Side and may The Force be with you.'

My new nickname on the wing was Obi-Wan, but I didn't stick around too long after that, as a few weeks later I got a letter saying my early release was approved and it was time for me to pack my shit. I was going home.

I let Misha raid all the food and Frosties I had hoarded in my cell – it wasn't like I was gonna need those discount cereal packs on the outside.

By pure coincidence, the movie showing on TV on my last night was *Terminator 2: Judgment Day*. It was the perfect choice – one of those long, classic films that by the time the credits roll and Arnie's thumb goes into the lava, you'll feel like you've just followed the characters to the end of an epic journey. And this leg of my journey, too, had come to an end.

6

I Cannot Self-terminate

I walked out of HMP/YOI Isis on the morning of 28 February 2014. I half-wanted the screws to say something like 'See you again soon' so I could tell them to go fuck themselves, but that never happened. Since I got told I was getting out the day before, there was no one waiting for me. I got into a taxi and took it home, where I waited all day to get fitted with an ankle bracelet as part of my conditional release – I had to be home by seven every night, monitored by the bracelet. I never actually found out what would happen if I broke curfew, but I always just assumed that the bracelet exploded and killed you like in *Battle Royale*.

After getting off tag, first things first. I had to see Rita. But every time I called, she seemed to be busy. Normally, if someone doesn't pick up the phone it can be for any number of reasons, but when you're in jail you get this really twisted, delusional view of reality, particularly if said person is an unresolved crush. I guess she stopped being a real person and started being a symbol. I knew by this point I had no chances with her, but if only she'd agree to see me that would be *something*. I started freaking out. We used to talk all the time. *Why* wouldn't she answer me? Was she trying to 'teach' me something? Was it her career? She couldn't afford to be associated with an ex-con? My calls got more intense, every day. I was turning into a stalker. Even if she told me to fuck off and die, that would be better than nothing – at least I'd know where I stood.

Nononononononofuckfuckfuckfuckfuck ... everything I feared was coming true! She was abandoning me. I knew it! I was just a worthless ex-con who didn't deserve even a glance from normal people. Why was a piece-of-shit like me still allowed to keep breathing? Time to fix that! But no ... no, that can't be it. I can't accept this, not after all that I've been through. It means *they've* won, and I'd rather die than let that happen. I couldn't let them win. I had to do something.

I couldn't take it any more. So I took the train out of town, found the quaint little cul-de-sac where Rita lived, and rang the doorbell. She wasn't at home, so I left the flowers with her dad. Unsurprisingly, after that she *did* call me back ... and said she never wanted to see me again.

I had to get a new obsession.

The common wisdom is if you're in jail you've committed a crime, and if you've committed a crime you deserve to be punished. But that didn't sit right with me. My conviction struck me not as unfair (I mean, I *was* breaking the law ...) but unjust. Sure, I was a drug dealer, but I wasn't exploiting any addicts; my market was mostly well-to-do university students, yuppies and hipsters, all of whom willingly paid for their gear. And while I did think a few people were smoking a bit too much weed, no one offered to suck me off for a ten-bag, d'ya know what I mean?!

Besides, just because something's *illegal* doesn't mean it's *immoral*, and vice versa. For instance, the ancient Greeks thought fucking twelve-year-old boys was pretty cool, whereas now we look down on that sort of thing. Meanwhile, people who hid Jews and gypsies in Nazi-occupied Europe were *definitely* breaking the law, but were they acting immorally?*

---

* Of course, some moral codes remain universal, but that doesn't apply to drugs: murder is and has always been regarded as a crime, ever since laws were first invented. The first written law is considered to be the Code of Ur-Nammu

While I was in jail, I'd figured that I might as well become one of those prison intellectual types; the subversive scholar. I tried to read everything I could about the drug war and the reasons behind my incarceration. I thought about how the issue of drugs not only landed me here, but has shaped the entire world: wars, scandals, coups, revolutions. I thought about Soviet dissident Alexander Solzhenitsyn, and the civil rights movement in America – Malcolm X, Angela Davis – and how their time in jail shaped their ideas about class, society and the nature of power.

Then again, if mental gymnastics was an Olympic sport, prisoners would be the fucking gold medallists: 'He deserved it'; 'She was asking for it' (the rapist's excuse). So was I making money off people's misery, or providing a valued service to the community? Either way, I wasn't gonna find out sitting there with my thumb up my ass.

After I got out, I was determined to find out more. I read every book, watched every documentary, from *Cocaine Cowboys* to *Marching Powder*. I saved up to buy plane tickets. I went to Colombia, Mexico, Russia, Italy, Japan and the Afghan border – all in all, fifteen countries across five continents. Call me Narco Polo. I sat down with cops, killers, junkies, senators, smugglers, Satanists, doctors, social workers, grieving parents, beauty queens, federal agents, Russian mobsters and the yakuza. I've marched in protests, barbecued with kingpins, and transcended the very fabric of space-time.

Saying this book isn't biased would be the most bold-faced lie since the Nigerian finance minister alerted me to a great investment opportunity. This isn't a bone-dry account by someone who doesn't care – I've been right there in the thick of it. I'm a writer, historian,

---

from ancient Sumer (modern-day Iraq), which had a lot to say about how you should treat your slave, but had nothing on what happens when you get caught sniffing in the pub toilets. But even 'Thou shalt not kill' is not accepted as a universal rule: it's more like 'Thou shalt not kill, except in war, self-defence, or if you're a samurai in feudal Japan and one of the peasants gets a bit lippy' (the right to strike lowly commoners over perceived insults was called *kirisute gomen*).

drug user . . . and a convict. Not to toot my own horn, but I feel like I have experience on this matter. In today's divisive times where everyone and their hamster has a fucking opinion about Trump or immigrants or Brexit, it's important to remember this issue doesn't revolve around any one political agenda: the war on drugs might have been started by American conservatives, but it's now being fought the hardest by Asian socialists.

To truly understand it all, we first need to dive deep into history. So let's begin our journey, starting with how we primitive carbon-based lifeforms got on the sesh in the first place . . .

Part 2

Everything Gets Banned

7

A Trip Through the Ages

The sun was setting over the horizon, which meant the mosquitoes were getting ready for dinner. It was time to get inside. I was way out in the sticks, in a small jungle compound sitting next to the muddy waters of the Amazon about two hours' boat ride from Iquitos, the nearest town and the world's largest urban centre unreachable by road. It was early 2016, nearly two years after my release, and since no one would give me a job I scrabbled together a few pennies writing essays for lazy students on the Internet and went backpacking through Latin America. A sense of adventure lured me here: *Raiders of the Lost Ark*, Percy Fawcett-type shit. Together with my fellow travellers, I'd come here to this remote part of the Peruvian Amazon to take part in an ayahuasca ritual. What is ayahuasca? Oh, only one of the most powerful hallucinogens known to man . . .

There was probably just over a dozen of us altogether, mostly gringo tourists and the support staff; Isabella, a super-chill Spanish hippy; and Tommy, who was basically a Geordie version of Dolph Lundgren; and a Russian chick named Sasha, on hand to make sure we didn't hurt ourselves crossing the astral planes. Some of my fellow participants were experienced trippers, veterans in psychedelics and well versed in the works of Terence McKenna. Me, I preferred stuff like hash, alcohol and cocaine . . . stuff that gets you fucked up but leaves you in the real world.

But ayahuasca was a whole different beast. It's a brew that's been prepared by the indigenous peoples of the Amazon for centuries, possibly millennia, which releases the chemical DMT (N,N-Dimethyltryptamine) and takes you to another dimension. And that's when all bets are off. Some people think they transform into an animal; a powerful beast like a jaguar or an eagle. Others meet 'things', beings that guide them and show them where they've been going wrong. In a way, ayahuasca acts as a kind of therapist, giving you space to work out your own personal issues.

It's not something to be taken lightly. Besides the powerful visions, ayahuasca's tendency to make you vomit and shit your pants makes it hard to recommend for a get-together unless you like it messy.

Our ceremony was to be led by three wise men. Well, two men and a woman: Wheeler, Ernesto and Angelina. I know Wheeler was for real because he only had one good eye; the other one he used to see into the spirit world or something.

We were all sat in a circle in the hut (*maloca*) while Tommy blew smoke around the hut like an Orthodox priest. I'm not quite sure what the purpose of this was, but it added to the ambience. Isabella and Wheeler called us over one by one, and when it was my turn to receive the 'medicine' I got up and walked over to the shamans, where Angelina poured me a mixture of reddish-brown sludge into a shot glass from an old Cola bottle.

The shot tastes like an ass smoothie from Simon Cowell's butt-crack but I down it and take my seat. Out went the flickering candle-light. We were now in complete darkness. Silence. Then the sounds of the jungle fill my ears. Frogs, snakes, birds, monkeys . . .

Nothing yet. Oh wait, here it is. I can make out something through the little light that gets through the windows. It's a giant spider. The window frames on the *maloca* have become its legs and it's crawling around, just minding its own business. I look up and there's some kinda frog or lizard hanging from the ceiling, staring down at me. Heh, I'm tripping, and it's kind of funny. I look back to where the spider used to be and there's another huge frog. It beckons me to come on its raft and starts paddling down the river. What I see next can only be described as an infinite, never-ending kaleidoscope of impossible shapes and colours, before plunging back into total darkness.

I start to panic. My heart's racing and I'm sweating like a priest in a playground. While ayahuasca's not usually dangerous by itself, it can be if you have a heart condition or in combination with anti-depressants or something called *toé*, a potent deliriant that can make your trip even more insane. I flash my torch over to Sasha.

'What's going on; where am I?'

'It doesn't matter where you are . . . let go, surrender to it.'

'I don't feel so good.'

'Do you wanna take a shower? It might help.'

'Yes . . . shower . . .'

Sasha takes my hand and leads me to the shower, which bathes me in rainbow as I bounce between the walls. This trip has the dubious distinction of having the weirdest shower I've ever taken . . . and I've showered in prison.

'Where am I?'

'You're in the shower!'

'Yes! I'm in the shower . . . what's going on?'

'You drank some ayahuasca, remember?'

Oh yeah.

'Have I been here for a long time?'

'About five minutes.'

It seemed like I'd always been in the shower, like Jack Torrance at the Overlook Hotel. Good thing I wore trunks.

'Is it gonna be like this for long?' I ask Sasha.

'It's just beginning!' she laughs.

On some level I understood I was in the shower, but in which plane of existence? It seemed like I was in two minds. One was conscious and understood things like language and directions, the other was somewhere in Kermit land. By the time we get back, the ceremony is in full swing. The shamans are singing *icaros*, songs to dispel evil spirits. I focus on my breathing, in and out, and as I do so it feels like the whole *maloca*, the whole hut, is breathing with me. I fall into a trance, rocking back and forth until someone comes up and sprays me with water. Lava pours down my face and fills my eyes. A hand reaches out of the darkness and gives me a towel. It feels so good to wipe myself down, like stroking the furry wall.

I am completely fucked. All sense of space and time have disappeared. Meanwhile, something awful is rising up from my stomach. I guess I can hold it in, but it's easier not to. As I reach for the bucket, who is holding it but none other than old Rafiki, the wise baboon from *The Lion King*. He looks at me knowingly. I acknowledge his presence before emptying my insides into the container, which is filled with a million jaguar faces rotating in a spiral. They are not impressed.

It's time for my own, personal *icaro*. I move towards the shamans and the chanting gets really loud. I wonder what the shamans are saying. Since it's all in Quechua and Shipibo, the native languages of Peru, it could be their grocery list for all I know. As I sit back down after listening to Wheeler and Ernesto spitting some mad bars, suddenly everything becomes perfectly clear.

We're sitting in total darkness, yet I can still see my mat, the shape of the hut and everyone around me as clearly as if it were broad daylight. Occasionally, Ernesto or Wheeler would light up a traditional *mapacho* cigarette and I'd see them, briefly illuminated, as the mighty Norse gods Thor and Odin sitting atop their thrones.

It feels as though someone is touching me, gently putting their hands on my face and moving their finger across my lips. I look around closely but there's no one there, yet it feels like everyone is. Everyone, everything, everywhere. It all seems to make sense somehow, like we all have our place in the universe. We're all the same: you, me, my parents, black people, white people, people who've left us behind, favela kids, refugees, even little bugs and creepy-crawlies. We all fit in there somewhere in the structure of the cosmos and I couldn't tell you if it's a 'God' that's responsible for it all, but there's something there in the natural order of things that seems very fucking important. I realise I'm a part of this system, and all my stresses and worries disappear as the universe wraps me in its loving arms.

I think about my parents. Everything they've done has been for me and my sister, and what have I given in return? They're humans, not gods, and they deserve something back. And Rita is only human as well. But she's not like my parents; she's not biologically programmed to deal with this shit. Her letting me go might not be the right thing to do, but thinking about how my behaviour must have been she doesn't need that shit in her life. For the first time in two years, I have closure.

As proceedings draw to a close, so does my feeling of Zen. Wheeler and the band sing one final *icaro* and the session is finished. Freakin' finally. I feel exhausted and can barely move.

'Right, that's enough weird shit for one night,' I say, before stumbling off to bed. The stars give a twinkle as I look up at the sky.

People have been getting high for literally thousands of years. Ayahuasca is just one of the many concoctions humans have invented to reach a different state of consciousness, often bringing them closer to the gods. Not content with blessing us with democracy, philosophy and mathematics, the ancient Greeks gave us the first techno house raves as well. They were the Eleusinian Mysteries, an annual festival held in honour of the goddesses Demeter and Persephone that was the equivalent of gurning your face off at Burning Man in 300 BC. Revellers drank the kykeon, a magical brew with similar effects to LSD.

While the Amazonians have ayahuasca, Native Americans venerate peyote, a Mexican cactus that they believe opens the door to another level of reality. Siberian shamans ingested magic mushrooms as part of their rituals, while *iboga*, West Africa's version of ayahuasca, is used in ceremonies that can leave you tripping for days.

Drugs, at least the fun kinds, generally come in five different flavours – stimulants (cocaine, caffeine, crystal meth) fire you up; depressants (alcohol, sleeping pills) bring you down; psychedelics (like shrooms, ayahuasca or LSD) make you see things; opioids (heroin, morphine, fentanyl), which come from opium; and cannabis, which is its own thing. All of these have wildly different effects, so which one you take depends on what you wanna do. But whether it's a cup of coffee or a line of Bolivian marching powder, people take mind-altering substances for the same reason we get together, play games, have sex, meditate or listen to music: for a thrill, to relax, to be sociable (PS: all these things are better on drugs).

Dopeworld is everywhere – from the high-rolling bankers to the street dealers. Everyone does drugs. Everyone knows someone who does drugs. Feeling a little grouchy because you didn't have an espresso this morning? Wah-wah, you fucking druggie. Yes, caffeine is a drug, one you can even OD on if you tried hard enough, and you are (in your own, more socially-acceptable way) also a drug addict. You could be sat next to someone on the train who has a gram on them. Doctors and lawyers take them, students take them, parents take them. All your favourite musicians smoke weed. The judge who puts people away has a massive coke blowout once a month. There's no escaping it.

Besides ayahuasca, Peru's also home to another one of the world's most popular poisons. From Iquitos I went to be a tourist in Cuzco, southern Peru. Climbing the Inca Trail to Machu Picchu, it became painfully clear I was woefully unprepared for the trip. Marching up and down through the mist-shrouded mountains, sometimes we were in the clouds *as it was raining*. It was wetter than wet, and since

I didn't bring any wellies, I was stuck wrapping plastic bags over my feet.

Meanwhile, our porters bounded effortlessly from one hilltop to another as they carried loads several times their size. The secret to their agility was the small green leaves they'd constantly chew in their mouths – coca.

We stopped to make a customary offering of coca leaves to the Earth Goddess, Pachamama. For over 4,000 years, the native peoples of the Andes have considered the coca plant sacred and a cornerstone of their civilisation: it would have been impossible to build the roads we were now walking on that high up in the mountains without giving the workers an energy boost and something to stave off altitude sickness.* These roads enabled the Incas to rule over an empire spanning the length of South America, from the northernmost reaches of Ecuador all the way down to Chile.

After four days, there it was: the lost city itself. Resting nearly 8,000 feet above sea level, Machu Picchu's stony mountaintop ruins are second only to Christ the Redeemer as the most famous site in South America, and a lasting testament to the Incas. And they couldn't have done it without coca.

Holy men took coca for their sacraments. Warriors chewed it before battle. The entire empire ran on coca. But all that changed in 1532 when a group of Spaniards led by an illiterate bastard named Francisco Pizarro landed in Ecuador. The Incas, weakened by disease and civil war, were no match for the musket-wielding, horseback-riding Spaniards, who went on to conquer the entire empire with fewer than 200 men. Pizarro had the Inca emperor executed after taking all his gold, then enslaved his people, putting them to work in the silver mines. At first, the conquistadors wanted to bring these uncouth savages to Christ and declared that coca was the devil's folly, then they turned around and called it the Lord's work after finding

* 'I must have had a lot of altitude sickness in London' said my friend Toby.

their captives would dig up more silver than they could carry for just a few more lines.

The coca magic would have probably stayed in South America were it not for German scientist Albert Niemann, who in 1860 isolated its active ingredient: cocaine. Nightclub toilets would never be the same. Sigmund Freud bashed out a few lines, then mumbled something about having sex with his mother. A cocaine-laced wine, Vin Mariani, got the enthusiastic approval of the Pope after fuelling a few late-night sessions at the Vatican. And one bright spark in Atlanta tried making his own knockoff version, swapping the alcohol for kola nuts. The name of this new drink? Coca-Cola.

Cocaine makes you feel good, really fucking good, and you can't wait to tell everyone how fucking good it is while your heart's going apeshit and your eyes dart across the room like marbles in a pinball machine. It also wears off quickly, costs a fortune and feels like a massive rip-off. That is, unless you take cocaine in Colombia.

'This is 100 per cent pure, local Mafia shit,' said Steve, an old-school hippy from the Woodstock era, as he racked up a line. 'I get it for practically nothing.'

We were in the sleaziest of sleazy hostels in the sleazy port town of Santa Marta. Turns out cocaine in Colombia ain't that hard to find, especially if you're a gringo tourist. Just stand outside for five minutes in any given part of town and you'll be approached by some kids peddling cigarettes, snacks and usually a gram or two of the country's national product. It's rarely cut and even if you get ripped off, it doesn't matter: at five dollars a gram, it costs even less than a Happy Meal. Steve got it even cheaper thanks to his connects in the local underworld.

I railed a line of Steve's powder and, *Oh my God*, it's so smooth going down you can't even feel it in your throat. This is real coke, not that worm pesticide they feed us in Europe. But even pure coke is one of the worst things you can put in your body. Cocaine floods then drains your brain of dopamine (the chemical that makes you happy), leaving you craving for more. Playing with dopamine levels screws up your brain's natural reward system: in your mind, the white stuff becomes synonymous with feeling happy and you start getting hooked. Snorting too much leads to heart problems, delusions of grandeur and paranoia, as well as generally being an insufferable asshole.

Good thing I was too busy waiting for Steve to stop babbling about his restaurant idea and give me another bump of yayo to care.

Weed, heroin, hash and cocaine all come from remote parts of the world, yet if you know the right person they're just a phone call away. Our worldwide drug culture is a direct result of globalisation – trade, transport, culture and business. How else do you explain why an indigenous Andean plant gets chopped up and snorted at a house party in Shoreditch? But what goes up must come down, and all good times come to an end . . .

8

Shanghai'd

The party couldn't go on forever. Eventually, one country was gonna have enough of its citizens snorting nose candy and huffing the devil's lettuce. That country was China.

I was excited to spend the day in Shanghai on my way to the Philippines to write another chapter of this book. A glitzy metropolis sitting on the Yangtze River, Shanghai now has more skyscrapers than Chicago. At the heart of it is the Bund, with the Oriental Pearl TV tower looming over the riverside like a giant needle going through a flying saucer.

Eighty-odd years ago, it was a different story. Shanghai in the 1930s resembled 1920s Chicago, a booming trade hub where East meets West. So I grabbed a taxi and made my way to what remained of Old Shanghai and its gangsterland, the French Concession.

Throughout history, heroin and its mother drug, opium, have both fascinated and repulsed humanity.

Opium itself is a sticky brownish gum that comes out when you slice open the pods of the *Papaver somniferum*, or opium poppy. The poppy is one tough flower and can survive just about anywhere, but it grows best in soil that's been dug up or ploughed in a warm, sunny climate that's not too rainy, not too dry. We don't know which society first discovered opium, but we do know it's mentioned in the earliest texts from the ancients. In the *Odyssey*, Helen of Troy slips some opium into the wine at a banquet in honour of the warriors who'd fallen in her love triangle. The veterans immediately forget their woes and spend the rest of the day wandering around the palace stoned.

In Victorian times being a drug addict didn't make you a loser: you could mainline heroin for breakfast, lunch and dinner and still ride your penny farthing to the country club. For commoners it was cheaper than going to the doctor; it cured cholera, dysentery and diarrhoea, which could be fatal back then. It was even used to calm crying babies, and since opium kills your appetite you also saved money on baby food.

In the nineteenth century, chemists started breaking down opium to get to the good stuff. In 1806, German scientist Friedrich Sertürner discovered morphine, naming it after Morpheus, the Greek god of sleep. During the American Civil War, both sides used morphine as painkiller, and thousands of veterans came home with crippling withdrawal – the 'soldier's disease'. Then, in 1898, heroin was synthesised by Heinrich Dreser, another German chemist, at Bayer Laboratories. Faster-acting and more potent than morphine, doctors first thought it could be a cure for the soldier's disease, but by 1910 they emphatically realised this was not the case.

Heroin can be sniffed, snorted, smoked and injected. For those who use it, heroin is an escape; you inject, blood shoots back into the syringe and you lie back in a cocoon of pure bliss. The problem is that, after getting cocooned a couple of times, you'll want to do it again and again. By the time you're an addict, you no longer get that magical feeling you had from the first time, but you have to keep doing it just to feel normal.

Medically speaking, if you took controlled doses of diamorphine (that is, clinically pure heroin) the only long-term side effect you'd have to deal with is the addiction itself, which means that when you don't have any, you start feeling like shit, maybe even like you're about to die. But although you might *feel* like you're about to die, you'll still live to tell the tale. Withdrawal from alcohol, however, if you're an alcoholic, could send your body into shock and that actually *can* kill you. Even then, you'd have to be doing smack on the regular to get to that stage: consider that hospitals give diamorphine to pregnant women for pain relief, and they don't get addicted. But in theory, other than the problem of dependence, you can keep taking it indefinitely. Keep knocking back shots, on the other hand, and that *will* kill you.

Unfortunately, most junkies have to deal with black-market skag, which comes with its own set of problems: blood poisoning, overdoses, HIV and hepatitis with a side-order of fucked-up veins from not injecting properly. After all their other blood vessels are out of business, some people even start sticking needles in their dick. Never underestimate a dope fiend's devotion to his fix.

Opium was first brought over to the Celestial Kingdom by Arab merchants on the Silk Road, the ancient trade route linking East to West. For hundreds of years, addiction wasn't really a problem, since most people ate it, which is a weaker way of ingesting, but then European sailors introduced them to smoking and the Chinese, wanting to join the cool kids hanging at the back of the playground, mixed opium into their tobacco pipes. The British Empire, or more accurately the East India Trading Company, saw there was money to be made and started shipping opium to China from their base in India, selling it dirt-cheap. Rightly or wrongly, the Chinese thought they were being turned into a nation of addicts.

In 1729 the Chinese emperor, fed up with the Englishmen poisoning his people, banned the poppy-based narcotic, punishable by death, strangulation, prison or exile. But since the Chinese navy consisted of about two rubber dinghies and an inflatable dolphin, the East India Company carried on business as usual, protecting their shipments with gunboats while having smaller boats meet them offshore to pick up the cargo.

And so in 1839 the emperor put his top cop, China's Dirty Harry, on the case. Lin Zexu surrounded the British enclave of Canton and threatened to lock up every dealer and crooked official inside – foreign or Chinese – if they didn't hand over their stock. The British commander reluctantly ordered all 20,283 chests of opium to be surrendered to Lin, who had them emptied into a massive pit, which was then filled with seawater and lime. One of the Chinese workers at the scene got caught stealing a few grams of opium and was beheaded on the spot. His work done, Lin packed his bags to go home.

That would have been the end of it, but then a British sailor killed a local in a drunken brawl. The Brits refused to hand him over, so Lin had Canton surrounded again. This time, alleged international smack kingpin Alexandrina 'Queen' Victoria called in the Royal Navy to bombard the shit out of the Chinese with cannon fire until they managed to re-open the smuggling routes (and also seize Hong Kong). So began the Opium Wars. The East India Company had effectively become the world's first drug cartel, and the Royal Navy its enforcers. By 1860, British redcoats made it all the way to Beijing and razed the Summer Palace, forcing the Chinese to sign a treaty that finally opened the country up to foreigners and legalised the opium trade on *very* favourable terms to the Crown.

The Opium Wars are now part of the Chinese national legend, marking the beginning of the Century of Humiliation that China spent under the boot-heel of foreign powers, her territory annexed or occupied. But as the celebration of Thanksgiving shows, national legends don't always paint the truest picture of the past. At the risk of sounding like an imperial apologist, was the opium scourge really that bad?

The Chinese knew about opium for well over a thousand years. It's not like the British suddenly rocked up one day and said, 'Hey guys, wanna try this?' and the Chinese just dropped whatever they were doing and hit with the pipe; this doesn't square with our modern understanding of addiction.

According to the UN, out of around 255 million people around the world who use illegal drugs today, only 29 million (just over 10 per cent) *at most* can be classed as 'problem users', in exactly the same way that having a glass of wine doesn't make you a raging alcoholic. Cocaine is not a healthy thing to be putting in your body by any means, but having a line or two won't turn you into Rick James; you need to be doing it every other day for like a month to start developing 'problems' (for that reason, the urban legend of dealers giving out freebies to get you hooked is a terrible business model).

Obviously, this varies from drug to drug; with something like crack or heroin, it can go all the way up to one in five. Nine out of ten druggies don't cause problems, just like most winos don't rampage through your town centre at night smashing up kebab shops. This distinction is very important. And this figure doesn't come from some whiny liberal pro-drugs group but the United Nations Office on Drugs and Crime, an organisation whose 1998 slogan was 'A Drug-free World : We Can Do It!' It's that remaining 10 per cent, those very extreme cases, that give this skewed impression.

So, while millions of strung-out Chinamen would lounge around opium dens, puffing on ornamented pipes, it's unclear how many were actually addicted, since most seemed perfectly capable of putting down the pipe if they needed to. It's certainly possible that 25% of the country was *using* opium (the same way most adults today drink), and in some cases a few people did lose everything over it. But why exaggerate? Because the Chinese were deadly afraid of foreign devils. Call it pride, call it xenophobia, but the Chinese wanted to protect their ancient civilisation from outsiders ... embodied, in this case, by opium. Not too disimilar, in fact, to how Chinese immigrants would soon be treated in America.

What Britain did was deplorable, but not that different from their other overseas adventures in Africa and India. It was British gunboats, not dragon-chasing, that cost China the war (no army has lost a war because they were all too baked – some individual battles, maybe). The idea that sneaky drug-dealing Brits caused the downfall of Chinese civilisation is preposterous, but convenient for the ruling party, as we shall see. It was domination by foreign powers *symbolised* by opium, rather than the effects of the drug itself, that brought about China's downfall.

Walking around the city, I could still see the tree-lined streets and colonial architecture that characterised the French Concession, a slice of the city that China was forced to surrender after the Opium Wars. Under the arrangement, the Concession was officially French territory, in which the native Chinese were regarded as second-class citizens.

The boss of the French Concession was Du Yuesheng, aka 'Big-Eared Du'. A peasant boy from the countryside, Du came to the big city to work for 'Pockmarked Huang' Jinrong, a crooked cop and boss of the Green Gang, which was one of the triads, or Chinese Mafia. The triads originated as secret societies sworn to overthrow the Qing dynasty, then forgot about their vows and started selling drugs instead.

Pockmarked Huang ran afoul of a local warlord and was thrown into jail in 1924, leaving Big Ears to run the gang. Shanghai was a perfect place for all sorts of nefarious deeds, being divided into British, American and French jurisdictions that rarely, if ever, worked with each other. Du ran his opium dens and whorehouses out of the French quarter, paying off the local police if they got too nosy.

A man like Big Ears could have a lot of enemies. In 1917, the Russian Civil War broke out between the Red Army and anti-Bolshevik forces, and soon thousands of White Russians who supported the tsar fled to Shanghai, where the domes of their Orthodox churches still stand over the rows of neat French houses. Du wouldn't go anywhere without a contingent of Russian heavies, along with a set of monkey heads (don't ask) he had sewn into his robes for good luck.

Like his bodyguards, Dumbo wasn't a fan of the communists. He was tight with the Chinese nationalist party, the Kuomintang, and its leader Chiang Kai-shek. In April 1927, his goons massacred thousands of Communist Party members in what became known as the White Terror. In reward for his services, Big Ears was appointed head of the Opium Suppression Bureau.

But the triads couldn't rule Shanghai forever. The communists and the Kuomintang briefly joined forces in the Second World War, but by 1946 they were again at each other's throats, and civil war broke out. The commies gained the upper hand and in 1949 emerged victorious, chasing the KMT and their Mafia goons out of the country. The gangsters fled to Taiwan, Hong Kong and Macao, setting up shop in what would become triad strongholds. Du died peacefully in Hong Kong in 1951.

Back at home, Mao set about rebuilding China's national identity. This meant ridding the country of opium, blamed for a hundred years of woes. Poppy fields were burnt, dealers were rounded up and shot, addicts were denounced by their relatives and sent to labour camps. Through mass executions and brute force, Beijing managed to 'solve' the drug problem in the world's most populous country. Meanwhile, Mao's government nationalised the tobacco industry, profiting off the deaths of millions of Chinese.

Every superhero has an origin story. So does every supervillain. The Opium Wars are China's origin story: the myth of an opium-addicted country, and the Communist Party as its saviour, is now taught in every school in China.

It was already night-time when I took a last look across the Bund, the pink glow of the Oriental Pearl reflecting in the water. China today is a very different country. Mao might have purged the country of drug dealers and other ne'er-do-wells, but after his death, liberal economic reforms in the 1970s re-opened the country to the world. Embracing decadent Western capitalism, China's fast-growing economy is now second only to the United States. You can find Gucci designer bags right next to the hammer-and-sickle.

At the same time, with all that spare change in their pockets, there's a fast-growing market for illicit intoxicants in China as young people discover Mao's *Little Red Book* wasn't all it was cracked up to be and relax, have fun and enjoy themselves.

But the memory of the Opium Wars remains strong and anyone having more than their allotted amount of 'fun' was, until recently, swiftly bundled off to a labour camp. And God forbid you get caught smuggling: China executes more people for that than the rest of the world put together. Death sentences are read out in sports stadiums before cheering crowds. It's fucking medieval.

With or without opium, by the mid-nineteenth century the country was falling apart anyway. There was widespread poverty, corruption and famine, followed by the Taiping Rebellion, an uprising far bloodier than the Opium Wars led by a guy who claimed to be a descendant of Jesus Christ. Because of all the troubles at home, many Chinese left to find a better life in America. Once there, though, most of them found themselves toiling away in slave-like conditions laying railroad tracks through the Old West, and facing white racism. In the nineteenth and early twentieth centuries, fear of the 'Yellow Peril' was in full swing, and Chinese immigrants were the target of xenophobic laws and race riots.

Not only were they taking jobs from decent, hard-working 'muricans, but those devious Chinamen brought their fiendish Oriental vices with them. They were setting up drug dens to ply pure, innocent white girls with dope before having their way with them, the slanty-eyed yellow bastards! And so, in 1875, San Francisco, the West Coast city with the highest population of Chinese, passed the first piece of American anti-narcotics legislation: an ordinance banning opium dens.

9

Dry Season

Ellis Island, 1906. A creaky boat pulled into New York Harbour past the Statue of Liberty, crammed with immigrants looking for their new home. They came from all over – Greeks, Italians, Germans, Polaks, Jews, Irish. After passing quarantine, they settled in enclaves like Greektown and Little Italy, often filthy slums and crowded brownstone tenement buildings. Among those huddled masses yearning to breathe free was nine-year-old troublemaker, Charles Salvatore 'Lucky' Luciano.

Born to an Italian family that barely spoke English, Charlie didn't care much for school, dropping out at age fourteen to run wild on the mean streets of Brooklyn. A juvenile delinquent, Charlie made his first forays into a life of crime shaking down Jewish kids from a nearby neighbourhood for their lunch money. But one of those kids, a scrawny boy named Meyer Lansky, stood up to Luciano. Lansky's family, like most Jewish immigrants, were fleeing pogroms (race riots) in Poland and Ukraine in what was then the old Russian Empire. Lansky told him to go fuck himself and they became best friends. Along with Lansky's hot-tempered friend, Benjamin 'Bugsy' Siegel,* their lifelong bromance would change the course of dopeworld forever.

* The man who'd later run Las Vegas, whose death by way of getting shot through the eye inspired Moe Greene in *The Godfather* (Lansky inspired Hyman Roth).

It started in the nineteenth century with the likes of Carrie Nation, a Midwestern woman with a grudge against alcohol after losing her first husband to the bottle. Together with a crew of hymn-singin', hatchet-swingin' vigilantes, Carrie went around busting up saloons across Kansas and Oklahoma for selling the devil's brew. Carrie was part of the Temperance Movement, in which those with more realistic concerns about the dangers of drinking teamed up with the ultra-Christian, Bible-basher types.

When it comes to altering states of consciousness, by far the most popular way of getting there is booze. It makes everything a bit funny, a bit wavy, and makes it more likely you will wake up in some alleyway with a traffic cone on your head and a sign that says 'I am a lamp.' And it's not only humans – chimpanzees have also been known to get buzzed on fermented fruit juice.

Alcohol probably first emerged around ten thousand years ago in the Stone Age when an unsuspecting caveman felt a little tipsy after having some honey that had been left out too long. Beer came along when those cavemen settled down and began fermenting grain, with the Egyptians and Babylonians drinking it as far back as the third millennium BC. Wine was invented a little later when people worked out they could do the same thing with grapes, and it later got incorporated into Jewish and Christian worship. Jesus turned water into wine, and Catholics drank it at Mass to symbolise his blood.

Although now, thanks to religion, most of the Middle East is as dry as the desert around it, the word alcohol itself comes from the Arabic *al-kohl*. The Persian alchemist Rhazes was the first to discover alcohol itself through distillation – waiting for the yeast to ferment yielded a maximum strength of 16 per cent, but boiling a mixture of water and alcohol and condensing the fumes gave something much more pure. The practice spread, and now each nation has its pride and joy – the Japanese have sake, Americans have their bourbon, Mexicans have tequila and us Russians drink vodka.

But drinking wasn't just something you did to find dates attractive. It was also a lifesaver. In 1854, when a cholera epidemic swept through London, the one area which wasn't affected was next to a local brewery, where the workers preferred quenching their thirst with beer. Filtration technology was only developed at the end of the nineteenth century – till then, drinking booze instead of water must have kept everyone constantly pissed.

But alcohol also had its downsides. During the Gin Craze that gripped eighteenth-century London, as prices dropped the unwashed masses had more money than ever to spend on cheap spirits that got them through their grim, meaningless lives. Drunkenness, lawlessness and depravity followed, until finally Parliament passed the 1751 Gin Act, which banned distilleries from selling their drinks to any John and Jane that passed by.

More than any other drug, alcohol's been ingrained in our culture, as our entire social lives revolve around drinking. Get that promotion? Have a drink! It's your son's bar mitzvah? Drink! Christmas Day, Boxing Day, Saint Patrick's Day, your best mate's birthday? DRINK DRINK DRINK!

And yet it's one of the most dangerous drugs you can put in your body. Short-term effects include a bad hangover, throwing up and calling the bouncer a cunt. Alcohol destroys your inhibitions and unleashes your inner warrior, leading to bar-room brawls and battered spouses, while getting behind the wheel after a round of Jägermeisters will most likely end with you slamming into a lamppost or a small child. Long-term effects include brain damage, liver failure, heart disease and death.

Carrie Nation saw drinking as the great social disease that needed to be cured and her movement grew in popularity, with some states putting their own anti-drinking laws on the books. Saloons, that classic, all-American symbol of the Wild West and

Manifest Destiny, shut down across Kansas in 1881, making it the first 'dry' state.

And then there was the 'ethnic' angle. In contrast to the Puritan code of abstinence that ran through American society, drinking was central to the culture and lives of the millions of immigrants that poured in from Europe: the Jewish tradition of Purim positively *demands* you get hammered once a year. Needless to say, many locals weren't too thrilled about their swarthy new neighbours and their rambunctious parties. As for the 'negroes', everyone knew *they* couldn't be trusted to handle their liquor.

But it was the First World War that proved the tipping point, as along came the Germans, storming across Europe and downing kegs on the way. It simply wasn't patriotic to share any bad habits with those nasty, beer-swilling Huns, and so in 1919 Congress passed the Volstead Act, making the favourite pastime of millions of Americans a criminal act overnight. Saloons across the country shut down. A few stayed open and tried to rebrand themselves by selling 'near-beer', but they were not successful because no one wants to drink piss.

The American incarnation of the Mafia grew out of the various small-time gangs formed in the squalid ghettos of Little Italy, as well as extortion rings like the Black Hand. The Mafia, or *La Cosa Nostra* ('This thing of ours'), is kinda like a parallel government for wiseguys, see? To get inducted into a Mafia family you had to go through an initiation ceremony and swear to uphold their oath of *omerta*, although being a bunch of cold-blooded killers, that oath is a little different from, say, the Boy Scouts. You also had to be fully Italian – the Mob only trusted *paisanos* straight off the boat from the old country. After that, you pay the boss his cut, and in return he makes sure no one fucks with you: the cops, other wise guys. And every now and then he might ask you to pop a cap in someone. It'd be rude to say no.

By 1929, Lucky and Lansky had grown into full-fledged gang-sters. They were mentored by Arnold Rothstein, the mastermind who fixed the 1919 World Series. Rothstein was a kingpin of the Jewish Mafia (the Kosher Nostra?) and encouraged Lucky to think of crime as a business, not just an endless game of cops-and-robbers. Such a business opportunity presented itself with Prohibition.

Bootlegging, like most crimes, is a crime of opportunity. Most crime doesn't happen simply because people are bad; it happens because they see the chance to get something (money, power, the thrill of exposing yourself to unsuspecting bystanders) and think they won't get caught, or that the risk of getting caught is worth the reward. That opportunity is provided by supply and demand: so, you've got a product that a good portion of the adult population want (and need), and that they can't get in stores. As long as they're willing to pay top dollar, Prohibition is doomed to fail.

Now, the nature of the black market means you need the connec-tions to be able to source your illegal product. You also need to have some sort of protection – after all, you can't sue or call the cops if someone robs you or screws you over. This meant that control of the market fell into the hands of those who could provide both. With that in mind, Lucky and Lansky began driving crates of whiskey over the Canadian border, with Bugsy riding shotgun.

Lucky had a problem. He worked for East Harlem kingpin Joe 'The Boss' Masseria, whose hunger for spaghetti was matched only by his lust for power. Masseria was a nightmare of a boss, always keeping Luciano on call 24/7 and demanding a cut of every criminal activity in New York, including Charlie's liquor business. In one hissy fit, he threatened to cut off and feed Lucky his Charles Dickens.

Like any disgruntled employee, Charlie started looking elsewhere. Rival boss Salvatore Maranzano was equally upset with Masseria, and Lucky drove to meet him one night at a Staten Island pier. But when Maranzano asked Lucky to kill his employer, the job interview took a sharp turn south. Lucky refused and immediately got a blow to the side of the head. When he woke up, he found himself strung up in a warehouse surrounded by Maranzano and several masked men, beating and stabbing him. Charlie summoned all his strength and lunged at Maranzano, kicking him in the balls. The old boss took a knife and slashed Lucky's face, leaving him with a permanent droopy eye, before taking a car and dumping him on the street, beaten to a pulp. A few days later when Lansky came to see him in hospital, Charlie said he was lucky to be alive.

'That's you,' said Lansky, 'Lucky Luciano.'

Meanwhile, the war between Masseria and Maranzano was heating up. They were hijacking each other's shipments and bodies were dropping all over New York. It was time to hit the mattresses.

Masseria was old-school and refused to work with non-Italians, but Lucky, who grew up with Jews, saw the future: crooks of all colours and creeds ripping off people together. Masseria had to go. Luciano took him out for lobster; then, when Lucky got up to take a leak, assassins walked in and pumped the fat cat full of holes. With the big man gone, Maranzano's days were numbered. Charlie never forgot that night in Staten Island. On 10 September 1931, Maranzano was shanked, shot four times and had his throat slit in his office over Grand Central Station.

To consolidate his hold over the New York underworld, Luciano then called his childhood friends, Lansky and Siegel, and formed Murder, Inc., a cutthroat army of fedora-wearing triggermen who exterminated rats like they were pest control. 'The yids and the dagos will no longer fight each other,' Siegel proclaimed at a Mob summit.

But the Big Apple wasn't enough. Lucky summoned Mob bosses across the country to the Blackstone Hotel in Chicago, where he laid out a plan that would shape the future of American vice for the next fifty years. To avoid another costly war, each Mafia family would get its own city (except New York, which would get five), and any problems would be ironed out by the Commission – a board of directors for Lucky's corporation of crime, with him as CEO.

After toasting the idea, the delegates retired to the very finest wine and women the Windy City had to offer, courtesy of their host, a man whose name is synonymous with Prohibition-era gangsterism: Mr Al Capone.

Like Luciano, Capone also ran with a Brooklyn street gang until age twenty, when he moved to Chicago to work for mob boss Johnny Torrio and his uncle, 'Big Jim' Colosimo. Colosimo conveniently took a dirt nap soon after, paving the way for Capone and Torrio to take over his operation and move into the bootlegging business.

Despite the law, people kept drinking in secret underground bars known as speakeasies. These places had to operate on the down-low, so you had to give the password to the guy through the peephole in order to get in. By 1927 there were some five thousand speakeasies in Manhattan alone, ranging from high-class joints to a sleazy set-up in someone's flat. Adventurous whites could head uptown for the night, which led to a perhaps unexpected consequence: the popularity of jazz. The more high-class of these watering holes hosted performances from the greatest jazz legends of all time. Duke Ellington got a gig playing at the Cotton Club in Harlem, run by Irish gangster Owney Madden, and audiences came from far and wide to hear some of that 'Cotton Club sound'. It was through speakeasies that jazz got introduced to white America and took off in the mainstream.

Gangsters and musicians often crossed paths. Pianist 'Fats' Waller was once snatched up and bundled in a car by four goons who forced him to play at a birthday party. It turns out this party was being hosted by none other than Al Capone, who was a huge fan. Three days later, Fats found himself drunk in the back of a limo, his pockets overflowing with thousands of dollars in tips. But most of the time, speakeasies were run by white mobsters who stopped the black musicians and their audience from mingling together.

Purveyors of these premises had to buy their booze from Mr Capone ... or else. Al's main competition was Dean O'Banion, an Irishman who ran both the city's North Side Gang *and* his own flower shop. As passionate about flower-arranging as he was about killing, in 1924 he was gunned down trimming daises at his shop. Gangland was about to explode.

On 14 February 1929, seven members of the North Side Gang got the worst Valentine's card of all time when four men dressed as cops, possibly out-of-town killers from Detroit's vicious Purple Gang, lined them up against a warehouse wall before spraying them with Tommy guns. No one was convicted of the attack, which isn't surprising considering that Capone had half of Chicago in his pocket: in case there was any doubt over who *really* ran the town, Capone once slapped the shit out of the mayor right in front of City Hall as the police looked on.

But after the Valentine's Day Massacre, the law started closing in on Capone. He was declared Public Enemy Number One, and a crack squad of federal agents known as the Untouchables was sent in to bring him down. Capone eventually got sent down ... for not paying his taxes. In 1931, just after the Blackstone meeting, a judge slapped him with eleven years in Alcatraz for not giving the government its cut.

But it wasn't big-time crime lords like Al Capone who felt the hardest impact of Prohibition laws. Rich white folks sipping cognac in their mansions escaped the watchful eye of the fuzz, but blacks, immigrants and downtrodden whites made easy targets for packing prison cells as America took its first steps towards becoming an incarceration nation. The open season on minorities also attracted another party – the KKK.

Millions of men, women and children were taken from Africa in shackles to work on Southern plantations, their bondage justified on the grounds that blacks were lazy savages who had to be disciplined by ol' whitey. Even after they lost the Civil War because slavery wasn't as cool as they thought it was, the good ol' boys in the South tried every trick in the book to keep blacks in chains. White folk were terrified that the newly-liberated slaves would come round their houses and make sweet *Mandingo* love to their wives and daughters.

A couple of those insecure limpdicks donned their white robes and formed the Ku Klux Klan, a gang of dunce-cap-wearing honkeys whose mission was to uphold Christian fundamentalism and white supremacy. The Klan's reign of terror extended to anyone who wasn't a WASP – White, Anglo-Saxon Protestant – but blacks were their main target and any coloured boy who looked at a white woman wrong could find himself strung up on a tree. The KKK got away with their crimes because mayors, judges and sheriffs were all members.

The Klan were not too keen on some greasy-haired dagos and Irishmen tempting their white Christian brethren with the devil's nectar, and even less keen on their ladies dancing the night away to that 'nigger jazz'. In Williamson County, southern Illinois, the KKK, with the full blessing of Prohibition Bureau chief Roy Haynes, began terrorising Italian immigrants, raiding their homes and livelihoods, before turning their attention to the French community. Houses were burnt down and suspects were paraded through town squares. Altogether, some three thousand immigrants and their families were forced to flee.

The Klan eventually got a taste of their own medicine by Tommy gun-toting gangsters, who after chasing them out of town turned on each other, with one side carrying out the first aerial bombing in the history of the United States by dropping three crates of dynamite over the other's fortified HQ (killing a dog).

But it was inner-city neighbourhoods that felt the worst impact of rising gangster violence. In 1931, a brazen drive-by shooting by

Irish mobster Vincent 'Mad Dog' Coll on a rival Italian crew in Harlem killed a five-year-old boy and left four more wounded.

Between public enemies and lawmen, you also had to watch what was in your drink. Genuine liquor was highly prized – boat captain William McCoy, who refused to work with gangsters like Luciano, smuggled rum from the Bahamas onboard his yacht, bringing along the real deal; 'the real McCoy'. Alcohol wasn't banned completely: those with a few bottles left in the basement could hold on to their stash, and alcohol could still be acquired for 'legitimate' (read: boring) uses – as a disinfectant, for example, or an industrial solvent. Besides, if there's anything I learnt from prison, it's that if you're desperate for a drink, you can always make your own. Just get together some bread, sugar and some sort of fruit, which in our joint usually meant an apple or an orange, and you blend it all together in a large bottle of water and let it ferment for a couple of weeks until you get a shitty kind of cider, which reeks like vomit, but hey, it gets you drunk! You can make different varieties depending on what you have to work with, and maybe if we had some grapes we could have made some wine (which is probably why we never had grapes). Amateur breweries also tried making their own bathtub gin, often with disastrous results.

Needless to say, neither industrial solvent nor moonshine brewed in someone's bathtub are something you should be putting in your body, and the lack of quality control meant thousands got sick. One batch of moonshine in Wichita, Texas, poisoned 500 people. In some cases, the government deliberately contaminated industrial alcohol to discourage people from drinking it. They paid no heed ... and then they died (the total death toll during Prohibition is estimated at around ten thousand).

By the 1930s, the Great Depression was taking its toll, and the federal government had a great idea: get everyone drunk. Knowing he was fighting a losing battle, President Roosevelt repealed Prohibition on 6 April 1933. That night a truck drove up to the White House loaded with booze. The Mob may have lost its top-earning racket, but some enterprising hoodlums were already looking at the next big thing: narcotics.

It started off with cocaine. Even after winning their freedom, many African Americans stayed on at the plantations in the Deep South, and some took cocaine because it was cheaper than liquor and helped get them through the long hours. And so at the turn of the century, articles started to appear in the *New York Times* with charming headlines such as 'Negro Cocaine "Fiends" are a New Southern Menace', claiming that a white-powder epidemic among Southern blacks gave them superhuman strength and whipped them into a wild frenzy, beating up cops, passers-by and members of their own family. Clearly these demented savages were out of control, and their coke-fuelled rampages made them impervious to bullets.

These stories terrified white, middle-class America, and so in 1914 the Harrison Act made it illegal to sell cocaine or opiates (remember those fiendish Chinamen?) without a licence, which doesn't sound so bad until you realise almost no one got a licence: in 1931, around 20,000 doctors were rounded up for prescribing heroin to their patients so they wouldn't overdose or steal. But was any of it true? Not really. Out of 2,100 blacks in Georgia's prison system in 1903, for example, only two (yes, *two*) were cocaine addicts. But who cares about facts as long as you can get cheap convict labour out of it, right?

At first, the dope game hadn't really been big business. Hatchet-wielding Chinese secret societies (sorry, 'respectable merchants' associations') known as tongs ran the vice and opium rackets in Chinatown, but they mostly kept to themselves and steered clear of the white man. That was about to change. Before he was assassinated in 1928, stumbling into the Park Central Hotel clutching a gunshot wound to his stomach, Lucky's mentor Arnold Rothstein saw which way the wind was blowing. He started buying heroin from Europe and had his men take care of distribution. By the time of his death, Rothstein's crew monopolised the drug trade on the entire Eastern seaboard.

With the Commission, Lucky had become the most powerful criminal in the country. But like his friend Al, the law was catching up with him. Prosecutor Thomas Dewey ordered a crackdown on organised crime in New York. His first target was one Dutch Schultz, who tried to have Dewey whacked. Lucky sensed that taking out a prosecutor would bring down too much heat, and Dutch was soon sleeping with the fishes. Dewey repaid the favour by having Luciano convicted of running a high-class prostitution ring and sentenced him to thirty years.

But don't worry, we won't miss him for long.

Mobsters weren't the only ones changing their business strategy. When the booze ban ended in 1933, Prohibition agent Harry Anslinger, who'd spent his time chasing Mexican beer barons, Canadian whiskey smugglers and rum-runners from the West Indies, found himself with nothing to do. Rather than sit around waiting to be made redundant, Harry, who'd been appointed head of the newly minted Federal Bureau of Narcotics (FBN), set about justifying his new position . . .

10

Keep Off the Grass

Night fell as I was hurried into a local farmer's abode, deep in the Rif mountains of northern Morocco. There was something disarmingly quaint about the sight of palm trees and mud-brick houses carved into the hillside under the pinkish glow of the setting sun. Our host was going to show us how to make hashish, the sticky brown resin made from cannabis, or marijuana.

Hashish has been cultivated in Morocco, mainly here in the Rif mountains, since the Middle Ages. It's as much of an institution as vineyards are in France: the only place safe from the alluring aroma of burning hash is the mosque. Historically, Moroccan kings have always had a hard time imposing their will on the fiercely independent Berber people, so they've been careful not to piss them off and cut off their main source of income lest they risk an all-out rebellion. When the hippy era came along in the 1960s, the European hash market exploded, and an armada of kids on jet skis, armed with kilos of the Rif's finest, lined up to make the run for Spanish shores.

There were only two rooms in the house; the living room, which also doubled as the kitchen and bedroom, and the storage room, which held only one thing: sacks upon sacks of crumbly brown hash. We went in the living room, illuminated by a lone bulb hanging from the ceiling, where a small TV showed a female newsreader while headlines crawled across the bottom of the screen in Arabic. They didn't have running water, and for a family growing thousands of pounds' worth of dope they didn't have much to show for it.

The farmer's ten-year-old son left and came back with two bundles of dried-up weed plants before chopping them into a fine powder, pouring it on top of a drum. He then fastened a sack around the top of the drum like a headpiece and started beating out a tune. But this impromptu concert wasn't just for good vibes. Beating a melody forces the pollen through the fabric of the drum, making it fall to the bottom where it's gathered up and pressed into bricks. It's that pollen which makes up the hash, and it takes hundreds of kilos of weed to get just one kilo of pollen. If you're in the mountains and you hear a rhythmic boom echoing across the valley, you'll know the Berbers are making hash.

There's different kinds of beats for different types of hash. The most powerful strain out there is called Zero-Zero, which is a shade of dark gold in colour and gives you by far the best, cleanest high in the world. I actually prefer hash to weed. With weed I just zone out on the sofa all day, but with hash I can actually get shit done. You can test the quality of hashish by seeing how quickly it catches fire and starts to bubble. I broke off a chunk of our produce and held it over a lighter. It lit up nicely.

Toking up is a tradition dating back to ancient times. For the past 4,000 years, Hindus have been drinking *bhang* – a kind of ganja milkshake – with the blessing of Lord Shiva, usually on special occasions such as Holi. Even the Sikhs, whilst generally against inebriation of any kind, picked up the habit when the great Guru Gobind Singh, in the midst of battle, gave one of his men a cup of *bhang* as they were being charged by an elephant, getting him so high that he single-handedly slayed the beast. To this day, certain sects of Sikhism still drink *bhang* with their Hindu neighbours.

From India, cannabis made its way to the Middle East in the form of hashish, where it made an appearance in *One Thousand and One Nights*. In 'The Tale of the Hashish-Eater', a stoned beggar falls asleep in a public bath, dreaming of a harem of curvaceous concubines, only to get thrown out after everyone sees his rising manhood. But it wasn't all bawdy dick jokes and belly-dancers. The word 'assassin' as well as *assassino* (Spanish and Italian: 'murderer') comes from *Hashishin*, a sect in medieval Persia which pioneered the art of taking motherfuckers *out*. Led by Hassan-ibn-Sabbah, the Old Man of the Mountain, his followers would spend months staking out their target and, when the moment was right, ice that sucker with no regard to their personal safety.

The Seljuk Turks declared them infidels, so Hassan had them murdered in their palaces. Disguised as monks, two Hashishin killers walked up to the King of Jerusalem and stabbed him to death. And one night, the mighty Saladin woke up with a dagger on his pillow, left there as a warning.

Hassan commanded such loyalty because he showed his followers a vision of paradise, full of beautiful naked women and all the hashish they could smoke, or so the legend goes. Sometimes he would go to the garden and bury himself from the neck down to make it look like they were speaking to his disembodied head ... really the kind of idea that only makes sense if you're high.

Today, the Assassins' mountain fortress in the peaks of Alamut lies in ruins, having been sacked by the Mongols. But hashish spread west through the Arab world, eventually reaching Africa and Morocco. Back in Europe, the Scythians, nomadic warriors who wandered the plains of what is now present-day Ukraine, were particularly fond of smoking weed from solid-gold bongs, and thousands of years later traces of THC (tetrahydrocannabinol – the chemical that gets you high) were found in a pipe belonging to William Shakespeare. But toking up was still something of a rarity in Western civilisation until the nineteenth century, when Napoleon's forces marched through North Africa, saw the locals blazing up and passed the blunt to trendy Parisians, including one Alexandre Dumas, author of *The Three Musketeers*. Dumas and his famous friends gathered at the Hashish Club in Paris's hipster quarter, where they'd sit around getting baked.

Aside from its more groovy side-effects, hemp fibre from the cannabis plant is some of the strongest in the world and was used as rope to fasten the sails of every power that sailed the Seven Seas – Greeks, Romans, Vikings, Venetians, Spanish, British, French, Dutch and Portuguese – as well as for paper, clothing and everything in between. So precious was hemp that, over in the New World, the first weed laws in America actually ordered farmers to grow *more* of the stuff.

Meanwhile, after the work of Irish scientist William O'Shaughnessy in the 1840s, doctors started prescribing cannabis for all manner of ailments. O'Shaughnessy, while serving in India, found that weed eased the pain of rheumatism and rabies, and brought a sample back to England, where it started being used for everything from childbirth to headaches and periods. It was even prescribed to Queen Victoria by her doctor.

People like to say weed is OK because it's 'natural'; it comes from Mother Earth. Well, getting eaten by a bear is also natural, yet the general consensus is it's something to avoid. Mostly, the effects of cannabis are good – a happy, mellow buzz that turns you into an amateur Socrates and makes movies starring rappers almost bearable. But on a level, it is what it is: being a stoner has consequences, and I'm not just talking about being fat and lazy and forgetting to pick your kids up from school. In some people, high levels of THC induce paranoia* and can push them to a psychotic meltdown: one of my neighbours in pen served nine years for attempted murder after stabbing and torturing his best friend for an hour during a skunk-fuelled psychosis.

---

* They all know ... EVERYONE KNOWS YOU'RE HIGH!

But the evidence for weed and schizophrenia is shaky; it's hard to say whether it actually causes schizophrenia, makes existing symptoms worse, or whether people who become schizophrenics *also* like smoking weed because it calms them. In my entirely non-medical opinion, it's best to err on the side of caution and say if you're already predisposed to certain issues, smoking a bowl a day is unlikely to make you the poster child for mental health.

In the 1930s, pot panic reached hysterical heights. Specifically, that it makes you an axe-swinging lunatic. No, really. In 1933, Florida man Victor Licata butchered his whole family with an axe. Prison shrinks examining him found he had a long history of batshit crazy and didn't even consider marijuana as a factor, but rumours spread anyway and inspired the film *Reefer Madness*, which depicts a group of stoners' descent into homicidal insanity. Against the advice of doctors and scientists, ex-Prohibition agent Harry Anslinger embarked on one of the wildest propaganda campaigns in American history, claiming that smoking pot can make you go on a murderous rampage.

Then, as with Prohibition, there was the ethnic angle. Marijuana was long associated with hot-blooded Mexicans and rumours it made them go *loco*. 'When some beet field peon takes a few traces of this stuff,' one lawmaker said, 'he thinks he has just been elected president of Mexico, so he starts out to execute all his political enemies.'

But it wasn't just those Hispanics causing panic. Thanks to their playing at unsavoury establishments like speakeasies, as well as being black in general, jazz musicians were a favourite target for law enforcement. Anslinger, in particular, wasn't a fan, so when word got round to him that performers of the devil's music were fond of smoking certain mildly intoxicating herbs ('Man, what's the matter with that cat there?' Cab Calloway used to sing. 'Must be full of reefer.'),

Harry, who was a massive racist even by 1930s standards ('Reefer makes darkies think they're as good as white men,' he once said), got right on it and successfully lobbied for ganja to be outlawed through the Marihuana Tax Act 1937.

And that's how the war on drugs started. Not because they were unhealthy. Remember, this was a completely different era: up until around the 1950s we didn't even know that smoking was bad for you and doctors actually endorsed cigarette ads. Adverts in the 1930s and 40s showed physicians happily puffing away under slogans such as 'More doctors smoke Camels than any other cigarette'. The real reason for banning drugs was straight-up racism.

These wild claims were challenged by New York's mayor Fiorello LaGuardia, who commissioned a scientific study into the effects of marijuana, which unsurprisingly found that most of Harry's arguments were fake news. The LaGuardia Report, published in 1944, found that:

- There's a lot of weed being smoked in the Big Apple, but it's mainly centred around Harlem.
- Most weed smokers are grown-up blacks and Latinos, not little white schoolchildren.
- Smoking weed is not an addiction in the medical sense of the word.
- There's no one single group dominating the ganja business.
- Smoking weed does not lead to hard drugs, and there's no scheme to push pot-heads to heroin.
- Weed's main effects are hunger, paranoia, euphoria, laughing fits, a dry mouth, short-term memory loss and some mildly psychedelic sensations. It certainly doesn't make you bury an axe in your whole family.
- The catastrophic effects of weed in the Big Apple have been grossly overstated.

Basically, the LaGuardia Report confirmed that most of what the Federal Bureau of Narcotics was peddling was pure BS. But no one cared and Anslinger dismissed the report as 'unscientific', even though he himself had conducted no research into the matter. The United States just declared war on a plant.

On 2 October 1937, fifty-eight-year-old Samuel R. Caldwell of Colorado became the first man convicted of selling marijuana. Anslinger himself came to watch his trial. He was sentenced to four years hard labour and a $1,000 fine, and died one year after his release.

But if you don't fancy a lazy night in with a doobie, and prefer bouncing off the walls of your local psych ward yelling incoherently about ants crawling under your skin, then maybe meth is the drug for you.

Chemical Warfare

Sanja Matsuri is a traditional Shinto festival that takes place in Tokyo in the middle of May at the Sensō-ji temple in the Asakusa district and is one of Japan's biggest, as millions take to the streets to celebrate the three men who founded Tokyo's oldest temple. It's also when the Japanese underworld comes out on parade.

As I approached the temple on a scorching-hot Saturday afternoon, the crowds grew larger and larger: old people, young people, all wearing kimonos; giggling schoolgirls slurping smoothies out of light-bulb-shaped cups; and a few gaijin tourists looking lost and slightly intimidated, perhaps because they saw a few of the men were rocking *fundoshi*, thong-like undies that showed a lot of *derrière*. I squeezed my way to the front of the crowd to get a better peek at what was going on.

A team of *fundoshi*-clad men – and a few women – were hoisting what looked like a miniature version of the temple on their shoulders, pausing only to clap their hands and chant something I didn't understand. These were the *mikoshi*, portable shrines that are home to deities or the spirits of the ancestors.

One after another, the processions spilled out of the temple grounds and into the streets, where they followed a pre-arranged route to their final resting place. There, the carriers could look forward to being treated to some snacks and a nice cold beer after a day spent appeasing the gods.

By five o'clock, most of the bells and whistles on the street had died down. It was time to make my way back home. I turned the corner to get out of the temple district and that's when I saw them, the whole crew.

A massive, sumo-looking bodyguard stood watch as a group of middle-aged men, one of them wearing an eyepatch, sat around some tables in the alley while their underlings scurried to bring over ice buckets and booze from the white van that just pulled up. A group of children played with toy guns as if imitating their fathers, while more people started to arrive including some women who had tattoos. I came up to one of the men, who seemed to be the ringleader, and asked for a photo. He smiled, got up, and promptly dropped his top.

Holy shit. I mean I'd seen that kind of stuff in the movies, but never in real life. His tattoos covered his body like a shirt, dragons and beasts fighting it out among the clouds; then he turned around, showing his entire back painted with the image of a samurai. It was like a scene straight from *The Godfather*, if the Godfather ate noodles instead of spaghetti and ran a tattoo parlour instead of terrorising young boys with orange peels.

'So, you're all yakuza?' I asked, just checking I hadn't accidentally stumbled into a *Kill Bill* cosplay event.

'Yes,' he replied with a grin. 'We are yakuza.'

They were members of the Sumiyoshi-kai, the second-biggest crime family in Japan. Still, for a group of people whose signature move is slicing off each other's fingers, they were pretty friendly. The yakuza can afford to be out in the open like this because they've got nothing to hide. You see, in the Land of the Rising Sun it's actually legal to be a gangster. They're tolerated as a necessary evil to keep the other criminals in line and as kind of an archaic throwback to Japan's feudal past. If you want to find out where they're at, all you have to do is run their office through Google Maps.

The word yakuza comes from ya-ku-sa (8-9-3), the worst possible hand in a game of cards. It means that the yakuza are born losers and, indeed, many of them come from the outcasts of Japanese society: the *burakumin*, the lowest social class in Japan, as well as ethnic Chinese and Koreans.

For a group of so-called 'losers' the yakuza sure keep up a fearsome appearance. Unlike your crude Western gangbanger with 'Thug Life' written across his forehead, the yakuza's bodies are beautifully adorned with traditional full-body tattoos, or *irezumi*, of mythical creatures like dragons and demons. Some of them are also missing fingers as a way of apology, because in the Japanese underworld just getting on your knees and grovelling like a naughty child before Santa for rigging the wrong pachinko machine simply won't do.

The yakuza emerged from wandering bands of hustlers, gamblers and outlaws during the feudal era, but it wasn't until the American occupation that they hit the big-time, making themselves useful by teaming up with far-right groups and the CIA to bash the commies. Then, in the 1980s, during the Bubble economy, they started making inroads into the corporate world through dodgy loans and real-estate deals through which yakuza thugs would chase out tenants for unscrupulous landlords.

As the profits got higher, so did the stakes, and a series of bloody gang wars broke out, including a violent split in the country's biggest crime syndicate, the Yamaguchi-gumi, which left twenty-five mobsters dead. In 1985, the gang's boss, Masahisa Taneka, and his two highest-ranking capos were waiting for an elevator at his girlfriend's apartment in Osaka when hitmen from a breakaway faction walked up and unleashed a hail of bullets. Shortly afterwards, Taneka's brother was arrested in Hawaii while trying to swap $56m worth of heroin and meth for a hundred handguns, five machineguns and three rocket launchers. He was released after claiming he was a humble Japanese businessman who'd come to Hawaii to book

Michael Jackson. The war finally ended in 1989 when the breakaway faction's boss was found floating off the Pacific island of Saipan with his ribs crushed; ears, tongue and middle finger cut off; and a bullet in his head.

Yakuza run drugs, guns, prostitutes, protection rackets and loan-sharking. During the 1980s, they'd also practise a particular (and very Japanese) kind of shakedown called *sōkaiya*, where they'd buy up enough shares in a company to be allowed to attend the annual stockholders' meeting. Once they got there, they'd act like dicks by shouting obnoxiously over everyone else, not letting them get a word in and making accusations about the company directors until they were quietly paid to go away. Others disrupted meetings with loud cries of 'Banzai!' and 'Praise the Emperor!', making it the most awkward blackmail racket ever.

There's also pimping. Near where I was staying in Osaka, Nishinari (the hood in Japan ... well, as hood as Japan gets), there was an Amsterdam-style red-light district where all these cute *kawaii* Japanese girls dressed as Pikachu sat by the door next to their mama-san soliciting customers. Because it's not an officially licensed prostitution area (prostitution is de facto legal in Japan), it's listed on the map as the 'Tobita Shinchi restaurants association', meaning they don't actually charge you for sex, but the mama-san brings up a plate of VERY expensive ramen noodles and an equally expensive glass of sake. There are also a few gentlemen standing around in gaudy suits – if you suddenly decide you're not hungry, they'll quickly work up your appetite.

And then there's drugs. Decades before al-Qaeda nicked the idea for 9/11, Japanese kamikaze pilots were dive-bombing their planes into US battleships in the Pacific, killing themselves and thousands of American seamen. They sacrificed themselves out of blind loyalty to the Emperor of course, but just in case that wasn't enough they got something to make that final flight a little easier – methampheta-mine, or crystal meth, invented by Japanese chemist Akira Ogata in 1919. Today, these suicidal tweekers are venerated as Shinto gods in Tokyo's Yasukuni shrine.*

The Allied troops and the Nazis were getting their buzz on, too: Berlin factories churned out 35 million 'energy pills' for the 1940 invasion of France alone. Hitler, a teetotal, non-smoking vegetarian, saw drug use as yet another Jewish degeneracy and had addicts shipped off to camps, but ironically he was just the sort of guy you would see stumbling out of the 1930s equivalent of Berghain at 3 a.m. gurning his 'tache off from getting daily doses of speed and morphine from his personal doctor, Theodor Morell. At one point, the Führer called Mussolini and ranted unstoppably in a meth-fuelled outburst that lasted three hours.

Meth will certainly make you chat a lot of shit. It's a powerful stimulant that'll keep you up for days, having amazing, tantric sex and obsessively cleaning your house like a serial killer. But once the effect wears off, there's a horrific crash, so you've got to keep tweek-ing to keep the sickness at bay. Before you know it, your teeth are falling out, you haven't slept for a week and you're staring at the mirror looking like Emperor Palpatine.

But Japan couldn't ride the ice pony all the way to victory, and by 1945 the country lay in ruins. Meanwhile, vast stockpiles of kami-kaze meth made its way to the black market, most of it falling into the hands of the yakuza. Like coke, meth raises aggression and para-noia, and it quickly became apparent why giving it to a population traumatised by carpet-bombing and imperialist warmongering was a bad idea. Meth was outlawed in 1951 but because of some quirks of Japanese culture, it remains the only place in the world where hard

---

* It's not just martyrdom the jihadis took from the Japanese. In 2014, when ISIS stormed across the desert, their fighters were high on captagon, a speed-like concoction made in Bulgaria.

drugs outpace the soft ones. Eighty per cent of drug convictions involve stimulants, the drug of choice for the Japanese salaryman. Speed fits the fast-paced, modern Nippon lifestyle like a glove – you need something to keep you awake on those twelve-hour workdays, not passed out in the toilets shooting up marijuanas.

In the US meth remained legal until 1970, used as a weight-loss remedy by bored housewives and a pick-me-up for truckers, who took it to stay awake on those long hauls coast-to-coast. After that, bikers controlled the market for a while, cranking it out in trailer parks using matches and cough medicine. Making meth is a delicate process, and many of these leather-clad chemists burst into fireballs after getting the recipe wrong. Since then, the laws around ingredients have been tightened up and, as any *Breaking Bad* fan will know, the biggest challenge for a cook these days is finding the right chemicals.

Since its meth outbreak after the Second World War, Japan's maintained a strict anti-drugs policy that can land you up to five years' hard time. Part of that's from the post-war meth craze; partly from inheriting America's reefer madness during the occupation; and partly from Japanese culture, which is extremely conformist. One thing about the Japanese: they're very law-abiding. No one questions the Rules and breaking the Rules is Very Bad – in 2017, actor Ryo Hashizume's samurai film was pulled from cinemas before being re-released with all his scenes cut out, Kevin Spacey-style, after he was arrested for meth. He was basically equated with a sex offender. The public's outrage, bordering on hysteria, means drug users are pushed further from society and closer to the bad guys.

Kenny doesn't look like a mass-murdering psychopath. In fact, he's rather handsome. As we sit in a rehab clinic outside Manila, he tells me his story.

'I grew up half-Spanish, half-Filipino. My father was a rough Spaniard and he'd beat me till I threw up, then force me to eat my own vomit. My mother looked for an escape out of this cruel marriage, so we ran away to Japan, where my mother met a Japanese man who treated me like a real son.

'But when I was thirteen my stepfather died and, after one month, my mother already had another man. I became rebellious and started fighting. Fighting felt good. I started smoking at school and all the other kids feared me; I even started fights with the teachers.'

But fate had something bigger in store for the teenage tearaway. At age sixteen he killed his first victim, another student, in a high-school fight. The boy's girlfriend was pregnant and Kenny handed himself in, but only spent a year or so in prison as he was still a minor. That's when he got the attention of a group who could make use of his talents – the Japanese Mafia.

The main business of the organisation was drugs. Kenny's partner had a meth lab in the Philippines and Kenny took the goods over to Japan, sometimes working with Iranian drug pushers. Iranians first started coming over to Japan as migrant workers after the Iran–Iraq war in the 1980s, mostly settling in the Tokyo area. But the yakuza also had a side hustle: double-crossing and robbing the dealers.

'We knew the Iranians were making a lot of money but couldn't deposit it because they overstayed their visas, so they usually kept it in their car or in their house. So what we'd do was rob the pushers and kill the Iranians. We dismembered their bodies, burnt them, smashed the bones into ash and scattered them in the ocean,' he says, mimicking the process with his hands.

Rip-offs and robberies are common in the drug world. As Mark Brandon 'Chopper' Reid, the scourge of the Australian underworld, once said, 'Why rob a straight guy of $20 when you can rob a drug dealer of $10,000 and he can't go running to the police?'

'My mother found out about what I was doing and told me, "Please stop, I will work hard; just stop what you're doing." That's when I realised by trying to be rebellious I'd become much worse than her.'

Kenny moved back to the Philippines, where he took English classes and got a cushy job as an accountant at a multinational corporation. But when he got sent to Japan as the company's representative, he was immediately detained by thirty immigration cops as a known associate of organised crime. After spending three months in jail, Kenny was deported back home. That's when he fell back to his old ways, smoking ice and nearly stabbing a man to death before some relatives checked him into the clinic.

While most people don't end up dismembering dealers and throwing their parts into Tokyo Bay, Kenny's story is otherwise typical of others in the dopeworld. People aren't born monsters – they're made. Exposed to violence at an early age and a chaotic home life, Kenny inflicted pain on others just as his dad inflicted pain on him. That's not making excuses, but we have to understand how he got there in order to break the cycle.

While there'll always be psycho killers regardless of laws, the drug market creates an opportunity to capitalise on that, to make it *profitable*. Even if you're not a cold-blooded killer, you have to act like one because those are the rules of the game. It gives people a fucked-up incentive where extreme violence is rewarded.

On 20 March 1995, five devices activated on the Tokyo subway releasing bags of deadly nerve gas, leaving thousands of passengers in convulsions frothing at the mouth. Thirteen people died in Japan's deadliest terrorist attack, which was carried out by members of *Aum Shinrikyo*, or the Supreme Truth, a doomsday cult combining elements of Buddhism, science fiction and end-of-days Christianity. The goal of Aum Shinrikyo was nothing less than the end of the world.

The cult was led by a half-blind former yoga instructor, Shoko Asahara, who relayed his visions of apocalyptic future wars and far-reaching conspiracies through the group's vast anime and manga franchise. Of course you'd have to be trippin' balls to believe any of this crap, so it's no surprise that most of them actually were. When police raided their compound by the slopes of Mount Fuji, they found gun factories, sarin gas and labs for making crystal meth, truth serum and LSD. Asahara himself was particularly fond of LSD, personally administering doses to new disciples to welcome them into the family.

They also sold these drugs to the yakuza, but after the Tokyo gas attack the gangsters realised why hanging out with these brain-washed manga nerds might be a liability. A month later, Hideo Murai, Asahara's minister for science and technology and head of their drugs and chemical weapons programme, died after being acquainted with the pointy end of a blade outside the group's head-quarters by a supposed 'right-wing activist' (really, a yakuza enforcer of Korean descent) before a crowd of shocked reporters and live TV cameras.

Lysergic acid diethylamide (LSD) is a powerful psychedelic first cooked-up by Swiss chemist Albert Hoffman. One day, in 1943, Hoffman took a hit back at the lab and the acid kicked in as he cycled home. It must have been terrifying – one minute you're riding your bike, the next you're being chased by a gaggle of interstellar clowns through a Dali painting. Hoffman thought he was dying.

I feel ya, Albert. My acid trip was six hours that will stay with me for the rest of my life. When you're dropping acid, you need to be in a safe, happy place, like in a nice sunny field on a warm summer's day, surrounded by people you trust. I bought twice the recommended dose from a man dressed as a wizard in a grimy, dingy nightclub in one of the most run-down and crime-infested neighbourhoods in the country. Over the course of the next six hours, I witnessed all my thoughts melting together, time going back and forth, the club's bar stretching to infinity, and, having watched *The Smurfs* earlier that day, instead of normal sentences coming out of people's mouths, soon all I could hear was *smurfsmurfsmurfsmurfsmurf*. It sounds funny now but it's fucking annoying when you're trying to work out what they're actually trying to say. Eventually, I'd had enough of this madness and caught a cab. By the time I got home I'd sobered up a little and was more or less back in the real world, but when my mum opened the door, she had a huge head but a really tiny body like in a cartoon.

In the 1950s, the CIA began secret experiments into the possibility of mind-control by feeding people LSD. The project was code-named MK-ULTRA. One scheme, taken straight from the pages of a cheesy 1970s porno, involved hiring hookers to lure unsuspecting men to a safehouse and plying them with acid as CIA agents watched through a one-way mirror. Since that wasn't sleazy enough, the agents gave their network of secret CIA-run whorehouses a name – Operation Midnight Climax.

Judging by their reports, a few spooks began getting high on their own supply.

'I toiled wholeheartedly in the vineyards because it was fun, fun, fun. Where else could a red-blooded American boy lie, kill, cheat, steal, rape and pillage with the sanction and blessing of the All-Highest?' George White, an FBN agent assigned to MK-ULTRA, wrote in a terrifying memo to his superior.

The world's premier intelligence agency stopped paying its drug whores after they found some crusties ready to get dosed willingly. Author Ken Kesey volunteered for MK-ULTRA while studying at Stanford University, giving him the inspiration to write *One Flew Over the Cuckoo's Nest*. Kesey then started touring the country on a brightly painted school bus with a group of his like-minded Merry Pranksters, holding mass parties where everyone took LSD known as the Acid Tests. With its mind-control experiments, the CIA had inadvertently started the hippy movement.

Despite Aum Shinrikyo and the CIA, LSD is fairly benign (unless you're driving, handling sharp objects or operating heavy machinery). It was no good for brainwashing but it *did* open people's minds up to new ways of thinking. A whacked-out Harvard professor named Timothy Leary went a bit loopy and believed that if everyone, from world leaders to children, dropped acid it would create some kind of New Age paradise. That also meant it was clearly un-American, goddamnit, and LSD was banned in 1966.

After getting jailed for drug charges, only to be sprung out by the Black Panthers – who announced he was joining the revolution – Leary went on the run to Algeria and Europe, where he was held hostage by a Swiss arms dealer. The FBN finally caught up with him in Afghanistan and flew him back to the States, where they put him in a cell next to Charles Manson. By the time Leary died in 1996, his son had abandoned him, while his daughter, to whom he'd been feeding drugs since she was a child, went insane and killed herself.

Leary's life story might be dark and disturbing, but it also shows how dopeworld intersected with the anti-racism, anti-war and anti-capitalism movements of an era that changed America – the 1960s.

12

Hail Satan

I first met Steve doing a line of coke in a hostel off the beaten track in Colombia. Originally from Boston, Steve's now an ageing gringo living in the coastal village of Taganga. The week before I met him, he got stabbed in a robbery, although to be fair it was kind of his fault for yelling 'Kill me you motherfucker!' in Spanish while they held a knife to his throat.

These days Steve mainly spends his time on the beach, drinking beer and watching the days go by, but he's had a crazy life and he'll gladly share a few stories if you have the time. I didn't believe them at first, until he showed me the pictures.

'There's Donald Trump,' he said, pulling out a snapshot of Studio 54.

'And there's me,' he added, pointing to a picture of a smiling, handsome, long-haired hippy. 'That was 1969. You know, I once spent three months in a Thai nuthouse.'

The 1960s were an interesting time to be alive in America. A tense showdown with the Soviet Union in Cuba brought the world to the verge of nuclear Armageddon. The Beatles, Jimi Hendrix and the Rolling Stones provided the soundtrack as young people started questioning what they'd always been taught: racial segregation, nuclear weapons and capitalism are good, sex before marriage is wrong, and rock 'n' roll is Lucifer's lullaby. Despite slavery ending a century ago, black people still couldn't vote, drink at the same water fountains or go to the same schools under the Jim Crow laws. Martin Luther King inspired millions with his 'I Have a Dream' speech, while the Black Panthers openly carried guns to challenge racist cops.

Nineteen sixty-nine was the year of Woodstock, the most famous music festival in the world. Over three legendary days in August, acts like The Who, Grateful Dead and Jimi Hendrix performed for 400,000 mud-soaked tree-huggers on a patch of land in upstate New York. It was the swansong of the era. Naturally, everyone was off their tits – even though dope had been around for a long time, it wasn't until this huge cultural shift in the 1960s that it became popular.

'A lot of the music was good but concerts in the 1960s didn't have good sound systems,' Steve said. 'But it was one of the first big concerts in the world and I was there, so I can say I'm a Woodstock baby! In the woods there were paths – LSD Lane, Reefer Highway – so you'd go to the woods and buy everything you need.'

Rebelling against society was all the rage. After Woodstock, Steve met a cool couple who invited him out West and he settled in San Francisco, the Mecca of free love and sixties counterculture: 'Nineteen and in the coolest part of the world, and at a time when it had an enormous effect, influence on our culture, politics and revolution in subtle ways,' he reminisced.

Through his new friends, Steve ended up joining the Church of Satan headed by one Anton LaVey, who led the Church from his Black House (so named because it was a house, painted black) on 6114 California St. LaVey founded the Church on 30 April 1966, the night of *Walpurgisnacht*, which according to legend is when witches assemble on the Blocksberg Mountain in northern Germany and get jiggy with Beelzebub. His teachings centred around how Satan, being the nemesis and rejection of God, encouraged Man to embrace his bestial nature and freed him from the shackles of organised religion – in particular, the Judeo-Christian values that dominated America.

Satanism was more an unapologetic embrace of hedonism than actual devil-worship, but that was enough to win over Steve to the dark side.

'We just gathered at his house, the church. After I went to a few lectures, I only went to the one service. I got to his house and I remember sitting there in the living room stoned out of my mind. Then the fireplace opens up in front of me and out came Anton dressed in a devil outfit. I was like, well, anything can happen here!

'We all gathered in a room for services. There was a fireplace, and on top there was a naked woman stretched out with a boa constrictor wrapped around her, both alive. People were dressed as Nazis like it was Halloween, then there were a lot of *Rege Satanas, Ave Satanas* and Hail Satans! After that, I got a membership card and that was about it.'

Steve hung around the Church for a while, but was mostly interested in hanging around San Francisco, jamming with his band and smoking pot. It was a glorious time.

Having saved the youth from a life of swing music and hanging out with Mexicans, Harry Anslinger set about promoting drug prohibition on the world stage. Now, this next bit is important because, although other countries (like China) also outlawed narcotics, it was America that forced the rest of the world to dance to its tune, bullying all the smaller, weaker nations into accepting its laws. Anslinger took his case to the UN, leading to the 1961 Single Convention on Narcotic Drugs. Signed by 186 countries, it banned all drugs, everywhere. Heroin, cocaine, hashish, marijuana . . . they were all outlawed from Trinidad to Timbuktu.

Peru and Bolivia were told to cut out their coca-chewing – a slap to their cultural heritage. Imagine if wine-drinking was banned in France. If it wasn't for thousands of years of tradition, booze would almost certainly be illegal. Imagine the French army descending on the vineyards of Bordeaux in Black Hawk helicopters and pulling out all the grapes. People would be pretty angry, right? Yet that's what's happened with the coca plant. The drugs used by Western society are deemed OK, but those of their colonial subjects are not.

A few nations resisted. India was not too thrilled at having cannabis, a Hindu sacrament for millennia, on the list, so the UN relented and made an exception for *bhang*. But most did not. Britain followed suit, like we always do, with the Misuse of Drugs Act 1971. Before that, you could get heroin from Boots.

But for a while, the war on drugs took a backseat to the Cold War. Angry rice farmers had just kicked the French out of Indochina and were about to throw out the bourgeoisie. Fearful of the domino effect and losing the whole of Southeast Asia, American troops poured into Vietnam.

Unsurprisingly, the public back home grew disenchanted after turning on the evening news to see US forces dousing Vietnamese children with napalm. Young Americans saw no point in going off to die, especially blacks and college kids.

'My conscience won't let me go shoot my brother, or some darker people, or some poor hungry people in the mud for big powerful America. And shoot them for what? They never called me nigger, they never lynched me, they didn't put no dogs on me, they didn't rob me of my nationality, rape and kill my mother and father,' said Muhammad Ali, refusing the draft. 'How can I shoot them poor people? Just take me to jail.'

A few American GIs picked up some bad habits while hunting Charlie through the rice paddies. Heroin and opium were all over US bases, being peddled by Vietnamese sellers or usually some enterprising sergeant, a cheap and plentiful escape from the horrors of war. Army surveys at the time showed that only around 10 per cent of soldiers liked getting high (usually on R&R, not active combat); shooting their sergeant in the face after getting shitfaced at some Saigon bar was a much bigger worry.

But the stoned soldiers story took hold in the media. Military historian William Allison called the drug problem 'among the most tragic elements of the war' (as opposed to the carpet-bombing of Vietnamese villages, Agent Orange, and so forth). Some observers even suggested it could be a nefarious commie plot.

In fact, the biggest dope dealers were America's allies. The US-backed Royal Laotian Army commanders Vang Pao and Ouane Rattikone grew and refined opium, and used the CIA-owned airline Air America to move their product. Being the enterprising sort, Rattikone diversified his portfolio by trading American guns for opium with rebels from Shan state in Burma. Shan state forms part of the Golden Triangle, the lawless tri-border area on the banks of the Mekong River between Thailand, Burma and Laos. The CIA's been snooping around this region since 1949 when the Kuomintang (KMT) army thundered into Shan state from southern China, commandeering the area's many opium plantations.

Shan state had enjoyed a high degree of autonomy since British rule, and the locals weren't too happy about having that taken away by the military junta that took power in 1962. So they sold smack to buy guns.

Occasionally the US's allies sometimes fought among themselves, such as in 1967 when an opium convoy belonging to Shan warlord Khun Sa was attacked by the KMT. Both sides lost when they were subsequently bombed by the Royal Laotian Air Force, who went on to 'confiscate' the entire shipment for themselves.

Khun Sa was the Robin Hood of the Golden Triangle, Southeast Asia's opium king. Two years after the 1967 war with the Laotian military, he was captured by Burmese forces and thrown into jail. His loyal men sprung into action, kidnapping two Russian doctors and holding them hostage until they'd secured his release in 1974. Back in business, baby!

The king of the Golden Triangle led a 20,000-strong militia and controlled around 80 per cent of the region's opium harvest. Khun Sa made no bones about his business, saying it was the only way he could provide for his people, and once offered to sell his entire crop to Western governments. They weren't buying.

A spate of defeats and defections led the opium king to surrender to the Burmese in the mid-1990s, after which he retired peacefully to Rangoon. Meanwhile, Burmese generals saw that decades of civil war weren't making them rich. 'Fuck it,' they said, and started growing poppies themselves. Burma is still the number-two producer of opium in the world after Afghanistan.

By the early seventies, support for the Vietnam War had reached its lowest point. Peace rallies were going on up and down the country and surveys showed over half of Americans believed going in was a 'mistake'. President Richard Nixon had already expanded the war, after promising to end it, by increasing the bombing campaign not only in 'Nam but also in Cambodia and Laos, costing thousands more American, Vietnamese and Cambodian lives; he needed to come up with a new strategy to distract voters from his fuck-up/lie. But Tricky Dick, as he was known, had an idea. Crime was rising. Frustration with unfairness and police brutality sparked riots: cities like Los Angeles and Detroit were on fire, and white voters were deadly afraid that one day the blacks would rise up and come for their crackers and milk.

Nixon's party, the Republicans, had already pioneered the Southern Strategy in the late 1960s, where they'd run on a platform of law and order that actually meant 'keep the darkies in check' (before that, the Democrats were the more outwardly racist party). As Republican adviser Lee Atwater explained to author Alexander Lamis: 'You start out in 1954 by saying, "Nigger, nigger, nigger". By

1968 you can't say "nigger" – that hurts you. Backfires. So you say stuff like forced busing, states' rights and all that stuff. You're getting so abstract now, you're talking about cutting taxes . . . totally economic things and a by-product of them is blacks get hurt worse than whites . . . if it is getting that abstract, and that coded, that we are doing away with the racial problem one way or the other.'

Drug laws were sneaky because, unlike Jim Crow, they weren't *explicitly* racist, so by Nixon's time he could even count on support from some black leaders who thought drugs were just another way to keep the black brother down. Hmm, now if only there was a way to put the blame for drug-addled soldiers on all those uppity negros and goddamn dirty hippies protesting the war . . . 🤫

There was some truth to the fears. After the free love and flower power of the 1960s had run its course, the burnt-out hippies looked elsewhere. In the late seventies, Steve moved to New York. Back then, pre-Giuliani, the Big Apple was a totally different place. There were prostitutes and peep shows on Time Square, and you couldn't ride the graffiti-strewn subway trains at night. That's where Steve found heroin.

'The first time was in 1972, I think, and I don't remember if I threw up or not but it was the best night of my life. Me and my wife went dancing all night. But I was making so much money with my bartending and photography it didn't even matter. When I first went to score in New York City I was so straight-edge they thought I was a cop. Then I started speedballing – that's when you mix coke and heroin – and that's when I lost everything. Lost my job, lost my business. There was one time I was clinically dead for two minutes. I'd overdosed. It was at Bellevue Hospital in New York, and the first thing I see is this big black orderly and he says, "You lucky mother-fucker, you was dead and I'd just gone to pick up the body bag and then poof you're back, you lucky motherfucker!"'

That's the thing with being a junkie. It's not so bad when you can afford it. Unfortunately every now and then, life throws you a curve-ball and you find yourself borrowing money, lying about paying it back, and stealing your mum's jewellery.

Harlem, with its grim, dilapidated apartment blocks and trash-filled alleys, was where Steve usually went to score. One time at his buddy's apartment on 125th Street, he came out to find his car wouldn't start because the battery had been stolen. So he went inside a gas station and asked if they had any batteries. They didn't, but when he came out there was a group of five lads.

'Yo man, do you want a battery?' they asked.

'Yeah, how much?'

'Thirty-five dollars.'

Steve walked over to his car, popped the bonnet and handed them thirty-five dollars.

'Now put it in,' he said.

'Why?' they said.

'I just paid thirty-five dollars for my own battery; you fuckin' put it in.'

So they did.

'The Nixon campaign in 1968, and the Nixon White House after that, had two enemies: the anti-war left and black people. You understand what I'm saying?' John Ehrlichman, a senior Nixon aide who did eighteen months in jail for the Watergate scandal, told *Harper's Magazine*. 'We knew we couldn't make it illegal to be either against the war or black, but by getting the public to associate the hippies with marijuana and blacks with heroin, and then criminalising both heavily, we could disrupt those communities. We could arrest their leaders, raid their homes, break up their meetings, and vilify them night after night on the evening news. Did we know we were lying about the drugs? Of course we did.'

If I was being conspiritorial, I'd say this was another system of control. Jim Crow's over and slavery's gone the way of the dodo, but decades of bing second-class citizens had created a situation where many saw the fastest way out of poverty as breaking the law . . . and then they could be arrested, thrown in chains, their families broken up and forbidden to vote (sound familiar?). Slavery's one thing, but who's gonna stand up for *criminals*?

And so, on 17 June 1971, Nixon declared in a now-famous speech that drugs were 'public enemy number one in the United States'. The Federal Bureau of Narcotics became the Drug Enforcement Administration (or DEA), and the War on Drugs had now truly begun.

Part 3

Cosa Nostra

13

Havana Nights

The lights dimmed as a tuxedoed gentleman ushered me into my seat. The waiters brought over a bottle of rum and a Cuban cigar, leaving me to enjoy the show as scantily-clad dancers, male and female, gyrated onstage in the great hall. There was something distinctly old-fashioned about the cabaret, like stepping back in time or *The Godfather Part II*, that scene when Michael realises Fredo has betrayed him in Havana. Which makes sense as in the 1950s when Cuba was the Mob's playground, the Tropicana club was their main base of operations.

I was on a stopover through Latin America. Havana's a city frozen in time. There's no advertising, of any kind, which is a relief; only huge murals of Che Guevara adorning old, colonial buildings. No Internet, either, so none of those sweet dopamine hits from someone liking your status. Everyone's driving these old cars; classic American whips from the fifties, just before the US embargo (they still work, too – Cuban mechanics must be the best in the world). If you didn't know any better you could think it was still the bygone era when the now-communist island was the site of the largest narcotics import–export operation in the world.

In 1942, Lucky Luciano was languishing in a cell in upstate New York when his lawyer got him an offer he couldn't refuse. The army and navy would use the Mob's control and influence over the New York dockyards to root out any German saboteurs. In return, Luciano would get released early from his thirty-year sentence for big pimpin' and deported back to Italy. It was the start of a beautiful friendship.

The Second World War put kind of a damper on international drug smuggling, what with all those U-boats torpedoing your cargo to Davey Jones's locker. But now it was time to get back in the game. Luciano settled in Naples, rebuilding links with the crime families back in the old country. In 1946, Lucky and Lansky called another Mob summit at the swanky Hotel Nacional in Havana. Chief on their agenda was narcotics.

After the death of Arnold Rothstein, Lucky picked up his mantle, buying opium from Turkey and the Middle East before shipping it to America via his friendly contacts in Cuba. To process the gear Lucky sent it through the French Connection, so named because it was done in conjunction with the Corsican *milieu* controlling the heroin-processing factories in Marseille, who in turn were supported by the French secret service running black ops in Indochina.* Marseille, a freewheeling port city on the Mediterranean, and Corsica, an island speaking a language closer to Italian, were the capitals of France's *grand banditisme*. After the Second World War, tensions grew between political factions in Marseille, and Corsican mafiosi were given cash, guns and support from the CIA and

---

* When those pesky Việt Minh started fighting the French for independence, the SDECE realised the colonial army couldn't fight its way out of a room full of toddlers and started paying various bandits and tribal militias to join their cause. To secure their loyalty, the SDECE launched 'Operation X', buying opium from the hill tribes and sending it abroad through the Corsican mob. To peddle their wares inside the country, the SDECE used the Bình Xuyên, Saigon river pirates with a vast network of opium dens. The Bình Xuyên was also an effective fighting force in itself and was hired by the French as mercenaries against the Việt Minh.

SDECE (French intelligence) to kick the crap out of left-wing unionists.

But in 1959, Fidel Castro and his ragtag band of Merry Men, despite being vastly outnumbered, managed to spook dictator Fulgencio Batista enough for him to flee the country.

The Mafia used to run drugs, casinos and prostitution, then lost it all once the communists came to power. With a shared interest in seeing Castro dead, the CIA reached out to Chicago boss Sam 'Momo' Giancana and Florida don Santo Trafficante Jr, and together they planned to slip poison in his food. Giancana had worked for the public sector before, helping deliver the Chicago vote to President Kennedy. Unfortunately, the Cuban whom they'd hired for the job hid the poison capsules in his freezer where they froze solid and stuck to the freezer coils, making them about as useful as the Swiss navy.

Overall, there were some 638 007-style plots to kill Castro, which ranged from exploding cigars to poisoned pens and even a booby-trapped seashell for the Cuban leader to pick up when he went diving. None of them succeeded, and dying at the age of ninety, old Fidel outlived most of his would-be assassins (Giancana wasn't as lucky – someone shot him seven times in the head as he fried sausages in 1975).

What we've seen in Cuba we're gonna see again and again: drug dealers working with government agencies, and getting squeezed out of one place only to pop up in another.

On 26 January 1962, Italian narcotics agents followed Lucky Luciano to Naples airport, about to arrest him for drugs trafficking. They never got their man. At the airport, just after meeting a Hollywood bigshot about making a film of his life, he suddenly had a heart attack. After a lifetime of bloodshed and betrayal, the world's most powerful mobster just keeled over and died.

After Lucky died, so did his pipeline. In 1971, an ex-SDECE agent was busted in New Jersey with a car full of smack and Nixon pressured Paris into shutting down the French Connection. With Fidel's partisans creating an increasingly hostile business climate in Cuba, the decision was made to move operations to Sicily.

14

The Pizza Connection

Sicily's the football kicked along by Italy's boot, an arid, sun-scorched island dotted with rocky hills and peasant villages. Its capital, Palermo, rests on the northern coast surrounded by mountains which loom over the motorway leading to the airport.

When I caught the bus to Palermo on Saturday night the whole side of the mountain was glowing with a raging inferno. *What the fuck was that?* I'd never seen anything like it in my life. I later learned that not only was it the season of wildfires, but a lot of them were started by disgruntled firemen looking for overtime.

The next day I hooked up with Edoardo Zaffuto, co-founder of the grassroots *Adiopizzo* (Goodbye, *pizzo!*) movement. Edoardo's in his forties now but looks a lot younger . . . must be that Mediterranean diet. In 2004, Edoardo and his friends set out to open a bar. When they sat down to work out the costs they realised they'd overlooked one crucial expense – the *pizzo*, or protection racket.

'On June 28th, we peppered the town with stickers: "a people that pays *pizzo* is a people without dignity,"' Edoardo said. 'People were scared of what may happen to them and some of them started tearing off the stickers. But there was no need for any one person, a single hero they can kill. If a lot of people do something, that's far more effective.'

These days shopkeepers proudly display stickers declaring that they don't pay *pizzo*, while those who stood up to the gangsters have been immortalised in statues, town squares and murals. In a window off the Four Corners, a four-way intersection in Palermo's baroque old town, one guy even wrote (in five different languages):

'In case someone intends to come and ask for money for prisoners or their family or to pay solicitors or similar . . . they must know that they can Fuck Off! #mafiashit'

'It's a sign things are getting better,' said Edoardo. 'Thirty years ago, no one even wanted to say the word "Mafia".'

Since the Mafia themselves usually aren't too chatty, Edoardo and his group of anti-Mafia activists were to be my guide. A lot of things in Sicily have changed since the early 1990s, when the Mob had gone to war with Italy itself and bombs were going off all over the mainland. But to find out how it got to that point, we need to go back over a hundred years, long before Sicily became ground zero for the world heroin trade.

Far from the canals of Venice and high-end fashion boutiques of Milan lies a land which, were it not part of Italy, might well qualify as a failed state. North and South Italy are like two different countries – the North is rich and prosperous; the South is broke, rural and doesn't even speak Italian (no one understands what the fuck the Sardinians are saying).

Until the mid-nineteenth century, the two actually *were* separate countries: the South was the Kingdom of the Two Sicilies, ruled over by the Bourbon dynasty in Naples. But in 1860 an adventurer named Giuseppe Garibaldi and a thousand like-minded patriots calling themselves the Redshirts landed in Sicily, before fighting all the way up Italy's boot. The country was united, but as the Bourbons' old feudal system collapsed, the South plunged into chaos. Brigands and outlaws roamed the countryside. In Sicily, wealthy landowners hired private armies as muscle; hired guns who went around shaking down the island's famous citrus groves. These greedy landowners and their thugs grew so powerful that they formed a parallel system of government: the laws may have been written in Rome, but have no illusions about who was really in charge. The Sicilians had a word for this secret power. They called it *Mafia*.

It fell on Il Duce to pull the brakes on these shenanigans. In 1922, Benito Mussolini and his Blackshirts marched on Rome, chanting their charming motto, 'Everything within the state, nothing against the state, nothing outside the state.' No fascist worth his salt will tolerate a challenge to their power, nor do they have to worry about such frivolities as 'due process' and 'human rights'. Thousands of suspected gangsters were rounded up across southern Italy and thrown behind bars.

But Cosa Nostra was too deeply entrenched in Sicilian society to go anywhere. The landowners claimed it was *they*, the good honest fascists, who were the poor innocent victims of *banditismo*. Then, in 1943, when the Allies landed in Sicily, the Mafia came crying to the Americans, saying their comrades in prison were poor innocent victims of fascism, and the Americans, who didn't know any better, let them all loose again as 'political prisoners'.

With every cop from Manhattan to Marseille out to nail the French Connection, the smack business fell into the hands of Tano Badalamenti, boss of the small seaside town of Cinisi. Tano flew in Corsican chemists from Marseille to teach his men how to cook, and even had the building work on Palermo's new airport moved a few miles down the road to be closer to his heroin labs. From here it was sent to America hidden in boxes of mozzarella, to be distributed by the US Mafia through a network of mobbed-up pizzerias. The French Connection had become the Pizza Connection.

Now that Cosa Nostra was getting fat, what to do with all the money?

Since the days of Al Capone, gangsters have been careful about some nosy investigator snooping around their account books. Let's say you made twenty grand selling PCP-laced honey to Winnie-the-Pooh. Awesome, but now you got the Feds on your back. So you set up a front business where your customers pay in cash, like a strip club, and keep feeding your dodgy bills through the bar until (on paper at least) you're running a very successful establishment. Or you set up an elaborate scheme where you move the money around so much that it will give any bean counters looking into it a brain aneurysm. This is money laundering. And what better way to do that than through some divine intervention?

Roberto Calvi was the chairman of Banco Ambrosiano, and was also known as 'God's Banker' for his close ties to the Vatican. His bank was used for all kinds of shady transactions, from laundering Mafia narco-dollars to funnelling money to anti-communist guerrillas in Central America. You see, Calvi was also a Freemason, part of the secret banned P2 lodge that included top judges, generals, police chiefs and politicians, including one Silvio Berlusconi.

But something must have gone wrong, because in 1981 Calvi was arrested for making illegal transfers to offshore accounts. In 1982, while out on bail, Calvi fled to London on a false passport, where he was found hanged under Blackfriars Bridge with his body weighed down with bricks and thousands of pounds in cash in his pockets. Shortly afterwards, Banco Ambrosiano went under after it became clear that over $1 billion had disappeared from its accounts. Calvi's murder remains unsolved to this day. Conspiracy theories abound: did he get greedy and try to make off with the Mafia's money, or did he know too much about the dirty secrets of the Vatican? Or both?

Tano Badalamenti wanted to build his airport at Punta Raisi, facing the rocky mountain slopes more than 30 kilometres west of Palermo.

But in order to get the runways where they needed to be, Tano had to force some peasants off their land. The peasants resisted, unsuccessfully. But what was curious was that among the protesters waving placards was the son of one of Don Tano's closest associates, Peppino Impastato.

Peppino Impastato grew up in the Mafia. His uncle, Cesare Manzella, was a major boss while his old man, Luigi, headed up a smaller clan. Living in the countryside by Cinisi, Peppino and his younger brother were far removed from the brutal reality of the family business.

'This was the happiest, most beautiful time of our lives,' Peppino's brother Giovanni told me as we sat in his old house. Giovanni's a weary, middle-aged man now, but he's always got time to school youngsters like myself, renovating his spacious old house into a museum of the struggle against the Mafia. Pictures and paintings of Peppino and his mother cover the walls. 'As a kid, you take it for granted.'

But reality has a way of slapping you in the face, and in 1963, a car bomb blew up their drug-dealing uncle. When he saw the scene, the fire burning and pieces of his beloved uncle scattered around, fifteen-year-old Peppino said, 'If this is the Mafia, I will fight it for the rest of my life.'

'He became very interested in all the movements in society – Woodstock, the marches for peace, the battles of 1968,' Giovanni continued. 'He made a political choice – he became a communist and a Marxist. He saw communism as a way of freeing the people, but also criticised it as a system of oppression. He was against world hunger, nuclear war, globalisation and American imperialism. He loved the landscape and wanted to protect it. He was for women's rights and he was a feminist.'

Peppino grew more involved with activism. He led peasants' protests when a new runway was being built for Palermo Airport on their land. He printed a socialist newspaper and called the Mafia a 'mountain of shit' – when others were scared to even utter the word. When their newsletter got shut down, Peppino and his comrades set up a radio station, Radio Aut. By that point, his mafioso dad had kicked him out the house, but Peppino didn't care. On his radio show, he ripped into politicians and mafiosi alike. Among the targets of Peppino's razor-sharp wit were the mayor of Cinisi, Gero Di Stefano, whom he called Geronimo, and the big dog himself, Tano Badalamenti, whom he called Sitting Tano, the Chief of Mafiopolis.

Peppino was playing a risky game. Peppino's father was a close friend of Tano Badalamenti, and maybe that's why he was able to get away with what he did for so long. They might not have been on the best of terms, but Luigi did everything he could to protect his son. But in 1977 he was struck by a passing car, and Peppino was all on his own.

On the night of 9 May 1978, his luck ran out. A group of thugs took him from the radio shack and drove him to a farmhouse just in sight of the airport he'd fought so strongly against. There, they beat the hell out of him. Then they laid his body on a railway track and rigged it with TNT.

'I'm not sure if he was still conscious when they put him on the railway tracks and put dynamite on his chest,' Giovanni said. 'They wanted to show he was a terrorist, but terrorists always act in the day.'

The Red Brigades had recently kidnapped Aldo Moro, the former prime minister, after shooting dead five of his bodyguards, and both his body and Peppino's were found on the same day. For a long time the police ignored clues and claimed that Peppino, too, was a left-wing terrorist, killed while planting a bomb. It was up to Giovanni and their long-suffering mother, Felicia, to find out the truth.

'We started collecting evidence ourselves – we didn't care about the investigation. We found the stones covered in blood at the stable. Of course, if you're set on blowing up the railway you won't hurt yourself before.'

In 2001 Tano Badalamenti, already serving time in the States for drug trafficking, was finally sentenced to life imprisonment for the murder of Peppino Impastato.

Giovanni got up to shake my hand. An old, black-and-white photograph hanging on the wall caught my eye, showing a group of black-suited men walking to the village feast. One of them held the hand of a small boy: little Peppino walking along with his dad. In the middle, looking like Mr Blonde from *Reservoir Dogs*, was Tano Badalamenti, holding the hand of his son, Vito. As we left the house, a series of brightly engraved paving stones pointed the way to Tano's house, now a municipal library. They lived only a hundred steps apart, Peppino Impastato and the crime boss who ordered his murder.

But in 1978 Don Tano had bigger things to worry about than some hippy slagging him off on the airwaves. From 1978 to 1983, the Corleone crime family (the real-life one, not the one led by Al Pacino) waged a vicious war against Tano and the established Palermo bosses over the booming heroin racket.

15

Corleone

Our next stop was Corleone – the very Corleone Marlon Brando takes his name from in *The Godfather*. Even in Italy, the name of this small town in the rolling hills south of Palermo is synonymous with the Mafia. Like me, Edoardo's a movie buff and we spent the ride discussing spaghetti westerns.

The Godfather and *The Godfather Part II* are two of my favourite movies. They transport you to another era: an expertly shot immigrant's tale in a bygone America. But it's not just a sprawling Shakespearean saga with a touch of gratuitous animal cruelty; it's also formed everyone's impressions about the Mafia: sucking up to gravelly-voiced, olive-skinned old Sicilian men in dark rooms murmuring in Italian on the day of their daughter's wedding, slurping spaghetti and ordering hits over baptism. But is that what it's really like?

One of the plotlines of the movie is that the Mafia isn't involved in drugs (at least, not the Corleone family), as Don Corleone regards it as a dirty business, until they get approached by a slimy drug dealer called Sollozzo. All that ends with a young Al Pacino blowing the drug dealer's head off. In reality, the Corleone family's had their sticky fingers in narcotics since the very beginning.

Corleone is one of those small Italian towns with narrow streets and crumbling churches where everyone knows each other, killer and victim, and old men sit outside sipping coffee in their coppola flat caps.

'You probably saw the sign coming in: "Corleone, capital of the anti-Mafia",' said Edoardo as we drove in. 'But last year the entire council was dissolved because of Mafia infiltration, so it's a little bit ironic.'

In the middle of Corleone sits a huge vertical rock, on top of which is a monastery. But what went on beneath was decidedly unholy. In 1974, Salvatore 'Totò' Riina and his lieutenant, Bernardo 'Benny the Tractor' Provenzano, took charge after Riina's boss, Luciano Leggio, caught a murder charge. Leggio himself had come to power after machinegunning his own boss, a diabolical doctor named Michele Navarra. Provenzano dropped out of school early to work on a farm, while his old boss Leggio couldn't read. The Corleone family were basically hillbillies.

But they were hillbillies with ambition. Badalamenti might have had the money, the Pizza Connection and the handshakes with officials, but Riina had the balls. The hillbilly hoodlums went around kidnapping or assassinating anyone close to Tano. Over a thousand people died during *La Mattanza* ('The Slaughter') as the Corleone gang wiped out judges, politicians and rival mobsters.

Eventually, the old don was allowed to retire, but others weren't so lucky. Salvatore Inzerillo, a major heroin trafficker who supplied a faction of the US Mafia known as the Cherry Hill Gambinos, had his face shredded by an AK. On the other side of the Atlantic, his brother Pietro was found beheaded in a car trunk in New Jersey with dollar bills stuffed in his mouth. The Corleones were hogging all the pizza.

Bloodshed spread to the Italian mainland over to the pirate city of Naples, that wretched hive of scum and villainy, where the Corleones tried to usurp the boss of the local Camorra, Raffaele 'the

Professor' Cutolo. The Camorra is the oldest of the Italian crime syndicates, having emerged as a prison gang in the early 1800s that grew into an unofficial police force in Naples' slums, keeping small-time criminals in check.

Unlike the Sicilian Mafia, the Camorra are more flashy, American-style gangsters: one capo even had his gaudy mansion modelled after Al Pacino's in *Scarface*. The Professor was one such colourful character – an eccentric crime lord who spent his time in the prison library waxing lyrical about the Camorra of old. The Sicilians supported a coalition of smaller gangs and even put a green light out on Cutolo, but their hitman got popped as soon as he stepped off the boat. When the Professor was defeated, the remaining *cammoristi* turned on each other. The war fractured the Naples underworld from a handful of crime families to dozens of warring gangs.

It seemed no one could stop Cosa Nostra. No one, except Giovanni Falcone and Paolo Borsellino, two judges who weren't scared to go for the guilty verdict in a Mob trial. As boys, they'd grown up kicking a ball around the ruins of post-war Palermo with kids who'd grow up to be gangsters. As men, they'd be responsible for putting many of them away. But it wasn't enough just to be fearless. They had to build an actual case.

Enter Tommaso Buscetta. Buscetta was an international drug lord who fled to Brazil after the Corleones slaughtered most of his family and friends, hiding out on his 65,000-acre ranch. But the Brazilian police had other ideas. They caught the fugitive in 1983 and, after pulling out his toenails, electrifying his balls and threatening to throw him off a plane, sent him back to Italy. Buscetta came up before Giovanni Falcone and offered to spill his guts on the inner workings of the Mafia – he didn't want any time off his sentence, only revenge on Cosa Nostra. Armed with the inside scoop from his blabbermouth, Falcone set about putting together the biggest Mafia trial in history.

Previously, those investigating the Mafia quickly found their life expectancy drop below the national average. This time was no different, as a leading detective was gunned down in front of his wife and even a whole train (the 904 express from Naples to Milan) was blown up in an attempt to derail the investigation. It was a grisly business. But Falcone and Borsellino doggedly persisted and brought the case to trial in 1985.

The Maxi Trial, which took place in a concrete bunker and lasted between 1986 and 1987, saw 338 mobsters convicted and sent down for a total of 2,665 years in jail, as well as 19 life sentences. Not only that, but for the first time the Italian government was forced to admit that La Cosa Nostra, 'this thing of ours', does actually exist. Falcone and Borsellino had to go.

On 23 May 1992, a powerful blast rocked the A29 highway linking Palermo with south-west Sicily as Falcone was making his way from the airport with his wife Francesca and a team of bodyguards. Antonio Vassallo, a photographer from the nearby town of Capaci, was the first to arrive at the scene. On hearing the explosion, Antonio grabbed a camera and jumped on his scooter.

'The scene was like something from one of those American war movies,' Vassallo told me. 'There was no road, no motorway at all. I had to drop my scooter and continued on foot when I saw this huge crater. The fireball obliterated the first car in the convoy, while the second car, which was carrying Falcone and his wife, slammed into the wall of concrete, which leaped from the road as the explosion ripped through the ground around it.

'As I climbed over the crater, I saw Falcone in his car. I didn't recognise him but he was still alive, just moving his head a little bit. When I think back to it now, I think that was his rage: "You finally did it, you bastards! You got what you wanted! You killed me!"'

As he looked around, Antonio saw a young man come out from a car in front of him pointing a rifle, maybe a Kalashnikov. Thinking it could be a hitman sent to finish the job, Antonio dived into the nearby bushes and only came back a few minutes later when the paramedics arrived. Thinking it was safe to come out, Antonio started taking some panoramic shots when he was approached by two plain-clothes men claiming to be police officers.

'They demanded I hand over my photos, but I said no unless they could show me some ID. So they twisted my arm and forced me to hand over the film,' he said.

Thinking the photos would be used in an investigation, Antonio waited to be called to testify. But months went by and he heard nothing, so he took a car with some friends and drove to meet the chief prosecutor in charge of the case.

'We told her everything we knew, but when we asked whether she'd got my photographs, she asked me what photographs? The next day I got a call from the police chief of Palermo, who told me, "Sorry, we have your photos, but we forgot to send them. We will send them tomorrow." But the photos never arrived.'

'And that's when I got scared. Maybe when I was there on the highway, at the scene of the blast, my camera took a shot of something no one was supposed to see? The killers surely wouldn't have expected someone to show up that early after the bombing and start snooping around. I never saw my pictures from that day again.'

But Antonio did get closure, of a sort. Seventeen years later he had the chance to meet the occupants of the third car; the rest of Falcone's entourage, including the man who threatened him with a gun.

'Yes, I was going to shoot you,' Angelo Corbo told him. 'All these years I was wondering, who is this man with the black box in his hands, peering at us after we'd just been blown up? You're telling me now it's a camera, but I was really going to shoot you!'

Edoardo walked me over to Piazza Magione, a wide-open space in the middle of Palermo. Bombed out during the Second World War, it was here that little Paolo and Giovanni came to play football among the rubble. These days, local children come to play here too in a playground crowdfunded by Adiopizzo.

'The Mafia collect money and use it for themselves. With the same money, voluntarily, we can do something good,' he said. 'It makes me feel good to see these children playing.'

There was some commotion on the other side of the square, with some yelling and chanting coming from the backstreets. We moved in to take a closer look, turned the corner and saw shitloads of *carabinieri* (paramilitary police) standing guard as protesters marched past chanting '*RESISTENZA! RESISTENZA!*' ('Resistance! Resistance!'), holding up banners of Falcone and Borsellino and little red notebooks. People stepped out of the cafés and clapped.

After the death of his childhood friend, Borsellino knew he was next. He'd wander off from his police escort to buy cigarettes, hoping that a single shot to the back of the head would spare them the massacre that took place in Capaci. But it was not to be. On 19 July 1992, a car bomb went off as Borsellino left his mother's house, killing the crusading judge and five of his bodyguards, including Emanuela Loi, a twenty-four-year-old police officer from Sardinia. An olive tree now stands in their place, representing hope and peace.

If the plan was to cow Sicilians into submission, it backfired. Hundreds of mourners showed up at Borsellino's funeral, chanting 'Justice, justice!' Soldiers were deployed to Palermo. Top boss Totò Riina was arrested for the murders, and in retaliation the Mob declared war on Italy itself, bombing the Uffizi art gallery (killing a nine-year-old girl) and planting more bombs across the mainland.

One of the crucial bits of evidence from Borsellino's murder, his little red notebook where he kept all his dirt on the Mafia, disappeared from the crime scene. Clutching their little red notebooks, the protesters made their way to the law school where Falcone and

Borsellino earned their degrees. The protesters demanded to know what really happened to Borsellino, and why he was killed. Did he know too much about the Mafia and their connections to the deep state and politics, and did certain politicians and members of the security services strike a deal with Cosa Nostra to put an end to their terrorist campaign?

'It's really frustrating because the answer to this mystery will never be solved. Every year a little bit comes out, but we have to wait a little bit more,' one of the speakers said.

A year later they were proved right. In 2018, a judge ruled that Berlusconi crony Marcello Dell'Utri helped broker a secret agreement between his party and the Mafia in the early 1990s and sentenced him to twelve years. Berlusconi was at the time running for prime minister and, sure enough, by the time he got to office in 1994 the bombings had stopped. An ex-*carabinieri* general was also convicted.

You know, in all of the *Pirates of the Caribbean* movies, you never see them doing any actual pirating: no raiding or pillaging seaside towns, nothing. Pirates were assholes in real life, but I guess enough time has passed to think of them as easy-going rebels who don't play by society's rules. Maybe someday we'll see a whimsical adventure about Somali pirates, who knows.

There's a widespread misconception that the Italian Mafia is somehow more noble than other criminals. That it has 'standards', a code of honour. It's the old 'our criminals are better' trope. Don Corleone thought blackmail and prostitution were absolutely acceptable sources of income, but drugs were not. Now I love *The Godfather* as much as the next guy, but the idea that they don't touch women and children, or that they take care not to hurt innocent people, is complete bullshit.

As the full might of the state came crashing down, snitches, or 'penitents', came forward to save their own asses. One of those rats was Santino Di Matteo, who, along with Giovanni Brusca (affectionately known as 'The Pig'), had helped assassinate Falcone. In return, Brusca kidnapped his eleven-year-old son, little Giuseppe Di Matteo, and locked him in an underground dungeon for two years to keep Santino from talking. In the end, the boy was strangled to death and dissolved in acid, all because of who his father was.

Honour.

One by one, the Corleone clan was hunted down. Giovanni Brusca was caught in 1996 after being holed up in a bunker with enough rifles, RPGs and hand grenades to outfit a small army. Ten years later, Bernardo Provenzano was found hiding in a peasant hut near Corleone, having been a fugitive since 1963. All got life sentences.

In the end, the Mafia got too bloodthirsty for its own good, alienating many of its one-time supporters including mobbed-up Prime Minister Giulio Andreotti and the Catholic Church, which gave the godfathers an aura of legitimacy in the Cold War by seeing the godless commie heathens as a greater threat. The Pope denounced mafiosi and in 2017 the Archbishop of Sicily banned them from taking the role of godfather at baptisms. At last, children all over this beautiful island were safe from strange old men with orange peels in their mouths.

These days Corleone is much quieter. But the scars of the past remain, and the people of Corleone still talk about Cosa Nostra in hushed tones – you never know who might be standing behind you.

16

New Blood

In the historic centre of Palermo lies Ballarò market, where for over a thousand years merchants have flogged fresh fish and fruits in the bright light of day. But as night falls, another type of market emerges. I sat down at a grubby bar table decorated with MJ leaves while everyone around me bought a one-way ticket to Bake City. The cops drove straight past as they rolled their zoots and no one gave a shit. This area was protected – a little Amsterdam in the middle of Palermo. But the mafiosi here weren't Italian, they were Nigerian.

The Nigerian Mafia emerged from an unlikely place: unruly frat houses. In the 1970s, student societies at Nigerian universities degenerated into bloodthirsty 'campus cults' such as the Black Axe. 'Hilarious' pranks they played included sneaking into rival fraternities and slaughtering everyone inside. Their alumni network gave them access to crooked officials. The Nigerians are also natural-born hustlers, and their worldwide diaspora enables many profitable smuggling opportunities.

But African dealers have to know their place in Italy. Shit got racial outside Naples in 2008, when a hit squad from the Casalesi clan went around the hood shooting black people at random, gunning down six West Africans and a local arcade owner. They wanted to show the Nigerians who's boss after the Africans failed to pay their monthly fees for pimping women and pushing drugs. Race riots broke out and the army had to be sent in to restore order.

Since then, racial relations have tumbled further downhill with the onset of the European migrant crisis. In 2011, protests toppled Colonel Gaddafi in Libya with the help of Western governments. Gaddafi might have been a real-life Bond villain, but without him Libya collapsed into anarchy, a playground for warring militias. The path was open for millions of Africans fleeing war and famine in their home-lands to make their way aboard rickety boats to the promised land of Europe, only to fall into the clutches of the Mafia. With these immi-grants packed into overcrowded migrant centres and desperate for work, the Mob became the newcomers' biggest employers, using them for cheap labour, drug runs and prostitution. Those who didn't play ball faced the wrath of their Nigerian taskmasters and their Italian handlers.

Another reason why the Sicilian Mafia is on its way out, aside from most of its top leadership being either in hiding or serving multiple life sentences, is that heroin is *sooooo* 1983. Nowadays all the cool kids are doing cocaine, much of it coming through the Gioia Tauro seaport in Calabria, on the tip of Italy's boot. The 'Ndrangheta, another secret society from the hills of Calabria, cashed in on the heat coming down on their Sicilian cousins by setting themselves up as the top dogs in the Italian underworld.

While the Mafia ran heroin back in the 1970s, the 'Ndrangheta's main business was kidnapping. In 1973, they snatched John Paul Getty III, the sixteen-year-old grandson of American oil tycoon John Paul Getty. Getty famously refused to pay his grandson's ransom until a Roman newspaper received his ear in the post, after which 2 billion lira of the 10 billion lira ($17 million) ransom was dropped off on the side of a road and the young Getty was released. Never getting over the trauma, young Getty turned to drink and drugs and fell into an early grave.

Like the Sicilians, the Calabrians follow their own weird traditions. Every year, 'ndranghetisti from across the world make an annual pilgrimage to a shrine of the Madonna on a wooded hill in Calabria, holding a SPECTRE-style meeting to discuss business, elect new bosses and recognise new crime families. Unlike the Mafia, which is riddled with squealers, the 'Ndrangheta has an advantage in that its crime families are *actual* families, bonded by blood or marriage that you can't walk away from.*

Probably no one outside southern Italy had even heard of the 'Ndrangheta until August 2007, when six men were shot outside a pizzeria (where else?) in the industrial town of Duisburg in western Germany. The killers fired fifty-four bullets, stopped, reloaded, then shot each of them in the head.

The Duisburg massacre was the culmination of a long-running beef between two 'Ndrangheta families that apparently began when one of them got egged at a festival. It woke the world up to the new Mafia it was facing, but by that point the 'Ndrangheta had spread its tentacles all over the globe, reinvesting its kidnapping loot in large-scale cocaine trafficking through Germany, Canada, Africa, Australia and South America.

'The American Mafia is more or less independent, but the Australians and Canadians take orders from villages in Calabria,' Professor Umberto Santino, an expert on organised crime, told me.

* Maria Cacciola learnt that the hard way. The Mafia princess was married off to another mobster when she was just thirteen and bore him a child two years later. When he got sent to the big house, her father and brother discovered she was Facebook friends with another man and beat her till she cracked a rib. Trying to escape her sadistic family, Maria thought about going to the police and entering the witness protection programme, but her family threatened to take away her kids. In August 2011 she was found dead, having downed a bottle of hydrochloric acid. She must have died in agony, the acid burning through her organs. Her family claimed it was suicide.

Meanwhile, over in Naples, the Cutolo war had thrown the old Camorra clans into disarray. One particularly vicious feud erupted over the open-air drug bazaars in the run-down housing projects of Scampia run by the Di Lauro family. Neighbourhood kids kept a lookout as pushers served up their customers the finest dope and coke in the city, while the clan's ruthless hit squad hit up the firing range before each job so they'd always have an excuse for gunpowder residue on their clothing.

Rumour has it that chieftain Paolo 'the Millionaire' Di Lauro once got his lieutenant Gennaro Marino to drink a cup of piss to prove his loyalty. Probably still remembering Paulie's warm, salty aftertaste, Genny soon mutinied, joining a large group of Di Lauro's capos, the Secessionists (including at least one transgender drug dealer – the Camorra's progressive that way), who stopped paying their weekly dues to the Millionaire in 2004. A series of tit-for-tat murders followed.

The Scampia feud in Naples has inspired another great work of art, *Gomorrah* (based on the book of the same name). I like it because, unlike such films as *The Godfather*, where the main characters are lovable rogues who you root for because the bad guys like Sollozzo are even worse, the heroes of *Gomorrah* are drug pushers and murderers who'll betray each other at the drop of a hat – which is more akin to real life.

Altogether, some sixty people died in the split, including Gelsomina Verde, a twenty-two-year-old factory worker who spent her spare time helping the elderly. On 21 November 2004, she was snatched up by Di Lauro loyalists demanding to know the whereabouts of her ex-boyfriend, who'd defected to the Secessionists. After torturing her for hours, they shot her three times in the back of the neck and dumped her body in a car they set on fire.

The Mafia's not nearly as trigger-happy as the Camorra these days, but that doesn't mean they're not around.

'It's much less dangerous, I have to be honest,' a sixteen-year veteran of Palermo's narcotics squad told me and Edoardo over coffee. 'But a couple of times I've received threats in my many years working against them, like threats to bomb my car. One time, the guards in prison found a picture of me and the magistrate in one of the inmates' Bibles. He said, "Yes, because I pray for them!"'

The story of the Italian Mafia – back home, in Cuba or America – shows how drug trafficking touches the highest echelons of power, how it adapts to a changing market (heroin to blow) and how, just like in London, the faces may change but the business stays the same.

There's one aspect of the Mafia *The Godfather* did get right. Towards the third act, the Mafia bosses gather for a meeting where they allow the drug trade in black and Puerto Rican neighbour-hoods. 'They're animals anyway,' says one of the dons, 'so let them lose their souls.' Little did he know that in a few short years, the 'animals' would run the zoo.

Part 4

Land of the Free

17

The Three Musketeers

The Blind Beggar pub, East London. It had been a while since I'd been here, but I wanted to show our American guests a slice of local history. It was over this very bar in 1966 that Ronnie Kray shot George Cornell for calling him a 'fat poof'. Although these days everything's gentrified to hell and the Beggar no more draws such a rough-and-tumble crowd, the Krays' pictures are still plastered all over the walls. I walked back from the bar, a drink in each hand, to Seth Ferranti and his lovely wife, Diane. After years of email and Facebook, this was the first time we'd got to meet.

The War on Drugs, as we currently know it, was born in the USA. We'll find out how the rest of the world got on in a bit, but first let's have a look at Nixon and Anslinger's legacy through the eyes of three of its survivors – one cop and two dealers; one black and two white; Seth Ferranti, Norm Stamper and 'Freeway' Ricky Ross.

Seth actually inspired me to write. His site, *Gorilla Convict*, is where you go when you want the true stories from the street. Stories about dudes like Kenneth 'Supreme' McGriff, the crack-dealing kingpin of NY's notorious Supreme Team, and his beef with 50 Cent. Seth ran the site while serving a quarter-century stretch in the belly of the beast, while his wife Diane typed up and posted the articles. Now, the ex-convict's making up for lost time.

'I'm blessed to have the most amazing wife in the world,' he said, looking over at her as they held hands. 'They have this expression in hip-hop, when you call someone your ride-or-die. Well, she's my ride-or-die!'

'Cheers to that,' I said, raising my glass.

Seth's a true American outlaw, having spent some time on the US Marshal's Most Wanted list after being indicted as a drug kingpin in the early nineties. Seth's a hench, rough-looking ex-convict, but back in 1987 he was just another skinny white kid into sex, drugs and rock-n'-roll. He started out much like me, having a really middle-class upbringing and moving around a lot as his father was re-stationed.

'I grew up a military brat. My dad was in the navy. I was born in California and grew up on military bases there, but also on the East Coast and even overseas, like here in London,' he began over a pint. But it was back in the Golden State that Seth had his first puff of reefer.

'When we were in San Jose one of the guys on my athletics team suggested we try it,' Seth explained. 'We scored some Thai sticks off this black dude with Jheri curls and smoked it. He never smoked again. I turned into a stoner.'

From there, it was a gradual progression from using to selling. Seth was the one all the other kids came to when they wanted to score, because he had the hook-up and wasn't afraid to stray to the wrong side of town. He quickly found he could always pocket some change and score some free dope just by going to pick up. By the age of fifteen he was dealing and by seventeen, he hit the big-time. Big-time for a kid, at least.

Seth's suppliers became a dude from Texas called Mexican Eddie and some good ol' boys from Kentucky, where the climate and soil is just right to grow high-potency chronic. Before long, Seth was driving hundreds of pounds of outdoor homegrown up to Virginia and East Coast colleges.

'At my height I was making twenty grand or so a month, selling drugs at fifteen colleges in five states. I had a little loop I used to drive: down Interstate-81 in Virginia and hit all the colleges, cut through Cumberland Gap to Kentucky and hit a couple of colleges, go up through Lexington then off to West Virginia University in Morgantown, my biggest customers, then into Pennsylvania and Penn State, then down into Maryland and hit the colleges there, stop in DC and then I'd be back in Virginia.'

Seth also expanded his operation to start selling LSD, which he did by going on tour with the Grateful Dead. Their music wasn't really his thing – he was more of an NWA/heavy-metal kinda guy and even played in a couple of bands – but hanging around Deadheads instantly gave him customers and connections.

He might live in a cabin on a faraway island off the Pacific Northwest with a beard that makes him look like a wizened sage, but Norm Stamper isn't your typical hermit. A thirty-four-year veteran of the police force, Norm rose through the ranks from a beat cop to be police chief of Seattle, before certain events fast-tracked his retirement.

Being a cop wasn't Stamper's first choice. Back in 1966, Norm was a twenty-year-old veterinary assistant in San Diego whose wife was getting tired of strangers knocking on their door at three in the morning demanding rabies shots for their kittens. One day, he went with a friend to take the test for the police academy and ended up passing, with flying colours.

'I remember putting on the uniform, looking at myself in the mirror and thinking, what have I done?' he told me in a Skype call from his cabin deep in the San Juan wilderness.

Norm worked his way to undercover, where he was assigned to catch a crew of burglars on a crime spree through Southern California. One night he was with his partner on a stakeout at a wealthy suburb when they spotted the suspects ransacking a house:

'They popped into their car before we could stop them and took off. I jumped into the car and gave chase. We were going zero-to-eighty miles per hour in a residential area, which is insane; we didn't even think about how reckless that was. We got to Interstate 8 and Mission Valley, doing eighty to a hundred. I was on the radio and my partner was driving. The driver of the getaway car went through a darkened area and cut his lights, but he'd tap the brakes every once in a while, so we could see them go into the intersection, and one of our marked police cars was there and pulled them over. I questioned one, my partner questioned the other, and we didn't even think twice how reckless we were in that pursuit.'

The perps turned out to be a couple of off-duty marines who'd gone down to San Diego from their base in LA. They had loot from all over SoCal, including an LAPD detective's badge.

From undercover, Norm climbed his way up the ladder and earned the rank of captain in 1975, becoming the youngest officer to hold that title at thirty-one years old. But then Seattle came calling and Stamper packed his bags, moving over a thousand miles to patrol the rainy Northwest. By 1994, he made chief.

Ricky Donnell Ross had a rough start to life. Born in the small town of Troup, eastern Texas, in 1960, Ross moved with his mother to Los Angeles when he was three years old. But it wasn't all purple sunsets and Hollywood Boulevard. In the 1960s, black Americans started moving en masse to the cities, escaping poverty and Klan lynchings in the South. They settled in Harlem, Oakland, Detroit and LA. But what they found up North was another form of segregation. Many landlords simply refused to allow African-Americans into their neighbourhoods. They were forced to settle in the poorest, most crime-ridden areas, cut off from basic services like schools and healthcare. Little Ricky moved to South Central. There, he witnessed his mum shoot dead his uncle in a domestic brawl. It was self-defence.

'That was the first time I saw anybody getting killed, but it wasn't the last,' Rick told me over the phone.

Ross went to Dorsey High School, but he wasn't big on classes. He preferred hanging with his friends, playing in the back alleys behind the sun drenched, palm tree-lined streets. In fact, he didn't even learn how to read.

'School was never for me. I never liked school, never wanted to go to school, and couldn't read or write before prison. School was just a place to have fun and socialise.'

There was one thing he *did* like doing, however, that could have provided him with an out. I remember when I was little my dad forced me to play tennis because he thought I should do some kinda sport, and I hated it because I had no hand–eye co-ordination.

'No-one forced me to play tennis, I loved it!' Ross laughed. 'I was looking for a way out of the ghetto. Playing tennis, and hanging out with wealthy people, gave me a whole new perspective on life. I thought my neighbourhood was the best in the world but when I saw and got a taste for the finer things in life, it gave me a new perspective.'

It's easy to say: if you don't wanna wind up in jail, don't do stupid shit. People say things like 'you always have a choice', but every choice we make is influenced by our genetics, upbringing and completely random events we have no control over. We're all products of our environment, and the environment of the ghetto isn't a very nurturing one.

'I look back on it now, and when I was growing up my neighbourhood was really dysfunctional,' Ross said. 'Some things we thought were important in life are really toxic: not caring about going to jail, not caring if you lived or died; those things are really toxic. That's what people say about rap music: it glorifies violence, or it glorifies drugs. It glorifies those things because that's where they [rappers] come from. In the black community, often the first entrepreneur that young blacks see is a drug dealer.'

After decades of ignoring the problem, the Feds finally set their sights on the Mob. In 1972, Richard Nixon signed the RICO (Racketeer Influenced and Corrupt Organizations) Act, which meant mob bosses could finally be prosecuted for the actions of their underlings. Before, the guys at the top kept themselves insulated from those doing the dirty work, but now whole crime families could be put away if it could be proved they were part of the same criminal enterprise. The heavy prison sentences this entailed led many a stone-faced mafioso to start singing like a canary. Pointing out where the bodies are buried could shave some time off your sentence and give you a new identity, so you could go make a fresh start in Alaska – easier that than spending thirty years in jail. Riddled with informants, Cosa Nostra was springing more leaks than the *Titanic*.

As the American government turned up its war on drugs, some bosses didn't want their soldiers dealing as it would bring too much heat. 'Big Paul' Castellano, boss of New York's Gambino crime family, forbade his men from dealing drugs, preferring they stick to more wholesome activities like robbing people at gunpoint or breaking their legs if they owed money. But he'd quite happily take any drug loot that came his way, so the rule wasn't so much 'don't deal' as 'don't get caught'. In December 1985, Big Paul and his bodyguard were shot dead in a volley of gunfire as they stepped outside Sparks Steak House in Manhattan after a dispute with one of his capos, John Gotti, over the family's ban on narcotics. The Feds busted Gotti's crew dealing drugs and Gotti was afraid Big Paul would demote him or rub him out, so he had Big Paul rubbed out first. After Castellano's death Gotti was crowned head of the Gambinos, until 1991, when his underboss, 'Sammy the Bull' Gravano, flipped after admitting to nineteen murders. But even after entering the witness protection programme, old habits die hard, and in 2000 Gravano was picked up along with his son for running an ecstasy ring in Arizona, ironically thanks to informers in his own organisation.

A rat infestation wasn't the only problem. The Mafia was going through a demographic crisis. These days, Italian-Americans (along with the Jews and Irish)* don't face the same discrimination and hardship their ancestors did and no longer have to live in the ghetto – all that's left of Little Italy in Manhattan is just one street (Mulberry St) that's completely surrounded by Chinatown. With their *paisanos* firmly a part of mainstream America, the Mafia's power base in the old neighbourhoods is all but gone.

At first, black kingpins like Harlem cat Nicky Barnes had to rely on the Italian Mafia for product and protection. But Frank Matthews, aka 'Black Caesar', was having none of that. A country boy from North Carolina, Matthews bought directly from the Cubans shipping cocaine and the Corsicans moving heroin in the late sixties. He wore mink coats and drove a pimped-out ride. When one of the Italian godfathers threatened to muscle in on his turf, Matthews warned him, 'Touch one of my men and I'll drive down Mulberry Street and shoot every wop I see.'

Matthews' organisation supplied dealers and pushers across the country, including Philadelphia, where he stepped on the toes of the Black Mafia. The Black Mafia were a rogue set of Nation of Islam Muslims whose most infamous crime was the 1973 massacre of seven Muslims, including five children, from a rival sect at the home of basketball player Kareem Abdul-Jabbar. In 1972, they shot

---

* The Jewish Mafia's still around, although now more in the form of immigrant Russians, Ukrainians and politically connected Israelis fighting over the ecstasy business. The Irish mobs gradually died out or became subservient to Italian organisations. The Westies, a gang of psychotic Irishmen in New York's Hell's Kitchen, flew under the flag of the Gambinos. James 'Whitey' Bulger and his crew managed to hold their own in the predominantly Irish-American South Boston projects until the mid-1990s, but only because Bulger himself was an FBI informant for decades during which time he committed dozens of murders, sold coke and smuggled guns for the IRA. Granted, the agent who took him in, John Connelly, was a corrupt piece-of-shit, but the higher-ups must have known the guy feeding them information about the Boston Mafia wasn't exactly a Boy Scout.

Matthews' lieutenant Tyrone Palmer, aka 'Mr Millionaire', in the face at a nightclub in Atlantic City, along with his bodyguard and three innocent women in front of hundreds of witnesses; a clear message to stay the hell out of Philly.

By 1973, Matthews was getting too high on his own supply and the law was catching onto him. Just after getting indicted by the DEA, Matthews made a run for it and disappeared with $20 million. That was over forty-five years ago, and no one has heard from him since.

The black godfather made history by being the first African-American drug lord of New York City. Matthews story was mirrored on the silver screen by the film *SuperFly*. Its funky soundtrack (courtesy of Curtis Mayfield) and cooler-than-cool hero, a Harlem drug dealer who outsmarts crooked cops, struck a cord with young Ricky.

'I loved *SuperFly*! He was my role model at one time. They redid that movie, but I only watched five minutes then I had to leave. If you remake a classic like *Scarface* or *SuperFly*, you gotta do it right! They took all the authenticity out of it, the stuff that makes it real.'

Ricky was still killing it on the tennis court. He was so good he almost won a scholarship to a university in Long Beach. But there was a problem – he still couldn't read. The uni turned him down and Ricky's life took a different turn. He was recruited by a car-theft ring, driving off with stolen rides during the night and bringing them back to the chop-shop. By the early 1980s, however, Ricky's friends introduced him to a new, more profitable venture, straight out of *SuperFly*: cocaine.

18

Ready Rock

Detectives called it the worst bloodbath they'd seen since the brutal Helter Skelter murders over a decade before. On 1 July 1981, the LAPD found four people with their skulls caved in at a house on Wonderland Avenue in the Hollywood Hills, western Los Angeles. They were members of the Wonderland Gang, a loose crew of drug dealers with a sideline in armed robbery that included porn star John Holmes, a man with a thirteen-inch cock who'd fucked 14,000 women as his alter-ego, Johnny Wadd.

Holmes began his thespian career in the early 1970s, back when porn films actually had a plot and you found out if the young lady's plumbing got fixed at the end. In those days, people thought it was acceptable to put on flares and platform shoes and spend your Saturday night dancing away to 'Stayin' Alive' under the influence of an old favourite making its comeback: cocaine.

The disco era was mercifully brief as the Bee Gees gave way to synth and hair metal, but the drugs remained. By the late 1970s, Holmes had become seriously addicted to coke, making his dick useless on-set. He was running out of money fast. Stealing from cars, airport conveyors and even his friends, Holmes took to sleeping in his car with his girlfriend Dawn, whom he met when she was only fifteen, and started pimping her out, eventually trying to sell her to a brothel. She escaped, but he tracked her down to her mother's house and begged her to take him back, saying he'd changed and only needed one big score. So he devised a scheme to rip off big-time crime lord Eddie Nash, aka Adel Gharib Nasrallah, a Palestinian refugee who went from running a hot-dog stand to being the biggest nightclub owner and coke dealer in LA. Holmes was friends with Nash and let the intruders into his house, where they held Nash and his bodyguard, Gregory Diles, at gunpoint, before making off with a million dollars' worth of jewels, cash and cocaine.

On the night of the murders, Holmes stumbled into his estranged wife's house, covered in blood. Knowing he'd fucked up, he probably led Nash to the robbers' house. The next morning, he wandered back to Dawn and fell asleep, mumbling something about blood. They both saw the Wonderland house on TV just before the cops kicked down the door and dragged Holmes away after his handprint was found at the crime scene. In the end, both John and Eddie bust case, although Nash later got three years for racketeering, including setting up the killings, but avoided being sent down for murder. Holmes died of AIDS a few years later, while Nash retired to suburbia and died in 2014.

The snowstorm that hit Tinseltown came from Miami, where thousands of anti-Castro exiles fled and settled in Little Havana. In 1961, the CIA trained a group of these exiles to land at the Bay of Pigs in Cuba and overthrow Castro. But the promised air and naval support never came, and the invasion failed. The men were thrown in Cuban prison camps. When they were released back to America, the militants began raising money for the struggle, using their working relationship with the Mafia from the Batista days to set themselves up in the coke business.

Cocaine would have remained a niche industry were it not for the machinations of the US justice system. You see, it would be nice if everyone in the pen learnt their lesson and came out fully reformed, but there's a reason prisons are sometimes called the Universities of Crime. The whole time you're there you're surrounded by other criminals, people who share your worldview. If you play it cool, they'll be more than happy to teach you a few tricks. I learned more about credit-card fraud and bank scams from Misha than I ever could browsing the web. Go in as a freshman studying for a degree in Burglary, come out with a PhD in Counterfeiting and Blackmail.

And so one day in 1974 Carlos Lehder ended up sharing a cell with George Jung, aka 'Boston George' (immortalised by Johnny Depp in the movie *Blow*). Jung moved to California in the 1960s, where he started selling pot on the beach before realising there was more money to be made by selling that dank Cali dro back home in Boston, after which he got air stewardesses to bring it over in their luggage. Raking in the moolah, Jung expanded his operation, buying it straight from Mexico and flying it over on his own aircraft. But he got caught, wound up in jail and ended up bunking with Carlos Lehder. Lehder was a half-German half-Colombian wannabe Nazi who got caught stealing cars, but after hearing what Jung was in for, he gave the Bostonian a far more interesting proposition. 'What do you know about cocaine?' he asked.

Like all good universities, prisons have an alumni network. Jung and Lehder met up again on the outside in 1976 and hatched a plan to flood LA with Colombian cocaine, selling $2.5m worth of coke. By 1977 they were bringing in a hundred kilos a week and moving it through Jung's ganja distribution network. But Lehder double-crossed his partner by approaching his distributors directly. George was out. It was the start of the Colombian takeover.

Florida was the perfect spot to unload cocaine, encompassing thousands of miles of Caribbean coastline. Lehder bought an island in the Bahamas, Norman's Cay, which he used as a pit stop between Colombia and Miami. Planes would land carrying hundreds of kilos of white gold, which got packed into speedboats that could easily outrun the Coast Guard.

Lehder ran Norman's Cay as his own personal fiefdom. His dream was to create an island with no laws, a kind of criminal utopia. Chasing the other inhabitants off the island, the drug lord hosted wild parties while German mercenaries riding in Jeeps patrolled for unwanted visitors. In 1980, a yacht belonging to a Florida couple was found drifting at sea, shredded by shotgun blasts and covered in blood splatter. In 1982, when the US finally indicted Lehder for drug trafficking, he flew a small plane over the Bahamas Independence Day parade dropping hundreds of leaflets with $100 bills stapled to the back reading 'DEA GO HOME'.

Back on land, the Colombians entered the Miami drug scene with a bang. Heading up the US side of Lehder's operation was an ex-prostitute named Griselda Blanco, also known as the 'Black Widow' because she whacked three of her husbands. The murder rate tripled as Colombian henchmen, dressed in Hawaiian shirts and pastel suits, went to war with the established Cuban bosses. There were so many shootouts between the cocaine cowboys that they ran out of room at the city morgue.

But just as the corpses were piling up, the money was too. Coke transformed Miami from a glorified retirement home into a glitzy metropolis, the city's nightlife taking off as thousands of clubbers lined up by the bathroom to shove white powder up their nostrils while bankers and property developers got their hands on more dodgy dollars than they could launder in their wildest dreams. In 1979, the Miami Federal Reserve Bank reported a cash surplus of $5.5 billion, more than all the other federal reserves put together.

Back in Los Angeles, the education system let down Rick Ross. Not only did it fail to teach him how to read, but it helped transform Ricky Donnell Ross, junior tennis prodigy, into 'Freeway' Rick Ross, South Central drug kingpin.

'I told a teacher from the field centre, which is kind of a trade school, what I was doing, and he introduced me to the Nicaraguan connect,' Ross said. 'He plugged me in properly.'

People had known all about smoking cocaine since the 1970s: Richard Pryor set himself on fire doing just that. But in the 1980s, some bright spark figured out that if you mixed it with baking powder, cooked it into a rock, and smoked it, you'd get a much stronger buzz than if you stuck it up your nose. Gram-for-gram, crack's not necessarily *cheaper* than coke, but the high was so intense that it gave better value for money in the ghetto, where blacks and Latinos could ill afford the more expensive (and much less addictive) powder cocaine used by whites. Anyone with a kitchen could make crack, but most people were too lazy to do it themselves. All Ross did was sell ones he made earlier. He called it Ready Rock, which sounds like the kind of cereal that would blow your socks off.

South Central at the time was divided between two warring street gangs, the Bloods and the Crips, who used to clash over who came from what hood, as well as fashion sense. You see, the Bloods wore red – red caps, flannels, T-shirts and bandanas – and the Crips wore blue.

'At first it wasn't quite Bloods and Crips, it was 107th Street versus Denver Lanes. I hung around with some guys that were from 107th, and one day when I was at school I turned around and this Denver Lanes guy's holding a gun to my face.'

Ross stayed away from the gangs at school, but now they were his best customers. Having no gang affiliation, Ross sold to the Bloods *and* the Crips. At the retail end of Ross's operation, gang members in appropriately coloured garb hung around shooting craps under the palm trees between dilapidated, low-slung houses, on the lookout for their lowrider-cruising rivals or the black-and-white squad cars of the LAPD.

Crack transformed these bands of wayward youth into underworld corporations, just as Lucky Luciano had done in his day. Some gangs had clear hierarchies and division of labour (treasurers, foot soldiers, street pushers and lookout boys), a board of directors and even expenses to pay funeral costs of dead homies. Fighting over a street corner meant not only who gets to control turf, but who gets to sling rocks at the local crack spot. South Central became an urban warzone as the Bs & Cs upped their arsenal to Glocks, AKs and MAC-10s.

Meanwhile, Ross was raking in the coin. Between 1982 and 1989, prosecutors claimed he sold three tonnes of cocaine, which in today's money would have earned him about $850 million.

'We were doing pretty good. I was working directly in about five different states myself. I was living young and wild, hood rich! Yeah, it could definitely be dangerous. I witnessed a couple of people getting killed. But I kept everyone at an arm's distance; nobody who'd want to come after me really knew me, or what I looked like, so that threw them off. And I never really came after anyone else either. I had a rule: "Never give anyone anything you can't afford to lose."'

Ross was low-key. No gold chains. His main concern was hiding everything from his mum. 'I remember I once had this massive rock, a quarter-kilo, of MDMA, which I kept in a see-through ice-cream tin. One afternoon I went out and my dad must have taken it upon himself to go in my room and do some J. Edgar Hoovering, because when I got back the floor was spotless *and my big jar of Mandy was sitting right there on the fucking desk*. My heart fucking stopped. But he didn't say anything so I guess my dad just thought I had a weird rock collection or something. Still, after that I thought it was safer to keep all my stuff stashed at my friend's yard around the corner.

'I kept my drugs away from my mother but one day she found my stash of cash under my dirty clothes. She was crying, like "Oh no, you're in the Mob, you gotta get out!" and I was like "Mom ... I *am* the Mob,"' Ross laughed. 'But she was scared I was gonna get killed.'

Crack devastated inner-city communities. The murder rate jumped as Jamaican and Dominican crews got in on the action. Abandoned or semi-abandoned buildings (where the owners really didn't give a fuck) became crackhouses where happy customers could go to take a hit from that sweet glass pipe.

As more young women started selling themselves, their prices would correlate to the price of crack. So if a crack rock cost five dollars, a blowjob cost five dollars. In turn, more men got the idea into their heads that all whores are crackheads willing to do anything, meaning all the 'clean' girls had to degrade themselves even more just to keep up. Meanwhile, pimps were icons of 1970s blaxploitation flicks like *SuperFly*, but the plummeting price of crack made the pimp game unprofitable. Score one for female empowerment? Not really. With no 'management', the girls were left on their own against cops and unruly customers. And that, dear children, is where crack whores came from.

'I tried crack, but then I saw it makes you spend all of your money,' said Ross. 'I wanted the money, so it didn't take me long to realise "Don't do it." *Scarface* put it best: don't get high on your own supply.'

It doesn't help that drug addiction proliferates in depressing environments such as ghettos, where desperation, hopelessness and poverty push people towards a chemical crutch that, of course, only provides more evidence of their moral failings. Upper-class people don't feel the heat of the drug war so much because they're protected by the safety net of their surroundings.

'When you're young, you get caught up in things you don't understand,' said Ross. 'I feel some penance and regret for getting involved.'

At the same time, the media blew everything out of proportion. TV crews and journalists tried to outdo themselves in tales of depravity: Crack babies!* Just one hit and you're addicted! Clint Eastwood

---

* News coverage showed skinny, crying babies in hospital wards, the product of their mothers smoking crack. Hysterical reports shrieked they were brain-damaged, a lost generation. But a twenty-five-year study following up on babies born between 1989 and 1992 showed that most grew to be healthy, normal adults. Most of those so-called 'crack babies' were actually just premature, with the same symptoms as any other. What *did* make a difference in their lives was growing up in the ghetto. It was easier to blame an evil force, drugs, than to tackle the serious issues of poverty, unemployment, mental health and so on.

and Pee-wee Herman appeared in bizarre ads warning kids to stay away from crack. Ironically, the media hype might have made suckers more curious to try it.

And where the media goes, politicians follow. In 1980, Ronald Reagan was elected and liberalism took a decade-long vacation. In 1986, Reagan released the long-awaited sequel to Nixon's War on Drugs, the Anti-Drugs Abuse Act, which handed out even harsher penalties to violators – five years without parole for getting caught with just five grams of crack, as opposed to half a key of regular cocaine. Crack was treated like it came straight from Peru, when it was mostly baking soda. It's probably no coincidence that crack was more popular with poor blacks and Latinos, while powder cocaine was the preserve of Wall Street fat cats, and having them share a cell with Billy Blanco from the Bronx was simply unacceptable. Meanwhile, Reagan's wife Nancy embarked on her Just Say No campaign ('What do you do if someone offers you drugs? JUST SAY NO!!!'), which even crossed over the Atlantic when it featured on gritty crime drama *Grange Hill* and became one of the most terrible songs ever.

While Nixon might have declared the War on Drugs, it was Reagan who turned it into an actual war, resurrecting an old, Civil War-era law that allowed him to deploy the army, navy and Coast Guard gunships to effectively mount a blockade of southern Florida. Seizures went up, but that couldn't stop the avalanche of Colombian snow headed towards America. With Miami locked down, the cartels turned their attention south of the border.

Over in LA, a special task force was formed to take down Ricky Ross. In many parts of the world, law enforcement is an entrepreneurial activity. Paid a pittance to risk their lives every day, maybe they deserve a little compensation. And if a little stuff goes missing, who's gonna know? It's not like anyone's gonna stand up in court and say, 'Excuse me your honour, but I was actually a bigger criminal than you thought.' And so your hard-earned drug loot ends up going towards egg-and-mayo sandwiches for the policemen's annual picnic.

Plus, drug lords can afford high-priced lawyers to get them off scot-free with a kiss and a handshake from the judge so, sometimes, to protect the weak and innocent, you've got to play dirty. And that can mean crossing a few lines, even if the chief will have your ass.

'Fabricating search warrants, fabricating witness, taking the oath on the stand and lying – some of the worst criminals you see are police officers!' said Ross. 'They caught one of my customers with quite a few keys, took one of them and planted it on me, in the trunk of my car. But that wasn't the only time: they'd plant it in drawers, any place that looked suspicious.'

Ross turned the tables on the Freeway Task Force, hiring a private detective, a former sheriff, to snoop on the snoopers.

'His report helped get the cops indicted. I think about thirty-five of them got indicted, but only six or eight went to jail. That was money well spent!' Ross laughed. 'By then I was out of the business, but then I caught another case – entrapment. That's when the government sends an informant to get you to do a crime you wouldn't normally do.'

Ross was set up by his supplier, and in 1996, as a twice-convicted felon (for drug trafficking) he was automatically handed a life sentence under California's three-strikes law. But where Ross's story gets *really* interesting is who his suppliers were.

I don't like conspiracy theories. Whenever I see someone sharing Facebook memes about vaccines, lunar landings, the New World Order and how Bush did 9/11, I shake my head in despair. I mean, is it really so hard to believe that some pissed-off Arabs could have hijacked a plane without involving an over-elaborate plan from a government that couldn't even cover up Watergate, a simple burglary? That's not to say there isn't some duplicitous double-dealing behind the scenes, but it's probably safe to assume we're not being ruled over by reptilian overlords from Alpha Centauri.

So when I was reading up for this interview, imagine my surprise when I found out the one about The Man bringing Crack to the Hood was actually true.

Well, kind of.

Ross's main coke connect was a man named Danilo Blandón, who was affiliated with the Contras, anti-communist guerrillas in the jungles of Nicaragua. During the 1980s, a brutal civil war was being waged in the Central American country, and the CIA was propping up the Contras against the ruling left-wing Sandinista Party since, despite Reagan proclaiming that the Contras were 'the moral equivalent of the Founding Fathers', Congress refused to fund Ronnie's little war.

Allegations had already begun to surface in the late 1980s, when a Senate Commission revealed that one of the airlines the CIA hired to send 'help' to the rebels belonged to a certain Juan Ramón Matta-Ballesteros, a top-ranking capo in Mexico's mighty Guadalajara Cartel. But this was conveniently forgotten until 1986, when journalist Gary Webb revealed that in order to fund the war effort, the CIA allowed the Contras to ship coke to America, where it was cooked into crack and distributed by Ross via Blandón. Keep in mind this was happening at the height of the crack epidemic, with addiction and gang violence both hitting their peak on the streets. The US government was complicit in pushing crack into the hood. So much for Just Say No.

The very public shitstorm that followed became part of the Iran–Contra scandal, as the CIA and 'military adviser' Lieutenant Colonel Oliver North stood accused of giving the Contra guerrillas covert support not only through cocaine but also through illegally selling arms to Iran and using the profits to bankroll the civil war. The ends justified the means.

I asked Ross how he felt about being thrust in the middle of this vast conspiracy.

'I didn't believe it at first,' he said. 'They [the Nicaraguans] told me they were fighting a war back home, but I wasn't keen enough to know about all that. I only found out about it when I was already in jail. Then I thought about the nerve of Ronald Reagan, George Bush and Ollie North to allow foreigners to come onto US soil and sell drugs to the black community. To me, that's more shocking than what the Nicaraguans did. The Nicaraguans were just trying to survive.'

Pissed that he'd beaten them to the punch, the mainstream media tried to trash Webb and his story, claiming he accused the CIA of being *directly* involved in the drug trade, as if Colonel North was stood on the corner of Malcolm X Boulevard slinging dime bags. Webb never actually said that; the CIA just enabled it by looking the other way. But eventually the pressure got so high that Webb was forced to resign from his newspaper, and in 2004 he took his own life by shooting himself in the head . . . twice.

There's a well-known saying that those who don't know history are doomed to repeat it. In a way, not a lot has changed. Replace Tommy guns with Uzis, jazz with gangsta rap, speakeasies with crackhouses, and Irish, Jews and Italians with blacks and Latinos, and you've got pretty much the same picture in America today as you did almost ninety years ago.

Rap emerged from block parties in black and Latino neighbourhoods in the Bronx, where DJs would start spitting bars or calling out their hoods over the beat. Rappers spoke of the problems affecting their communities, which inevitably involved rapping about drugs. In the beginning, when rap emerged in the early 1980s, it tried to convey a social message: 'D-d-d-don't do it, baby!' went the chorus in Grandmaster Flash's 'White Lines'. Then gangsta rap flipped the genre on its head by embracing those very same problems – instead of 'don't do it' you now had the 'Ten Crack Commandments' by Biggie (an essential guide for purveyors of black-market pharmaceuticals everywhere). While sometimes being a little over the top ('There's gonna be a lot of slow-singin' and flower bringin' / if my burglar alarm starts ringin'', Biggie warns us), the lyrics of gangsta rap represented a sad reality for large parts of black America, and the rappers themselves.

While Biggie was signed to Bad Boy Records in New York, his main rival, 2Pac, was signed to LA's Death Row set-up by Marion 'Suge' Knight, a heavy-set man with notorious gang ties who once dangled Vanilla Ice (of 'Ice, Ice Baby' fame) from a hotel window. 2Pac, a classically trained actor, fully embraced his gangsta persona, tattooing 'Thug Life' across his belly and getting into scraps with cops.

The start-up money for Death Row came from Michael 'Harry-O' Harris, a member of the Bounty Hunter Bloods (a set, or faction, of the Bloods gang) and an occasional customer of Freeway Ricky. Harris also branched out into Broadway, producing a play starring an up-and-coming young actor named Denzel Washington.

The feud between Biggie and 2Pac escalated from diss songs ('That's why I fucked your bitch, you fat motherfucker', 2Pac brags on 'Hit 'Em Up') to murder. On 6 September 1996, 'Pac was gunned down in a car on the Las Vegas Strip, while Biggie was shot dead six months later leaving a *Vibe* magazine party in LA. Both murders remain officially unsolved, but a group of rogue cops from the LAPD's Rampart division were implicated in the Biggie murder. The affair, which became known as the Rampart scandal, showed that the elite anti-gangs unit of the LAPD had basically become the biggest, baddest gang in the city. The Rampart cops were, among other things, robbing banks, framing witnesses, stealing cocaine from the evidence locker and working security for Death Row. A few of them had been on the Freeway Task Force.

Meanwhile, things weren't exactly great for Seth Ferranti, either. A cop got shot and wounded by a kid tripping off acid, and the Feds started cracking down hard.

'It was like an LSD witch-hunt in Fairfax County. Dudes were flipping and eventually it led to me. All my so-called friends snitched on me to save their own asses. I don't blame them, but I wasn't going out like that,' Seth said. So he faked his own death at the Great Falls National Park, Virginia.

'I knew from living in the area that a lot of people used to commit suicide at Great Falls by jumping off the cliffs into the raging rapids below. So I left hints and started telling people I was gonna kill myself, and set up a scene with my wallet, cigs and alcohol to make it seem like I was distraught and jumped.'

Unfortunately, Seth staged the suicide at the wrong end of the dam. The Feds had park rangers trawl the river for two weeks and when no body showed up, they declared it a hoax. The twenty-year-old metal-head was placed on the US Marshals' Top 15 Most Wanted list.

'Being a fugitive was cool in retrospect. Back then, though, I was really paranoid. I felt like the Feds had superpowers and were tracking me by my thoughts. I was this closeted suburban drug dealer who never believed this all could happen and I was really in shock. Imagine facing twenty-five-to-life for a first-time, non-violent offence when you're twenty years old! My instincts took over and I ran. I didn't wanna do the time, didn't wanna snitch on anyone, just wanted to get the fuck outta Dodge.'

For the next two years Seth was on the run, taking off to California and then St Louis, where he went back to running weed for Mexican Eddie. It was there that he met his future wife, Diane, while staying over at her sister's friends' under a new identity.

'She told me there might be someone there I might like, and I did,' she smiled.

She knew he sold weed but didn't know the full story until the US Marshals kicked down the door. In 1993, at the age of twenty-two, Seth Ferranti was sentenced to twenty-five years in jail. The suburban white boy was plunged into a world of hardened convicts and brutal guards.

19

Incarceration Nation

The prison world is quite unlike the outside; all of society's rejects and the worst specimens of humanity are brought together under one roof. Even now, Diane complains, Seth rarely smiles in his photos because he hasn't learnt to take off his mask – the same tough-looking gaze that got him through two decades in the joint.

'You have to stand tall and not back down, let people know you can handle your business. Without the mask on, the threat of violence is very real,' he explained.

One time, Seth was heading to recreation at FCI Manchester when a guy stumbled in front of him, covered in blood from head to toe, before collapsing just as he went past. Apparently, he'd got jumped in the bathroom by a few other inmates. The man had to be taken to hospital, but survived.

Another risk is getting turned out – turned into a bitch. That is, if you're in the showers and you lose control of the soap, those buck-wild booty warriors are gonna be on you like a pack of hungry cats.*

---

* The closest I heard to something like that happening was a weird story about a guy getting violated with a hair comb. Basically, one day he was taking a dump, and for some reason he stood up mid-way through while little nuggets of shit were still falling out of his crack and going all over the floor. His cell-mate was totally grossed out and expressed his displeasure by poking him in the arse with a hair comb. By complete coincidence, the comb ended up actually going into his asshole and our hero screamed in terror before running out of his

In a place where everyone's trying to fuck you over, some prisoners will try to stick together. Safety in numbers and all that. A group of prisoners banding together is called a car and they're usually racially or geographically based, so you'll have the New York car, the white boy car, the Italian car, and so on. Usually (but not always) the cars are run by a gang; so, for example, the fearsome Aryan Brotherhood could run the white-boy car.

While a car is just a group of homies who've got each other's back, a gang is a more organised group that sells drugs, bribes the guards, extorts and pimps out other inmates and so on. Since most career criminals end up spending a significant part of their life behind bars, the shot-callers on the inside have tremendous control over what goes down on the streets: drug deals, mob hits, you name it. They're also drawn on racial lines; so, for example, the neo-Nazi Aryan Brotherhood doesn't get along too well with Black Guerrilla Family.

'The kitchen was segregated,' explained Freeway Ricky. 'I saw them all sitting at their tables – the blacks, the Aryans and the Mexicans. But the only time racism really affected me was there was this white guy called Todd McCormick, and the Aryans told him he couldn't hang out with me. Then one day when I wasn't around, two of them beat him with locks-and-socks.'

Seth, meanwhile, found some allies in unexpected places.

'I met some wacked-out motherfuckers and some straight-crazy motherfuckers. But Johnny Deathrow, a homosexual who could fight his ass off, was the strangest. If you needed some back in a beef, Deathrow was the guy to get,' Seth explained. 'He had motherfuckers shook.'

One time, some new black guys appeared and, not knowing the volatile racial politics of the unit, started watching TV in the

---

cell, pants dangled around his ankles, waving the shit-covered comb in the air like the Olympic Torch and yelling at the guards that he'd been raped. He then ended up being moved from our wing to protective custody, while the other dude got done for sexual assault.

white-boy room. The other white boys came running to Seth, who came back with Johnny Deathrow. Seth explained that this was the white boy room and there was a black TV room on the other side of the hall they could use. They looked at Seth like he was crazy, but before they could say anything, Johnny Deathrow piped up: 'You heard the man. Get the fuck out of here.'

One of the black dudes took offence.

'Fuck you, cracker.'

That set Johnny off. He lunged at the black guy and clocked him on the nose. Blood started flowing. Seth tried to calm the situation before it escalated and dragged Johnny back to his cell with the other whites while he went to speak with the black shot-caller on the wing to get the situation straightened out before a full-on race riot broke out.

'Johnny Deathrow didn't give a fuck and was thrown in the hole [solitary] later that day for calling some black guys niggers in the yard,' Seth said. 'He may have been a homosexual but he was a tough motherfucking country boy who didn't give a fuck.'

Since the days of Richard Nixon, US presidents – George Bush, Ronald Reagan, Bill Clinton – have been trying to one-up each other in a dick-measuring contest over who could come down on crime the hardest. Clinton knew he couldn't back out of this race or he'd look like a liberal pussy, so his Democrats oversaw a massive expansion of the prison system via the 1994 Federal Crime Bill, which paid extra money to states whose inmates were serving 85 per cent of their sentences. The prison population almost doubled. Of course, keeping so many people under lock and key came with a hefty price tag, so the government started subcontracting the job to private enterprises. Incarceration became a business. Companies got millions of dollars for keeping men and women in cages. It's one of those things (like Israel and military spending) that both parties, Republicans and Democrats, could agree upon. Bipartisanship!

When you take a group of people you once considered 'lesser' people, tell them they're on equal standing now but don't give them any help – let them pull themselves up by their bootstraps (if they even have bootstraps) – and force them to settle in the worst neighbourhoods where the quickest way to success is to break the law, what do you think's gonna happen?

'We were promised forty acres and a mule, and we never got that,' said Rick Ross. 'Blacks never get anything in this country.'

With 5 per cent of the global population but 25 per cent of all prisoners, America has the dubious honour of having more people behind bars than any other country in the world, beating Russia, China, Iran or any Third World hellhole. Land of the Free, indeed. And when you consider that this whole affair has been horribly racist from the very start, it won't be surprising to learn that, despite evidence that they don't use or sell drugs any more or less than whites, black people make up over half of all drug arrests in America. When it comes to imprisonment, apartheid-era South Africa only put away 853 out of every 100,000 black men it could get its hands on. In America it's 4,919, versus 934 for whites. More black Americans are in prison today than were enslaved in 1850.

'Being in prison really opened my eyes,' Seth remarked. 'White people were the minority in the Feds.'

Mass imprisonment creates a cycle that's extremely corrosive: a boy falls in with a bad crowd, sells drugs and goes to prison. He comes out, gets his girlfriend pregnant, but can't find a job because of his record, so where does he go? Back to selling drugs, and back to the slammer. Meanwhile, his kid grows up without a father and starts hanging out in the streets.

With so many black men in prison, the jailhouse culture seeps back into society. Can't work, can't vote: you've created a permanent underclass.

With few other options, the competition gets intense. To this day, South Side Chicago, Al Capone's old territory, is home to some of the most dangerous hoods in the country. From 2001 to 2016, more people have been killed there than US soldiers in Iraq and Afghanistan, giving the city a catchy nickname, Chi-Raq. The victims were overwhelmingly young and black. Where does it stop?

And while we like to think we're above that sort of thing here in the UK and we don't have the same problems as the Yanks, we're just as bad. Here in Great Britain we, too, adopted a 'tough-on-crime' policy back in the 1990s. Black people are eleven times more likely to be thrown in jail for drugs offences than white people, and Asians three times. So, without being in-your-face about it, Britain and America have both managed to subtly outdo one of the most explicitly racist regimes in human history. Well done.

Between gay thugs and prison Nazis, Seth found a way across the colour divide.

'I played baseball and football with the blacks, soccer with the Spanish and softball with everyone. Sports was my equaliser,' Seth explained.

From shooting hoops Seth went on to writing the prison sports newsletters, and from there, articles and books. He started writing about guys he was locked up with ... and guys like Freeway Rick Ross. It was Seth who suggested I get in touch with him.

'He's a real gentleman,' Seth said of his pen pal. 'It was cool to reconnect once I'd hit the streets, but I'd been writing him for years and we knew the same people so it was like we'd known each other for years.

With all the time in the world, Freeway finally learned his ABCs.

'I went around with these little cue cards, so I knew how to sound them out – "Ah", "Buh", "Kuh",' Ricky explained. He buried himself in law books, where he found a technicality that annulled his life sentence: technically, his two previous convictions should have counted as one continuous criminal enterprise. The judge agreed and reduced his sentence to twenty years.

'It was reading that set me free,' he said.

Needless to say, Seth's sentence weighed heavily on his family. While his dad had enough clout in the navy to get him out had he been caught on a military base, in a civilian court he could do nothing. It was the same with my parents and I remember my mum coming in on a visit, berating me for not telling them what happened and how they could have paid for a lawyer. But I'd already looked at the sentencing guidelines and I was looking at a minimum of two years – with these mandatory terms, a judge couldn't let you off the hook even if they wanted to. We were both fucked.

Seth was separated not just from his friends and family but from the love of his life. It was Diane who ran his site and posted his articles on the outside. They got married in the visiting hall of one of the prisons before the chaplain, his case manager and one of the guards. The newlyweds got to spend fifteen minutes together after the ceremony.

Seth got out in 2014, having served twenty-one years of his sentence. Twenty-one years is a long time. While he was inside, the world saw Nelson Mandela and the end of apartheid; peace in Northern Ireland; the new millennium; 9/11; the Iraq invasion; the Second Intifada; the global banking crisis; *Harry Potter*, *Lord of the Rings*; America's first black president; WikiLeaks; the Arab Spring; iPhones; Myspace; Facebook; Instagram; Dolly the Sheep got cloned; Princess Di bit the dust; and I made it all the way through kindergarten, school and university (and here I was, crying like a little bitch over one lost year). After so much time out of the loop, I wondered how Seth got on.

'I got used to everything pretty quick when I got out. It took me a while to figure out the difference between cellular and Wi-Fi. All the automated stuff on the phone kills me. I just want to talk to a person and you get stuck in this cycle of robot replies and pushing numbers. I feel justified now that weed is on the way to legality. I was a marijuana outlaw and I still am.'

His life sentence annulled, Rick Ross got out a little earlier, in May 2009, into the waiting arms of his girlfriend. Since then, he's been on the warpath: giving talks, interviews, writing books and steering kids away from crime. He's also trying to get the money together for a film about his life.

'You're gonna see it – *SuperFly 1980*. It's gonna gross a billion dollars!'

Seth's now an actor, filmmaker and journalist. But what happened to the third wheel of our holy trinity? I hope you haven't forgotten about Norm Stamper.

20

#BlackLivesMatter

It was 30 November 1999. Forty thousand demonstrators and anti-capitalists descended on rain-soaked downtown Seattle to rally against globalisation and corporate power, blocking intersections to stop delegates reaching the Paramount theatre where the World Trade Organization was holding a conference. What happened next became known as the Battle of Seattle.

'I authorised the use of tear gas to clear an intersection occupied by hundreds, maybe thousands, of demonstrators,' Norm Stamper recalled. 'I was on three to four hours' sleep each day, it was raining, and my sweater reeked of tear gas and water. All of downtown was pretty much clogged, and we needed to get somewhere to help someone who was bleeding from a stab wound. But it made the situation so much worse. It cleared the intersection, but at an enormous cost. We radicalised the non-violent protesters, and their anger pivoted to the Seattle police department.'

Over the next few days, the peaceful protests spiralled into chaotic street fighting between police and activists. Black-clad riot squads, looking like occupying stormtroopers, fired cans of tear gas, spreading clouds of noxious smoke.

Stamper resigned later that week. While now Norm describes his order to deploy tear gas on the protesters as the 'worst mistake of my career', for five years he was convinced that he'd made the right call.

'Once I was at a book signing and I saw a man without a book. He told me, "I used to respect you." I said, "Do you wanna say something more about that?" And he said, "Yeah, I was there, I got gassed, you got what you wanted but you lost me and a lot of other people."

'By the time I finished my book tour, there was a tectonic shift. We did not have to do what we wanted to. We didn't have the right to gas fellow Americans who have the right to assembly and protest. Those wonderful people were protesting against injustice, and I was their enemy.'

The Battle of Seattle made Stamper rethink his whole attitude to police violence. He's now a member of LEAP, Law Enforcement Against Prohibition, an organisation of current and serving police officers, judges and prosecutors who've taken a stand against the drug war.

It was 6 July 2016. Just an ordinary Wednesday. Thirty-two-year-old Philando Castile got a haircut, had a Taco Bell with his sister and went to pick up his girlfriend, Diamond Reynolds, and her four-year-old daughter. Philando was black and, like any honest-to-God American, also a gun owner. As they were driving through Larpenteur Avenue in Falcon Heights, a suburb of Saint Paul, Minnesota, they were pulled over by officers Joseph Kauser and Jeronimo Yanez of the Saint Paul police force.

'Sir, I have to tell you that I do have a firearm on me,' said Castile as the two officers approached.

'OK,' said Yanez, putting his hand on his holster. 'Don't reach for it, then.'

'I'm not pulling it out.'

'He's not pulling it out,' Reynolds added.

'DON'T PULL IT OUT!'

BANG-BANG-BANG-BANG-BANG-BANG-BANG.

'FUCK!!!'

Jeronimo Yanez fired seven shots. What happened next was streamed live by Diamond Reynolds on Facebook. Philando can be seen lurched over in the driver's seat, his white shirt covered in blood. He'd been reaching for his licence. And then he stops moving.

Chauntyll Allen, a local schoolteacher and activist with Black Lives Matter, was one of the first at the scene.

'I was actually on-scene as they cleared out the car and all that stuff,' she told me over Skype. 'I once worked at the same school district as Philando. He was basically me: we grew up in the same community and he was a victim of racial profiling, which we all were. I've actually been pulled over on that strip before.

'When you have a black son, you tell them not go down Larpenteur Avenue. You can't ride three black people in a car; you're gonna get pulled over. If you have a third, it better be a girl, and she better be small. They'll pull you over to see if they can find anything on you.'

There's this obsession, both in the public and the media, with perfect victims – unless they're a bona fide saint like Mother Teresa, if there's any hint of dirt on them, then they're a 'thug' and they had it coming. Regardless, you can't just go round popping rounds in people, then try to rationalise it later by pointing to something that had nothing to do with you shooting them in the first place.

But Philando Castile was such a perfect victim. The man worked in a school serving food to kids before he was gunned down in front of his partner and four-year-old child at a traffic stop. He told the officer, because he wanted to avoid trouble, that he had a gun in the car, but the officer opened fire anyway because he thought he could smell mari-jah-uana.

'I thought I was gonna die, and I thought if he has the guts and the audacity to smoke marijuana in front of the five-year-old girl and risk her lungs and risk her life by giving her second-hand smoke and the front-seat passenger doing the same thing, then what care does he give about me?' Yanez later told investigators. A glass jar with a small baggie of weed was also found in the car. Now, thanks to Officer Yanez's keen sense of smell, a little girl has lost her dad.

The Black Lives Matter movement began after a series of deaths of African-Americans at the hands of police made the headlines in 2013–14, including Tamir Rice, a twelve-year-old boy shot while playing with a toy gun, and forty-three-year-old Eric Garner, suffocated in a police chokehold while selling bootleg cigarettes. Rallying online under the hashtag #BlackLivesMatter, thousands of protesters took to the streets in sometimes-fiery demonstrations calling for justice and an end to America's long history of police brutality.

Police shot dead 990 people in 2015 alone, ninety-three of whom (around 10 per cent) were unarmed. Two hundred and fifty-eight of them were black, 15 per cent of whom were unarmed (compared to 6 per cent of whites). That might not seem like a lot, but even if the rest were all gun-crazy desperadoes, over the years those numbers add up to hundreds of victims. Most of those on the receiving end of police gunfire in the United States are white, and Black Lives Matter gets attacked for focusing on black victims. But colour's not the point. In July 2017, Chauntyll and Philando's mother Valerie marched in Minneapolis in memory of Justine Damond, a white Australian woman gunned down by a black officer after calling the cops to report a rape.

Cops, then, shoot plenty of white people too, for equally stupid reasons, but *proportionately* speaking an unarmed black person is far more likely to be shot dead by cops than a white person. Philando Castile, though, *was* armed, so the next question we must ask is: were they aiming that gun barrel? For 17 per cent of whites and 24 per cent of blacks, the answer was 'no'.

'Even if Black Lives Matter critics were right that police killings in America are not racially suspect, that would not be a sufficient argument against police reforms,' wrote Conor Friedersdorf in *The*

Atlantic. 'It would still remain the case that American police officers kill many more people overall – and many more unarmed and mentally ill people in particular – than do police officers in other democratic countries.'

Alternatively, Blue Lives Matter, the police and conservatives' answer to Black Lives Matter, will point to the fact that, statistically, a cop is 18.5 times more likely to be killed by black hoodlums than to kill an unarmed black person. That's certainly one way of looking at it. Another is that cops are *supposed* to be the ones putting themselves in harm's way, as opposed to, say, random black motorists. And as Jon Stewart once said, 'Why all the interest in holding police officers to a higher standard than gangs?'

And yet, despite thousands of civilians (of all races) being pumped full of holes each year, only forty-seven officers were prosecuted for their shootings between 2005 and 2014, and just a handful of those were convicted. You can take their word that they were dealing with violent criminals, but unless there's video evidence or statements from other cops showing otherwise, that's all you have to go on. And what are the odds they'll be betrayed by their brothers-in-blue?

On 16 June 2017, Jeronimo Yanez was acquitted of dangerous discharge of a firearm and manslaughter in the second degree. The fact that cops can shoot so many people, especially black people, and get away with it, suggests that black lives *don't* matter.

So why do black people keep getting used as target practice? I had to speak to someone on the inside to break through the blue wall of silence, the police's own *omerta* – Norm Stamper.

Of course, most people in the ghetto don't turn to crime and drugs, and power to them. But in order to look like they're doing their job, cops need to make arrests.

'If you're a good cop in San Diego, you get five tickets, at least one criminal arrest per day, and maybe a few traffic citations. You wanna make detective? Get out there and get those numbers!' Stamper told me. 'Cops across the country are comparing their *activity*, not their *productivity*, which defines good police work: problem-solving, relationship-building and preventing crime. Every day you check the score card to see how you're faring against Smith and Jones.

'Blacks and Latinos represent the most visible manifestation of drug use, sales and government neglect. You just don't see street gangs working corners in affluent communities. Your numbers are down? Go to 30th and Imperial in San Diego. You'll get your weeks' worth of activity in a day.'

In other words, when a young man of darker complexion walks down the street, cops will typically assume he's got his finger on the pulse of the drug-trafficking community. Since black people are more likely to be searched, they're more likely to be arrested, which in turn makes them more likely to get searched. They wouldn't get away with this in the lily-white suburbs, as white people can call up their lawyers and kick up a fuss.

Freeway Ross concurred.

'It's simpler for the cops to arrest people in the ghetto so they focus on areas where people are less desirable. It's much harder to get a search warrant for Beverly Hills than in South Central.'

The relentless focus on stats and the obsession with taking X amount of 'dangerous drugs off the streets' has ruined regular police work, creating a climate in which officers make up any bullshit ('Uh, sir, this area's known for Bob Marley impersonators and you look like you know your way around a bong') to justify their stop-and-searches – an easy way to get that all-important promotion whilst simultaneously alienating the very communities they're supposed to protect and serve.

Police will hound drug dealers not only because it looks good on their stats, but because it pays their salaries. Civil asset forfeiture is the practice of seizing someone's property because you merely *suspect* them of committing a crime, then selling it off and keeping the proceeds. It's essentially legalised robbery.

'States do it, local departments do it, it's done everywhere,' said Stamper. 'Departments who make a lot of drug busts usually have one or more desks who spend their time processing seized property. It's not personal corruption, it's more systemic. Taking from your fellow citizen their house, home or a boat, so they can be seized and used to underwrite something on your budget. To me that's corrupt; sending out cops to make money.'

Over a quarter of deadly police encounters in America take place in small towns like Ferguson, which don't get FBI-style budgets and have to resort to catching speeders or asset forfeiture to survive. And who's a good target for some possible asset forfeiture? Drug dealers (read: black people).

If a black guy and a white guy are driving down the road, who's more likely to get stopped? The black guy, of course, because police (whether black or white) are more suspicious of them. Now, both the black guy and the white guy could have drugs in their car, but because the white guy doesn't fit the typical profile of a 'thug' he's more likely to get away with it. Obviously, there's more than one factor at play – it also depends on how they're both dressed, how they're driving and whether their car smells like Willie Nelson's porch – but generally speaking, it's the black guy getting busted for a bit of green.

OK, so you pull someone over for driving while black in Hicksville, Tennessee ... now what? It doesn't have to end in fireworks. What makes the encounter go south? Part of it is racism. In the Jim Crow South, many local cops were part of the Ku Klux Klan – that's not a legacy that disappears overnight. The KKK might now be a thing of the past, but more subtle prejudice remains.

'Cops shoot unarmed black men in part because they're afraid of black men. The taller, the darker, the greater the fear. They've grown up in an all-white environment, gone to an all-white school … they've never been around people like that before. Every ethnic slur, every story you hear in the locker room about someone getting a gun pulled on them in Logan Heights, that fuels the behaviour on the streets. Where ignorance thrives, that creates an environment for fear. If you're scared, your perception is affected. You see things that aren't there. And you can't shoot straight.'

A professional officer knows how to handle himself and avoid escalation. But in America, some sheriffs in a rural backwater will give any redneck a badge and a gun.

'A cop can put on his uniform and say to himself, "No one dies today,"' said Stamper. 'That applies to him, but also to the citizens he interacts with. If you have that kind of mentality with an officer who is well trained and mature, you're saving lives. But we don't have that in American policing. Our officers have literally murdered fellow citizens.

'Slowing things down, speaking more smoothly, ducking behind your car, that's not cowardice. But cops are taught you can't back down. And what's the great equaliser?'

In August 2014, the killing of unarmed teenager Michael Brown by a white officer in Ferguson, Missouri, sparked days of riots. The protesters were accused of burning down their own city. The police response wasn't exactly calm and dignified either: SWAT teams riding around in armoured personnel carriers dressed like they were about to invade Iraq. How did they even get this hardware? Yep, the drug war.

'The federal government threw military surplus to local police departments. This won't be used by military, they said, so let's just grant it to local law enforcement with virtually no strings, no inspections, no requirements to train or maintain the equipment, all in service of this country's drug war,' said Stamper.

The 1980s saw a militarisation of the police force. SWAT teams, previously only deployed in extreme situations like hostage raids or a terrorist attack, now routinely kicked down doors in military-style drug busts. That created an arms race between gang members and the police. If someone's facing twenty-to-life, what've they got to lose?

'We are getting more militarised, they get more militarised, the streets get more militarised,' Chauntyll told me. 'So something's gotta give.'

And remember, most dealers aren't tooled-up maniacs with itchy trigger fingers. Back in the day, I could open a can of whoop-ass if it needs be, just ask Mickey Foreskin, but I probably wouldn't show up at your door with a baseball bat. A drug dealer is simply someone who supplies drugs – that can mean anyone from an ageing hippy selling ditch weed, to Lucky Luciano organising shipments of heroin across the Atlantic.

The racial situation in America hasn't changed all that much, whether under Clinton, Bush, Trump or Obama. What's changed is the technology. The LA riots kicked off back in 1992 after white cops were caught on camera beating Rodney King. The same inner-city rage once rapped about in NWA's 'Fuck tha Police' spilled out onto the streets. Six days of mayhem saw city blocks torched, shops looted and sixty-three people killed before the National Guard was sent in. The police brutality's always been there, but now anyone can whip out their phone and start filming. Now there are dozens of Rodney Kings each year.

On the face of it, it might look like mindless violence, but since when has any struggle been won without a fight? 'A riot is the language of the unheard,' said that famous pacifist, Martin Luther King. It took the Stonewall riots to show the world a bunch of fairies can smash some shit up. Even in India, do you think the British would have listened to Gandhi if they weren't shit-scared of mobs burning down their colonial houses?

I'm not hating on the police. It's a high-risk job and, sometimes, keeping us safe means pulling the trigger.

'There are situations where police will need to use their guns. I was at the McDonald's massacre of 1984. It was the worst scene of carnage I'd ever witnessed: moms, dads and kids blown away mid-bite by a madman. Everyone was moaning and groaning on the floor. Twenty people died at his hand before we got to him. Could we have got him sooner if we had an armoured carrier? We could have. So there is a time and place for what people call police violence, where lethal force is the answer. But it ought to be happening much less in this country.'

But despite those cases where shooting was fully justified (like, the perp was literally *asking* for a .44-calibre hole in his forehead), trust has deteriorated to such a point that *any* death involving the police automatically becomes suspicious. And whose fault is that?

In 2006, plainclothes cops in Atlanta burst into what they thought was a traphouse in the middle of the night on a 'no-knock' warrant, hoping their unexpected courtesy call wouldn't give the occupants a chance to flush away evidence. But inside they found only ninety-two-year-old black grandmother, Kathryn Johnston. Johnston lived alone in a rough neighbourhood, so all she saw was two men barge into her home brandishing guns. The terrified old woman, who thought she was being robbed, fired an old revolver over the heads of the officers, who returned fire with thirty-nine shots.

'Ten to twelve officers raiding a house, maybe the wrong house, and you hear all these horror stories; a baby in Georgia getting severely burnt by a flashbang grenade tossed in the living room,' Stamper said. 'Pets killed, elderly killed, police officers killed.'

The logic of these surprise raids seems to be that the life of a pet, family member or ninety-two-year-old grandma isn't worth the risk of flushing. It later turned out that not only did they get the wrong house, but as Johnston lay dying the officers planted crack vials to set the scene like a geriatric *Boyz N The Hood*. They would have got away with it too, if their informant hadn't refused to play ball (even snitches got standards).

The drug war has created an absolutely toxic atmosphere between African-Americans and the police. It singles them out as criminals and drug dealers while giving police carte blanche to use whatever means they need to end this menace, then gives them bonuses and promotions based on how many perps they catch or how much gear they find.

We might look down on the Yanks but we've got the same problems in Europe. In January 2017 riots broke out in Paris after a police officer 'accidentally' slipped his baton into a twenty-two-year-old black man, 'accidentally' tearing his rectum during an anti-drugs sweep through the *banlieues*, crappy high-rise projects thrown up after WWII to house migrant workers from the former colonies. Decades of harassment of African and Arab youth has created a mistrustful, stand-offish atmosphere not unlike the US ghetto. Add to that prison's not an environment for healthy personal development (many future terrorists served time for drug charges), and that terrorism attracts the same kinda individuals up for a fight as gang-banging, and you've got a recipe for mayhem.

'One friend said to me: why do black people get upset and say black lives matter, when *all* lives matter?' said Stamper, sympathetically. 'But for the Black Lives Matter movement it represents aspiration. If you're a white American, your life matters as a fact. But if your black, that's an aspiration.'

21

Interlude: Planes, Chains and Automobiles

On May 1 1994, the most brutally oppressive racist regime in recent history fell to (no, not the United States): South Africa. Nelson Mandela was elected president, signalling the end of apartheid and holding the country together against the vicious inter-ethnic blood-bath that engulfed other parts of Africa. But the Rainbow Nation faced a new set of problems.

Some say the fall of apartheid led to one of the most vicious crime waves of the twentieth century. But life in the townships, the squalid ghettos for blacks and coloureds created by apartheid, had always been nasty, brutish and short. Street gangs and violent crime had long festered in the townships of Cape Town and other cities; it was just ignored by authorities and the media because if a black boy dies on the outskirts of Joburg, who cares, so long as he wasn't rising up against whitey. Once apartheid ended, being black was no longer automatic grounds for arrest, so the police were powerless to stop white neighbourhoods getting a taste of what black South Africans had been living with for decades. Murder, rape, robbery, carjacking – crime hadn't so much gone up as spread out.

At the same time, the collapse of border control and massive corruption turned South Africa into a huge traphouse. The Nigerians brought the cocaine, while Cape gangs like the Firm and the Americans handled distribution. The corruption went right the way to the very top: in 2007 the head of Interpol, Jackie Selebi, was nailed for racketeering after letting his pal, international kingpin Glenn Agliotti, know, in exchange for a fancy pair of shoes, that he was under surveillance by British intelligence.

But Bridget had nothing to do with any of that. In the early 2000s, she was working as a barmaid in Johannesburg when she met CJ, a white Afrikaanners man who invited her on a trip to Mauritius, an idyllic island in the Indian Ocean.

'He said he was from Cape Town but I don't think CJ was his real name because no one could pick him up afterwards,' she told me on Skype. 'I knew him quite well, or well enough that he'd give me lifts home. And one day he said, let's go to Mauritius together.'

Unless you count cigarettes, my only brush with international drug smuggling was once when I was catching a flight to Morocco, I reached in my jacket for my passport and found I was still carrying a half-ounce of Buddha. I wasn't about to be busted smuggling weed *into* Morocco so had no choice but to flush it down the toilet. I remember speaking to this Brazilian guy I knew in jail who got girls to hide coke up their snatch. But my girlfriend, always the feminist, told me I should talk to one of the girls he sent instead. So I got in touch with Locked Up, a charity that helps captured drug mules and their families, and they put me through to Bridget.

As far as she knew, she was just getting a free holiday to Mauritius. But at the last minute, CJ backed out; he said he had a group of tourists to take on safari and Bridget would have to fly to Mauritius on her own. He did, however, leave her with a pair of shoes, which he insisted that she wear:

'That's when it set in. At the time I didn't think it was actually heroin; working in a bar you see people spend ridiculous money on a gram of coke, so my guess was it was diamonds. But by that point you're so far deep ... I mean, he knew where I lived, where I was living with my mother and grandmother. Once they know where your family live it's too late to back out now.'

The bringers of contraband pharmaceuticals have to think outside the box to slip their cargo across borders undetected. Over the years, people have used the following methods to sneak their goods past those stuck-up killjoys at customs:

- Dissolving the cocaine in chemicals or water, then soaking it up into clothes or fabrics. The clothes get dried out again once they reach their final destination.
- Mixing the cocaine with other materials, such as plastic, then moulding them into an object. Statues of Jesus are an old favourite, but people have crafted everything from plaster casts to their very own suitcases out of the white stuff.
- Body-packing. That's when you swallow condoms full of powder, usually heroin or cocaine, and poop them out on the other side. Dissolving the drugs in water makes them harder to spot, showing up on X-ray as part of the intestines. This method is pretty common in West Africa and the Caribbean, but it's very risky – if those condoms burst and the drugs get into your system, you're gone.
- Piggybacking, when the contraband is hidden inside a legit cargo container, shipped halfway round the world and quickly offloaded by dock workers before anyone's the wiser. This is where the Mafia's trade union contacts come in handy.
- In 2017, US border agents clocked a group of men welding a catapult onto the Mexican side of the fence. The medieval siege weapon was being loaded up with two massive bundles of pot.
- In 2005, a set of plywood doors arrived at a middle-class family home in Guildford, Surrey, where they were picked up by a Colombian gang and shaved into chippings with a cheese

grater. Police caught them red-handed as they were about to extract 17.3 kilograms of cocaine with industrial solvent, which had been impregnated into the wooden doors. Bankrolling the scheme was Paul Sneath, a twenty-four-year-old public school-boy and university dropout who'd recently inherited £250,000 and thought it would be a good idea to spend it on coke. If you thought things couldn't get any more middle class, his mum, the lady's captain of the Puttenham Golf Club, later told her fellow golfers that he'd gone away for the ski season.

- In 2011, prison guards in Colombia (where else?) spotted a pigeon struggling to fly into the jail in the north-eastern city of Bucaramanga. But the 45-gram (1.6-ounce) package of coke was too heavy for the poor bird and it landed right by the jailer's feet. Six years later, at a prison in Argentina, guards shot down another pigeon with a backpack carrying 7.5 grams of cannabis, sleeping pills and a USB stick (what could inmates possibly want with a USB? Music, porn, the prison's architectural plans . . . ?).

- Cocaine labs used to be based in Chile, but the good times came to an end in 1973 when a coup overthrew socialist president Salvador Allende, paving the way for Generalissimo Pinochet to start throwing leftists out of helicopters. But in 2005, Manuel Contreras, Pinochet's former chief spook, claimed that his boss had a clandestine laboratory built twenty-four miles from Santiago in the 1980s, where his chemist Eugenio Berríos, moonlighting from his usual duties making sarin gas and biological weapons, made 'black cocaine'. Black cocaine is just regular cocaine mixed with other substances like cobalt (to get past colour tests) or activated charcoal (to hide the smell), making it almost undetectable to customs agents in America and Europe. Black cocaine resurfaced in 2015 when two tonnes of coke disguised as printer ink, bound for Mexico, were uncovered at El Dorado airport in Bogotá.

- In 2017, Argentinian police uncovered a drug ring operating out of the Russian embassy in Buenos Aires. Just like the bad guys in *Lethal Weapon 2*, they schemed to slip sixteen suitcases of cocaine onboard a diplomatic flight to Moscow, where it would have been waved through all the usual customs checks.
- As the Soviet Union collapsed, Russian military hardware was being sold off by the shitload to the highest bidder. An Israeli 'businessman' in Miami saw an opportunity and tried to sell a nuclear submarine from a naval base in St Petersburg to a Colombian cartel. While the deal fell through, a few years later the narco-subs plot became reality. Built deep in the jungle, far from prying eyes, the cartel's DIY narco-subs are equipped with crew quarters, GPS, fibreglass and engine shielding so as not to show up on scanners. In 2000, Colombian authorities found a vessel under construction on the outskirts of Bogotá that was 100 feet long and could dive to up to 30 feet, carrying 200 tonnes of blow at a time.
- In 2014, sniffer dogs at Manchester airport picked up the scent of 50 grams of heroin carefully woven into a load of handwoven carpets from Pakistan.

The vast majority of smugglers aren't bringing over tonnes of white gold on Soviet nuclear submarines like a coked-up remake of *Red October*. Mules are the poor sods walking through Heathrow with a condom full of white powder stuffed up their ass. They might get caught through random checks, or because their shifty behaviour or suspicious itinerary gives them away. If they're lucky, they might end up spending a few years in a Third World hoosegow like San Pedro in Bolivia, which isn't so much a prison as a little gated community run by gangs with its own shops and restaurants and even whole families living there. At one point, the jailed mules were even giving backpackers tours.

If they're unlucky, they'll end up on Death Row somewhere like Indonesia which happened to the Bali Nine, who were caught smuggling eight keys of heroin. The H they were smuggling wasn't even meant to end up there; it was passing through en route to Australia, but that didn't stop two of them being lined up in front of a firing squad. The rest of the gang are serving life sentences.

The mules don't usually get much sympathy: 'Oh, they knew what they were doing.' But even if we agree they were stupid, stupidity is not grounds for ending someone's life. You might say Indonesia has different standards, but shooting someone in the face doesn't magically become OK just because you're standing on a sandy beach in Bali. The runners need to face something proportionate to what they've actually done – that's the whole concept of justice.

By that standard, Bridget was one of the 'lucky' ones. As she sat on the plane, she had a gut feeling this wouldn't end well, a suspicion that was confirmed when she saw a herd of customs officers waiting for her at the arrivals lounge. She'd been stitched up and CJ, of course, was nowhere to be seen. He'd pretty much sent her to get caught.

'Once you get inside, you meet some of the big importers – they do occasionally get caught – and you find out they put six people on one plane, one of them gets caught while someone else slips through with a suitcase of the stuff. That's pretty much how they roll.'

Inside the Mauritian jail, it was a whole new world. The cells were filthy and overcrowded, there was no running water, most of the prisoners and guards spoke either French or Creole, and half of the inmates were drug addicts.

'They'll put a person full of life in a cell with them and they're sick and vomiting, and you're stuck with them from six in the evening till six in the morning.

'It was suicidal in there. You want to end your life, but you don't know how. Sometimes, the guards would send in a special team with bats to beat the prisoners. I know on the men's side of the prison they used to beat them terribly and wouldn't give them any food or water. They're not big on human rights in Mauritius.'

Since this was to be her home for the next ten years, Bridget had no choice but to adapt to her new surroundings. She learnt French and Creole, and started teaching the other inmates how to speak English. She made some new friends, including a few pen pals from the men's side of the prison. She became quite popular, and everyone called her Café Aulait, or 'Coffee and milk'.

As time went on, old prison mates got released and new ones came in. Bridget saw how the different nationalities of the women reflected the changing smuggling routes to the island: first Indians, then South Africans, then Madagascans and Zambians. But in the grand scheme of things, they were still all small fry. Elsewhere on the continent, drug lords control entire nations.

The tiny West African nation of Guinea-Bissau lies between Senegal and Guinea, the westernmost point of Africa and the shortest possible route across the Atlantic. In 2005, mysterious packages of white powder started washing up on the coast. The locals didn't know what to do with it. It definitely wasn't fertilizer because it killed all their plants – someone used it to mark their football pitch. Then two Colombian gentlemen landed in a private plane and offered to buy it all back, and that's when the gold rush started. The country has now been all but taken over by Colombian and Nigerian gangs moving their product into Europe. It doesn't help that, for a long time, the only 'prison' in the country was an old one-storey house with a broken gate where inmates and captured mules were dropped off and asked politely not to escape. The military coup of 2009 (President João Bernardo Vieira has the dubious distinction of being one of the few world leaders hacked to death by machetes) was as much about political infighting as it was a struggle between different factions of the military over control of cocaine.

Eventually, it was Bridget's turn to go, too.

'When I came out, it was almost unreal. Sometimes you see people leave for the airport and come straight back. Even when my plane took off, I kept thinking about it, and only when I landed on South African soil did I realise it was finally over.'

Since she was released three years early, Bridget kept having nightmares that she'd have to go back and serve the rest of her sentence. But unlike other prisoners who get kicked out on the kerb, she quickly found a job with a family friend and is now happily married with a baby daughter.

'Sorry, I have to go now; I've got a furniture business to run. We've only been here two months and it's been hard, but we have to survive. I can't sell drugs any more!' she laughed.

No one's heard from CJ since.

Part 5

Gangster's Paradise

22

Plata o plomo

Somewhere in the jungles of southern Colombia, a dodgy guide runs 'special tours' for 'special tourists'. A more ethical traveller might say no, but I'm not an ethical traveller. Ernesto claims to have worked for Pablo Escobar, a claim I find unlikely, but then again, the Medellín Cartel was a massive operation employing tens of thousands of people, so perhaps he worked for Pablo Escobar in the same sense that a janitor at the CIA works for Donald Trump.

The emerald-green hills were no cinch for vehicles so we made our way down the valley on horseback, something I didn't enjoy as riding on horseback feels like repeatedly being punched in the nuts. Thankfully we arrived at the spot with my testes intact and Ernesto got to work.

We were on a coca plantation near guerrilla-held territory. Coca grows best in damp, humid conditions, and the cocaine content gets stronger the higher you go, which is why it's specifically grown here in the Andes. I told myself that if we ever bumped into any Marxist rebels, I'd tell them my mum was in the youth wing of the Communist Party – we're on the same team. But paranoid thoughts still filled my mind: like at any moment an army helicopter would land, soldiers would jump out waving M-16s and we'd have to flee through the jungle, where my gringo ass would immediately be caught by one of their boys hiding in the bushes, and I'd have to make some awkward calls back home: 'Mum, it happened again . . .'

First, Ernesto poured the coca leaves into a bowl before crushing them with a rock; then he added sulphate, ammonia, cement and gasoline as two younger guys went past, holding machetes. The gasoline is there to help extract the coca alkaloid from the leaves, leaving a dark, icky paste which he then poured through a rag to filter it from the leaves. He next added baking powder to the sludge and his assistant, a young peasant girl, began heating it over a stove. He slaps her ass and she laughs. Maybe they have a thing going.

Ernesto poured away the excess fluid ('That's crack,' he told me, 'no good') and heated the batch some more until we were left with a kind of white-ish paste. Leaving it to bake under a lightbulb, we came back in ten minutes to find the powder dried into the purest, most potent cocaine on the globe.

Colombia is the biggest producer of the white stuff in the world, a title it occasionally shares with Peru (and once upon a time, Bolivia). A kilo of coke costs a mere $2,500 from a dealer in Colombia, but that goes up to around $54,000 stateside or $87,000 in Great Britain. Even taking into account logistics and shipping expenses, the profit margins are ridiculous. Although it's (sadly) what Colombia's best known for, not that many Colombians actually do cocaine. In fact, some of them might look at you in disgust for even bringing it up. Our pleasure is their pain. But like it or not, cocaine's been one of the most important forces not only in Colombia's history, but also the rest of Latin America.

And from the late 1970s to the early 1990s, it was synonymous with one man, a man who made Al Capone look like a prissy schoolgirl: Pablo Escobar.

Medellín, Colombia's second-biggest city, lies in a lush green valley 250 kilometres north-west of the capital, Bogotá. Its inhabitants, descendants of Basques from northern Spain, speak with a lively, sing-song *paisa* accent. Its red-brick neighbourhoods snake up and down the mountain slopes: the poorer the neighbourhood, the higher it is.

I honestly don't wanna talk too much about Pablo, one of the greatest supervillains of the twentieth century, because it's been done. But this is the history, and you can't talk about the history of cocaine in Colombia without Pablo Escobar. He started out stealing grave-stones to sell on the black market and probably would have stayed a small-time bandit had the gringos not begun snorting inordinate amounts of disco dust in the 1970s. By 1987, his fortune, officially estimated as shitloads, got him listed by *Forbes* magazine as the seventh-richest man in the world. His company? The Medellín Cartel.

What do you do when you have more money than God? Together with the rest of the Medellín capos, Pablo and his men bought their own football teams and started playing fantasy football IRL. And then there's *this* . . .

Halfway between Medellín and Bogotá lies Hacienda Nápoles, a 3,000-acre property purchased by Pablo in 1978. Hanging over the main gate is a small plane which once carried the first load of cocaine Pablo ever smuggled. Hacienda Nápoles is HUGE. After a long, bumpy ride on a rickshaw cabby past the hills, fields and dozens of small lakes, I arrived at the ticket booth. Since Pablo's death, the Nápoles ranch has been converted into a bizarre theme park. With the booming African drums and the colourful tribal designs, the emphasis is definitely more on the safari theme than the sordid, drug-dealing past.

Maybe I'm here in the off-season, but it's surprisingly deserted. One family's lounging around the pool. I've got the whole place to myself. Imagine going to Disneyland and not having to wait for any of the rides. Yep, that was me. It's so relaxing to take a dip in the pool by the giant, water-spouting octopus without any little scamps screaming and peeing in the water.

A family of capybaras – mama, papa and their litter – relaxed in the shade near a lake next to a trio of turtles, who plopped into the water as soon as I walked past. In addition to building a full-scale replica of *Jurassic Park*, Pablo was so loaded he had this place turned into his own, personal zoo. Further up the path there's a safari park, complete with lions, ostriches, tigers, elephants, meerkats and a hippo named Vanessa. Fun fact: after Pablo's death, no one wanted to look after the animals in his zoo, so all the other hippos escaped. Now there's a herd of wild hippos living somewhere in Colombia, all because of Pablo Escobar.

Hacienda Nápoles is kind of a weird place, filled with life-size statues of dinosaurs (because if you had billions of dollars in coke money, why *wouldn't* you have dinosaurs all over the place?) complete with thundering sound effects. Then there are other monstrosities that I can only describe as a 'zebraptor' and 'tricera-shark', though I'm not sure if these came from the park's owners, or Pablo's coked-out imagination.

But apart from a small museum of newspaper clippings dedicated to Pablo's atrocities and a couple of burnt-out cars (including the one driven by Bonnie and Clyde), there's very little drug lordy left about the place. The old bullfighting arena has been repainted in bright colours into a slightly patronising African museum. I thought back to how it must have been: the tropical drug lord and his private airstrip, colonial palace and pet hippos. It's not every day you find yourself in a Bond villain's lair, and Pablo was the ultimate supervillain.

Far from the roaring pterodactyls lies a disused landing strip, where planes would land carrying coca paste and fly out carrying processed cocaine to Mexico and the Caribbean. Originally, there wasn't that much coca being grown in Colombia, so the cartels had to buy it from abroad. Pablo's supplier in Bolivia was wealthy coke-dealing landowner, Roberto Suárez Gomez, who took over the government with a bunch of Nazi war criminals. In 1980, just before democratically elected Hernán Siles Zuazo was about to take office,

Gomez seized power with the help of German mercenary Klaus Barbie, aka 'the Butcher of Lyon', installing General Luis García Meza as president. Of Bolivia's 189 coups, this was one of the bloodiest. Left-wing unions tried to mount a resistance, but their headquarters were stormed, their leaders shot and the women gang-raped. Meanwhile, Gomez embarked on a counter-narcotics crusade (of sorts) by liquidating all his rivals and stealing their coke, which was flown to his customers by the Bolivian Air Force. In 1981, Meza was overthrown in yet another coup, but even with democracy restored, years of corruption and mismanagement had fucked the economy so hard that inflation reached the dizzying heights of 11,750 per cent. So, what remained the only viable industry? You guessed it: coca.

Pablo's man in Peru was said to be Vladimiro Montesinos, spy chief/chief executioner for President Alberto Fujimori. In the 1990s, Montesinos led the ruthless campaign against South America's most bloodthirsty rebels, the Shining Path. The Shining Path's calling card was stringing dogs up on lampposts, and had they actually siezed power, they would have been the most fucked-up far-left regime since the Khmer Rouge. Fujimori declared martial law and handed most of the military apparatus over to Montesinos, who unleashed death squads on left-wing students and the peasantry.

As the most powerful man in the country, Montesinos offered drug lords protection in exchange for briefcases of cash. He even once spent a grand weekend at Hacienda Nápoles. In 2000, Fujimori fled to Japan and his government spectacularly collapsed after Montesinos was caught on camera bribing a congressman, revealing him as the mastermind behind all manner of under-the-table schemes, including gun running, drug smuggling and pilfering government funds.

But it wasn't all lavish, tacky, dino-decadence. Pablo was also known for his reign of terror. When confronted with a troublesome cop or official, Pablo offered them a simple choice: *plata o plomo* – silver or lead. They could either accept the bribe and walk away, or find themselves staring down the barrel of a gun. In 1983, the new Minister of Justice, Rodrigo Lara Bonilla, was appointed and began an anti-corruption drive, upsetting Pablo's bid for Congress and ordering raids on his cocaine labs deep in the jungle. Lara passed on Pablo's generous offer of fat stacks, so in 1984, two *sicarios* pulled up on a motorbike and peppered his car with bullets.

After the Bonilla hit, Escobar lay low in Panama with his pal Manuel Noriega. In the 1980s, the general ruthlessly outmanoeuvred his opponents in a kind of telenovela *Game of Thrones* and got cosy with Escobar: letting him move coke through his territory, use Panamanian banks to launder his money, and even crash until the heat died down. At the same time, Noriega was working for, you guessed it, the CIA, providing intel on Nicaragua's Sandinistas and communist Cuba.

Eventually though, Noriega's habit of having his political opponents tortured and beheaded got too much even for America, and so in 1989 the US invaded in Operation Just Cause. Noriega, a well-known opera lover, hid out in the Vatican embassy. Since going in uninvited would effectively have amounted to declaring war on Catholics everywhere, the American Delta Force surrounded the building and started blasting out AC/DC at full volume until the pineapple-faced dictator surrendered. Noriega spent the last few years of his life suing the makers of *Call of Duty* for using his likeness and depicting him as a treacherous buffoon.

By 1985, the Colombian authorities amassed a pile of evidence on Escobar, which they stored at the Palace of Justice in Bogotá. In an odd coincidence, left-wing militants stormed the Palace in November that year, torching all the paperwork and murdering a bunch of judges. Escobar was safe . . . for now.

But one man refused to back down: presidential candidate and hope of Colombia, Luis Carlos Galán. Galán stood up to the cartels, not because of any moral convictions about the dangers of drug use, but because of the corrosive effects of drug money on society. Escobar had him assassinated at a rally, the sound of machinegun fire ringing out into the night. It was a murder that shocked the country.

While Escobar had had journalists, judges and other politicians killed before, this was a turning point. Enough was enough. But when the Feds moved to bring him in, the Medellín Cartel went to war with Colombia itself, planting bombs all over the country, gunning down cops and blowing up Avianca Flight 203, killing all 110 innocent passengers on board.

Escobar and his organisation managed to cause so much mayhem that the Colombian government had no choice but to give in and let him surrender ... on his terms. He would go to prison, but not just any prison: La Catedral, his own custom-built luxury gaol, with a bar, jacuzzi, football field and a giant doll's house for his daughter. That's how much power he had. He bought off all the guards and lived like a king, hosting drugs-and-hooker orgies that would make Charlie Sheen proud, until, one day, he got a visit from his business partners, the Galeano brothers. After accusing them of stealing money, Pablo cut them to pieces.

Throwing wild parties was one thing, but killing people was a step too far. Yet when the authorities tried moving Escobar to a different prison, he simply walked out, sparking a nationwide manhunt. While Pablo moved from safehouse to safehouse, making calls on his clunky radiophone from the back of a moving car, the Feds were listening in with high-tech surveillance equipment from their spy planes circling around Medellín. They finally got a fix on his location while he was calling his son and, after a gun battle, the world's most infamous drug lord lay dead on a Medellín rooftop in 1993.

'The Colombian government doesn't like us giving these tours; they call us the narco-tours,' said the guide, as five of us gringos clambered into his van, 'but it's a part of history.'

He's right. Middle-class Colombians hate their country's association with drugs and violence, but Medellín today is a battlefield of historic memories. The Monaco building, where Pablo's enemies planted a bomb that deafened his daughter, has now been torn down, but when I was there it was covered in posters dedicated to those brave judges, politicians and lawmen who stood up to *El Patrón*. While he was the worst criminal, terrorist and mass-murderer the country had ever seen, for many he was a hero, building schools, churches, football stadiums and even an entire neighbourhood for the poor: Barrio Pablo Escobar.

Meanwhile, local tour guides are making bank off the drug lord's notoriety. You can go paintballing in Pablo's old mansion on the banks of a jaw-dropping artificial lake in Guatapé, while on this excursion we got to meet Señor Escobar's brother himself, Roberto.

The driver pulled up to Roberto's hillside house and we went for a look inside. The walls were covered in bullet holes – a few years ago, some bandits showed up looking for Roberto, who'd been released from prison in 2003, looking to kidnap him and force him into leading them to some of Escobar's hidden loot. To this day, they keep finding bags of money all across Colombia. Police arrived, they exchanged gunfire, and two of the gangsters were killed.

Roberto himself came out to greet his guests, shake our hands and pose for photos in front of his Wanted poster. He doesn't talk much owing to having had a mail bomb explode in his face, which also deafened him in one ear. It's kind of sad; he and Pablo were kings, but now the lone remaining brother is basically a tourist attraction.

Our tour ended at a graveyard overlooking the city that is the final resting place of Pablo Escobar Gaviria and his family, along with the one bodyguard who stayed with him to the end. To this day, people still come to leave flowers or piss on his gravestone.

The official version is that Pablo was gunned down during a shootout with a special forces team, but many in Medellín doubt that theory. Pablo always kept a pistol handy with a spare bullet, just on the off-chance they'd try to take him alive. However, Pablo was pursued not only by the police, but also by *Los Pepes* (People Persecuted by Pablo Escobar), a death squad made up of disgruntled policemen, vigilantes and his rivals from the Cali Cartel, who made it their mission in life to slaughter anyone even remotely connected to Pablo. So, another version comes from Pepes boss Don Berna, who claims his brother Rodolfo fired the fatal shot.

Don Berna, aka Diego Murillo, used to run with Marxist guerrillas before becoming an enforcer for the Medellín boys under the Galeano brothers. The guerrillas shot him for his betrayal, leaving him with a permanent limp. When Pablo butchered the Galeanos in La Catedral, Berna joined Los Pepes, along with former Medellín *sicarios* Carlos and Fidel Castaño. Whether or not Berna's men were there on that fateful day, they played a huge part in the cocaine king's downfall: the bodies piled up as the police sent the Pepes to do their dirty work, and the group also worked closely with the DEA. Don Berna and his militia would also play a key role in the next phase of Colombia's cocaine saga: civil war.

Rain gently drummed on the tent roof as night fell and I settled into my new surroundings – a bed of leaves is surprisingly comfy. I was in a rebel camp, but I wasn't being held hostage. It was early 2019 and the Revolutionary Armed Forces of Colombia (*Fuerzas Armadas Revolucionarias de Colombia*, or FARC), having demobilised, now welcomes visitors to their camp, which doubles as a makeshift museum. That's right: Latin America's most formidable guerrilla army has a fucking gift shop.

The next morning, I had breakfast in the kitchen – chicken and rice, with sweet plantains – and sat down with Lucas, a former commander with the FARC and a thirty-year veteran of Colombia's civil war. Lucas isn't his real name – when you join the rebels you take on a new identity, in case someone wants to get back at your family – but after living with it for over thirty years it's hard to go back.

'All right, Nikolai Ostrovsky, what do you want to know?' he chuckled.

Nikolai Ostrovsky, the famous Soviet writer. Lucas, an old-school communist, grabbed my passport and passed it round to his friends to show my birthplace, Leningrad. I'd also put on my CCCP T-shirt, just so they'd know I was one of the boys.

Lucas was born in Sincelejo, near the Caribbean coast, and seeing the great inequality between rich and poor, joined the communists in 1987 when he was in his early twenties. At the time, a ceasefire was in place between the FARC, the government and other rebel groups. In 1964, oppression at the hands of brutal landowners drove the impoverished peasantry to take up arms and unite into the leftist FARC and, later, their urban counterparts, the 19th of April Movement (M-19).

But revolutions cost money, and because they couldn't exactly host a bingo night, the rebels turned to kidnapping to make ends meet. In 1981, the M-19 snatched Marta Ochoa, the sister of one of Pablo Escobar's partners. In response, the cartel formed MAS (*Muerte a Secuestradores* – meaning Death to Kidnappers), a ruthless death squad that proved far more effective at tackling the leftist menace than the Colombian army: hundreds of guerrillas were captured or eliminated. Sure enough, shortly afterwards the young lady was returned.

Under the ceasefire, FARC was allowed to form a party (the Patriotic Union – UP) and go into politics. But as soon as the fighters laid down their guns, MAS was lying in wait.

'They were targeting everyone of the left – the social left, the communists and the FARC. They assassinated two presidential candidates from the UP. Altogether, some 5,000 people were killed,' Lucas explained. 'That's why we went back to the mountains.'

The peace process collapsed. There were mass defections back to the armed wing of FARC, which took refuge in those parts of Colombia, far from cosmopolitan Bogotá, where the rule of law was effectively abandoned. No roads, no electricity, no tax collectors, no nothing. The guerrillas disappeared into the mountains and jungles, occasionally wandering into villages to . . . not threaten, exactly, but subtly imply with their weapons that the villagers should hand over their food.

'We were changing our camps every three days,' said Octavio, another one of the fighters. 'We couldn't have fires at night because they're easily detected. There were moments in the day when we could cook, but never regular times. And we could only cook for small groups, never the whole unit.'

'We always had to sleep next to our guns,' added Cecilia, the nurse (the rebels were equal parts men and women). 'I had three mortar rounds strapped to my legs at all times.'

The rebels' homes were their tents and all they could fit in their backpacks. Bugs were a problem, and Octavio showed me some nasty scars on his arm where he was savaged by some creepy-crawlies. But other than that, life on the run wasn't too bad. The rebels had regular classes in Marxism and military warfare, and even gadgets like smartphones, Internet and a TV, which they powered with a generator. They could afford this extravagance by cashing in on the most lucrative business around these parts – coca.

'In our zones the peasants (*campesinos*) grew it and sold the coca paste to the narcos. We imposed fees and taxes, but we didn't touch the stuff,' Lucas explained.

They also protected the coca crops, laying landmines out for any pesky soldiers. The narco-profits allowed them to buy more weapons and, getting rich off that white gold, their numbers grew. In 1998, more than a thousand fighters overran the town of Mitú in the Amazon, killing dozens of police officers and taking many more hostage. As with Escobar, the Colombian government gave in and awarded the rebels a 42,000-square-kilometre demilitarised zone in the south of the country – about the size of Switzerland. As with Escobar, that was a mistake. FARC used the territory to regroup, hold hostages and grow coca.

The demilitarised zone held out from 1998 to 2002, when President Álvaro Uribe came to power. Uribe bore a personal grudge against the FARC, haunted by memories of his father who was murdered by guerrillas. Uribe also got help from the Americans. Since the drug business is international, it follows that drug enforcement too must be international. And in this respect, the United States has taken it upon itself to be the world's policeman. Under Plan Colombia, Presidents Clinton and Bush sent over billions of dollars in aid and Black Hawk helicopters that the Colombian military unleashed on the guerrillas and narco-traffickers. The rebels responded with terrorist tactics: bombing nightclubs, kidnapping for ransom and using child soldiers.

Uribe pounded the rebels with his fancy new Black Hawks. At the same time, his forces worked hand in hand with the most bloodthirsty side of the Colombian armed conflict – the paramilitaries.

With MAS, Pablo Escobar was the father of the paramilitary movement in Colombia. His death left a power vacuum that was first filled by the Cali Cartel. Cali was less violent, more business-minded, than Escobar, who just wanted to blow everything up: Colombia's biggest newspaper writing shit about you? BOOM! Who's next? Whereas Cali took a more low-key approach: they bugged the US embassy and the DEA's informant hotline, and even managed to rig the 1994 presidential election. But their reign didn't last long – in 1995, all the heads of the Cali Cartel were arrested.

But hey, remember Los Pepes? While narco-traffickers and wealthy landowners had long had their own private militias, in 1997 the Castaño brothers united them all under the United Self-Defence

Forces of Colombia (*Autodefensas Unidas de Colombia*, or AUC). The paramilitaries were even worse than the guerrillas, massacring entire villages with chainsaws and machetes, then stealing the murdered peasants' land.

At some point, the brothers reunited with their old comrade Don Berna, who was heading the remnants of the Medellín Cartel under a new crime syndicate, the Office of Envigado. It's not clear when the Mafia boss made the switch to extreme right-wing politics, but aligning himself with chainsaw-wielding psychos clearly had its upsides.

The cable car swings a little when I get on it. I never feel totally safe climbing onboard one of these things. Below, the red-brick buildings are piled on top of each other like rice paddies in the hillside slum. This was Comuna 13, formerly one of the most dangerous neighbourhoods in Medellín and recruiting ground for teenage *sicarios*. The metrocable system was built to help residents cross 'invisible borders'; unofficial boundaries marking territory controlled by gangs and paramilitaries.

I was here, fairly innocently, on a graffiti tour. As we climbed off the gondola, we were met with a spectacular array of street art. One mural in particular caught my eye: a trio of elephants, tears in their eyes, waving white flags. This symbolised the first operation against the slum. In the early 2000s, the *barrio* was controlled by FARC and a smaller guerrilla outfit, ELN. The population was made up largely of native and Afro-Colombians fleeing the civil conflict, but even here they were not safe. In May 2002, the government launched an all-out assault on the hood, laying siege with gunfire and heavy artillery. In the midst of the fireworks, one brave woman ran out clutching a white bedsheet, begging to take her children to the hospital. Her neighbours came out too, and pretty soon the whole neighbourhood was out in the streets, waving white flags. The fighting stopped. These elephants never forget.

But the worst was yet to come. As we got to the top of the hill, we were treated to a panoramic view of the city. My guide pointed to a garbage dump in the distance, La Escombrera. There, she said, the remains of hundreds of people are buried, victims of Operation Orion. A few months after the first operation, the soldiers came back together with Don Berna's henchmen. On paper, only about a dozen fatalities were recorded, but armed men went door to door rounding up suspected 'terrorists', and hundreds of civilians are still missing. Exhumations at La Escombrera are still ongoing, and the mass graves there might hold up to three hundred bodies.

Why would the crime lord side with the army to flush out the rebels? Well, Comuna 13 lies next to the San Juan highway, which leads north of Medellín and towards the Caribbean coast. He who controls the highway, controls all the drugs moving in and out of Medellín and, by extension, most of Colombia.

Flicking through these pages, you'd be forgiven for thinking I'm an arrogant, pedantic son-of-a-bitch who's written a 400-page treatise because he doesn't wanna admit he's wrong. But I'm sorry. I'm sorry to my family for everything I put them through. I'm sorry to my friends for driving them away. I'm sorry to my customers for under-weighing my baggies. I'm sorry to my editor who has to read through this. And I'm sorry to Colombia.

I have blood on my hands. Appeasing my customers' craving for some white powder has contributed, even if indirectly, to torture, massacres, disappearances, kidnappings and the driving of millions from their land. Over 260,000 people have been killed and many more displaced in Colombia's coke-fuelled nightmare.

Having said that, let's not pretend drugs are uniquely evil in this regard. The Congo is the world's most important source of coltan, a mineral forming vital components in laptops, mobile phones and other electronics. From the late 1990s to the early 2000s it was the scene of the deadliest battlefield since the Second World War, sometimes known as the African World War, where a multitude of neighbouring countries and their proxy tribal armies fought each other in a conflict that killed over 5 million people. Today, children still toil away in mines controlled by rebels, warlords and crooked officials. And in addition to all the human misery, the mountain gorilla has been driven to the brink of extinction by miners destroying their habitat and hunting them for bushmeat.

So if snorting a line leaves death and destruction in Colombia, sending nudes over WhatsApp is causing genocide in Africa. Did I do my bit of damage? Sure, but it's nothing compared to the *system* that allows this to happen, and keep happening.

As in the Congo, coke has a huge environmental impact, acres of pristine rainforest having been cut down for coca plantations and waste chemicals left to enter the soil (it's safe to say the kind of person who sets up a cocaine lab doesn't care too much about their carbon footprint). If that wasn't enough, army helicopters go around spraying coca fields with glyphosate, a poison that not only destroys coca plants but also contaminates the water supply, ravages the local ecosystem, may cause cancer in humans and ruins crops like bananas and corn, which the farmers depend on to survive.

Of course, as one plantation falls, another appears deeper in the bowels of the Andean jungle. By 2017, coca production in Colombia had reached record highs. Even as more land got sprayed or uprooted, growers developed advanced techniques to get more cocaine out of each plant. The United States put pressure on Colombia, threatening to blacklist it for not doing its part in the struggle. The result was a massacre. On 5 October, a group of farmers peacefully protesting against the destruction of their crops was attacked in the town of Tumaco on the Pacific coast. A renegade FARC unit was originally blamed, but footage on social media soon uncovered the truth: the security forces opened fire on a group of unarmed peasants. At least seven people were killed.

Back at the FARC camp, I took a quiet moment to take a look around. The climate here was a little different from other parts of Colombia, dusty and dry like the African savannah. We were surrounded on either side by the mist-shrouded mountains of the Sierra de Perijá.

On 23 June 2016, the Colombian government and its largest rebel group signed a historic ceasefire agreement, ending (officially, at least) over five decades of fighting that have claimed hundreds of thousands of lives and driven millions more from their homes. 'The horrible night has ceased,' said President Juan Manuel Santos, wiping back a tear, as he and FARC leader Timochenko, both dressed in white, signed the historic treaty with a pen fashioned out of a bullet casing in the coastal city of Cartagena. A year later, Lucas, Cecilia and Octavio handed over their weapons.

'There was a big container here where we threw in our guns,' said Cecilia, pointing to a patch of land at the bottom of the camp. 'There was one container for guns and one container for ammo. One hundred and fifty people threw their guns in there, and the UN took care of them. They were melted down and used to build monuments in Cuba, Colombia and the United States.'

The battle-hardened fighters had to get used to a life in which they weren't living in the jungle, with the animals and the birds and the trees, being chased by Black Hawk helicopters. They're still communists, but they continue their fight with the ballot. After decades in the jungle, fifty-five-year-old Lucas is now expecting his first child – a baby girl.

'We have ten people in Congress now,' he said as I high-fived him. 'Now we want to live in peace with social justice, equality and respect for human rights.'

But that might not be so easy. Medellín's a much safer place than it was in Escobar's day, when car bombings and shootouts were daily occurrences. Part of that is because of new developments and infrastructure, yes, but part of it is because Don Berna decreed there was to be no more killing. The Mafia still reigns supreme.

In 2003, Berna became the first paramilitary leader to disband his troops, in a deal with the government. Five years later they betrayed him, shipping him off to a cell in the United States just as ties between the warlords and certain politicians were becoming apparent. The rest of the paramilitaries officially disbanded in 2006, but since most of them lacked any transferrable skills for the job market other than being handy with the steel, many turned to gangsterism full-time. With Don Berna gone, the murder rate started climbing again as the Office of Envigado fought off encroachments from the paramilitary-outlaw Usaga Clan.

That's not all. The rebels in the demobilisation camp have put down their guns and committed to the peace process – a peace process the government's abandoned, with no guarantees for the rebel's future or safety. Then just a few months after my visit, I heard that someone attacked two people from the camp, a young couple, and killed their fucking baby. Seven months old.

This is happening all over Colombia. Since the peace deal was struck, hundreds of activists and community leaders, largely indigenous and Afro-Colombians as well as former rebels, have been murdered by hired killers working for narcos and landowners in a bloody rerun of the massacres of the 1980s. And dissident factions of FARC who didn't accept the peace deal still roam the forests, guarding the coca farms.

'We need people like you to tell the world what's happening here,' Lucas said. 'We've completed 100 per cent of our side of the deal, but the government hasn't held up its side, and that's why our comrades are still fighting. But we're strongly behind the peace, so we'll wait.'

Recently, outsiders have started appearing in Colombia, buying up the coca plantations. These outsiders come from the most important nation in narco-trafficking in the Western hemisphere. Once upon a time, the Mexicans were the errand boys of the Colombians, moving their packages across the border. Now, it's the other way round.

23

The Boys from Sinaloa

I flew into Mexico the night of 31 October, the Day of the Dead. The streets were alive with the not-so-deceased: skull-faced children holding up candles; skeleton mariachis dancing a jig; Lady Death's jet-black eyes peeking out under a wide-brimmed hat. For four days a year, the spirits of those who've left us behind come to be with their loved ones. For a country that's seen so much death, they've sure found a jolly way of dealing with it.

In 2018, Mexico hit a grim milestone. The annual body count for its drug war, which started in 2006 when President Felipe Calderón deployed the army against the powerful narco-trafficking cartels, reached over 33,000 murders, making it the second-deadliest country in the world after Syria. Mexico's meth labs and poppy fields feed the needs of American junkies, while the country also serves as the main waypoint for Colombian coke on its way to rich gringo noses.

Obviously, I wasn't just here for the sunshine and margaritas. My guide in Culiacán was Miguel Ángel Vega, a journalist and filmmaker who knows a thing or two about the cartels. He actually grew up around the narcos and even wanted to be one, but chose a different path. With his beard Miguel looks a bit like a Mexican Spielberg, but vampire flicks cost money so in between churning out Mexi-horror films Miguel also works as a fixer, his upbringing giving him access to every strata of the cartel hierarchy. If you're a TV crew and you need something done here, Miguel's your guy. RT, CNN, BBC; he's worked with them all, and after nearly a decade on the job it's never ended in tears. Well, I say that ... one time these two dudes were driving around the town, waving their camera out the window, and he told them to stop filming. But they didn't stop filming, and a group of big, burly Mexicans pulled them over, pistol-whipped the camera guy, and took all their shit. Miguel managed to get everything back, though.

'There are lookouts everywhere,' he said as we drove to my hotel. 'You see someone on the street corner, on the intersection, or maybe waiters or taxi drivers. They're all informers, so if they see something wrong, they'll pick up their phone and call their guy.'

I'd better behave myself.

The blame for the drug war can be laid squarely at the feet of Mexico's great northern neighbour. During Prohibition, the country was the source of whiskey and tequila, and after that, marijuana. In the 1930s, Mexico's chief drugs tsar, psychiatrist Leopoldo Salazar Viniegra, pissed off the Americans by recommending allowing marijuana and fighting alcohol and heroin addiction. Harry Anslinger got him fired, then threatened Mexico with sanctions if it didn't play ball.

The gringos came back again in the 1970s, shortly after Nixon declared his War on Drugs. Mexican farmers had been busy filling American hippies' demand for groovy greenery and, in response, Nixon ordered Operation Intercept, dispatching 2,000 customs agents to search every single vehicle coming over the border. Every. Single. One.

Of the 5.5 million drivers searched, not a single major smuggling attempt was thwarted, but traffic was delayed for so long that everyone wished they hadn't had tacos for breakfast. Then, under the supervision of American agents, the Mexican authorities launched Operation Condor, flying helicopters over the hills of the Sierra Madre and spraying the ganja fields with herbicide.

In the 1980s, after Reagan deployed the Coast Guard and Lehder's insane little Bahamas adventure came to an end, the Caribbean route was getting too hot and the narco-business moved to Mexico. It's like a game of whack-a-mole: if you smash it in one place it simply pops up somewhere else. That's when the Mexicans started making real money, not shifting ditch weed across the border.

Back then, there was only one single Mafia running the show – the mighty Guadalajara Cartel, led by its godfather, Miguel Ángel Félix Gallardo. Since its revolution, Mexico spent most of the twentieth century governed by the Institutional Revolutionary Party or PRI, a big-tent, catch-all alliance that included everyone from leftists to arch-capitalists. The PRI sat atop a grand pyramid of corruption where everyone knew their place: drug bosses paid off the cops and politicians to maintain control of their *plazas* (drug-trafficking territories). Everyone got paid and everyone was happy.

But the Mexicans got cocky when they kidnapped, tortured and executed undercover DEA agent Enrique 'Kiki' Camarena. In 1985, Kiki was jumped while leaving the US consulate. His body was discovered hundreds of miles away, beaten to a pulp with a stick shoved up his ass. Cause of death: blunt force trauma.

The Americans went apeshit, leading to a crackdown that led to the fall of the cartel. First, the DEA kidnapped the surgeon who'd kept Camarena alive during the torture, and brought him to El Paso, Texas. In 1989, Félix Gallardo was arrested, and all the cartel bosses met in Acapulco to divvy up the turf. It was in the interests of everyone involved – police, politicians and the cartels – to make sure order was restored and the machine ran smoothly. The Italians call this state of affairs *Pax Mafiosa*, the 'mafioso peace'. But where once there was one cartel, now there were many.

Culiacán is the capital of Sinaloa state in the north-east and the birthplace of many Mexican drug lords, including Félix Gallardo and

Amado Carrillo Fuentes. Carrillo Fuentes, aka the 'Lord of the Skies', ran the Juárez Cartel on the border with El Paso. Not that it mattered much, because borders didn't matter to him anyway: Fuentes just paid off the military to shut down their radar systems while his fleet of Boeing 727s flew across the desert, carrying loads of white gold. By 1997, he was a wanted man and had plastic surgery to change his appearance, but years of crack smoking had taken their toll on his heart and he died under anaesthetic. The surgeons who botched the job were later found stuffed into steel drums.

Miguel drove me first to meet Andrés Villarreal, a local journalist who runs the local newspaper *Ríodoce* and Miguel's occasional boss.

'One of the first stories I covered was the death of Carrillo Fuentes. I was so young back then,' Andrés told me. 'We were surrounded by doubts whether he was really dead. Keep in mind he was most powerful drug lord in Mexico. We thought drug lords don't die like that, they get shot to death. Add to that, his body wasn't there when the family tried to recover his corpse – the police were trying to do some DNA tests.

'There was this mystery surrounding the whole thing. To this day I still don't know if it was him or someone else. When the corpse finally came from Mexico City, the narcos tried to recover the body, but the soldiers tried to stop them, in shorts – they weren't wearing uniform – and they were all holding guns. Us journalists in the middle didn't know who was who!'

Culiacán is the stronghold of the Sinaloa Cartel led by Joaquín 'El Chapo' Guzmán (aka 'Shorty'), the most powerful faction to emerge out of the post-Gallardo era. While Chapo's nickname makes him sound like the coke-dealing cousin of Grumpy, Sleepy and Bashful, don't let that fool you – he's not a man to be trifled with. Born to a simple peasant family in the village of La Tuna, deep in the Sierra Madre mountains, Chapo started growing poppy when he was fifteen, taking his first steps up the ladder of the Sinaloa Cartel.

Chapo's success eventually put him at odds with the Arellano-Félix brothers, who ran the Tijuana Cartel. In 1993, assassins looking for Chapo gunned down an archbishop at Guadalajara airport. Guzmán was captured not long afterwards in Guatemala, before being sentenced to twenty years at a maximum-security prison. But Chapo had other plans and in 2001 he escaped in a laundry basket. Some say he paid his way out, but I prefer to think he hid under a pile of dirty undies.

After leaving *Ríodoce*'s offices we drove over to the outskirts of town. For a redneck backwater, Culiacán sure is flush with cash. We turned into a cemetery that looked less like a graveyard and more like a posh gated community, with vast tombs shaped like colonial houses and even a replica of the Taj Mahal. Jardines Del Humaya is the final resting place of Arturo 'the Beard' Beltrán, as well as (it's rumoured) Carrillo Fuentes. It costs at least $2,000 to be buried here, or more if you want one of those swanky tombs with a roof, air conditioning, etc. Some of these tombs are better than most of the places I've spent alive. It was just after the Day of the Dead, and there were still plenty of beer cans and tequila shots lying around so the deceased can keep getting loaded in the afterlife.

Sinaloa is steeped in narco-culture. The muchachos walking around with cowboy hats and gold-plated Magnums have spawned their own movie genre, the narco-cinema: cheap B-movies filmed on a shoestring budget where producers hire real-life prostitutes and fire real-life guns for an action extravaganza that's less Stanley Kubrick and more like the poor man's *Desperado*. Like Antonio Banderas's guitar-swinging gunfighter, the narcos also have their own style of music: *narcocorridos*, traditional folk ballads played with accordions and twelve-string guitars in which the lyrics are closer to gangsta rap (gettin' money and screwing over the gringos). Banned from the radio, artists are sometimes commissioned by the narcos themselves to sing about their daring exploits at private parties.

'At these parties there's a lot of guns. Sometimes they'll ask me to play a song while I hold their AK,' said Baldomar Cazares, Miguel's friend from the mountains who's also a narcocorrido singer, as we sat in a bar off the main square of Culiacán. 'In this atmosphere you can find anything at all – guns, bulletproof cars . . . it gives you an idea of what these people are like. Once, I was at a party with El Chapo himself, in and out and then he left. Then I came out with my first song, "Bulletproof Vest".'

Baldo comes from a village that's a cradle of drug trafficking. Starting out as a weed farmer, he found that his true talent lies in writing songs. Drug lords now pay him thousands of pesos to immortalise their stories in verse. Baldo's inspiration was the 2Pac of narcocorrido, Rosalino 'Chalino' Sanchez.

'Chalino Sanchez was very popular, he used to come to my village all the time,' Baldo said. Chalino, a Sinaloa farm-boy-made-good, toured Mexico and the United States dressed in his trademark cowboy hat. But like 2Pac, the bad boy of gangsta rap, the violent world of the narcos was never far behind.

'Sanchez was a hitman not because he wanted to be, but because when he was eleven years old a man raped his sister, so when he grew up he killed that man. But he was so talented he became a singer. He was killed in a dispute about drugs, but actually the murderer said he was so good, "Play one more song before I kill you." And then he was dead.'

In 1992, Chalino Sanchez was found with two bullets to the head after getting arrested at a concert in Sinaloa.

The narcos' power lets them have any woman they desire. Miguel suggested we head to a film-set in a sleazy motel where one of his buddies was filming a clip for a low-rent Enrique Iglesias. There were waterbeds, Jacuzzis, all the girls were wearing tight dresses and the walls were a shade of blood red that's more creepy than sexy.

We managed to pull away Helena between takes. She's short and not as skimpily dressed as the others, but she doesn't need it. With her fair skin, soft, gorgeous jawline, deep-red lipstick and long, dark eyebrows, she looked every bit the femme-fatale straight out of a 1940s noir or pulp detective novel as she lit up her cigarette. She agreed to tell me her story but told it hypothetically, like it could be the story of any girl tangled up in the dopeworld of Culiacán. After running away from home at the age of fourteen, Helena was approached by a drug lord:

'At an event they'll come up to you, ask you for your number. If you say no, they'll come back with a present – sometimes it could be flowers, jewels, sometimes a 1,000-peso bill with their phone number. A bottle of whiskey, wine, or they'll pay your bill at the restaurant. They'll watch wherever you are, modelling or in a bar, and they'll come up to you and ask you if you want to go anywhere . . . the most expensive restaurants in Cancún, Los Cabos . . .

'They'll buy you anything you want, anything at all. They'll give you any luxury you ask for; they like to please their princess. But at that point, they feel like they own you. So that means you can't go out, hang out with other people or girls. You're like an object. They get jealous, abuse you mentally, physically, every imaginable way. You have everything, but when they take you to bed you can't say no. And then they leave. You're just one among many.

'If you say no, they beat you. They terrorise you in so many ways. They send someone to keep an eye on you, watch every step you make. If you talk or hang out with other narcos, they kill you.'

It's easy to be drawn to the allure of being a gangster's moll. But once you're in the grip of such dominant, controlling men, you're trapped. Helena was lucky. She got away and a few months later, the narco was killed, leaving her with a six-year-old daughter.

'After his death she has nothing, but that's a price I'm willing to pay,' she said. 'One thing I've learnt is you can have everything, but even if you have the best clothes, the best jewellery, all that means nothing if you're not happy.'

I've been to some strange places in my life, but Mexico was quickly starting to top my list of crazy. Unlike American gangbangers or Sicilian mafiosi, the narcos have their own patron saint. Jesús Malverde was a nineteenth-century outlaw who stole from the rich and gave to the poor, a sort of Robin Hood of Sinaloa. Malverde might not have actually existed, but around these parts he's venerated as a saint. People, mainly drug dealers, come to his shrine and leave dollar bills on the walls as an offering beneath portraits of the moustached brigand standing between bundles of weed, AKs and AR-15s. The money plastered over the walls comes from all over the world; there were notes from China, Cuba, the US, Canada and even Mozambique.

Another saint is *Santa Muerte*, or Lady Death, the sultrier female version of the Grim Reaper. Denounced by Catholics as devil-worship and more morally flexible than Francis of Assisi, she speaks to all those left behind by the Church – criminals, gays, the poor ... and the narcos. Day of the Dead is, of course, her big day.

And then there's the cults. The Narcosatanists (*Los Narcosatánicos*) were founded by Adolfo Constanzo, a Cuban expat from Miami who worshipped the gods of Palo Mayombe, an Afro-Cuban religion with origins in the Congo. The kid had a knack for prophecy and moved to Mexico, where he amassed a small group of followers who also became his gay lovers. They began making sacrifices, torturing rival drug dealers before ritualistically slaughtering them, lopping their arms and legs off and cooking their body parts in a pot. When one narco-trafficking family tried to stiff him, their bodies were found in a river without their fingers, toes, ears, brains or spines. But the gods grew bored of feasting on gang members, so in 1989 the cultists abducted Mark Kilroy, a twenty-one-year-old Texas student on a spring break.

As with Kiki, if you piss off the Americans there'll be hell to pay. Kilroy's family kicked up a shitstorm, and a massive manhunt soon led police to Constanzo's ranch, where they found Kilroy's body, along with fifteen others and a massive stash of coke, weed and guns. Constanzo later died in a police shootout in Mexico City, but he wasn't the last egomaniac with a messiah delusion.

In 2006, a gang burst into a crowded nightclub in the southern state of Michoacán and tossed five severed heads onto the packed dance-room floor. Along with their present was a lovely card which read: *'The Family doesn't kill for money, kill women or kill innocents. Only those who deserve to die will die. Let everyone know that this is divine justice.'*

La Familia were a cartel doubling as a cult, mixing up meth and coke operations with heavy doses of evangelical Christianity. Their leader, Nazario Moreno, aka *El Más Loco* ('The Crazy One'), wrote his own twisted version of the Bible in which he channelled both Jesus Christ and legendary Mexican revolutionary Emiliano Zapata, and claimed he could talk to donkeys. He held bizarre initiation ceremonies where new recruits dressed as knights were forced to eat the hearts of their victims. Whether Dr Doolittle believed his own hype we may never know, but it's definitely easier to rally an army of uneducated, gun-toting young men when you claim to have God on your side. Just ask ISIS.

Moreno also forbade his men from taking drugs and made them watch *The Godfather* for its family-values content. Together, they took over most of the narcotrafficking and protection rackets in the state. Unfortunately for Moreno, it wasn't the 1980s any more. The PRI was losing its grip on power. In 2000, Vicente Fox became the nation's first non-PRI president, a tough-talking cowboy who declared high noon on the narcos. Though Fox left the Sinaloans curiously untouched, the political shakeup had cartels spooked: what if the next president waged an actual war on drugs?

The next president, Felipe Calderón, did just that. In December 2006, Calderón ordered the military to take down the drug lords, starting with his home state of Michoacán. But the narcos were ready. After getting a pep talk from William Wallace in *Braveheart* (as well as being a deranged psychopath, Moreno was also a cinephile), El Loco's men launched an insurgency, blocking off highways with barricades of burning cars and launching guerrilla raids on Mexican troops.

But while the cartel could hold off the government's forces, there was another group they hadn't counted on: the vigilantes. La Familia was rapidly sinking to new levels of depravity. They'd hang around outside schools, picking out which girls they wanted to rape. The people had had enough. With the government unable or unwilling to defend them, the villagers formed vigilante groups. At first, only a few farmers armed with rusty old shotguns stood up to La Familia, but their numbers grew and before long they were clearing out whole towns and taking out the trash. It was real *Tombstone* shit.

Moreno's time was running out. In 2014, he was finally eliminated, either gunned down by marines or (more likely) turned in to vigilantes by his own bodyguards, beaten to death, then handed over to the authorities. But not all the vigilantes were brooding gunslingers with a righteous thirst for revenge: the movement to oust La Familia included rival gangsters including a rock-hard gang of meth cooks calling themselves *Los Viagras*. Before long, Michoacán descended into a battleground between invading cartels, ex-Familia associates and squabbling militias.

The worst bloodshed was on the Texas border as the Sinaloans, led by Chapo Guzmán, moved in on territory held by the Juárez Cartel. It was *barrio* against *barrio* as the cartels fought a proxy war with local gangbangers. It wasn't just bad guys killing bad guys: everyone was a target. On 31 January 2010, gang members opened fire on a birthday party in the neighbourhood of Villas de Salvárcar. When the smoke cleared, thirteen high-school students and two grown-ups lay dead; none had anything to do with the cartels.

The police were targets too, on both sides: the local police were on the payroll of the Juárez Cartel, while Chapo paid off the *federales* (federal police). Later that year, police and paramedics responded to an emergency call in downtown Juárez – officer down. As officers and paramedics approached the wounded man, a nearby car bomb exploded, taking out a medic, an officer and one passer-by. It was a booby trap: the cartel kidnapped some random guy, shot him and dressed him in police uniform to lure in their victims.

Between 2008 and 2011, Ciudad Juárez was dropping around three hundred bodies a month and beating Cape Town, Caracas, Baghdad, Detroit and all those other honeymoon spots as the most dangerous city on the planet. Literally across the bridge on the other side of the Rio Grande, El Paso was the second-safest city in the United States, with only eleven murders for the whole of 2009. It was control of this bridge, which the cartels used to send their mules over the border, that sparked all the mayhem. It's precisely the fact that these checkpoints are so few and far between that makes them so valuable, and the competition so fierce.

For years, Americans watched in horror what was going on in Mexico and anyone's inability to do anything about it. They didn't want the warzones of Juárez and Michoacán on their doorsteps in Wisconsin. That's understandable. But, as always, people want simple solutions to complex problems.

'When Mexico sends its people, they're not sending their best,' Donald Trump said at a rally announcing he was running for president. 'They're sending people that have lots of problems, and they're bringing those problems with us. They're bringing drugs. They're bringing crime. They're rapists. And some, I assume, are good people.'

'I will build a great, great wall on our southern border,' he added. 'And I will have Mexico pay for that wall.'

There's not much love for Agent Orange down in Mexico. You can't call Mexicans a nation of rapists and get away with it. Stalls everywhere were selling T-shirts saying 'FUCK THE WALL'.

'Trump and [then-President] Peña Nieto, the two assholes fucking this country,' my taxi driver grumbled as we drove past Trump's mural on a wall next to a swastika. Perhaps ex-president Vicente Fox put it best when he said, 'I'm not going to pay for that fucking wall!'

But over in America, Trump's supporters claimed he was only doing what any good leader should. Every country has a right to defend its borders. But would a wall be enough to stop Mexican bandidos turning sleepy Idaho into *The Wild Bunch*?

Could China's Great Wall keep out Genghis Khan?

24

The Wall

Trump's response to the Mexican rapists, criminals and drug dealers coming over the border was to announce that a wall would be built along the 2,000-mile (3,200-km) southern border. Unfortunately for him (and the American taxpayers footing the bill), the Mexicans build tunnels.

The US–Mexican border's been heavily policed since Nixon launched Operation Intercept. Millions cross each day, and that's just through the official checkpoints. Vehicles are searched by hand, scanners and sniffer dogs, and border agents are moved around to avoid corruption. Tyre shredders are deployed in case anyone tries to make a break for it.

But in 1989, El Chapo, then just a logistics guru for the higher-ups, came up with an ingenious idea – with all this security, why go over the border when you can go *under* it? So in 1989 he hired a team of engineers to dig the first tunnel from Tijuana to San Diego. As time went on, these tunnelling operations got more sophisticated, complete with lighting, rails and ventilation systems (features that would come in handy later on).

We knocked on the gate of a fairly nondescript house in Culiacán. A wiry, middle-aged man let us through to a little open-air garage, where he plopped three buckets down on the ground. Paco's days running with the Sinaloa Cartel might be long over, but his piercing eyes instantly made me think this was not a man I wanted to upset.

'I saw my first killing when I was eight years old. There was a shootout between two cars, and the gunmen killed three men. That was the first time I saw blood,' he said, occasionally breaking into broken Chicano English. 'My family was involved, so they brought me in, but now I don't want this any more. I want nothing to do with my old life in the organisation.'

Paco started out doing small drug runs to the United States, with a little heavenly assistance.

'Early on in my criminal life, I was smuggling three keys of heroin when I hit this checkpoint to the United States,' he reminisced.

'They had four dogs barking at my hidden compartment and I prayed to Jesús Malverde, please save me. They couldn't find my stuff in the car, even on the X-ray, so I drove all the way to New York. When I came back, I went to Malverde's shrine to thank him.'

As he rose up through the dopeworld, Paco graduated from cars to aeroplanes, flying Colombian cocaine from Oaxaca all the way to Tijuana through Mexico City.

'I used to smuggle by plane. Not just on a Cessna, but commercial flights as well. I used to smuggle 10 tonnes at a time. Once we were gonna smuggle several tonnes, but there were some problems with the officials running the airline. They told me, "We like money too, asshole!" But we had to get rid of these drugs, so we stole an aeroplane and filled it with coke, then we flew it to the beach in La Paz, Baja California [near the American border], and we buried the plane in the sand. If we just left it there, the Feds were gonna find it and pay close attention to that location, but we wanted to use it again.'

So who were Paco's partners across the border?

'La Eme, Mexican Mafia, you understand what I'm saying, Holmes?'

I did understand what he was saying. The Mexican Mafia, or La Eme, is a California prison gang formed in the 1950s to protect

Latino inmates from the blacks and Aryan Brotherhood. Since then, it's morphed into a sophisticated crime syndicate, rallying most SoCal street gangs under its flag. Every gang or pusher on its territory pays a weekly tax to La Eme or gets smoked. This is something Paco was familiar with as, in addition to being a big-time smuggler for the Sinaloa Cartel, he was also a hitman.

'An order is an order; if the boss says you gotta kill this person you gotta kill 'em. If he says kill the president, you gotta do it.

'Sometimes I have dreams that the devil is chasing me and I can't run and the devil is on my back. And I see the red figure of the devil with this long red tail. He's coming to get me because of all the bad things I've done in my life.'

Over the years, Paco reckons he must have made at least $50m, but in the end he lost it all over a woman.

'I was in love with this woman. But when you're in love you're so stupid, you don't do anything right. I used to kill for her all the time. She took everything from me, all my money. I was doing so well and then it was like a free fall. I had businesses in Guerrero and Michoacán and everything just collapsed. And by then I was an addict and using coke and heroin, and even the guns I had, I exchanged them for drugs. Why do you think I don't want anything to do with this life?'

Paco now works as a mechanic and also, apparently, as an amateur chiropractor; he offered me a Bane-style massage to fix my posture as we walked out. I politely declined, but Miguel was only too happy to have his spine snapped back into place by this headcase. He's a braver man than I.

The next day, we met with another representative of the Mexican shipping industry. Miguel, Baldo and I were sat at a Burger King in Culiacán when a heavy-set, burly man walked in with a shaven head and a cholo moustache. Hector was a mid-level trafficker with the Sinaloa organisation, so it was only right that I buy him a Whopper

Meal (while I nibbled on some chips, assuming my meeker place in the hierarchy).

'I'm from Badiraguato, the same area as El Chapo,' he explained. 'All my family are drug dealers there. If you're born in the mountains, you have two choices: either you work for the drug lords, or you sow poppy and marijuana. It's like they make you do these things; it's the decision we make because we don't have other options.'

It's hard to exaggerate how much power the cartel holds over Sinaloa. A few days later we met Major González, a thirty-year veteran of the state police's homicide squad. He's seen a lot of shit in his time on the Force – chopped-off heads, dead bodies – but he won't even investigate if he suspects it's a narco-murder.

'Sometimes, you've just got to let things go,' he told me in a parking lot. 'The Sinaloa Cartel's gunmen wear the same uniform as marines and they drive around in the same trucks, so you can't even tell them apart. The bad guys are better equipped than us – better guns, better radios, better cars. If you pull over a drug lord, and you can tell he's a big fish by who he has with him, you let him go if you don't want any trouble.'

The days of Carrillo Fuentes shutting down the country's air defences may be over, but that doesn't mean other 'arrangements' can't be made.

'A cop around here makes around 800 dollars a month, and that hasn't changed for decades,' said González. 'That's why there's so much bribery. When you graduate from the academy, you think you can change the world, but then you realise that you can't, so you just chill and make money.

'We make arrangements with the narcos. We call them: what are you bringing? Coke, weed, heroin? OK, you have one hour to move the coke through my territory, from five to six for example. After that, if you don't have time, call me and I'll give you more time.'

Is it even greed if you're risking your life five days a week and can barely scrape together enough change for one last Happy Meal? Back at the Burger King, Hector laid down how this all works.

'The police don't work for the people, they work for us,' he said, biting into his Whopper. 'Every single officer is afraid of the cartel because they know if they don't co-operate, we're gonna kill them. So they can't be clean. And they have families. They think about their mother, father, sister, brother, and they think "OK". But that's good because they're making money now on the side. Usually, we pay the commander 20,000 pesos a week, and he splits it with all his other officers.'

But it's not just the cops who the drug lords have in their pocket. Since the PRI days, drug trafficking in Mexico has long rested on the cartel's ability to control or manipulate elections.

'Police, governors, mayors, congressmen, city officials, they all work for us,' Hector explained. 'Whenever there's an election, our bosses talk with some of the candidates and ask them: are you gonna be with me or support someone else? Every single governor, before they even reach their office, has already made a deal with the criminal world.'

If they don't, the consequences could be fatal. At least 175 candidates or officeholders were killed in the bloody run-up to Mexico's 2018 presidential election, putting Al Capone's 1928 Pineapple Primary (named for all the hand grenades lobbed at opponents' houses) to shame.

But once they're in, the upper- and underworlds merge to the point where it's hard to tell the difference between your friendly local councilman handing out parking permits, and coked-up lunatics who'll cut your head off and use it as a pleasure device. In one of the darkest episodes of the Mexican drug war, forty-three students were marched off their buses while en route to a protest in Iguala, southwest of Mexico City, before being handed over to the *Guerreros Unidos* ('United Warriors') gang in cahoots with local police. One of the students was found with his face flayed off and his eyes gouged out. The rest were never seen again, and though the government kept unearthing more and more mass graves, none of them seemed to be the students; instead, they were more cartel victims *they didn't even know about*.

One version of the story is that the mayor of Iguala disliked the students' radical left-wing politics and had them 'taken care of' by the United Warriors gang. Another is that they were mistaken for a rival cartel, while a third implicates the army and federal police. Either way, the green light came from someone close to the establishment.

If law enforcement suspects you of carrying drugs, get ready for a strip search that's as thorough as a prostate exam. They'll lead you to a back room, take off your clothes and make you squat while a fat, sweaty officer peers up inside your asshole (God, he must love his job).

But these searches take a lot of time, so it helps if they've already been alerted by some Very Good Boys. A dog's nose is over a hundred times more sensitive than a human's, and they're also incorruptible (unless you give them treats). Sniffing out sachets of meth hidden up your grandad's butt is like a game to them. They find the Bad Man's stash and get a reward. Dogs smell like we see – instead of soup, they smell carrots, potatoes and onions, so it's no good hiding it in a coffee jar because the dogs will just smell the coffee beans, a plastic bag and your stash of dank Cali bud. You might be able to slip past if the coffee jar's made of glass (because smells take longer to leak through glass), but I wouldn't stick around to find out – it was a dog that busted me that night in 2013.

Then there are the scanners. An X-ray can tell not only the density of an object, but whether it's organic (which includes most drugs) or non-organic (metals, etc.) as well. Organic materials show up as orange on-screen.

One way to get around this is making your stuff un-X-rayable. Curtis 'Cocky' Warren grew up on the tough streets of Toxteth in Liverpool, rising through the ranks to become the Cali Cartel's man in Europe. Using his international connections, the scouser brewed up a plot to smuggle cocaine to the Netherlands from Venezuela, hidden inside a shipment of lead ingots. But his phone was being tapped by the Dutch police. They intercepted the shipment and raided his property, finding £125m worth of drugs as well as pistols and hand grenades. After serving out his sentence, Cocky was sent back to Britain, but only tasted freedom for five weeks before being caught smuggling a shitload of weed into Jersey.

But even with all this technology and Fido's sharp nose, only a small fraction of drug shipments is seized. With millions of passengers, cars and shipping containers passing through docks, airports and border crossings each day, authorities will be lucky if they can search even 1 per cent of them. Occasionally they'll get a lucky break, such as in 2007 when a Mafia plot to import 15 million ecstasy tablets, enough to get half of Australia dancing the Macarena, was uncovered in Melbourne. But even then, it was discovered through pure luck – the gangsters hid the pills inside tomato tins under the name of a legit farm company, and would have got away with it had the freight manager not called the company's actual number instead of the fake one the goombahs supplied. Fuggedaboudit!

So does Trump's border wall stand any hope of reining in the cartels?

'No, amigo,' said Hector, now tucking into his French fries. 'The gringos are the biggest customers in the world. If we can't smuggle it, they will come get it themselves.'

With all the ways of getting drugs across the border, as far as the flow of coke, meth and other goodies goes, a wall ain't gonna do squat. It's just a massive waste of taxpayer money. The one thing it might stop, though, is all those people risking their lives making their way across the desert, but something tells me it's not being built with humanitarian goals in mind.

'Besides,' he added with a smile, 'I bring all my stuff by boat.'

25

Dinner at El Chapo's

When a tropical storm and heavy floods hit Sinaloa in October 2018, washing away homes and communities, help wasn't far behind, but not from the authorities. In the villages around Culiacán, families who'd lost their homes were given stoves, blankets and mattresses with a logo bearing the initials of their benefactor, JGL – Joaquin Guzmán Loera. A viral video showed villagers smiling and waving, as an elderly woman faces the camera and says, 'God bless you, Chapo Guzmán.'

In other countries, celebrating an outlaw behind the deaths of thousands is usually frowned upon. But, like Escobar, Chapo's something of a local legend. He gave money to the poor; built hospitals, schools and churches.

'The truth is, people think El Chapo is this murderer, but they don't know him,' Baldo explained. 'People here love and respect El Chapo because he was very humble and if there is a problem he tries to work it out. He doesn't want to kill anyone but he tries to fix the problem. If the problem is not fixable he kills, yes. But he creates jobs, helps people. If the kid is sick, he takes them in his plane to the hospital. If the family doesn't have any food, he gives them some money. He is a fair man. In my eyes, he's a great man.'

The law caught up with Chapo after tracking a henchman's Blackberry to a hotel in the coastal resort of Mazatlán. As marines

stormed the building room by room, they found two American stoners, one of whom, thinking a platoon of soldiers armed to the teeth
was kicking down his door because he was smoking pot, held up his
California medicinal marijuana card. Chapo and his henchman were
found in another room and gave up without a fight.

But it wasn't long before Mexico's Most Wanted was on the loose
again. Eighteen months later, Chapo escaped from the highest-
security prison in the country (even in Mexico that has to count
for something) through a tunnel leading from his cell to an abandoned house one and a half kilometres away, complete with aircon
and a motorbike.

It was too late for me to pull a Sean Penn and try to interview the
man himself: after a massive manhunt, the world's biggest drug boss
was caught after succumbing to the one weak spot of all red-blooded
men – a beautiful woman. Mexican telenovela star Kate del Castillo
said that only Chapo could solve the problems of the country and
suggested that he 'traffic in love' on Twitter. Chapo sent her over some
flowers and Kate agreed to meet the hopeless romantic, asking if Penn
could tag along. Chapo hadn't seen *Fast Times at Ridgemont High* but
agreed to the interview anyway, so long as he'd get to meet Kate.

Kate and Sean were brought to a remote meeting spot in the
jungle, where the drug lord informed them he didn't want to be
'portrayed as a nun', since he supplied 'more heroin, methampheta-
mine, cocaine and marijuana than anybody else in the world'. But
what he didn't know was that Kate was under surveillance by the
Mexican security forces, who started to zero in on his location. The
world's most wanted criminal was recaptured in January 2016 after a
massive gun battle. The GoPro footage is worthy of a John Woo film.
Not taking any more chances, the Mexican government agreed to
extradite Chapo to the United States. There, he faced the biggest
narco-trafficking case in US history.

With him knowing what he does about Mexico's dirty laundry,
I'm surprised he made it this far without falling inexplicably

depressed and finding himself on the end of a rope. But given how he's locked down in an American cell twenty-three hours a day, it's probably harder to reach Chapo now than when he was a fugitive. Instead, I did the next best thing. I went to La Tuna.

In order to get to La Tuna, the birthplace of Chapo Guzmán, we needed a four-by-four. You can't get through the twisty-turny mountain roads in a normal car, and if it rains it's impossible to drive through at all. But none of the rental spots we checked in Culiacán had a spare four-by-four that weekend, and that's when I remembered – Pedro, a heroin cook we met earlier, was selling his pickup truck. We went back to his village and persuaded him to lend it to us. Baldo came along too; he wanted to get a lift with his wife.

So with Baldo's pregnant wife in tow, we drove through the mountains in a smack dealer's truck. Every few miles or so there were a couple of teenage boys, maybe about fourteen or fifteen, standing around with quadbikes and walky-talkies. Their job was to keep a lookout on everyone who goes in and out of the valley (especially the army and other *enemigos*).

After dropping off Baldo, I asked Miguel if doing this kind of work was dangerous. A few months ago, his friend Javier Valdez, a well-known journalist and the founder of *Ríodoce*, was gunned down just a few short steps from his office. Mexico's the most dangerous country in the world for journalists. Those reporting on cartel activity will soon find themselves in early retirement by way of bullet or hand grenade, like the one thrown at *Ríodoce's* office a few years earlier. Fortunately, that time no one was hurt.

Valdez was a caring and sensitive reporter who joked around with his colleagues and often stayed in touch with his subjects long after interviewing them. But he'd clearly pissed someone off. As he left his office in May 2017, two gunmen forced him out of his car and shot him dead. A small memorial cross now stands in his place, one of hundreds more scattered around Culiacán.

After four hours driving through the mountains, we finally arrived at La Tuna. The houses here were a little nicer than some of the others we drove past. Miguel spotted a guy he knew and asked him to take us to Don Angel. Sure, he said, and led us to this huge mansion where three young guys stood posted outside in full camo gear and bulletproof vests, with ammo belts across their shoulders, each clutching a heavy machinegun. They let us through and we walked inside, where there was this guy with a massive gold chain and a silky-white shirt, looking up at us from his family dinner with a look of total surprise.

'Hello, we are looking for Don Angel?'

'Yes, I am Don Angel. What do you want?'

It turned out that Don Angel was El Chapo's *brother*, whereas we were looking for El Chapo's *cousin*, who also goes by the name Don Angel, aka 'El Indio'. We scuttled out, offering our apologies, and before long found the other Don Angel, who was waiting for us. He looked like a typical Mexican cowboy, a fifty-something-year-old with a huge sombrero and a twirly moustache.

After inviting us over for some dinner, El Indio took us to his friend's house in the nearby village. I noticed all over the walls there were these framed photographs of a young guy – can't have been older than his mid-twenties – in exotic places like the Taj Mahal and Machu Picchu.

'Who is that?' I asked.

'Oh, that's just my son,' said the man, 'but he doesn't come round here much any more. He's one of the top most wanted fugitives in Mexico.'

Everyone in this valley is involved.

Nightfall. Through the clear mountain air, far from the city lights, you could see the whole Milky Way. That's when this trip started getting really bizarre. We headed back to La Tuna. Back at Don

Angel's house, a small crowd had gathered round. You see, one of
Don Angel's businesses is a small sushi stand, and as mariachi music
played in the background, the locals were having what I can only
describe as a Mexican cartel sushi party: around twenty or so armed
guys, AR-15 rifles swung around their shoulders, Glock pistols
sticking out of their jeans, standing around eating sushi.

I've never seen so many straps in my life. Here I am, in the drug-
trafficking heartland of the world, hundreds of miles from the nearest police station. If the Mexican army tried to come here, these
people are ready for war. I could be killed here without a second
thought. Shit just got real. Then I thought, with all those lookouts
dotted over the hills, if they didn't want us here we would have found
out a long time ago, and my heart rate dropped back to normal.

Another of El Chapo's cousins (they're all related in this village)
walked up and started quizzing me. What do I think about Putin?
Did he help Trump? (I don't know.) Who is more powerful, Putin or
Trump? (Putin, because even though Trump is the head of the most
powerful country, he doesn't know what to do with it.) It was basically the opposite of an interview. He also claimed to be related to
Pancho Villa, the legendary outlaw hero (or bandit) that led a rebel
army during the Mexican Revolution. Then he asked me what I
thought about Albanians, which I thought was a weird question, but
then it turned out he was a big fan of *Taken*, with Liam Neeson, and
of Harrison Ford and Arnold Schwarzenegger. So I'm sitting down
with a Mexican drug lord in the middle of the mountains at night
discussing the finer points of Liam Neeson's filmography over sushi,
while surrounded by his bodyguards, who are all also eating sushi.

This almost beat ayahuasca as the weirdest night of my life.

The next day was a lot more chill. We stayed over at Pancho's
house watching eighties action movies and woke up the next morning to a BBQ. Pancho led us for prayers, laying his Bible on the table.
Considering how many tacos we ate, it would, perhaps, have been
worthwhile to check what the Good Book has to say about gluttony,

for with all this red meat, the greatest danger here, despite the guns, was probably having a heart attack. After that, Don Angel and Pancho settled down to tell me about their cousin.

Chapo was a man of action but he was a practical joker, too. One day, back when when they were all just simple farmers, a girl died in the village. They couldn't yet afford her a mausoleum in Humaya, so Chapo sent a friend to steal a gravestone from a cemetery. The friend broke in at night, digging up the gravestone and apologising under his breath, promising he'd give it back, when he saw something moving through the darkness. Two ghostly figures approached, wailing the agonising howls of the undead. It was Chapo and another cousin, wrapped in bedsheets. The boy almost filled his pants.

Every so often as we spoke, a gunshot crackled in the distance, probably just those boys shooting a few rounds in the air. A couple of times, a small plane flew overhead carrying opium from the poppy fields, probably on its way to someone like Pedro. So what does the family think about how Chapo's wares are blamed for so much misery and death?

'They are not obliged to use drugs. No one is holding a gun to their head and forcing them to use drugs.'

So why, with all his money, did Chapo stay in Mexico and not run away to some island in the Caribbean?

'Why would he go to a place he doesn't know? Here he is protected by the people.'

What about the whole episode with Kate del Castillo?

'That was his downfall; he lost everything because of one woman. We don't know how many children he has because of his addiction to women, but too many. He may have over fifty kids! But Kate Castillo is such a beautiful woman, we don't blame him!'

In January 2019, Chapo was convicted on all counts after an eventful trial where, amongst other things, it was claimed he bribed the Mexican president with $100 million. With a mandatory life sentence at a maximum-security jail, it doesn't seem likely he'll taste freedom ever again. Can we look forward to another dashing escape?

'One day, he will come back here, either released from prison or escaped. But it won't be because of him, it will be because of God.'

In all of yesterday's excitement I forgot to take any photos of armed men to blow up my Instagram. No matter. Don Angel's son-in-law came running around the side of the house, cheerfully waving a Kalashnikov. Take pictures, he said, but no faces.

We wanted to go and check out some poppy fields, but it was now getting late and Pedro probably wanted his truck back. The ride home was relatively uneventful, apart from that one time we almost drove off a cliff.

El Chapo's family are really chill. It kinda reminds me of a friend from uni who knew the bin Ladens: just a normal family, for the most part – Osama was the black sheep. If it wasn't for all the guns, La Tuna would be just another Mexican village, not the home of the world's most powerful Mafia.

But since the mid-2000s, cracks began appearing in the Sinaloa organisation. The government, led by President Calderón, pursued the 'kingpin strategy', in which they tried to cut the heads off drug-trafficking organisations by going for the guys at the top. But you see, by taking out the king, all his lords and minions scramble for the throne . . . at the same time. Like Iraq after Saddam Hussein, disrupting the old order only leaves you with chaos.

The troubles began in 2008 when Chapo's partners, the Beltrán-Leyva brothers, accused him of setting up one of their siblings and gunned down his twenty-two-year-old son, Edgar Guzmán, outside a shopping mall in Culiacán. Two days later, there was not a single red rose left in the state for Mother's Day as Chapo bought them all for his son's wake.

'It was a really heavy war. We're talking about two powerful factions that used to be just one group, the most powerful in Mexico.

Hundreds of people were killed,' Hector recalled between slurps of his soda. 'I was in La Tuna once and they called me to say they killed my *compadre*. I asked who, and I knew this guy, so I called all my shooters and we knew where to find them.

'We've got an intelligence system that leads us and watches all over. For example, they'll tell us "There's a group standing outside a restaurant, then you go left and see a red car". We don't know who's inside, we just know our people told us to go and kill. Every single entrance to the city is being watched twenty-four hours a day, three hundred and sixty-five days a year. So if we're gonna do a hit, they guide us, and when we hit, we hit twice, we don't ask questions. And sometimes it's the wrong people, but if it's a mistake it's a mistake. But that time, it was personal.'

The cops got caught in the crossfire, too. González was driving along when his convoy was ambushed by *sicarios*.

'They shot at my car eighty times; I got hit in the leg, hand and side,' the old officer recalled, showing me his scars. 'One officer was dead and three were wounded, including me. Back then, many colleagues of mine were killed.'

In December 2009, Alfredo's brother Arturo, aka 'The Beard', was tracked down to an apartment block in Cuernavaca, a spa town near Mexico City. The building was surrounded by marines and Arturo called one of his heavy-hitters, Edgar Valdez, aka 'La Barbie', for backup. But Barbie refused, and so, after a two-hour siege, Arturo and five of his bodyguards went down like Tony Montana: in a glorious hail of gunfire.

The marines pulled down The Beard's pants and covered his body with banknotes, then invited journalists to come and take photos. But the marines lost one of their own in the siege. In retaliation, Beltrán-Leyva gunmen shot up the funeral and gunned down the rest of his grieving family – mother, brother, sister, aunt.

This little family spat in Sinaloa sent ripples across the whole of Mexico. Acapulco, a seaside resort on the Pacific coast, was once known for its sandy beaches and posh hotels that hosted celebs like John Wayne, J.F.K. and Frank Sinatra. After the death of Arturo The Beard, control of the seaport fell to his lieutenant, La Barbie. So naturally, once their boss was dead, Barbie and the other capos sat down to resolve their territorial differences with all the grace and humility of a raging chimpanzee on steroids. Acapulco transformed from party central to Mexico's murder capital.

La Barbie – that's gotta be the least intimidating nickname ever, but don't let it fool you. Barbie was a bit of an odd character, a gringo high-school jock from Texas who loved playing on his Wii and had a soundproofed torture chamber built in one of his safehouses. It was he who started one of the most disturbing trends of the Mexican drug war. Like the insurgents in the Middle East, the cartels embraced a key aspect of warfare – propaganda.

Four hitmen from a rival group arrived to take out the drug boss on his home turf. Barbie ordered his men to grab the assassins and was surprised to find that one of them had brought his family along (because, fuck it, if you're off to commit bloody murder in Acapulco, you might as well make a holiday out of it). His wife and two-year-old stepdaughter were bundled into another car, while the four mobsters were tied up in a safehouse. Barbie came up with a camera in his hand and a pistol in his jeans. As the captives frantically spilled the beans on who sent them, Barbie calmly shot them one by one in the head before putting the video up on YouTube. The wife and stepdaughter were released the next day with a thousand pesos for bus fares.

La Barbie's tape went viral. Since then, the internet's been bombarded with more novelty deaths than *Saw*. Killing someone wasn't enough; you had to send a message. The cartels tried to outdo each other in brutality as the deaths got increasingly elaborate: beheaded, skinned alive, blown up with dynamite, or some combination of the three.

Some bosses preferred to send out their messages old-school, leaving burnt bodies hanging off bridges. In 2012, the following banner was unfurled over a pile of dismembered corpses in Nuevo Laredo, near the Texas border: 'We have started to clear Nuevo Laredo of the Zetas because we want a city that is free and because we want the citizens to live in peace. We are narcotraffickers and we don't mess with hard-working or business people. I am going to show these filthy Zetas how it's done Sinaloa-style; without kidnapping and without extortion. And this goes to you, Z-40. You don't scare me. I know you sent H to dump those heads on my turf because you don't have the balls to do it yourself. Signed, El Chapo. PS: Don't forget I'm your daddy.'

The Sinaloa Cartel was squaring off against Los Zetas, a ruthless hit squad of elite ex-Mexican army commandos gone rogue, ready and eager to terminate with extreme prejudice. The Zetas started out as mercenaries for the Gulf Cartel before turning on their masters and going into business for themselves.

While the Sinaloans are old-school gangsters who prefer bribery to bloodshed, the Zetas made their name through a level of cruelty that those blubbering yakuza manginas could only imagine in their wettest dreams. In one massacre, they executed seventy-two immigrants, including one pregnant woman, at a ranch in San Fernando. In another, they ran buses carrying 193 men, women and children off the road; raping the women, drowning the children in acid and forcing the men to club each other to death in gladiator-style death-matches. When the Zetas' head honcho, Miguel Treviño, aka 'Z-40', got word that the DEA was onto him and the rat came from somewhere in the town of Allende near the Texas border, he expressed his displeasure by having the town razed to the ground, leaving it looking more like Syria or Iraq than a couple of hours' drive from the Alamo.

As they prepared to move into Nuevo Laredo, the Sinaloans hired MS-13 gangbangers for the first wave of attack. MS-13, or *Mara*

Salvatrucha, began in the 1980s when thousands of Salvadorian refugees banded together in Los Angeles to stop getting picked on by the local Mexicans, covering themselves with face tattoos to scare off the Cholos. When the war ended in 1992, it was time to send them home, and it doesn't take a genius to work out what happened next. The Americans deported a bunch of gangbangers to a former warzone with no rule of law but plenty of unhinged veterans carrying guns. Now, thanks to MS-13 and another LA gang, Barrio 18, El Salvador is actually deadlier than it was at the height of the 1980s civil war.

But despite their fearsome reputation, these G'd up homeboys were no match for the Zetas' professional exterminators. The bodies of five gang members were found in a Zetas safehouse next to a note: 'Chapo Guzmán . . . send more *pendejos* like this for us to kill.' After that, the Sinaloans stepped up their game. Hector told me the cartel was even taking applications from abroad.

'We've come face to face with the Zetas and, yeah, you can tell some of them are special forces, but we have those in Sinaloa too. We have the money to bring in the Guatemalan special forces. So yeah, they are good, but we have enough money to hire anyone.'

The special forces Hector was referring to are the Kaibiles of Guatemala. From 1960 to 1996, the Guatemalan army carried out a brutal genocide of indigenous Maya peoples under the guise of fighting a leftist insurgency. The Kaibiles were especially known for their brutality, butchering whole families and leaving their heads as a warning to the rest.

But the cartels aren't just looking down south for reinforcements. Since the Contra era, the countries south of Mexico have been used like a trampoline to bounce shipments of the devil's dandruff from South America. Nowadays, Honduras, El Salvador and Guatemala have the highest murder rates on the planet, and while MS-13 and their face-painted gangbangers get all the attention, the cartels, who sometimes use the street gangs as muscle, have quietly taken power. In Honduras especially, where a 2009 coup saw the then-president marched onboard a military plane in his pyjamas and given a one-way ticket to Costa Rica, political instability has opened up a new smuggling route from Colombia. Planes carrying cocaine from Colombia and Venezuela land on hidden airstrips in the jungle, while the Honduran authorities are even cheaper to bribe than in Mexico.

Having got a foothold, the narcos began buying up acres of pristine rainforest to build more landing strips and set up logging and farming operations to launder their money. But oh no, what's this? Here come some annoying activists, screeching something about indigenous rights and protecting the environment. No matter. With all this gang warfare in the streets, who's gonna notice if some soy boy eco-warriors go missing? Honduras is now the deadliest country in the world for environmentalists.

Facing barbarians at the gates, traitors from within and its chairman caged in America like an animal, the Sinaloa Cartel's senior management is again falling into disarray. Guzmán's remaining sons, Ivan and Alfredo, appear to run the cartel, but in 2016 the boys were briefly kidnapped from a restaurant in Puerto Vallarta and released only after the intervention of 'El Mayo' Zambada, Chapo's main ally, who's so far avoided the spotlight on his partner. Meanwhile, another, more militant wing has broken off to form the Jalisco New Generation Cartel (CJNG), a trigger-happy outfit with a predilection for shooting down army helicopters.

Make no mistake, this is a war. The government sent the army to fight the cartels, and the cartels are winning.

'Back in the old days, the cartels could negotiate with us,' mused González. 'You let them do their thing and they left you alone. But that all changed once the wars began. They used to respect codes, family, but that's all gone. Before, they never used to kill women and children. Now the new generation is making its own rules.'

I'm usually wary of this 'good old days' bullshit – ah, back when women couldn't vote, they still sacrificed people to the Sun God and you had to wallow through nine miles of polio-infested no man's land just to get to school? Those good old days? – but the level of bloodshed in Mexico is unprecedented: since 2007, more people there have died in cartel wars than in the 'real' wars in Afghanistan and Iraq. This is a bloodbath on a scale that makes Al Capone-era Chicago look like a family picnic.

Back at Paco's crib, I asked him: with so much death, does the carnage in Mexico stand any chance of slowing down?

'Look here,' he said, crouching down, using his finger to draw a circle in the sand. 'In my days, this was the criminal organisation, the Sinaloa Cartel. The cartel gets more violent for one reason.'

He stopped to draw a bigger circle around it.

'It gets bigger, and as time goes by and there is more money, it gets more violent. As a gunman I can tell you this: narco-traffic is so deep in the bowels of our society, it won't ever stop. The violence will not stop, it will increase.'

But has the war at least reduced supply? Has it fuck. The amount of coke, dope and meth seized at the border remains the same. So it was all for nothing.

26

Interlude: Shottingham

Outside Nottingham Castle stands a tall, copper-green statue of Robin Hood. A little ways away lies Sherwood Forest and the Major Oak, a great big oak tree where the outlaw hero and his Merry Men used to hide out from the Sheriff. These days, though, with police helicopters and CCTV, highway robbery isn't such a viable option, so instead of hiding in trees Nottingham's outlaws now prefer growing them.

Growing weed is an artform – you've gotta get the light, temperature, humidity and the soil's nutrients just right. A big guy with a big personality, Paddy was my old business partner. If weed is an artform, then Paddy is Michelangelo. Turning your house into the Eden Project can bring lots of unwanted attention, but Paddy used to grow whole warehouses of the green stuff and drive it down to me in London. But back then, I didn't know too much about him, so I figured writing a book about drug dealers was the perfect opportunity to catch up. If he's not got a joint in his mouth he's usually rolling one, and his living room table was littered with papers, grinders and little green nugs. He can be quite difficult to get hold of, Paddy, and for a man his size he has an uncanny knack for falling off the grid. As our conversation turned to his life in the weed scene, it quickly became apparent why.

'One of the things I like about the weed game is people who sell weed, smoke weed, so it's a bit more chilled out,' he said, relaxing on the sofa. 'One of my mates – when you go out with him, it's like you're in Manchester and you're with Ronaldo. Everybody waves you over. If you see some black lads honking in their car, that's him. And the way he made his money was he robbed all the other dealers: take them to a warehouse, pull their teeth out. But the ones at the top didn't get touched cos they were all in the same firm. The ones at the bottom couldn't do anything. But that's the way you gotta be in this game. You can't show any sign of weakness. That's how it is in the coke game in Nottingham.

'One time, I got into some nasty shit with some coke dealers and I remember I was in this black guy's living room, four of them holding me up against the wall with a pistol to my head. I was shitting myself, I thought I was going to die. But then his mum walked in the house and she's shouting at them, "What's all this commotion?" They all turned around to talk to her and that's when I legged it.'

'Damn, homie, that's intense,' I said, taking a drag.

Paddy called up his old man and told him he was knee-deep in shit. They rented a van and he skipped town.

'Once I woke up with a knife open in one hand and a handgun in the other, with the safety off, and I'd fallen asleep just like that. I remember thinking, at this rate, I'm gonna kill myself. And that's why I have such a paranoid life now.'

He laughed and pulled out a baseball bat from behind the sofa. There's a weapon in every room of the house – a sword in the kitchen, a baton in the dining room. Since he's come back to Nottingham, Paddy always sits facing the front door every time he's at a restaurant, ready to jump if anyone walks in. But it's paid off – he's a survivor, a veteran of the drug game for the past fifteen years. Not once has he been arrested or charged with a major crime. For all their brazen lawbreaking, Paddy and his crew have proven extremely slippery to catch – his brother's on the Force.

'One time, I was picking up a load of Buddha when I got a text from my brother saying "Get out now." Seeing my big bro's number flash up on my burner phone, what the fuck?! So I took the three grand from my pocket and slipped it in the back of the sofa. I didn't want them to know I got tipped off. Then I looked at the weed, said it was shit, and left. Just as I went outside, a police car pulled me over. They asked me what I was doing. I said I was at my friend's house but they were busy so I left. They searched me but didn't find anything. I tried to say thank you to my brother afterwards, but he told me not to say anything about it ever again.'

In the early 2000s, Nottingham was ruled by a roided-out psychopath named Colin Gunn, who ran his Mafia-like empire from the Bestwood Estate. It was Gunn and his crew's propensity for fireworks that gave Robin Hood's old stomping ground the nickname 'Shottingham'.

'I didn't have much experience with guns, but I was running a café once and my mate drove up with another guy who used to run deep with the Bestwood lot,' Paddy told me. 'He then fled to Thailand cos he was wanted for some murders, then got a bit excited and tried to smuggle some coke into England, where he got caught for the coke and the murders. Anyway, they told me to come round the back. They popped open the boot and there were about four assault rifles and a shitload of handguns. He said, "Let's go for some target practice," so we drove down to the woods. That was fun.'

Welcome to the Drug Wars: Great Britain DLC.

Just because severed heads aren't rolling down the street like in Mexico doesn't mean gangland Britain isn't full of ruthless cunts. After an attempted hit on his nephew in 2003, Gunn exacted his revenge by tracking down the parents of the man responsible and shooting them both, execution-style, outside their seaside bungalow.

Neil Woods was one of the officers sent to infiltrate the gang. He quickly found himself, however, in a *Departed*-type situation where, at the same time as he was infiltrating the gang, the Gunns had their own mole in the police department.

'It was about four months into the job, and I'd just managed to get introduced to one of the lieutenants of Colin Gunn, the Bestwood Cartel,' Woodsy told me as we sat for a pint in the Sherlock Holmes, a pub just off Trafalgar Square which I thought was appropriate.

'My cover officer had gone off sick, so I was introduced to two new cops. One of them I had no problem with, but the other one literally made my hair stand on end. I instinctively knew something was wrong with him. I told my boss I wanted him out and he told me there was no problem. I didn't think much of it until twelve months later when it turned out that cop was an employee of Colin Gunn, being paid two grand a month on top of his salary, plus bonuses for good info.'

In the end, Gunn was sent down for thirty-five years for the bungalow murders and now spends his time complaining about the price of prison stamps. Woods, meanwhile, spent fourteen years undercover infiltrating drug gangs up and down the country. Undercovers have been a fixture of drug enforcement since Prohibition times, when 'Hooch Hound' Izzy Einstein and his partner Moe Smith busted speakeasies dressed in drag. Undercovers act as spies, posing as potential customers or fellow lowlifes to get in with drug dealers, earning their trust and gathering evidence before making a bust.

It's a dangerous vocation, and you've got to have a knack for improvising and talking your way out of a situation. While he'd technically have backup, Neil preferred them sitting with their walkie-talkies as far away as possible so their eagerness to get involved wouldn't screw up his operation. Once Woods was sent to infiltrate the Burger Bar Boys in Birmingham, named after the fast-food joint where they used to hang out (presumably, Mickey D's Mandem was taken). They were a nasty bunch, using rape for intimidation and building their notoriety. One of their names came up in police intelligence reports for multiple murders. Neil's source, a smalltime user-dealer called Angus, agreed to take him to the Boy's HQ.

He's skinny and bald so Neil's usual cover story was he was a junkie, but Angus didn't know him well enough so they went in the toilets, rehearsing a cover story on the cover story, when the gang walked in.

'This guy came in saying, "What's this?" Then four more came in, all hooded, all dressed in black, and began circling me,' Neil explained. 'One of them headbutted me as he was walking slowly around me. While this was going on, the lead guy started interrogating me, asking me and my mate the same question in different ways to trip us out. The sense of immediate violence in the air was incredible and I was convinced we wouldn't get out of there without at least a very serious beating. It went on for fifteen minutes, but it felt like hours. But as soon as the main guy said I was all right, they all walked.'

The dangers of undercover work are manifold: living your life with one foot in the underworld can put pressure on your own home life and identity, as Woods found when his hectic work schedule slumming it with scumbags tore his marriage apart. The temptations of always being around money and drugs. Being beaten to death by the Burger Bar Boys. And finally, empathising a little too much with those you're meant to be arresting. That too happened to Neil.

In his last assignment, Neil was posted to Brighton and tasked with finding the source of one of the worst heroin epidemics in the country. Brighton comes across as the British version of San Francisco – a liberal seaside town full of rainbow flags – meets Balamory, and not the sort of place that harbours a sinister secret. The city was suffering from one of the highest overdose rates in the country so Neil, disguised as a tramp, was sent to investigate.

But every time he approached one of the dealers, no one wanted to sell. They were suspicious of new faces. So he made friends with some addicts – vulnerable people living on the street – because they knew everyone and they were easy to manipulate. What he found was horrifying: drug dealers, having grown wise to the tactics of undercover cops, sealed themselves off from street activity using homeless addicts so that they'd be the ones getting arrested. If anyone thought they were snitching, they'd end up dead from a heroin overdose. The whole city lived in fear.

'I can't say there were definite casual murders going on – that needs an investigation – but a large portion of the population were convinced that murders were happening, and Brighton had the highest overdose rate by a considerable measure,' he told me. 'The idea was to create a buffer zone between the police and the gangsters. If you brought anyone close, you would be killed.'

The cops didn't seem to care. They only wanted arrest stats. Every overdose is just one less problem to worry about. In fact, most of Neil's new friends got rounded up along with the most vicious thugs and killers.

'They get it from both sides. Year after year, the drug trade becomes more violent and vulnerable people get caught in the crossfire. They're intimidated by the police and intimidated to make it harder for undercover police, then they get arrested and trampled on by the criminal justice system as well.'

Brighton was the last straw. Woodsy left the Force and began campaigning for drug reform. He wanted people to see drug users as something other than freaks and fiends.

Part 6

Freaks and Fiends?

27

Nisha

'I have a special place in my heart for heroin because it's the one drug I can see myself getting completely fucked up for. That's what scares me about it. It's exciting and intoxicating. It's the best thing in the world. It's mysterious, it's dark, it's seductive, it pulls you towards it in such a way you can't say no . . . you don't want to say no. You never want to quit it, and you want to give everything up for it.'

So Nisha tells me.

I've never had much luck on Tinder. What do girls mean when they ask me what I'm looking for on there? I never know what to say; like, what are YOU looking for? Yesterday when some chick asked me, I told her I was looking for a virgin to appease the Ancient Ones. She blocked me. ☹

Nisha's a sexy, curvy twenty-something brown lady I met on Tinder. Though we never bumped uglies, we bonded over our love of doggo memes and cocaine. She's also done ecstasy, ketamine, acid, shrooms, crack, skunk, Ritalin, Valium, OxyContin, laughing gas, methadone and Xanax, but heroin is her favourite. Just looking at her, you wouldn't know she is, or was, a drug addict, although her deep, smoky eyes give off a bit of heroin chic. She has a small scar from when she tried kissing a sausage dog and it bit her on the nose.

But what even is addiction? Well it's not a precise, clinical term, but generally it means doing so many drugs that you start depending on them, taking them compulsively to stave off the feelings of depression or withdrawal, until it starts wreaking havoc with other parts of your life. But how come millions of people spend every weekend railing white lines and don't get addicted?

People with lower levels of dopamine receptors in the brain find it easy to turn to chemicals or overeating (comfort food) to seek happiness, and harder to cope without them. Some of that's genetic, but it's also shaped by your surroundings. Sadistic experiments on monkeys showed that dominant monkeys, who get more attention and grooming, abuse less cocaine than sad, lonely monkeys. Take a dominant monkey and put it in isolation, on the other hand, causes it to stress and bash out more yayo to calm its frayed nerves. So does drug addiction cause misery, or do miserable lives cause addiction?

What a lot of people don't understand is, if drugs are so awful, why even do them? Is it not enough to take pleasure in life and being alive? If it's alternative states of consciousness you seek, why not try yoga or meditation? Who knows, you might achieve enlightenment.

Nisha lives in London now, but she grew up in a well-off family in India. One night, we sat together bashing out coke on her bedroom mirror. Nisha can do drugs like a fucking champ, writing out her name in white powder and sucking it up like a hoover. Even by my standards, that was a lot, but she only laughed when she saw my jaw drop.

'This is nothing,' she said. 'Once, my ex-boyfriend got me more than an ounce of cocaine as a present for my graduation. I did that all by myself in two or three days. I was so fucked up by the end of it I couldn't speak. I had so much up my nose, I physically couldn't do any more. I used to do big fat lines that I called N-lines in the shape of an N; they were half a gram by themselves. And I just did them one after another after another.'

Nisha was the biggest wreckhead of everyone I knew, and a 'bitch in heat' to use her expression. Sex and drugs were part of her identity, and there was a time when she'd be with a different man every other day of the week.

'I did a lot of crazy shit because maybe I wanted to be crazy, maybe I just had a crazy streak and I knew nothing other than that,' she reminisced. 'I remember one time I fucked two guys in one night. I met one guy, we did maybe three grams of coke together. I said I had to meet another guy. He said for what? I said sex. He was very turned on, and I could see he was touching himself. I told him to take me to his car and I sucked him off in full view. Then he dropped me off at the other guy's house who was around fifty, and I fucked him while he called me mummy.'

There's an old saying: it's all fun and games until somebody gets killed, and Nisha came close to the edge of oblivion more than a couple of times. Sometimes, she'd overdose accidently, writhing on the floor as her heart tried to rip out of her chest; sometimes on purpose, loading up on vodka and downers before having second thoughts and calling the ambulance. Then she'd indulge in other erratic, self-destructive behaviour; for example, marrying a man she met after only a month.

'He used me: physically, emotionally, sexually, every way he used me; he used to get knives out and threaten to kill me; he'd hold a knife to my throat and threaten to stab me; he used to drink every day, do coke every day,' she told me.

Nisha and her husband were both damaged goods, using liquor and narcotics to excess. It's easy to look down on addicts as hopeless losers who've messed up their lives with their insatiable thirst for pleasure, while society's paying the price. What happened to choice, and personal responsibility?

While it's debatable how much 'choice' people already hooked on drugs actually have, some might say just trying them to begin with, knowing the consequences and what might happen, is on you (just like selling them and ending up in jail is on me). That's true, but you also have to look at *why* people do the things they do.

It took a couple more rounds of the Colombian truth serum before Nisha revealed her dark secret. Back at her family home in Delhi, between the ages of six and fourteen, she was repeatedly molested and raped by someone she trusted – a family friend.

'He was a grown-up, I was a child. I was too scared to tell my parents.'

We're both lying on the carpet as she says this, staring blankly into the ceiling. I didn't know what to say. I wanted to find this man, whoever he was. I wanted to kill him. No, that's too good. Make him suffer. Make him jump off a two-storey building, so that he breaks both legs but doesn't die. You know, like that scene where Batman tosses Julia Roberts' brother off the roof. Let him know, let his family know what he's done. Then maybe, if he's not so overcome with shame that he does the right thing, let him grovel on the ground for forgiveness.

Drugs – heroin, opium, cocaine, vodka – all helped dull the memory of her stolen childhood. Trauma, especially childhood trauma, is the single biggest predictor of drug abuse in someone's personality. For sure there are people who've been through worse and come out clean the other side, I don't doubt that. But remember, bad experiences can make a person, but they can just as easily break them. If you're going to sit there and tell me that a little girl who had her childhood destroyed and went on to use heroin in order to cope is a bad person, you can fuck right off and take your fucking yoga classes with you.

And yet, Nisha's managed to succeed. Her rampant drug-taking didn't stop her from studying hard and earning a Master's in psychology on the topic of depression. She's actually done much better than most of those casual, part-time druggies I sold to at uni.

Junkies are seen as pathetic degenerates whose minds have gone to mush so all they think about is getting their next fix. But neuroscientists have proven that this simply isn't true. In the late 2000s, Dr Carl Hart invited crack smokers into his lab at Columbia University and gave them a choice between five dollars or a free hit on the pipe, fully expecting to find more evidence that crack was the Big Daddy of all drugs; try it once and that's it, game over, man! Game over! You can forget about having a job or washing the dishes, because all you'll be doing is smoking crack.

But Dr Hart found that more than half the time, the crackheads preferred taking cash. When he upped the stakes to $20 or a hit of crack (worth more than $20), almost all of them chose the money. The experiment was then repeated with methheads, and tweekers had even better impulse control than crack fiends. Clearly, even hardcore addicts can think beyond their never-ending quest to get high, to say nothing of casual users. It's entirely possible to be a drug addict and a productive member of society, much in the same way you can be a 'functioning' alcoholic. The fact that we see the latter more than the former could have something to do with us trying to lock them up all the time. We don't give addicts a chance.

The list of accomplished drug users is long. There's the Beatles, the Rolling Stones, and Lil Wayne and his cough syrup, but let's ignore the rock stars and Hollywood icons and instead note some other celebrated druggies.

William Wilberforce, the nineteenth-century philanthropist and general do-gooder who ended slavery in the British Empire, before founding both the Royal Society for the Prevention of Cruelty to Animals (RSPCA) and the West African country of Sierra Leone – smackhead. Carl Sagan, esteemed astronomer, noted pothead and author of over sixty scientific papers on the cosmos. Steve Jobs, who described tripping off acid as 'one of the two or three most important things I have done in my life'. Or how about that massive coke fiend and father of modern psychoanalysis, Sigmund motherfucking Freud? Or Barack Obama, who went from a teenage stoner to the most powerful man in the world?

Clearly, their drug use did not result in a downward spiral that must be prevented at all cost. Only a tiny proportion of drug users actually go out and commit crimes. Most of them just get high and ... that's it. In the 1980s, a study was conducted of all drug-related homicides in New York. Two per cent were robberies by junkies gone wrong; 7.5 per cent were drug-induced: someone thought they were fighting alien invaders after snorting enough coke to kill the village elephant. And over three-quarters were committed not by drug-crazed loons but by gangsters killing each other over turf; just the cost of doing business. Another, more recent study in 2017 found that users of psychedelics such as magic mushrooms and LSD were around 22 per cent *less* likely to commit violent crimes than an average person.

Even among addicts, the number of those boosting TVs and sticking up old ladies is still fairly low. They represent the extreme end of the spectrum, those who've hit rock bottom. My cousin in Russia told me about how *narkomani* (junkies) robbed and killed her neighbour in their village, then set his house on fire. Obviously, those individuals should be caught and punished, but because they are murderers, not because they're drug addicts. And who's to say they weren't already bad news? If you were a cunt before drugs, you're probably going to be a cunt after drugs as well. There aren't many drug users who've done a 180 on their personality and slipped from a straight-A student and volunteer at the local puppy shelter to a neighbour-killing arsonist after a bit of coke.

It's also important to look at the wider context in which these events occur. If addicts commit crime to pay for their habit, then logically it follows that's because drugs are expensive, and they are expensive because they are illegal. The guy who supplies them, i.e.

me, has to be compensated for risking their freedom every time they leave the fucking house.*

If you have a drug problem is prison, and spending day after day in a drab cell, really going to help? We lock them away from their families, throwing them in with a bunch of other misfits, so inevitably they feed off each other's negative energy. We give them a criminal record, which means they can't find a fucking job. Then we're surprised when they get out and go back to doing the exact same shit.

Then there's this culture of shaming. For instance, someone might be drawn to cocaine or crystal meth because it boosts their confidence, something they might not have in their everyday lives. You can't just *be* confident – either you are or you're not. Someone who got bullied in school and now enjoys a fruitful career in data entry simply isn't gonna have as much confidence as, say, Dan Bilzerian. So if you call someone who does meth a freak, is it *more* or *less* likely they're gonna clean up?

Nope. It's more likely that they'll get drawn in even deeper into the addict lifestyle. Once someone's named and shamed as a criminal degenerate – whether they be addicts, subcultures, minorities, or so forth – it becomes a self-fulfilling prophecy. You can only hear yourself being called a lowlife, a useless junkie, so many times before you start to believe it: 'You know what? Fuck you. I *will* go out and steal things!' Then, once you've been rejected by society, there's no place to go but the waiting arms of the dope-fiend community, where you can

---

* It's not just because dealers are greedy. Drug prices are governed by the laws of supply and demand, just like everything else. Try as I might, I could not pull off the hustle that Kevin Spacey's neighbour runs on him in *American Beauty* by selling him an ounce of 'top-secret' G-13 weed, supposedly developed by the US government, for $2,000. Shit, with that kind of money, the motherfucker could have booked a first-class flight to Amsterdam, taken a limo to the finest hash bar in town, before staying overnight in a five-star hotel and still have enough change left over for a Subway back home.

get high, help each other score and boost stuff together. They called you a junkie, so a junkie you became.

Since that night in her bedroom, Nisha's managed to break the cycle. She only gets high occasionally now, and has a new boyfriend with whom she's bonded over Marvel movies.

'I think now I'm in a fairly good position. I'm very grateful I got out of it. I can see how drugs can destroy people and completely change a person, and that's not what I want to be for the rest of my life. I don't need drugs, I've got me. Drugs are fun, but only for a while. You don't control the substance; the substance controls you.'

28

Jack and Torin

I was a little anxious about meeting Ray Lakeman at first. Considering my prior involvement in certain enterprises, a sense of foreboding loomed over our rendezvous, like British weather over a picnic. In all my time dealing, I'd never really faced any serious side-effects from drug use – the odds of dying from ecstasy (around 1 in 10,000) are less than those from falling off a horse. It's usually stuff like heroin people think of when they say that drugs kill: squalid junkies camping out in run-down, needle-strewn council flats, 'getting what's coming to them'.

But I couldn't relate to that – I never messed with smack – and that's why I wanted to meet Ray. Our rendezvous was set up by Anyone's Child, a group of grieving parents who've lost their children to drugs, gang violence and more. I spent a few minutes mulling outside the dockside café in Bristol, getting into character. But I needn't have worried, as Ray, a former teacher, was more than happy to talk to me, a former dealer, about his sons Jacques (Jack) and Torin.

'When they were about nine or ten, my wife or I would drive them to drama lessons and the only thing we had in the car was the comedian Tony Hancock,' Ray recalled over a cup of coffee. 'They absolutely loved Tony Hancock, and it's quite bizarre because he was quite big in the sixties and most of their peers had never heard of him, but we'd play the tapes constantly. We used to have every one of his series on cassette, even the TV specials, because you didn't actually have to see him.'

Growing up on the Isle of Man in the Irish Sea, the boys were incredibly close. Born just fifteen months apart, they went through various phases together.

'Jacques had fads when he was little. He wanted to be a wizard, and then he got into *Grease* and wanted to be John Travolta, so he got a leather jacket, and Torin got a leather jacket. Then it was spaghetti westerns and he got a hat and poncho, so Torin got a hat and poncho. They had separate bedrooms but Torin never slept in his; he preferred the futon at the bottom of Jacques' bed.'

They'd been a funny pair, the boys. Torin had small handwriting at school, so tiny that the teachers couldn't decipher it. And each time his teachers complained, his handwriting got smaller. It got to the point where, every time Torin wrote an essay, Ray had to blow it up and photocopy it to make the letters bigger.

Jacques was also a talented musician and guitarist, and Ray took him to open-mic nights around the island. But as he got older, the troubles began. He started experimenting with drink and drugs. One night he just collapsed on the kitchen floor and Torin, his younger brother, berated him, calling him every name under the sun. The Lakemans got rid of all the liquor in the house.

In 2014, Jacques moved to London to live with Ray's mum, while Torin went to Aberystwyth University in Wales to study astrophysics. It was the first time they'd been apart for any period of time. Torin was nineteen, Jacques was twenty. The months went by, and Jacques called to say he'd be working and couldn't make it home for Christmas, but he had tickets to a Manchester United game. His mate pulled out at the last minute, meaning that Torin could come instead. The game was on the Saturday, so they'd meet up in Manchester and then come back home on Sunday. At least, that was the plan.

'I rang my mother as I usually do on a Sunday and she was already worried because it was already half past six and they'd always go to the pub quiz at five. It wasn't like Jacques to let her down. I tried to ring and got through to Torin's voicemail. Half past ten, and Jacques still hadn't arrived, Torin still wasn't answering and we were getting seriously concerned.'

Ray called the Manchester police to see if they'd been arrested at the match – boys will be boys, after all – but no answers. He then tried ringing round the local hospitals, but no joy there either.

'The police told me they'd probably met some girls and stayed over for a bit, but we knew from instinct this isn't the way they would have behaved. You know your own kids! The next day we reported them missing and started calling round hotels. Someone answered that Jacques made a booking and paid in advance but hadn't turned up. This confused us even more. Were they even in Manchester? Did they even go to the football? Because I helped book the tickets, I called to confirm if the seats had been occupied. The guy told me, "Give me a minute, I need to redirect you."

'I got put through to the legal department and ran through the scenario again; this time the guy gave me the number of a police officer I could ring for some more information, which of course I did. But when I rang, I was told they were in a conference and would call me back. Then we got a knock on the door from two police officers. My wife asked them if they'd come to tell us what we already knew.'

The two brothers had been found dead that Sunday afternoon in a room over a pub. They'd taken six times the lethal dose of ecstasy. It turned out it was Torin, the more straight-edged one, who'd ordered the drugs from an encrypted site on the Internet, the 'Dark Web'.

'It's the sort of thing that would intrigue him, that undercover thrill. That and also people were using drugs at university. Talking to his friends, it's obvious he liked the effects. It made him feel happy.'

No parent should have to bury their child. I'm old enough to remember the Leah Betts case in the nineties, when the eighteen-year-old's parents allowed pictures of her dying in a hospital bed to be printed in the media to warn about the dangers of ecstasy (she'd actually died of drinking too much water – something easily preventable if the proper precautions were in place). But despite losing both his sons in one night, Ray takes the opposite view.

'We have a law. If that law doesn't work at stopping people doing things, that law is useless,' he said. 'Torin's death hasn't stopped his friends at uni taking drugs. They just think he was unlucky. And he *was* unlucky. If people are going to keep taking drugs, all you can do is make it safer. So, if people like [drug-testing group] The Loop are doing what they're doing, that can only be a good thing.'

All right, now it's time for the big question. Although I personally don't feel like a merchant of death, Ray might not feel the same way. There's always that one in ten thousand. Three years later after that fateful night, the law caught up with the online entrepreneur who sold them the X, slapping him with sixteen years in jail. Cautiously, I asked Ray what he made of that.

'The way I look at it, he's just a businessman. It's not as though he approached them on the street and forced drugs on my sons. They approached *him*. They looked *him* up and said *that's* the product we want. So from that point of view, the only thing he did wrong was not make it absolutely clear what his product was. There's no quality control. He sent out a packet of MDMA that was probably enough for thirty doses. He didn't know they were going to take it all in one go, and they didn't know how much they were meant to be taking.'

I felt myself gently unwind. Ray doesn't blame the dealer. Well, maybe he does, but not as much as he blames the system. It's the system – the laws which create the black market – that keeps every-one in the dark: what they're buying, what they're selling.

The chemistry drop-outs churning out pills in secret underground labs don't exactly follow the same rigid health-and-safety standards as Boots, who'd get sued into poverty if someone died using their product. By the time you're getting it from someone calling themselves Candyman ('Call me if you need anything, yeah?'), it's been passed through so many hands no one has any idea what the actual dosage is. Imagine if every time you took a swig from a bottle, you were taking a gamble on it being anywhere between a normal beer (about 4 per cent) or absinthe (up to 80 per cent). That's how people die.

Then there's whatever other random shit the dealer happens to throw together in his kitchen. I amateurishly used to mix ground-up paracetamol (that shit *destroys* your nose) and then dental powder (for the numbness) into my coke to pass one gram off as one and a half, before I realised I could stop tainting a perfectly good batch and just charge people extra for the better stuff. It got to the stage where, in court, the prosecutor claimed my charlie was 80 per cent pure, at which point my housemate turned to his friend and whispered, 'You can accuse Niko of a lot of things, but you can't accuse him of selling good coke.'

The Loop is the only organisation that carries out drug testing at music festivals in the UK, where you can take a break from partying to walk over to their tent and have a sample run through their specialist equipment to check whether those Es you bought are genuine, pharmaceutical-grade ecstasy, vitamin tablets or some next-level wizardry that will leave you twitching and vomiting in a puddle of your own shit. Normally, people very rarely die from ecstasy if they take the proper precautions, like drinking plenty of (but not too much) water. A lot of the time when someone suffers an overdose it's from taking PMA, not MDMA, which unlike MDMA genuinely is risky business. The cooks make PMA when they can't get what they need for the real thing. Of course the police would probably chalk this up as a success, because they've managed to 'disrupt the supply', but what they've really done is help poison everyone by being dicks.

In the past, The Loop's team has found drugs containing insecticide, malaria pills and even concrete. Once they find their sample has something dodgy about it, most people throw the rest away. No one gets in trouble, and in fact the scheme has won the support of several local police forces, who issue a joint, public warning with The Loop if there's a bad batch going around. After The Loop pitched their tent at one festival in Cambridgeshire in 2016, hospital admissions dropped *95 per cent* (from 19 to 1) from the previous year it was held. Checking if your coke has worm-killer in it makes you less likely to wind up in hospital. Who knew?

Even now, there are some who complain that this is 'normalising' drug use. But what if it happens to your kids? If one of them made a mistake, would you be happy about them overdosing in a corner, or going to jail? Oh, I know it won't happen to *your* kids, but hey, I was a professor's son and look where I ended up. So why should it be OK for anyone's child?

At their sons' funeral, the Lakemans played a tape of Tony Hancock, their favourite comedian.

'If I lost only one son, it's just another statistic. But I find myself talking to journalists, and in another context I would be talking about them for a whole different reason because they would have achieved things,' said Ray, fighting back tears. 'And I want to talk about them because they deserve to be talked about. They don't deserve to be just a statistic.'

29

Treasure Hunting

It's like logging onto eBay. We fired up the browser to start browsing the catalogue – Afghan heroin, Peruvian premium, DMT, 2-CB, PCP, and of course sticky nugs of Big Green Buddha – all handily broken into categories and so lovingly photographed you could see every crystal. I was like a drug-addled kid in a candy store.

'Great stuff, bro,' wrote one happy customer. 'I haven't had my face numb like that since I had a stroke.'

We were on HYDRA, the Russian Internet's Amazon of Drugs.

In 2016, I moved to Moscow after landing a gig at Russian media outlet RT. It was the first 'real' job I'd had since getting out. Since coming from the UK, I had quite a culture shock. First of all, the customer service – it doesn't exist. Like, at all. In Britain, the customer is always right and their happiness is a matter of priority: 'Good afternoon, sir! How may I help you, sir?' But Russian shopkeepers will look at you through their cold, dead eyes and say, 'Take cigarettes, take vodka, and get fuck out of here.' People say it's because they're not paid much, but you think the staff manning the tills at Tesco's are millionaires?

But HYDRA stands out for its customer service. The admins do quality checks of the product themselves, posting their results on the site's forums. There's even a clinical service through which you can get expert dosage and safety advice. The advice given on HYDRA is more practical than Just Say No. Scare tactics don't work: once you survive smoking your first joint, you might suspect everything else you've been taught is bullshit too.

Since I have the technical proficiency of a toothbrush, I have barely any idea how to turn on an Xbox, let alone work any of this. Luckily, Katya, a hot twenty-two-year-old student from Moscow State University and fellow narcotics connoisseur, does and orders 10 grams of high-grade Buddha through her boyfriend's account.

But there was a catch. We had to go get it.

Jack and Torin bought their drugs over the Dark Web, a part of the Internet only accessible through a special browser that hides your location from any nosy authorities. TOR, The Onion Router, was originally developed by the US Navy in the late 1990s to hide their online spying activities, but has since been released to the public to be used by anyone who doesn't want to be found: activists, whistle-blowers, paedophiles, drug dealers and paranoid survivalist types prepping for the end days. It's called The Onion Router because, like ogres, it has layers. Your online address gets randomly routed through several of these layers, or servers, around the world, so you might be browsing at home in Shropshire but to anyone tracking your physical address, you're somewhere in Algeria.

While shopping for forbidden wares online might seem like a new craze, it's actually been around since before the Web as we know it existed. Students from MIT used ARPANET, a kind of proto-Internet linking several universities across the United States in the early 1970s, to buy a bag of weed from their buddies at Stanford. It was the first thing bought and sold over the Internet.

But it was TOR that revolutionised the drug trade in the early 2010s. In 2011, a mysterious rogue calling himself 'Dread Pirate Roberts' (after the swashbuckling hero in *The Princess Bride*) set up Silk Road. The site was named after the trade route that once connected ancient China to the Mediterranean, but the goods were entirely different.

Roberts was a straight-up libertarian; he wanted to create a space where buyers and sellers could do business in peace, far from the watchful eye of Big Brother. And it worked. You could log in through TOR and browse a catalogue of any and all psychotropic substances you could imagine: China White, Peruvian flake, LSD, DMT, PCP ... anything and everything was available and at the highest quality. There was no more risk of getting ripped off or jacked by a mean-looking dude in a back alley; no more drive-by shootings for a piece of turf. The worst you'd get is a nasty email.

Before, when you got ripped off, you'd have nowhere to turn: 'Hey uh, that coke you sold us tasted like sherbet.' 'Well, you got a receipt, motherfucker?' Here, anyone caught selling crushed-up vitamin pills as Peruvian flake would face the wrath of the eBay-style customer review system, so all the shit-peddlers were taken out of circulation and you'd only be left with the good stuff.

The goods would arrive right on your doorstep. You'd think that mail is routinely checked with scanners and sniffer dogs, but with thousands, if not millions, of parcels posted each day, the chances of something getting through are high. If caught, you could always claim ignorance: 'I'm outraged that someone is trying to send me these drugs!'

Since bank transfers, Western Union and most other payment systems leave a paper trail, Silk Road merchants used Bitcoin, an online crypto-currency that, like cash, isn't linked to anyone's real-life identity. Of course it's possible to track down which exact bitcoins were involved in drug deals, but you can launder them through an online 'tumbler', which mixes your dirty bitcoins with clean ones and leaves the trail cold. DPR was earning millions in commission from the transactions done on his site.

But by 2012, Dread Pirate Roberts suspected that one of his underlings, Chronicpain, a Mormon from Utah, was working with the Feds and had made off with $350,000 in bitcoins. He asked another user on the site, a Dominican cartel member known as Nob, to have Chronicpain whacked.

Little did he know that Nob was actually undercover DEA agent Carl Force, part of a joint inter-agency operation against Silk Road. Chronicpain was indeed working with the Feds, having been set up in a real-world sting by Force. The pair acted out Chronicpain's murder and sent Roberts photos as proof of the deed. DPR might have gone too far . . . his idealistic stance against the war on drugs led to him ordering a hit, just like a real crime boss. But neither Force nor Chronicpain knew who he was.

All it took, though, was one dumb move for everything to come crashing down. After hours browsing the web, another federal agent with too much time on his hands found a forum post that Roberts had made using an email address under his real name – rossulbricht@ gmail.com – asking how to run an online black market using Bitcoin. Inconceivable! Ross Ulbricht, a young American entrepreneur living in San Francisco, was put under surveillance and arrested in October 2013. Undercover agents pounced on him as he sat working on Silk Road in a public library; they snatched away his laptop before he could shut it and lock valuable files of evidence.

In May 2015, Ulbricht was sentenced to life imprisonment without parole for drug trafficking, money laundering and computer hacking, although he escaped the murder charge. Life without parole. Even Charles Manson got a hearing every once in a while. The judge who put him away told him he was no more than a common drug dealer, which he was anything but. He was a pioneer who made a nasty, criminal business that little bit safer and more honest for everyone.

There's one more twist in the Silk Road story. Carl Force, the DEA agent who busted Chronicpain, was arrested and pleaded guilty to money laundering, obstruction of justice and extortion. It turned out he was behind a series of rackets on Silk Road, including selling Ulbricht information and being behind the $350,000 Bitcoin heist that put Chronicpain in hot water. He's now serving a six-and-a-half-year sentence.

But while the world's largest online drugs bazaar might have been shut down, cyber-junkies didn't have to wait long to get their next fix.

Ross Ulbricht was the original gangsta of the cyber-dopeworld, but he wouldn't be the last. Six thousand miles away, RAMP, the Russian Anonymous Marketplace, saw a gap in the market dominated by dirty cops and tracksuit-wearing hooligans. This wasn't your papa's *baryga*. Inspired by Silk Road, RAMP nevertheless steered clear of the libertarian politics that defined Dread Pirate Roberts. Perhaps that's why it lasted longer in Russia's opinion-hostile but cybercrime-friendly environment – RAMP stayed online for a good five years before being shut down in 2017. But by that point, Moscow's meth-heads and Petersburg's potheads had already migrated to another platform: HYDRA.

Silk Road delivered right to your doorstep, but in Russia, it's a little different. Getting a package delivered in Russia means filling out more paperwork than a Tolstoy novel, so instead of having the drugs sent to your door the sellers give you the location of a dead drop somewhere in the woods, sending you on a little Easter Egg hunt. And so me, Katya, her boy-toy Slava and another friend, Vanya, set off on our quest to find the magic potion, not a level-five paladin with healing spells among us.

It was a sunny morning, and the streets outside were littered with autumn leaves. I was still a little groggy from the night before. We'd been at a party, and all I could remember was dancing with a pair of bald strippers wearing Bane masks who might possibly have been twins. As we were walking to the bus stop, I noticed Vanya was wearing a green bobble hat with the word *Amsterdam*.

'Are you trying to attract attention?' cried Katya. 'Why don't you carry a pair of shovels while you're at it?'

After a long ride through the underground (most things in Moscow are shittier than London, but I've gotta give a shout-out to our gorgeous Metro and its free Wi-Fi), we arrived at the Kolomenskoye Park, south-east Moscow. A royal estate from Tsarist times, this park, and especially the ravine that runs through it, is well known, according to legend, for mysterious happenings. Rumours speak of travellers getting shrouded in a deep green fog, emerging only to find that decades have passed. Maybe it has something to do with Veles, the ancient Slavic trickster god whose sacred stones lie in a pagan shrine between the running streams and woodland groves at the bottom of the valley.

There were many people walking through the park – old ladies with their dogs, families with their children. I wondered how many more were here looking for a stash? All of them, perhaps, with each of us eyeing the other like we were in some Orwellian nightmare. *No, no, guys, we're just here for the sacred stones.* As our party of adventurers climbed a steep wooded hill, it started to rain. The sun's yellow rays still shone brightly through the raindrops.

Slava stopped on top of the hill to check his GPS. Yup, we were there. The buried treasure should be two centimetres below the ground by the tree to our right. We rolled up our sleeves, got on our knees and started digging. It's always best to do these things during the day – who the fuck goes digging holes in the park at three in the morning? Then again, I thought about how we must look: a group of drugged-up fiends in the throes of narcomania frantically clawing through the dirt like a pack of wild hogs. Any cop who walked past would instantly know what we were up to, although it's always possible to come to an 'arrangement'. Meanwhile, Katya stood guard by the footpath taking selfies to distract passers-by. Our treasure hunt had turned into a photoshoot.

Vanya stood up and pulled a dead branch off a tree, using it as a shovel and tossing aside a load of dark earth to reveal a lump of aluminium foil. Is that it? Nope, just someone's rubbish. Oh, look, a small white bundle of sticky tape wrapped around a sachet. Inside was a packet of densely packed kush smelling like Snoop Dogg's greenhouse.

Vanya hastily slipped the loot into his pocket and we headed down to a restaurant, where we had a private booth. There, we ripped a homemade bong, and the whole room filled with smoke.

The image of the typical drug user is the crackhead, the junkie or the tweeker. But in all my years of dealing, not one of my customers came crawling to me in rags trying to pawn off their mother's jewellery for one more dose of the sweet stuff. Not one. You could argue, as my probation officer has, that because I hadn't seen much of the damage this stuff can do first-hand it made me blind to what I was unleashing on the community. But, naturally, as a probation officer he had to deal with the shitstains of society on an everyday basis, whereas as a purveyor of these forbidden goods I had access to a much wider demographic. And my experience has to count for something, right?

But he had a point. I couldn't sling grams to London yuppies and brag about it like I'm some kind of middle-class Che Guevara, then chat shit as if I knew what the hellish, day-to-day life of an addict was all about. After all, that's why we're fighting, right? It was time to actually go see for myself what's going on in the capitals of Eastern Europe.

While America was busy locking up black people and China was putting everyone who didn't worship Mao on Death Row, the Soviet Union largely sat things out. We had our own vices, namely alcoholism. Vodka was the Party-approved ailment of choice. The government controlled the liquor stores and kept the prices low. It was one of the ways to keep the dysfunctional socialist economy afloat. Low prices kept the people constantly wasted, which sounds like fun until you realise that heavy drinking has given Russia the highest rate of alcoholism in the world and the lowest life expectancy in Europe (sixty-five for men). For a long time, beer wasn't even considered alcoholic.

Other drugs weren't really a problem. A few people planted poppies at their *dacha* and there were wild tracts of weed growing in Kazakhstan's fabled Chui Valley, but it was a really niche activity because the Soviet Union was a police state. It *is* possible to keep drugs at bay through mass repression.

That all changed in the 1980s. Soldiers coming back from Afghanistan got a taste for opium, which seeped from Red Army conscripts to the rest of the country. After the collapse of communism, drug addiction swept across the country, riding the wave of hopelessness and poverty that followed as the former superpower plunged into social, political and economic meltdown.

It's impossible to talk about the history of modern Russia without mentioning that lawless period of free-for-all mayhem that was the 1990s. During the chaotic switchover from communism, the country took a sensational nosedive into a big, steaming pile of shit. Russia, which only decades before had sent the first man into space, now had old ladies queuing up for a ration of bread. Chechens were rebelling in the south; communist hardliners went rogue and tried to restart the Cold War, with tanks rolling through the streets of Moscow for the first time since the Second World War; and ordinary people didn't know when their wages were gonna come, if they would come at all.

Russia is now the single biggest consumer of heroin on the planet.

In the autumn of 2016 I moved back to Russia after somehow landing a gig typing out stories in RT's newsroom. I'm proud of the work we did there, presenting an alternative point of view to Western media. Although I have some reservations about what we printed, it taught me a lot about sources, journalism and working in the media.

At the time, I was living in a crappy Soviet communal-style flat with three adults, six kids and two cats. I wanted to get the fuck out of there as much as possible, so on one freezing November night I found myself standing around in the grim Soviet housing projects on the south-eastern outskirts of Moscow with Maxim Malyshev and Lena Remneva, two outreach workers with the Andrey Rylkov Foundation. The Foundation is one of the only charities that works with drug users and HIV-positive people in Russia without passing judgement or chasing them into detox. Max is pretty normal-looking, but he used to be an addict. Every night, Max and the volunteers stand around handing out information leaflets and medical supplies such as naloxone (a lifesaving remedy that can bring you back after an overdose, as if by magic).

It was only around minus five degrees, but it sure felt a lot colder, even with my patriotic hammer-and-sickle *ushanka*. You could see your breath. We stood outside a twenty-four-hour pharmacy while people came up to us to get their goodie bags.

'Nice hat,' one of them said, before turning to the volunteers and telling them about his upcoming court case. The cops got him on charges of selling speed and were getting another tweeker to turn witness. That's common in drug cases – the Feds find someone who's busted and get them to squeal, or sometimes they plant drugs to help their case. More often than not, they're trying to get a bribe. Rich people don't go to jail in Russia.

As time went on, more people came up to us. Sasha did heroin in playgrounds with his best friend back in the 1990s. Now his friend's dead, and he only takes *vint* ('vitamins' – meth). Abdullah from Dagestan was homeless, and had spent some time in a German prison. Someone else told us about their pet chinchilla.

Not everyone was stereotypically junkie-looking. One of them was even plump, bearded and jolly, like a smack-addled Santa. But with others, whether it was drug abuse or simply an unhealthy lifestyle, something had definitely taken its toll. So why did so many of them look like extras from *Night of the Living Dead*?

'Well, first, when they become addicts, they believe they don't have a future,' Max, a former drug user himself, explained. 'You and me, we have plans for the next few years. Go somewhere, earn some money, learn another language, buy an apartment. But that stuff goes to the back of their minds. Looking after themselves is no longer a priority when they have so many other things to deal with: the cops, someone trying to rip them off, where they'll get money from. And then it's the physical factors – opiates and stimulants wear your body down.'

A man came up to us high as a kite, coughing and sputtering. Max jumped back. The man had just been kicked out of rehab for breaking the rules, and had tuberculosis.

'OK, here's our number; call us and we'll help you,' said Max. 'But wear a mask, for fuck's sake!'

Max is jumpy because he's HIV-positive, so any infection, like TB, could be fatal. Back at the office, he told me how it all happened. In the late 1990s, Max was living in Tver, north-west of Moscow.

'I never really liked drinking, but then I tried weed and I felt relaxed, this is for me,' he said. 'To this day, I don't drink. Maybe I'll have a glass of champagne, but that's it!'

Max and his friends would go to this gypsy (Roma) neighbourhood to smoke weed and make fun of all the 'real' druggies passed out. Then one of his friends went to study in Moscow and there were some Africans from Patrice Lumumba University who were selling heroin. At first, he didn't like it, he didn't like what it was doing to people, but when he tried it, he found it gave him 'inner peace'. For the next fifteen years, Max was a full-time smackhead.

'Everything revolved around this gypsy neighbourhood,' he continued. 'Every morning I'd wake up, get some money – maybe I stole something, maybe I tricked someone – and I went to the gypsy neighbourhood. And that was the whole day.'

Every time he went to the gypsy settlement, it was like a quest, constantly scrounging for money and dodging the cops. He wasn't always lucky. One time, he headed over and it was dry; no one was selling apart from this one house where a huge queue was forming outside. Everyone was shoving money through the window as the gypsies were packing up doses. Max met some friends and asked them where they could shoot up.

'Let's do it behind the house,' one of them said.

'OK, do you have water?'

'Yeah, and I have some spoons with me.'*

So they got behind the house and Max started cooking it on his spoon, getting the needle ready, when suddenly two guys in tracksuits came round the corner and stuck a gun in his face. Max, thinking they were some local hoodlums trying to rip them off, tried to wave them away.

'I was trying to work with the spoon so I told him to fuck off, waving the pistol away from my face, and he's like "what the fuck" and I'm like "fuck your mother!"'

This exchange of expletives went on until the cop grabbed his spoon and threw it on the ground.

---

* Heroin's a powder, so to inject it you need to mix it with water and boil it on a spoon.

'That was my second conviction,' he laughed. 'Another time, some cops picked me up and they saw I had a spoon, some money, but no drugs. They sat me in the back of their car and said, "What are we going to do with you? How about we just take the money and let you go?" And I said, "No way, I hustled all DAY for this money; I'm not giving it to you." And they said, "Come on, are we really gonna drive around all day?" So we drove around all day and I outlasted them. They turned to me and said, "Fuck it, get outta here."'

Like their American colleagues, Russian police use arrest figures as a sign of how well they're doing their job. Russian cops will plant evidence to bump up their stats, or extort bribes, or threaten and beat suspects to force out confessions. Anything over seven grams of cannabis or a half-gram of heroin is a 'significant amount' for which you can get fifteen years, the same penalty as murder. It's even said that some officers possess otherworldly powers to double or triple what they find in your pocket to attain this magic number (unfortunately, they've been unwilling to share this secret with the rest of us). Although ostensibly they've got to search you in front of witnesses, those can be rookie cops or their drinking buddies. And if you're arrested together with your friends, you can be charged with organised crime, allowing the officers to round up a group of potheads and claim they've smashed the Medellín Cartel.

America might be the incarceration nation, but in Russia our police state is different; it's more a leftover of the Soviet era. Nearly a third of Russia's prison population are there for drugs. Having spent the last few years in the belly of the beast, they'll come out useless and unemployable, immersed in jailhouse culture like the thieves-in-law (Russia's homegrown prison Mafia). So it's no surprise there's an 85 per cent recidivism rate. Russia's huge prison population means that diseases like TB spread quickly as well.

In 1997, Max was driving back from uni when a policeman pulled him over and found some doobies in his cassette case. He got booked and sent to see a doctor, and when they tested him for HIV, the results came back positive.

'We weren't really watching our needles in those days,' he said. 'That's it, I thought, I've only got two to three years more to live because, back then, there was little knowledge or treatment available. I couldn't accept it for a while, so I wouldn't tell anyone. My dream was to make it to the new millennium, see what it's like.'

But Max did survive, and taking a pill every day kept the HIV from turning into full-blown AIDS. He started working in harm reduction, handing out needles to fellow addicts, while going in and out of rehab. He finally kicked the habit after police tried getting him to squeal on his buddies.

'I went for rehab because the pigs had really got to me, they wanted me to give up some dealer. We were working with some Tajiks who were bringing in 10 grams, 100 grams. So I knew this wasn't going anywhere good. The second reason was they suddenly took off and left me with 5 grams, and I'd already ticked off everyone else. And the third reason was I fell in love with a girl, another junkie, and that gave me the illusion everything would be OK. And this all came together.'

These days, Max works at the Andrey Rylkov Foundation and helps organise Positive Moments, a project in which they give clients a camera and get them to take pictures.

'It's usually something simple like a cat, or a ray of sunshine. We have two goals. The first is that drug users themselves realise . . . when you're caught up in this cycle, it's very easy to think "Why bother? Everything's out of my control anyway." The second is to set up an exhibition and show people that drug users have the same moments of positivity as everyone else.'

The US always gets the blame for its racist war on drugs (as it should), but other countries also realised they had their own pesky minorities they needed to supress. In Australia, the Aboriginals Protection and Restriction of the Sale of Opium Act 1897 treated Aborigines as though they were incapable of making their own decisions and had to be shielded from the malign influence of civilisation, which meant in practice that their white 'protectors' had a free hand to take away their rights. In pre-war Europe, the Jews were said to be behind the narcotics trade. And in 1919, years before Harry Anslinger caught a whiff of reefer madness, the Egyptian ambassador to the League of Nations (a kind of proto-UN) claimed that Cairo's madhouses were filling up with ganja-crazed lunatics (in reality, only 2.6 per cent of patients at the Abbasiya Asylum in Cairo between 1920 and 1921 were pot smokers, while 48 per cent were winos and alkies).

People are fine with America-bashing until I tell them to look at their own country; then they tell me I shouldn't lecture them because I don't know what's going on. They may have a point. So I bought a few plane tickets, did my research, went over there and talked to some people. So eat my shorts.

Part 7

The New Guard

30

Just Say *Nyet!*

Ghosts. The cemetery was deadly quiet, with only the far-off sound of a woodpecker breaking the silence, and even though the snow was starting to melt it was still chilly enough to see my breath. It wasn't quite Humaya, but here in Yekaterinburg, on the frontier between Europe and Asia, lay another kind of gangster graveyard.

Their gravestones stand tall above the rest. Dima, Misha, Vova – here lie some of the *bratki* who died fighting for a slice of the capitalist pie back in the wild old days of the roaring 1990s. Etched on their large black tombstones are life-size engravings of young men, many in their early twenties, dressed in tracksuits and leather jackets (the pinnacle of gangster fashion), standing like spectres between the trees. They were members of the Uralmash crime family, one of the city's three main gangs who fought a bitter war in the 1990s in which Uralmash came out on top. Several of these guys died in the same shootout. Further along the path, under close surveillance, stand three busts, the heads of the Uralmash crime family. They used to be the kings of this city. Now they're just ghosts.

Four hundred and fifty miles to the west lies Kazan, a city on the banks of the River Volga. A former Tatar khanate conquered by Ivan the Terrible, it sits at the crossroads of European and Asiatic civilisation, evenly split between Russians and Tatars. In the 1980s, a moral panic erupted in Soviet newspapers about gangs of feral youth running wild through its housing projects.

'It was a completely different country then. We had this ideology of fighting for your patch, and then we started getting money,' said Sergey, a former racketeer and a veteran of the 1990s street wars. 'There were around a hundred and fifty crews in those days, not counting the ethnic ones. Almost every street had one. Zhilka, Pervaki, Gryaz ... You could write a whole book about the Kazan gang wars.'

The first major gang in Kazan was Tiap-Liap, which started out as a street-fighting alliance and moved on to shaking down black marketeers. During the communist era, there was a thriving business in contraband goods. Jeans were wildly popular – my mum used to smuggle them back from Poland. But everything changed in 1988 when the first laws were passed allowing private business. Suddenly, everyone seemed to be doing something that could get you a nice long spell in Siberia not too long ago ... and all the victims were out in the open. The courts didn't know what a contract was or how to enforce it. The police were were too underfunded, stretched out too thinly, and had no idea what to do to be of any help. No one knew what the fuck was going on. Meanwhile, crime shot up as honest shopkeepers found themselves at the mercy of robbers, thieves and hooligans.

Since the law couldn't protect you, you had to look outside it. You had to get a 'roof', or a *krysha*. *Krysha* is Russian slang for 'protection', as in you hand over X amount of money each month to a corrupt politician, your old-school buddy who joined the police, a private security firm or the racketeering organisation of your choice in order to avoid having problems. If you failed to keep your end of the bargain, you'd risk having an accident, like having your stocks spontaneously combust. In Russia, it doesn't pay to be clumsy.

In 1978, Tiap-Liap rolled up to a rival gang's turf in a show of force and started blasting fools at random, killing a seventy-five-year-old war veteran. The Soviet authorities quashed them with an iron fist, but more gangs had emerged.

'When I was young, all the lads were in a gang,' Sergey explained. 'In my class, thirteen out of sixteen guys were in a gang. Kazan's always had a lot of gangs, but in the 1970s there were only twenty or so. By 1990 it was over a hundred, and that's when we started getting weapons.'

When he was fourteen, Sergey served his first jail term for murder.

'You understand, if a guy from another street wants to cave your head in with a brick, you gotta do it first,' he shrugged.

By the time he got out, the Soviet Union had fallen, and his group had taken control of a local market and was exacting tributes from merchants and drug dealers alike.

'No one saw it as a criminal career, but around the 1990s everyone thought about how to make some money out of it and monetise their position. So we started putting the squeeze on merchants, taxi drivers. It wasn't hard – they all came to us. Everyone wanted a roof. There was hardly any police in those days,' Sergey recalled. 'Around that time, the dealers showed up and we taxed them as well. If they didn't pay up, we broke their legs.'

The stakes were higher as well. Before, they fought with sticks and stones; now, when there was a business dispute, out came the automatics. Sergey's gang, Kaluga, fought it out with several larger outfits.

'I remember once we fought with Pervaki, running around throwing Molotovs and setting their cars on fire. It was like Stalingrad. We also fought with Zhilka ... many, many bodies,' Sergey remembered. 'One time, I was living on the first-floor apartment reading a book when someone fired a shot through my window. I just happened to lean down at that moment, and the bullet whizzed right over my head and took out half my window. That's when I had to skip town.'

The biggest mob at the time was Hadi Taqtaş, formed on a street named after a famous Tatar poet. Led by Radik 'Raja' Galiakberov, who liked to quote Marlon Brando in *The Godfather*, the gang was extremely violent, even by 1990s standards. One of their victims was dismembered with an axe after Raja told them to make him the Venus de Milo, the famously armless Greek statue.

'We had a war with them; they threw a Molotov cocktail at my friend. Burnt him all over,' said Sergey. 'But they were some real psychos. And they killed all their elders. By that time, it was mainly narco-business. That's why their war started with Pervaki. They took something like 200 grams of coke and didn't pay. But all the stories about them, that they wanted to kill the president of Tatarstan, that's all bullshit. They didn't have that kind of power. All those documentaries made them into monsters.'

There was only so much money, though, to be made in Kazan, so the mobs made their way to my hometown, St Petersburg, where they ran afoul of local godfather Vladimir Kumarin, who earned the nickname 'the Night Governor' by ruling over the northern capital's bars, nightclubs and protection rackets as the boss, or *avtoritet*, of the Tambov gang. In 1994, Kumarin's arm got blown off in an assassination attempt. Eager to prevent further appendage loss, Kumarin decided to go legit and in 1998 became the vice-president of the Petersburg Fuel Company, awarded exclusive rights to the city by the then-deputy mayor, Vladimir Putin.

Meanwhile, over in Moscow, a few goons approached car dealer Boris Berezovsky.* They were from the Solntsevo Brotherhood, a gang of toughs known for scaring the borsch out of terrified merchants. It's a dangerous world out there, they said; an entrepreneur like yourself could use some protection. But there was a problem: he already had a roof with the Chechens.

---

* He'd later become an oligarch, the man behind the throne of President Yeltsin, and had basically the whole country in his pocket before Putin kicked him out.

The Chechen Mafia were fast emerging as the most ruthless motherfuckers in the city. Their leader, Khozh-Ahmed Noukhayev, was more than just a gangster; he was also a patriot and great supporter of the Chechen cause. Chechens had been itching for independence ever since they'd been conquered by the Russians hundreds of years ago. They were also known for their shoot-first-ask-questions-later style of negotiating, and so the sit-down between Solntsevo and the Chechens at the Kazakhstan Cinema resulted in ten deaths – six Chechens and four Russians. It was time for payback, revenge-style.

To do this, the Solntsevo enlisted the help of the *vory-v-zakone*, or thieves-in-law, the closest the Soviet Union had to the Mafia. A thief-in-law is kind of an arbitrator, a mediator in criminal disputes. Say you and your boys just held up a bank but Joey Four-Fingers demands a bigger cut of the loot. Who do you call? It's not like you can take him to court for breaching his contract. That's where the *vory* comes in. Emerging from Stalin's gulags in the 1930s – prison camps only a touch better than the concentration camps of Nazi Germany – the *vory* turned thug life into an ideology, constantly defying prison authorities and living purely off criminal proceeds. The most hardcore thieves hailed from Georgia, a small land on the mountainous Black Sea coast between Russia and Turkey – during the civil war of the 1990s, the most powerful armed group was the Mkhedrioni, who answered to a thief-in-law called Jaba Ioseliani and came damn close to taking over the country. The *vory* also iden-tified themselves through their tattoos, an elaborate system of ink that could be used to read your life story like a book. For example, stars on your knees meant you'll never kneel before authority.

But it was their pals in the KGB, not a bunch of tattooed ex-cons, that won the day. Russia's infamous spy agency (now called the FSB but operating more or less the same way) was growing worried about Noukhayev's links to guerrilla leader Dzhokhar Dudayev. Noukhayev and Dudayev were tight, so tight that Dudayev even helped organise his jailbreak in 1991. So the FSB and the Brotherhood joined forces to chase the southern upstarts out of town, the gangsters taking care of business when the Feds couldn't get their hands dirty. It was the beginning of a beautiful friendship. At the same time, some agents of the police, FSB and other divisions started doing private work on the side, running protection rackets. The state–Mafia merger had begun.

For the first time in my life I was scared of flying. I don't know why – maybe it was because I was on-shift when the Saratov airline went down earlier that year, or maybe because I kept hearing the engines cut out as if the pilot had taken his foot off the gas – but for three butt-clenching hours I kept picturing my fiery death over the frozen wastes below. I was on my way to meet Evgeny Roizman, Russia's vigilante king. To his fans, he's the Russian Robin Hood standing up to the rotten establishment. To others, he's a thug who kidnaps people and holds them in a barn. All I can say is, he's an interesting character.

After that terrifying plane ride, I landed in Yekaterinburg and made my way to the Nevyansk Icon Museum, Roizman's collection of Orthodox paintings. Oh, did I mention he's an art collector? And a champion rally car driver? At the age of fourteen, he left home and wandered the USSR. Roizman, whose father is Jewish, went around in a Star of David T-shirt to troll anti-Semites. In 1981, the young troublemaker served a short stint in jail for theft, fraud and weapons charges.

'Prison plays an important part in the Russian psyche,' Roizman said as we sat surrounded by haloed saints. He's a stern, no-nonsense kinda guy and his phone's always going off. 'All the Bolsheviks went to prison, then they sent everyone else through prison too, so it's important for understanding the Russian soul.'*

---

* In the 1930s millions were sent to the gulag for petty or political offences, like saying Stalin's moustache looked shit. This was the beginning of Russian mass incarceration.

As Hitler advanced during the Second World War, the Soviets moved tank production further east to the Uralmash plant in Yekaterinburg. After Roizman got out, he found work there, as did future members of the Uralmash gang. By the late 1990s, the fearsome crime syndicate was trying to soften their image and so, in the year 2000, after a hard day's work bleeding local businesses dry, these family-friendly gangsters joined Roizman's latest venture: ridding the city of the drug menace.

'Here we had, simply put, a narco-catastrophe,' Roizman said. 'I saw what drugs does: it turns people into animals. The situation was so monstrous, something had to be done.'

There was a gypsy village in Yekaterinburg, which was the heart of the city's smack business. The gypsy peddlers sold openly there, having paid off the cops. If they couldn't pay with cash, the junkies could barter with stolen goods. Together with some Uralmash heavies, Roizman went down there and announced that his group, the City Without Drugs, was declaring war.

They mounted patrols and, using more or less the same techniques that they used to consolidate their hold over the underworld, the Uralmash set about ridding the town of the drug problem. One dealer was tied to a tree before having his pants pulled down and used syringes stuck into his backside, all in front of a local TV crew.

'They [the police] told us we don't understand: you have to go after the big fish, but you guys target the small dealers, and then what? You close one down, another one pops up. And we said, "OK, but if we don't let anyone deal here there won't be any drugs. If another one comes up, we'll shut him down, too." It's like doing the dishes; you use one and it gets dirty so you wash it again.'

Meanwhile, junkies were dragged away, kicking and screaming, to a 'detox centre' in the woods, where they were handcuffed to a radiator, not allowed to use the toilet even as they shat themselves (something that happens a lot in withdrawal), periodically beaten and fed only bread and water till they went cold turkey.

Roizman justified his harsh approach: 'When you're working with addicts, you need a closed space, clear of drugs. Liberals tell me, "We don't support you; you're holding people against their will." I tell them, "Look, their parents brought them to me in chains, in the boots of their cars. Now tell me what you did." It turns out they didn't do anything. It's some kind of abstract humanitarianism, helping people out of someone else's pocket. They were brought to me, and I did what I could.'

Keeping addicts in chains isn't based on any understanding of modern medicine, but then again, Roizman's never been one for conventional science. He once warned kids on the devil's lettuce they better get ready, because that's not all they'll be smoking on.

'Marijuana is the first sign of homosexualism,' he declared.

Sounds legit. Remember lads, next time your mate asks if you've seen his grinder, it's time to call it a night.

Asked which groups were responsible for the drugs scourge, Roizman was unequivocal: 'We drove out the gypsies, but we only chased them for drugs. We put up their pictures, pressed the police to work. Some are in jail, some are living somewhere else, but they all left, so such a phenomenon as the gypsy village no longer exists.'

In 2001, activists armed with sledgehammers tore down the home of an alleged gypsy drug baron. Then, two more houses were burnt down by unknown assailants.

Closed off from the rest of society, many gypsies steal, beg or sell drugs. Modern life is geared towards people in cities, but the nomadic Roma never signed up for the deal, so having no fixed address means there's no incentive to send their kids to school or find 'proper' jobs. Not like anyone will hire them, anyway. Hundreds of years of slavery, persecution and attempts to erase their culture have made gypsies distrust us sedentary folk. Anti-Roma is the last acceptable form of racism: polite, intelligent people will talk about exterminating them over a cup of tea.

Roizman also had few kind words for the city's migrant population:

'All the heroin here came from Tajikistan. They tried to be politically correct and call it Afghan heroin, but hell, I don't care if it was Martian heroin, the people bringing it and selling it were Tajiks.'

The communists tried to stamp out ethnic discord, but the collapse of the Soviet Union brought national differences front and centre. After Tajikistan suffered a civil war with the death toll in the hundreds of thousands, its economy now depends on immigrant street-sweepers cleaning up Moscow. They, along with the Roma, are seen as the nation's street pharmacists.

Roizman denies he's against gypsies or immigrants, just the ones committing crime. However, he's also said that the reason Russia has such a drug problem is because it has so many immigrants, which sounds an awful lot like he blames immigrants for the drug problem. Xenophobia paid off. In 2013, he was elected mayor of Yekaterinburg, the first mayor not belonging to Putin's United Russia Party in a long, long time. Bizarrely, he's also become kind of a hero to a few liberal Russians because Putin equals bad; therefore anyone who isn't Putin equals good.

A tough Jewish ex-convict who collects Orthodox art, races cars in his spare time and became the only mayor in the country not beholden to Putin, Roizman isn't the only one with a murky past who's made it in Russian politics. In the early 2000s, Alexander Khabarov, the head of Uralmash, registered the Uralmash Social-Political Union, or Uralmash OPS (OPS also stands for *Organizovanoe Prestupnoe Soobshestvo*, or 'Organised Crime Syndicate' – Khabarov was trollin'), while the current president of Crimea went by the nickname 'Goblin' in the 1990s. The gang bosses always wanted to go legit one day.

I put it to Roizman that, in the West, sending gang members to fight drugs would raise some eyebrows.*

---

* Wouldn't be the first time, though. The IRA famously took a dim view of drug dealing, shooting suspects in the knees.

'We all live in the same city,' Roizman replied, his eyes suddenly widened. 'Drugs don't discriminate if your father's a factory worker or a general. We had a narco-catastrophe here, so everyone from teachers to convicts was united. Who are you to tell someone they can't fight drugs? So we got help where we could.'

'You understand, the only ones who can do this are those with a "past" – either ex-policemen, or ex-hooligans,' added his associate, Alexander Shumilov. Shumilov heads a regional chapter of the City Without Drugs Foundation. 'An engineer's not gonna go to a house where they're selling drugs and tell them to cut it out. But a hooligan knows how to talk to these people.'

While never charged with overt mobsterism, Roizman surrounds himself with very dubious company. One of his associates was found guilty of the gruesome murder of a pensioner. Another, Evgeny Malenkin, the vice-president of the Foundation, was convicted of planting drugs on people and holding others captive, including twenty-nine-year-old Tatiana Kazantseva, who died after being refused emergency care. Bruises on her body also showed she'd been beaten during her involuntary stay at the clinic.

These days, Roizman told me, heroin is yesterday's problem. Now the latest craze is spice; synthetic cannabis cooked up in Chinese labs. In 2015, authorities blamed the spice racket on the Ukrainian Mafia led by Ihor Kolomoisky, a business-tycoon-turned-wannabe-warlord who heads his own private militia in east Ukraine. Kolomoisky's certainly a slippery character, but it seems a little too convenient that our enemies get the money to take up arms against us by poisoning the nation's youth.

Roizman claims he sees them every day, the people he's helped, usually on one of his morning runs (unlike other Russian politicians, Roizman drives his own car and doesn't roll with a posse of bodyguards). But in 2016, an HIV emergency was declared in Yekaterinburg, with one in fifty people carrying the virus. Russia has the worst HIV epidemic outside Africa, much of that from junkies sharing needles. I respect Roizman tried to do *something*, and I'm no saint myself, but perhaps kidnapping smackheads and handcuffing them to a radiator wasn't such a hot idea after all?

Russia's stern outlook stems from the Mongolian clusterfuck it experienced in the 1990s, as well as the rise of religious conservatism. The Orthodox Church has experienced a revival since the militantly atheist Soviet empire, and AIDS, homosexuality and drug use are all Western imports to undermine Holy Rus'. An objective, evidence-based approach is also derailed by the Soviet junk science of narcology, which tries to frighten patients into thinking they'll die after taking just one more dose (in real life, dying from drugs is a slow and steady process and there's no telling which dose will be your last). Anti-drug campaigners make terrifying pronouncements like 'marijuana can alter your DNA', which sounds like the plot of a Cheech and Chong *Spiderman* remake.

Other countries let addicts take methadone, which gets you through the day but gives less of a high.* But in Russia, even trying to wean yourself off the hard stuff is illegal. Viktor Ivanov, the moustached chief of the Federal Narcotics Control Service (FSKN – Russia's equivalent to the DEA), said that this just encourages addicts. Courts can order them to get treatment, but since there's no methadone, many don't make it through rehab. It's not clear where else they're supposed to go – high-end private clinics? Sent to live in a monastery? Roizman's prison camp? Ivanov suggested they can work on a farm.

And with desperate times come desperate measures. When the smack supply dried up in certain areas, addicts began making their own out of codeine pills. The result was affectionately known as

---

* However, the withdrawal symptoms are *much* worse, so it's not for everyone.

krokodil (crocodile). Why? Because it literally eats you alive, rotting your flesh and leaving you with greenish, decomposing skin, festering sores, abscesses and open wounds that go all the way to the bone. A krokodil user is the closest thing we have to a real-life zombie, wandering around with dead, corroding limbs that have to be amputated lest they play host to maggots and gangrene. Not that I've got a burning desire to try either, but if I had to choose between heroin and doing *that* . . . shit, I'm rolling up my sleeves already.

What's decided in the Kremlin is felt far beyond its walls. When Crimea was taken over by 'little green men' in 2014, addicts lost the methadone supply they previously got from Ukraine so they switched back to heroin. Within a year, a hundred were dead. The official policy seems to be 'just let them die'.

Max mentioned that he used to deal for a group of Tajiks, so it was time for me to head to the source. It was a gruelling thirteen-hour drive through spectacular alpine scenery along the Panj River from Dushanbe, the capital of Tajikistan, to the Afghan border. While still appreciating the landscapes, the roads can make you feel like you're stuck in a washing machine.

Most Russians know Tajikistan as our version of Mexico: a poor country full of brown people south of the border where we source cheap labour and drugs. Tajikistan was poor even in Soviet times, but in 1992, shortly after getting independence, an alliance of ethnic and Islamist factions took up arms against the government in a devastating civil war. The war weakened whatever tenuous grip the authorities had, and forces were stretched thin across the empty goalposts they called the southern border.

'We patrolled here mainly on foot,' said a former border guard, 'covering ten kilometres in four-hour shifts. We caught a few smugglers sometimes, but they were mostly small-time guys. I think they were mainly bringing it for themselves to get high.'

After spending the best part of the day being tossed around like a leaf in a hurricane we reached Khorog, the biggest town in the Gorno-Badakhshan region of the Pamir mountains. This was the frontier of the Russian Empire in the nineteenth century, during the Great Game over who would rule Central Asia. The Russians and British divided the border along the Panj River. It was one brother living on one side, one brother on another. Afghans, Iranians and Tajiks are all Persians, and many still have family on both sides of the water.

The proud Pamiris are a distinct ethnic group from other Tajiks, but picking the losing side in the civil war they found themselves on the brink of famine, only saved from starvation by their spiritual leader, Aga Khan. Under the terms of the 1997 peace deal, this is warlord country. Armed clashes broke out here in 2012, and I had to get a special permit to Gorno-Badakhshan with the help of Maram Azizmamadov, who runs a local NGO helping drug addicts.

'Welcome to Pamir,' Maram greeted me, 'a little piece Russia left behind.'

Even though they fought on the Islamist side, there's no fundamentalism here, or women wearing hijabs. There's even a 'MACDolands'. We walked over to Maram's drop-in centre for addicts, a little junkies' community. If anyone knew this corner of dopeworld, it would be them. Across the river, resting between the mountain slopes, lay Afghanistan.

'Up till the late nineties it used to be an open border. In the winter, the water would freeze and we'd play ice hockey across the river – one team Afghan, one Pamir,' said Farkhad, a middle-aged man.

This, supposedly, is where the Northern Route begins, a Silk Road of heroin leading across the 'stans (past dirt-poor Kyrgyzstan and its Mafia-sponsored revolutions) up to Russia. I've seen the river – you could probably throw a plank across to make a bridge, or wade across if you had some wellies. Coupled with the – shall we say, loose? – border patrols, it should be pretty easy to get across, right?

'Someone gets shot every month,' said Farkhad. 'Sometimes they set them up; shoot them and claim they were smugglers trying to get across the border, but it was only some guy fetching firewood. It's something they do to fill their quotas so they can look good. If they see you, they'll just shoot without warning. One Afghan I was in jail with in Dushanbe, they shot him about five or six months ago. As soon as I saw it on TV and they said his name, I knew it was him.'

Maram walked in holding a tray. Now, I've been round the world, seen a lot of weird shit, but I've never seen motherfuckers drink tea with salt before. Well, it was more like soup with tea, but I can see why this hasn't taken off elsewhere. As I tried to hold it down, I wondered, where are all the sports cars? Where is the Tajik narcomafia? If heroin costs $5,000 a kilo here, and $15,000 in Russia, somebody must be making a killing.

'There's no organised cartel like in Mexico, or in Russia,' Maram explained. 'There's a few people in the villages, who people respect, who solve problems. Occasionally one of them will buy a new car, but there's no one who's really rich. So none of the money goes back here.'

Makes sense – Khorog's still far from Russia, where the big money's made. But high-level trafficking still goes on: Moscow's appetite can't be filled by some Afghan wandering the mountains with his backpack. So who does it?

'Now it's mostly the Chekist [KGB] faggots; without them it's impossible,' snarled Farkhad.

Commanders on both sides of the civil war made their money through heroin and got to keep their business as part of the peace deal, enjoying protection at the highest level. Since the Tajik drug agency could barely scrape two roubles together, foreign aid poured in – which was immediately deployed to crush private competition, effectively national-ising the narcotics industry. In other words, Western money paid for Farkhad's friends getting shot while the president's cronies lived large.

And then there's the Russians. The Russian army's 201st division was stationed in Tajikistan when fighting broke out and started engaging in some extracurricular activities, like sneaking smack onboard military flights. They're still there.

'Yes, of course, it's the generals. They bought directly from Afghanistan and flew it out on their helicopters. And they sold weapons across the border to anyone who'd buy. Then they all went out and bought expensive apartments in Moscow,' said Maram.

So what about Russia? When Vladimir Putin came to the throne in 2000, he set about restoring law and order, and he did this partly by incorporating the Mafia into his 'power vertical'; chasing out the oligarchs who wouldn't get in line, a lot of whom were crooks who looted Russia in the 1990s. Gangsters fell in as well, with an implicit understanding there'd be no more of the lawlessness of the 1990s. To fit in, crime bosses reimagined themselves as legitimate businessmen, politicians, art collectors and so on.

Putin might have laid the groundwork out himself. As deputy mayor of St Petersburg in the early 1990s, Putin had to deal (as did any other official) with the Mafia. As well as giving the Tambovs the contracts to St Pete, Putin sat on the advisory board for SPAG, a joint-venture company on which Vladimir Kumarin was one of the directors. In 1999, before Putin even became president, SPAG was named in a German intelligence report as being a money-laundering front for the Tambov and Cali organisations, and in 2001, two of its co-founders were charged in Lichtenstein with money laundering and fraud (Putin, who'd become president by this point, wasn't named in the indictments). The pair got a slap on the wrist for scamming their investors, but were acquitted of money laundering for lack of evidence.

Putin, an ex-KGB agent, surrounded himself with *siloviki*, a tight circle of ex-military and intelligence officers from his St Pete days. These included Viktor Ivanov, who was appointed head of the newly formed FSKN in 2008, as well as his deputy, Nikolai Aulov.

In 2007, Kumarin was arrested and is now serving a lengthy sentence for a litany of crimes after refusing to step aside from his business interests to Putin's inner circle. Three hundred police commandos flew in on government aircraft to snatch him up during the night.

'Kumarin's in jail, and they got everyone else they needed to get,' an ex-federal agent told me. 'Now the FSB protects everyone.'

In a jailhouse interview, Kumarin admitted to journalist Zoya Svetova that he knew Aulov in the early 1990s. Allegedly, coke was coming into the St Petersburg ports from Colombia, and Aulov wanted a slice.

'I knew Aulov well, from the time he was a [police] captain, when the first shipment of cocaine came through Vyborg in cans of stew,' the one-armed bandit told Svetova. 'There was a meeting with Aulov in 1992 or 1993 in which, as I understood it, he hinted to me to take drugs [trafficking] under my control, arguing that the one who takes it under control stands to make a lot of money. Those who make more money will get stronger than us and will beat us or have us thrown in jail, which is basically what happened in the end.'

Eventually, power did go to those other players. In 2008, Spanish police in Mallorca arrested ex-boxer Gennady Petrov, the leader of a rival faction. Petrov moved to Spain in 1998 and lived in a lavish mansion with stone lions, Roman-style pillars and priceless Orthodox icons. Wiretaps revealed he had contact with high-level officials including none other than Aulov, whom he'd called seventy-eight times in one year. Two years later, the WikiLeaks scandal broke out, and in the leaked documents Spanish prosecutors claimed that crime syndicates had been incorporated into the official hierarchy, creating a so-called 'Mafia State': government agencies offered Russian mobsters protection in exchange for wet work like running guns to Turkey or political assassinations.

The FSKN was widely known to be corrupt. In the most egregious case, a retired army colonel, his wife, daughter and her aunt were slapped with eight years in prison for opium trafficking for having traditional poppy-seed buns in their family bakery. Aside from the absurdity of addicts gorging themselves on copious amounts of poppy buns to get high, the family had earlier been approached by FSKN agents demanding they pay 50,000 roubles a month towards their protection racket (they refused). And that's without mentioning all those times the Feds got caught with bricks of heroin.

In 2016, the Spaniards issued a warrant for Aulov's arrest. Ivanov insisted Aulov was just using Petrov as an informant, but the growing scandals were too much even for Moscow, and the FSKN was disbanded, its agents transferred to the Interior Ministry (MVD).

Russia's not the only one standing accused. Near the statue of Gagarin in the south of Moscow, hidden in the basement of a parking lot, lies a restaurant named Koryo. It's supposedly run by a branch of the North Korean secret service tasked with making money for the regime. Sure enough, in the corner a TV's showing nuclear warheads obliterating America to patriotic music, and there's a free magazine with all the latest news from the socialist workers' paradise. I was very disappointed, however, to find they were serving Coca-Cola, the imperialist dogs.

Since it's under sanctions and has few other ways of earning cash, Pyongyang runs, through its secretive Room 39 intelligence division, one of the biggest crime syndicates in the world. One of its operations is making Superdollars, counterfeit 100-dollar bills so accurate you can't tell them apart from the real thing. North Korea also produces a shit-tonne of meth, or *bingdu*, which it exports to its neighbours, as well as opium grown on its state-run collective farms (workers were even ordered to grow poppy during the great famine of the 1990s). Within the country, meth itself is supposed to be as common as having a cup of coffee.

It's important not to get too carried away with this Mafia State thesis lest we stray into tinfoil-hat territory. After all, in October 2018 most of the officials implicated in Petrov's case were acquitted in a Spanish court, which had every reason to find them guilty (Petrov himself skipped bail and the warrant's still out on Aulov). The Kremlin will deny everything of course and say Russia is a normal country. There's corruption, yes, but isn't that true of everywhere? The UK are the biggest hypocrites: they pretend they're squeaky-clean but half the world's dirty cash flows through London – a lot of it from Russia. However, it's a different kind of corruption: no coke dealer I know has had to pay kickbacks to MI5.

One mistake a lot of people make is that, in Russia, a bear can't shit in the woods without Putin's say-so. But he's not some all-seeing puppet-master. Think of it like a king and his court. The king reigns supreme, but his lords are always one-upping on each other. One night it's the Interior Ministry, one night it's the FSB. One of those transferred when the FSKN was dissolved was Yuri, whom I met through a mutual friend in a café that's a favourite hangout spot for the MVD.

'We used to be part of the FSKN, but our powers were transferred,' he said, eyeing me up as I clocked the pistol poking out under his leather jacket. 'We don't have as much pull as we used to. If it's an important investigation, they [the FSB] will railroad us as much as they can.'

These turf wars between different agencies have replaced the gang wars of the past as everyone struggles for a piece of the action. I asked Yuri what they do for fun.

'Yeah, sometimes we go out, drinking, women,' he said. 'But me, I don't drink, I don't smoke, I only get my high from the gym. With us operatives, it's difficult to know who to trust because you never know who is with whom, because of all this corruption. So you have this circle of maybe three to four people, but you don't let anyone get close to you.'

The underworld has become the upperworld. No wonder Yuri's paranoid.

Meanwhile, the war in Chechnya ended when the Kremlin found the most powerful warlord, Ramzan Kadyrov, and got him to switch sides. Since then, he's ruled Chechnya with an iron fist and Sharia law. In 2017, reports emerged of hundreds of gay men being rounded up and tortured in concentration camps. Three were allegedly killed.

'If such people existed in Chechnya, law enforcement would not have to worry about them since their own relatives would have sent them to where they could never return,' Kadyrov's spokesman said.

A few months later, they repeated the operation, this time against drug users. Thankfully, Kadyrov only rules one province. Imagine if he was given control of an entire country . . .

31

The Golden Crescent

I touched down at Imam Khomeini International Airport in Tehran a day before *Nowruz* (Persian New Year). Since I was flying from (relatively) liberal Turkey, there were maybe five or six women onboard, all over the age of fifty, who were already wearing hijabs. But as soon as the plane landed, *all* the headscarves came on.

Just before New Year's there's a fire festival, a day when people set off fireworks in the street and jump across bonfires. Climbing to the roof of my hostel to get a good view of the mountains rising over the city, I could hear bangs and crackles in the distance, while gunpowder smoke filled my nostrils. If it wasn't for the joyous atmosphere you could think it was a warzone.

When the smoke cleared, it was time to party. I got the heads-up about a shindig going down at a house in the leafy suburbs of northern Tehran. It was a Thursday, because Friday is their holy day, and the bar was well stocked with forbidden fruit.

'It's not in my culture and it's forbidden, but . . . *salamati*!' said my new host, toasting a glass of *arak* (a kind of vodka made with grapes). There were a few dozen people here; boys and girls in their early twenties, dressed less for mosque than a night out in Camden. We didn't have a DJ but the TV was switched to full blast on one of those satellite channels from overseas, with bikini-clad honeys cavorting around the pool with Persian rappers.

Fun fact: since the Islamic Revolution, booze is illegal in Iran, but only if you're Muslim. Many Iranians are not very religious and some are even atheist and actively despise fundamentalist Islam – which they see as having been imposed on them by the Arabs – but as far as the Ayatollah's concerned, they're all God-fearing Muslims. This means the Armenians (and a few renegade Jews and Zoroastrians) have earned themselves an unsavoury reputation as booze barons. Need a six-pack? Call Aram. Beer and spirits are smuggled in through Turkey and Kurdistan to the west, as well as Armenia, Azerbaijan and the ex-Soviet republics to the north. The Islamic Revolutionary Guards (IRGC) militia is said to have its hands in the racket.

The headscarves came off as a group of girls walked through the door, and my eyes couldn't help but wander as they walked over to pour themselves a drink in their tight black dresses. Since Iran has no nightlife to speak of, drinking takes place at private gatherings or house parties such as this one, where the girls' twerking would make Rihanna blush. One in particular caught my eye; a tall, beautiful lady with purple hair cropped at the sides who smiled at me as she walked past.

'You can do whatever you want,' said my friend, pouring another shot, 'as long as it's not politics.'

Just then someone turned on the smoke machine and the crowd disappeared into silhouttes lit up only by the disco lights. It was a big house so we had lots of privacy, and no one was particularly scared of police. At most, they'd come knocking for a few bribes.

By early morning Friday someone had given me a lift home. Since alcohol is illegal anyway, there's no rules. Everybody drinks and drives, or drinks till they pass out. If they get caught, they're liable to get lashes. But I was too ratted to care.

Before the Arab invasion, Iran (or Persia) was home to drinking, dancing and other debauchery under Zoroastrianism, the traditional

Persian religion. Then Islam came along. The early verses of the Qur'an praised wine but, as the word of God was gradually revealed to the Prophet Muhammed, later verses condemned it. Islamic scholars believe Muhammed got fed up with his uncle's drunken antics and so banned his followers from drinking. Wine (and usually most alcohol) is therefore expressly forbidden in the Qur'an, because wine is a *khamr* (intoxicant) that befuddles the mind.

The Muslim position on other drugs is a little more ambiguous. I've got some Muslim friends who won't drink, but there's nothing in the Qur'an about popping Molly or doing ketamine. Remember, all the teachings would have had to make sense to people at the time, and I guess it was hard to imagine the rise of acid house in the desert of seventh-century Arabia. So, much hinges on interpretation – while most Muslims agree that anything which befuddles the mind is *khamr* and therefore forbidden, followers of scholar Abu Hanifa have managed to narrow *khamr* down to the very particular kind of wine that would have been around in Muhammed's time.

The Qur'an said nothing about opium, but hash was generally looked down upon in the Arab world, being associated with Sufis, a mystical branch of Islam that uses music and dance to draw themselves closer to Allah. This put them at odds with mainstream Muslims, who saw them as weird, drum-banging hippies.

In 1631, the Turkish Sultan Murad IV banned alcohol, tobacco and coffeehouses and personally beheaded anyone who broke the rules. Anyone caught operating a coffee shop could be bundled into a sack and thrown into a river. But this wasn't so much out of piety as paranoia, since Murad thought bars, cafés and the like were a gathering place for radical dissidents. Opium and hashish remained legal.

But unless you're ISIS or the Spanish Inquisition, religious teachings aren't usually taken at face value. Especially not by the Persians, whose adherence to scripture was chequered at best.

'Drink wine. This is life eternal. This is all that youth will give you', wrote the poet Omar Khayyam. 'It is the season for wine, roses and drunken friends. Be happy for this moment. This moment is your life.'

Shah (King) Ismail was the founder of the Safavid dynasty that ruled sixteenth- to eighteenth-century Persia. Once, in an absolute baller move, he cut off an Uzbek warlord's head and used the skull as a gold-encrusted chalice. His son, Shah Tahmasp, felt guilty about his own drinking habits and, swearing to total abstinence, outlawed booze, gambling and prostitution. One official caught partying with hookers was stuffed into a barrel and thrown off the top of a minaret. The rest of Safavid rule in Persia varied between strict Sharia law and a free-for-all fuckfest.

In 1951, Iranians voted in their first secular, democratically elected prime minister, Mohammad Mossadegh, who kicked out British and American oil companies to give the country's oil wealth back to Iranians. If there's one thing the British and Americans hate, it's not having oil, so in 1953 they engineered a coup and deposed Mossadegh in favour of the Shah. The Shah basically ran a dictatorship, his secret police arresting anyone with dissenting views. He also alienated conservative Muslims with his radical reforms – women walking around in *skirts*!

But in 1979, an unholy alliance of communists and Islamists – every right-winger's worst nightmare – marched through Tehran, causing the Shah to flee. Ayatollah Khomeini, the firebrand preacher at the heart of the protests, then turned on his left-wing allies and declared an Islamic Republic.

Iran is now under one of the most repressive regimes on Earth. Women's rights were rolled back after the revolution and they had to cover themselves from head to toe. Forget about social media, this is a country where you can get arrested for the wrong haircut. Facebook is blocked. YouTube is blocked. Porn is obviously blocked. You can still go on it through a VPN, but that's a lot of effort just for a wank. The authorities seem determined to suck every last bit of joy out of life – in 2014, six young Tehranis were arrested and publicly humiliated after filming a video of themselves dancing to Pharrell's 'Happy'.

Iran's ominous reputation reaches far beyond its borders. Hezbollah was the strongest faction to rise from the rubble of the Lebanese Civil War. Lebanon, an Arab country nestled between Israel and Syria on the eastern Mediterranean, is evenly split between Christians and Muslims. In 1975, the Christian far right took it upon themselves to 'fix' the Palestinian refugee crisis by driving them out of their camps, igniting a three-way battle between Christian, Muslim and Palestinian militias that turned Beirut, once the Paris of the Middle East, into shorthand for a bloody mess.

The Americans and Israelis got involved, but quickly found themselves in over their heads. In 1983, with Iranian help, Hezbollah carried out the world's first Islamic suicide bombing at an American barracks, killing 241 marines, after blowing up the US embassy in Beirut. The Americans shit their pants and pulled out. Today, Hezbollah's reinvented itself from a suicide squad that would kaboom your ass to pieces to a legitimate political party and anti-Israeli resistance movement, as well as Iran's proxy army in Syria.*

---

* And an alleged drug cartel. During the war, the Bekaa Valley in eastern Lebanon became one of the world's top producers of heroin, opium and hashish. As the gear made its way to the Mediterranean the militias, including Hezbollah, charged 'taxes' on all the product moving through their territory.

Hezbollah now takes donations from the Lebanese community worldwide, allegedly including South American coke barons. In the late 2000s, the DEA accused Hezbollah's top financiers of working with cocaine smugglers and the Cartel of the Suns, a group of Venezuelan generals, officials and even members of the president's family, facilitating cocaine shipments at the highest levels. At Hezbollah rallies, supporters chant 'Death to America!', but who knew death would come slowly from heart disease and high blood pressure? Of course, Hezbollah denies all allegations of drug running as a Zionist ruse.

And yet the first thing you notice about Iranians is their hospitality. They really roll out the red carpet for foreigners. Of the three weeks I spent in Iran, I only paid for a place to stay about three times, because people will just invite you into their homes. From Tehran I took a bus east through the vast, flat, open desert, where I met Hossein, a cheery student who invited me to stay with him in Kerman, a city of ancient bazaars and Zoroastrian fire temples.

Hossein led me through the long arched galleries of the bazaar, past mounds of exotic spices and handwoven Persian carpets, and round the corner to a mud-brick building that looked like the Skywalker farm in *Star Wars*, where he lived with his mum, dad and sister when he wasn't studying for his exams in Tehran. After putting down our bags in the bedroom, I wandered over to the living room, where his old man and some friends were lazily sprawled out on the carpet holding a traditional, rounded opium pipe, known as a *vafoor*, next to a tray of smouldering coals.

Kerman is basically Opium City. It seems like every family here has at least one person who smokes opium, or *taryak*. Opium's been a part of Persian culture for thousands of years, especially since alcohol was declared verboten by the Qur'an. Mostly confined to the lower classes, opium use was so widespread in the Safavid era that French visitors likened it to their own drinking of wine. My man Hossein's dad was blazing 24/7.

'Opium is like a medicine for old man, is good,' the father said, scraping the leftovers off the pipe, which he'll later sell to his friends. It's more potent, apparently, but imagine someone hitting the bong, then selling you the ashes.

'You want to try?'

Sure, why not. To smoke, light a piece of charcoal over the tray and puff into the pipe, holding the coal up to the opium. Then, when it starts bubbling, start breathing it in short, sharp bursts (don't try this at home, kids).

I was looking forward to the next phase of my life as a Middle

Eastern skag fiend, but found myself severely underwhelmed. Don't get me wrong, I love illicit narcotics as much as the next man, but this tarry black stuff is fairly weak and you need a good five to six hits just to get even mildly stoned. It's a nice feeling – kind of warm, light and heavy, drowsy and alert at the same time – but you might as well just get some hashish, which is very affordable round these parts, with the added bonus that it's safe to drink alcohol afterwards (thanks for telling me that after I downed half a bottle of your dodgy Iranian homemade vodka, guys).

After a short time chasing the dragon, Hossein said we should go and meet his friends. It was already night-time as we went to pick up some hash (*VERY* cheap, around £1.20 per gram), then headed over to a park where everyone was getting fucked up: weed, heroin, vodka, meth, you name it. There were boys and girls there, all hanging together, and everyone wanted to take selfies. A fat sixteen-year-old named Biggie Smalls kept trying to play me Persian trap music (yup, that's a thing) and talked about how much he loved LSD. An older, paler, skinnier boy kept plying me with moonshine while explaining his take on altered states, peppered with nihilism.

'Drink alcohol, snort cocaine and smoke marijuana, that's what life's all about,' he said. 'There is no God.'

Buzzing on hashish, opium and moonshine, we got up to get some food, but Persian Nietzsche and a fat dude we saw smoking crystal meth earlier waved us into a sports car. We got in and the fat man started showing off his best Paul Walker impression at 120 miles an hour down the wrong lane while pounding the ceiling and screaming 'I AM IRANIAN TERRORIST!!' before spinning his car into a drift, the smell of burning tyres filling our nostrils.

I've noticed Iranians take a very *c'est la vie* attitude to road safety. Crossing the road in Tehran is like a video game, except you've only got one life. The traffic just doesn't stop and comes in five different directions. There are people driving motorbikes on the sidewalk and through shopping centres. There are no rules.

Fortunately, our terrorist compadre dropped us off at a restaurant, where we got picked up again an hour later by Hossein's mate and fellow stoner Reza. He had the weirdest rolling technique I'd ever seen. He emptied out a cigarette and mixed the hash with the tobacco, then sucked it all back into the cigarette, all the while still driving and holding the steering wheel with his knees. Hossein rolled the windows up and lit the joint.

Smoke filled the car as we drove around the city bumping 2Pac until we got to a lonely stretch of road, where Reza reached into the glove compartment and pulled out a baton and taser before handing me his phone. On it was a photo of him smiling, holding an AK up in the air, dressed in the smart white shirt and epaulettes of . . . holy shit, I'm getting hotboxed by a cop!

A cop, that's right. Every man has his vices – after all you've read, are you really surprised that one of the boys in blue tokes a doobie every now and then?

Reza handed me the taser, and me and Hossein sat at the back zapping each other like fourteen-year-old boys while he drove us home. In a country where you get ninety-nine lashes just for drinking a beer, this was one of the safest places to be.

Despite the regime's strict moral outlook, every other person here seemed either drunk or stoned – even the police. All this pompous religiosity's a front; in reality, they're just as depraved as the rest of us. I guess you have to be high to deal with the repression.

'As soon as they prohibit things, the people become curious,' a friend later told me over shisha. 'The government should let us decide, what is good for us and what is not.'

One notion we have to get out of our minds is that drugs are inherently bad. Drugs aren't bad. They are inanimate objects, like a

chair or an iPhone. They can do bad things to you if you're not careful, but so can smoking cigarettes, drinking beer, eating McDonald's
and spending too much time in the sun. Legally speaking, a cop
might know the difference, but your body won't.

With religion, everything depends on who you ask: Pachamama
is absolutely fine with you chewing the coca leaf, the sacred plant of
the Andean peoples, while the American Prohibition was driven
largely by Protestant moralists who just couldn't rid themselves of
the notion that someone out there was having fun. Iran's a funny one
because their religion looks down on alcohol, our most popular drug,
but what we call 'hard drugs' are more socially accepted – to the point
where Iran has one of the highest opiate addiction rates in the world.
And of course, they like to blaze as much as everyone else. You can't
change human nature. Dopeworld is everywhere, even in the Islamic
Republic.

Kerman in particular is awash with narcotics, since it's next to the
chief drug-producing region in the world – the Golden Crescent,
which lies across the rugged lands of Pakistan, Afghanistan and Iran.

Once upon a time, Iran was a major opium producer, but poppy
cultivation was banned under the pro-Western government of the
Shah. Although it was re-legalised in 1969, the revolutionary government banned it again and threw dealers before a firing squad. But
druggies still needed their fix, so the poppy fields moved further east
– to Afghanistan.

Afghanistan's entry into the murky world of international heroin
trafficking was facilitated, in no small part, by our old friends in the
CIA. In the 1960s and early 70s, Afghanistan (along with Iran and
Pakistan) lay on the hippy trail to India, where Western backpackers
went to discover themselves in the exotic aura of the Orient. They
were all smoking dope, of course, but the Afghan king let it be – he
had bigger things to worry about.

In 1979, the Soviets invaded Afghanistan, unleashing mass destruction and creating one of the world's worst refugee crises. Thousands of volunteers joined the Mujahideen resistance in their holy war against the Red Army. The CIA's policy at the time was to arm anyone who wanted to mess with the Russians, which they did by sending guns through their contacts in Pakistan's notoriously shadowy spy agency, the ISI (Inter-Services Intelligence). Since Afghanistan's got no natural resources to speak of, resistance leaders sent hash and opium back through the same mountain paths the CIA and ISI used to smuggle guns. Neither government was too concerned. After all, they were giving those godless commies what-for! By the time the Soviets withdrew in 1989, 1.5 million Afghans (around 10 per cent of the population) and 15,000 Russian soldiers lay dead. They'd got their Vietnam.

But there was trouble in paradise. With the Russians gone, the Mujahideen morphed into the Taliban and began dynamiting Buddhist monuments and executing 'sinners' in football stadiums. Things got even more complicated when it turned out they were hiding that infamous miscreant, Osama bin Laden.

While the CIA's broken its ties to the Talibs, the Pakistanis have not. Engaged in a constant secret (and sometimes not-so-secret) battle with its bigger and richer neighbour, India, the ISI often tries its hand at geopolitical influence. But as one senior Pakistani official put it: 'We have no money. All we have are the crazies. So the crazies it is.'

On 12 March 1993, Pakistan unleashed the crazies. Twelve bombs detonated across Mumbai, killing 257. The bombs were revenge for the riots earlier that year in which 900 people died, mostly Muslims, and were planted by men loyal to Dawood Ibrahim, an underworld boss with an empire stretching from Nepal to Dubai. Dawood's gang, D-Company, received training and equipment from the ISI, including the eight tonnes of RDX explosive used in the blasts. Although his principal business interest used to be gold smuggling

(Indians don't like to pay the high import tax), Dawood switched to the heroin business through the ISI and their links to Afghanistan. India's Most Wanted now lives in the port city of Karachi under the watchful eye of his guardian angels at Pakistani intelligence.

Pakistan was also, along with the Saudis and the UAE, one of the only countries to officially recognise the Taliban's leadership. In those early days, the Taliban were trying to get more international standing and figured they could win some friends over at the UN if it seemed like they were doing something about the opium scourge, which was beginning to look like a serious problem. In 2000, the Taliban declared opium un-Islamic and, despite the fact that it kept their entire economy afloat, almost managed to eliminate poppy growing altogether (they did this by being a bunch of bloodthirsty maniacs who'd chop off your head if you disobeyed, but never mind).

The only parts of the country that kept growing were under the control of the Northern Alliance; the kinder, gentler face of Afghan warlordism. It was the Northern Alliance that provided NATO with much-needed manpower during the 2001 invasion, so naturally, once the Taliban fell, they rose right to the top of the political hierarchy. While on one hand, the Afghans' counter-narcotics forces were trained by the US military, Blackwater mercenaries and the DEA, at the same time, high-up officials like the ex-president's brother, Ahmed Wali Karzai (assassinated in 2011), protected the bigwigs and made sure they never stayed in jail too long. In other cases, anti-drug efforts were complicated by the fact that the most prolific offenders were actually warlords working for the CIA. The West didn't wanna put too much pressure on its allies in the War on Terror.

But the whole system is broken from the bottom up. Four decades of nonstop warfare and occupation have destroyed whatever prospects farmers might have had outside of growing poppy, while destitute refugees are paid to carry drugs across the border. If they lose a package, they have to marry off their daughters to pay the debt (in a male-run society such as this one, the girls have little choice).

Meanwhile, Taliban chieftains, having rolled back their edict on the godlessness of opium, sell smack to restock their armouries. And so the war rages on, with no end in sight.

Bigger loads weighing hundreds of kilos cross the desert in heavily armed convoys, and thousands of Iranian border guards have died in shootouts with the smugglers. Iran has responded by walling off part of the border with trenches and barbed wire, and the death penalty. Executions take place in public, with crowds gathered to see masked prisoners being hanged off cranes. That hasn't stopped the flow of drugs: since 2011, the number of addicts has doubled.

All over the world, minorities are picked on for drugs. In Iran, it's the Baloch people on the border with Pakistan getting the short end of the stick. In 2016, it was reported that in one Balochi village, every single man had been hanged for drug smuggling. While the number of executions has tailed off in recent years, Iran's drug laws are still very conservative. Punishments include lashes, forced rehab and imprisonment. I wanted to meet someone who confronted the system head-on.

It's risky getting an interview from inside Iran, as the secret police have an annoying tendency to snatch journalists they don't like, throw them in a darkened dungeon and electrify their balls. Luckily for me, Dr Arash Alaei had been in exile for the past seven years. I could see him in the corner of my Skype window with his long, bushy moustache (thick moustaches are very much in vogue here).

Born to a popular teacher, Arash and his brother Kamiar grew up during the Iran–Iraq war. Saddam rained missiles on Tehran, and the Iranians responded with human-wave attacks reminiscent of the suicidal bravery of the First World War. The impact of the war was devastating. On every major street in Iran you can see portraits of the *shaheeds*, martyrs who laid their lives down for their country. The Alaeis' hometown of Kermanshah lay near the front lines of western Iran. Arash remembered one bombing raid.

'One day there was a huge attack from an Iraqi plane,' he told me. 'The attack was very close to our house, and I saw my youngest brother, who was eight-years-old at the time, had a huge injury in his arm and leg. I took him to the hospital but there wasn't enough staff because so many people were killed or injured, so we had to take him to Tehran, where one of my father's students did the surgery free of charge.'

From that point on, Arash wanted to be a doctor. As he and Kamiar were getting their medical degrees, the brothers saw how people around them were dying of overdoses and HIV, usually spread through sharing needles. The authorities didn't want to admit this was even happening, much less do anything about it: HIV was something to do with gays, and only those depraved Western homos have the gay.

'I saw many clients over the years who were injecting drugs,' Arash says. 'They were very smart, friendly and supportive. I can't say 100 per cent, but most of them.'

In 1997, the Alaeis got permission from their local health board to start up a free health clinic for HIV-sufferers in Kermanshah. It was small at first, only a room, but it was the first clinic in the Middle East and Central Asia that offered injecting drug users clean needles so they wouldn't infect anyone else (or get infected themselves). The idea was to contain the HIV outbreak.

'We increased from one patient a week to between fifty and sixty a day. Then the government supported our project, as did the Global Fund, and we were called the best-practice model by the WHO. We expanded our programme to around sixty to seventy cities and named our clinics Triangular, because of the three-way stigma surrounding our patients: drug users, sex workers and HIV/AIDS.'

Wait a minute ... sex workers? Believe it or not, prostitution exists in Iran. A man and woman can go before an imam to get a 'temporary marriage' certificate, spend the night together and get divorced in the morning. It's all very official, and the contract even sets out terms for the 'divorce settlement'.

For Arash and Kamiar, it was important to look at their clients as more than just patients.

'For us it was important to look at drug users as human, not just someone who commits crime. It's not like an assembly line, where I give you your prescription and you go. Because of the huge stigma and discrimination, they need lots of social and emotional support. So we say to them, "I am here as your doctor and also your friend."

'In Iran, when you have guests, you have to offer them gifts. Once, one of our patients saw we had three international visitors at our clinic. He was homeless and didn't have any money, but later, when they were leaving, we saw him running towards them to give them some flowers. I asked him later, "Where did you find these flowers?" Next to the clinic we have a square, and he cut the flowers there and gave it to them as a gift. It was the most wonderful gift because no one told him to get those flowers, but he did it because he wanted to support me even though he didn't have any money.

'People think homeless and drug users are dirty people, but it's a social issue. Society sends them a message, and they react. But if someone appreciates you, you appreciate them.'

The Alaeis even got the support of some clerics, who saw their project was getting results. But in 2008, the brothers' lives got flipped upside-down. The new president, Mahmoud Ahmadinejad, was like an Iranian version of Trump: always saying ridiculous things to appeal to his rural working-class base. Arash was arrested on 22 June, and Kamiar the day after. They were charged with spying.

'But they couldn't prove I was a spy, so they said I had relations with an enemy government because we were working with foreign universities. They asked us in court, "Do you have contact with foreign universities?" I said, "Yes, of course, I can't deny that." They said, "That is evidence." The previous government gave us a medal for our work!'

In the end, Arash got sentenced to six years and Kamiar, to three. The brothers were sent to Tehran's notorious Evin prison. For the first two months, Arash was held in solitary and denied access to a lawyer. A couple of times he was tortured, 'but not too much'. Sometimes, they'd send jailhouse bullies to mess with him in the yard. But like Andy Dufresne in *The Shawshank Redemption*, the wrongly imprisoned brothers set about making the inmates' lives better.

'We asked the prison officials to give us the regulations and laws for prisons. We had to know what we could do. Then we wrote a letter to the head of the prison, asking if we could work in the department for education. He said, "Sure, who cares, go ahead." The head of faculty was a great man. He said, "I don't care what your crime was, I just see you as a prisoner." That was fantastic, because in Iran, killers and thieves get more rights than political prisoners.

'Then we looked through the rules and we saw there is a guideline for publishing a prison newspaper. We asked for printing paper, a computer and gathered all the prisoners who could write. We then asked the prisoners to send their articles, edited them and published them in the *Voice of Evin*.'

In 2009, allegations of vote-rigging by the Ahmadinejad government sent thousands of Iranians to the streets in protest, only to be beaten up, shot at and arrested by the security forces. The paper's usual columnists of scoundrels, thieves and ruffians were soon joined by activists, journalists and academics.

'Prisoners who'd been forgotten about for many years by their families now had their name in print in weekly newspapers. It was a huge change for them, a lot of prestige, and it became very popular!'

It was less popular, however, with the prison administration. The paper ran for twenty-three issues before the Alaeis were accused of fomenting dissent and were moved to another facility in the desert. But even there, they wouldn't stop their work: the doctors put together an exercise regime for the prisoners in the yard. Then the brothers found out that two of their friends had been executed.

'It was one of the saddest nights. We didn't know them on the outside, but in prison they became our friends. It's one of the worst things when they change your location, because you become familiar with one group of people, then they move you and you hear they are dead. It's one of the tortures they do. It's worse than physical torture, because the pain in your body disappears but the pain in your mind doesn't go away.'

Kamiar was eventually released in late 2010 after an international outcry, while Arash was released the following year. The amazing thing was, while the doctors were imprisoned, their Triangle clinics stayed running – they were too entangled in official bureaucracy to go anywhere.

'We were too far integrated into the primary healthcare system of our country, so they couldn't get rid of us without a long process that would have to go through parliament,' Arash chuckled. 'They arrested my brother and me, but they couldn't arrest everyone.'

Nowadays, the Alaei brothers are based in Albany, New York, where they continue to run HIV/AIDS projects around the world and have even set up a remote learning course for students in war-torn Syria. So would they ever get to return home?

'I can go, but it's not clear whether or not I can leave,' said Arash. 'When the government changed again, they sent some people to say "We are very sorry about that." We said that we understand, but in our country you never know what happens tomorrow. The good news is our clinics are running and providing our services, no matter who's in charge.'

Iran's war on drugs has simmered down in recent years, as the number of hangings has dropped and detox clinics have opened for alcoholics. But it's not the Muslim world, or even America these days, that's fighting the drug war the hardest . . .

32

Killers and Karaoke

'The one thousand will become one hundred thousand. You will see the fish in Manila Bay getting fat. That is where I will dump you.'

Jomar Libo-on might have sensed he was going to die that day. Early in the morning, he came to his wife Dhavie, held her close and asked her forgiveness for all the wrong he'd done, as this could be the last time they'd see each other. Don't talk like that, she told him.

That night, Jomar finished work and made his way home through the slums of Quezon City, a sprawling urban jungle east of the Philippine capital of Manila. Dhavie was already back from her shift, and together with their three oldest kids they sat down to watch TV. The family were gathered in the front room next to the staircase when suddenly, around 11 p.m., there was a knock.

Dhavie got up to check who it was. The men outside were dressed all in black; black masks, black jackets and black pants, with only their eyes visible through their balaclavas. It was hard to mistake their new guests for well-wishers.

'Don't move, don't make a scene,' they snapped. Three men stayed outside while three more barged into the house, ordering Dhavie and the children under the stairs, just out of sight of her husband. As she held the three terrified kids, she heard Jomar begging, pleading for his life. Just then, one of the intruders pulled out a pistol and shot

Jomar straight in the head. Petrified, Dhavie could only hold her children tighter. More gunshots. As the men turned and walked away as if nothing happened, a pool of blood slowly crept across the floor.

It was 13 June 2017. Altogether, Jomar had been shot six times; once in the back of the head, twice in the front and three more in the spine. His murder, like most extra-judicial killings in the Philippines (or EJKs, as they're known here), remains unsolved.

In the 1970s and 80s, the Philippines, a collection of some seven thousand islands in Southeast Asia, was ruled by a piece of work named Ferdinand Marcos, who – in the name of fighting communism – suspended the constitution and declared martial law, which of course won him big props from Washington and the CIA. Under his spectacularly corrupt regime, Marcos and his cronies siphoned off billions of dollars in public funds while his people lived in shantytowns. But by 1986, the people had had enough and rose up in mass protests all across the country. Even some army commanders joined the revolt, sending the dictator packing to Hawaii. The People Power Revolution, as it was called, had won.

Leading the protests in Davao City on the southern Philippine island of Mindanao was a teacher and activist named Soledad Duterte. The mother-of-five was here from the very beginning, braving martial law to hold marches while Marcos assassinated his opponents. After the revolution, when the authorities needed someone to take charge of the city, they approached her, but Soledad, already in her seventies, declined. Instead, her son, Rodrigo 'Rody' Duterte, took up the post.

It wasn't just her activism that rubbed off on Rodrigo. His mother ran a mini-dictatorship of her own, hitting Rodrigo so hard when he was a boy that she wore out her whip. Perhaps unsurprisingly, little Rodrigo developed violent tendencies. At the age of fifteen he carried a gun, and by the time he finished law school he'd already shot and wounded another student for bullying.

It was 1988 and Davao was fast earning a reputation as the Wild West of the Philippines. Communist rebels waged urban warfare while rapists and muggers prowled the streets. But there was a new sheriff in town. As mayor, Duterte took a hands-on approach to law and order, unloading his assault rifle at kidnappers and forcing tourists breaking his smoking ban to swallow their cigarettes at gunpoint. His crime-fighting strategy seemed to be modelled closely on 1980s action movies: just shoot the bastards.

'I grew up in Davao,' said businessman and Duterte fan Jerry Perez De Tagle. 'It was like a warzone. Every morning there were dead bodies found in the street, there was lawlessness and killing. Duterte went in and turned it around.'

Politics in the Philippines has long been conducted at the barrel of a gun. Politicians and powerful clans have fielded their own private armies, particularly in Mindanao, an island wracked by conflict with communist and Muslim insurgents, as well as the head-chopping Islamists of Abu Sayyaf. These militias are used not only for providing security but also as muscle for settling scores: in November 2009, gunmen massacred fifty-seven people in the province of Maguindanao for opposing the powerful Ampatuan family. The Davao Death Squad (DDS), a crew of killers who Mayor Duterte tasked with cleaning the streets of one of the country's most dangerous cities, fitted right into this pattern.

During the 1990s and 2000s, the DDS rode around on motorbikes carrying out targeted assassinations of suspected lawbreakers. Their targets were mainly drug dealers, addicts and small-time thieves, along with a few journalists and human rights activists ... you know, just collateral damage. Arturo Lascañas, a former DDS chief who later came clean at a Senate hearing, admitted to killing over 200 people (including his own brother) on Duterte's orders, receiving between 20,000 and 100,000 pesos ($400 and $2,000) per hit. Far from dashing crimefighters, Lascañas also claimed that some of the police officers who moonlighted in the death squads jacked drug hauls, selling these on themselves.

The actual death toll varies, depending on who you ask. Some sources put the figure at between 700 and 1,000, but Duterte himself boasts it was around 1,700. In 2015, after denying for years that he was behind the DDS, Duterte finally admitted to a reporter: 'They say I am the death squad? True, that is true.'

Elsewhere, this kind of Robert-De-Niro-in-*Taxi-Driver* logic might not fly, but in a country plagued by gun violence, corruption, insurgents and piracy (the Jack Sparrow kind), Duterte's shoot-first-ask-questions-later approach resonated with Filipinos. It was time to roll out his model nationwide. So in early 2016, Duterte ran for president on the tough-on-crime ticket.

In many people's minds, crime meant *shabu*, or crystal meth. A cheap, powerful high, *shabu* kept you going through the long hours of the night and offered slum-dwellers an escape from lives of extreme poverty. People were scared of being stabbed or raped to death by tweekers. They feared too that the Philippines was turning into a narco-state. Drug lords were protected by corrupt police and officials, and even being behind bars was no major obstacle. Take the New Bilibid Prison outside Manila, for instance (one of the biggest correctional facilities in the world, housing over 25,000 inmates). There, gang leaders lived in palaces on-site, complete with lavish offices, aircon, paintings and widescreen TVs. One even had a framed picture of himself with the then-Justice Secretary, Leila de Lima.

In his presidential campaign, Duterte promised to solve the nation's crime problem in an eco-friendly manner by feeding 100,000 criminals to the fish in Manila Bay. Never one to play favourites, Duterte even vowed to kill his own children if they became involved in drugs.

'Just before the campaign back in 2015, I was able to talk to him as part of an exploratory discussion on whether he'd run for president,' Senator Antonio Trillanes told me. 'We talked for an hour. I was really hoping I'd somehow be inspired by his thoughts about governing and reforms, but sadly during our conversation he really never talked about the country and only boasted about the people he'd killed and how he killed them. I believe he had the sick mind of a hitman.'

Rather like President Trump, Duterte was seen as a man of the people – a voice for everyone ignored by the metropolitan elites. And like Trump, Duterte had a potty mouth with no filter.

'How is your health?' one reporter asked.

'How is your wife's vagina?' he replied.

A psychological evaluation of Duterte conducted as part of his divorce proceedings revealed a 'pervasive tendency to demean, humiliate others and violate their rights'. But Filipinos were unperturbed. On 30 May 2016, the Killjoy Pinoy became president of a country of 100 million people.

The killings began straight away. Every night, bloodied bodies would turn up wrapped in plastic sheets with cardboard signs around their necks that read 'Pusher'. One of the early deaths was Maria Moynihan, daughter of the third Lord Moynihan, who at the time of her death was out on bail for drugs charges. In September 2016, she was found with a sign next to her body saying, 'Drug pusher to the celebrities'.

However, most of the victims came from the lower echelons of society. On the night of 16 August 2017, seventeen-year-old Kian delos Santos was just chilling outside his house when a group of plainclothes officers approached him. An hour later, the teenager's body was found. He'd been shot in the head at the end of a filthy alley.

At first, the cops claimed that he was a pusher who went out guns blazing. Usually when suspects are killed 'resisting arrest' the officers invariably find a sachet of meth or a firearm lying around, putting them in the clear. But this time they were caught with their pants down. Witnesses said they saw the officers beating Kian before taking him away, while CCTV showed three officers marching the terrified boy down the alley, begging to be let go; he had school in the morning. There was no way they could spin this as anything other than a cold-blooded execution.

Thousands showed up for Kian's funeral, and thousands more took to the streets demanding justice, smashing through Duterte's cast-iron personality cult. Eventually (which I'm sure had nothing to do with the unfolding PR nightmare) three cops were sent down for murder. The irony is that Kian had supported his president and wanted to be a policeman when he grew up. He was one of thirty-two people killed that weekend. So far, no evidence has emerged that he was ever involved in drugs.

To put this in context, the security services killed or 'disappeared' some 3,240 people over the whole of Marcos's twenty-year reign. Officially, more than 5,000 people have been killed in anti-drug operations since President Rodrigo 'smoke pot, get shot' Duterte took power in 2016, but unofficially the body count might run into tens of thousands: Human Rights Watch places the figure at over 12,000, while Senator Antonio Trillanes, the loudest voice in the Philippines' opposition, claimed a figure as high as 20,000. Duterte himself seemed to encourage the bloodshed, telling any would-be vigilantes that if they shoot a drug dealer, 'I'll give you a medal.'

'The numbers are unprecedented,' the Commission on Human Rights' (CHR) public affairs officer Jacqueline Ann De Guia told me. 'All previous administrations have had human rights issues, but never before have we had a moment where we've been so overwhelmed with cases. We're currently investigating a thousand cases, 50 per cent are the result of police operations and 50 per cent are vigilante killings.'

At the same time, Duterte took aim at his political opponents. In 2017, Senator Leila de Lima, the former Justice Secretary who oversaw the CHR's investigation into the Davao Death Squad, was thrown into jail for her alleged ties to the New Bilibid gangs. Duterte's supporters also threatened her with a sex tape. It's a bit mysterious as to how the knowledge of whether she spits or swallows will help shine any light on the Philippine drug trade, so I can only assume this invasion of her private life is an attempt to frame her as a harlot whose whorish words cannot be trusted by good Catholic Filipinos.*

In 2018, Senator Antonio Trillanes was arrested. In 2003, he led a mutiny of 300 naval officers as they seized a downtown hotel to protest against corruption. He was pardoned, but Duterte reversed the pardon.

I landed in Manila in January 2018, hoping dearly that no one had told Duterte about my former occupation. Manila's a mess of a city, an eclectic urban sprawl where skyscrapers and shopping malls rise up a stone's throw away from shantytowns and open sewers. Metro Manila itself is made up of sixteen different towns, including Quezon City (location of the Libo-on residence), and, as you might expect, the traffic is awful. Winding our way through the rickshaws and jeepneys, I finally understood why EJKs always take place at night – anyone planning a getaway between 17.00 and 21.00 will quickly find themselves up shit creek. We drove up to the Philippine National Police (PNP) headquarters to speak to their spokesman, Dionardo Carlos, whom I hoped would shed some light on Operation Double-Barrel, the government's campaign against drugs. Carlos greeted us dressed in his dark-blue uniform and full regalia.

'The plan against illegal drugs is in two parts: Operation Tokhang, and High-Value Targets. Tokhang is to knock and plead, going door to door to plead with known drug personalities to change their ways,'

---

* Duterte himself brags about being knee-deep in pussy and how he 'can't imagine life without Viagra'.

Carlos explained. The idea is that High-Value Targets includes the Chinese crime lords and corrupt officials bringing in *shabu*, while Tokhang is ostensibly to give low-level users and dealers a chance to hand themselves in.

'Based on the feedback from the community, they feel safer outside,' Carlos continued. 'They can go out in the street. Before, the public was afraid; now, it's the addicts who are on the run.'

In the first year of Duterte's term, street crime dropped 10 per cent (except murder, murder went way up). So OK, the public feel safer. But how do they come up with this list?

'We confer with the *barangay* [village or community],' he told me, 'as they are the ones who provide the list. We then cross-check that with our intelligence and, together with the *barangay*, we go to them and tell them to change their ways, to please go to the *barangay* centre where they will be provided with assistance. But along the way, Tokhang got demonised. Now the thinking is you will be killed, which is not the aim of Tokhang.'

I'm glad Carlos brought this up, because for many people, once they get that knock it's time to say your prayers. So what does he make of the killings?

'In the first six months there were a lot of deaths. Why? Because the drug syndicates normally liquidate their underlings. There were a lot of vigilante killings, and people were also killed during police operations when they opted to fight it out. As the president explained, the tendency to use *shabu* makes them suspicious and violent. There was no specific order to kill drug lords. But if it's a choice between the one who died, and the life of the officer . . .'

Given Duterte's rhetoric, I'd debate Carlos when he says there was 'no specific order', but more on that later. Part of what he says, however, is true. There are a lot of gangsters in the Philippines, and most of them carry heat — so yes, many police shootings are legit cases of self-defence, and dozens of officers have been killed in the line of duty.

It was time to see how the police worked. Bien, my fixer, suggested we go on a ride-along. I was already locked up when the Met ransacked my flat, so I've never witnessed a drug raid, and I wanted to see how things looked on the other side. So off we went to Station 6 in Quezon City, where the lead detective waved us into his car. The first thing I saw was that he was a big dude, and you gotta give credit where credit's due, his shirt was pretty badass: the words 'SDEU – Station Drug Enforcement Unit' over a giant skull logo, just like Frank Castle in *The Punisher*. As heavy rain poured down, we drove down to the slums, where I promised myself I'd look the other way if I saw anyone getting away. But by the time we got there, everyone was already in cuffs. Three old geezers had been arrested in a bust-buy operation, where the cops sent in an informant to score off the suspects. On the living-room table in their three-room house lay 300 pesos in banknotes, a set of baggies, and about £40 worth of meth. I asked the Punisher: 'How long are they gonna get?'

'For selling? Probably twenty years.'

At first I was like, 'no way'; like probably the maximum is twenty years, so maybe that's the *most* they're gonna get. But then I asked around and, yeah, twenty years sounds about right . . . they don't fuck around here.

After the drug bust, we went to see a rehab clinic, the Department of Health Treatment and Rehabilitation Center in Bicutan, south of Manila. Cornered between forced detox or death, many on the *barangay*'s hitlist weighed up their options and handed themselves in to the authorities. I'd heard stories about thousands of addicts being herded into overpacked prisons, but the vibe was a lot more positive: wearing the same uniform of bleach-white shorts and T-shirts, all the patients wished me 'Good day, sir!' with a smile, even the ones doing time-out on the naughty step. Of course, it could all have been for show, but I'd be less concerned for them here than on the outside, where the president does not even consider them to be people.

'These human rights advocates did not count those who were killed before I became President. The children who were raped and mutilated [by drug users],' Duterte told his critics. 'That is why I said, "What crime against humanity?" In the first place, I would like to be frank with you: are they humans? What is your definition of a human being? Tell me.'

Dr Alfonso Villaroman, the practitioner who runs the facility, disputed the notion that his patients are crazed baby-raping maniacs.

'Their problem is basically addiction. Some of them sell or are forced to sell, or go into petty crimes or prostitution, but generally drug dependents are not bad people. That's why we're here to give them a chance,' he said.

'We're the only centre which has a formal school, offering both regular and alternate learning and vocational courses. We try to cover all domains – health, spiritual and psychological. I did a study with the WHO where we found the best catalyst is to establish education and vocation. It helps their low self-esteem so much, so it can be a catalyst for recovery as well. At the same time, we have other programmes like TB, HIV and others as well. And all our medication here is free. Our patients don't pay a single cent.'

I liked Dr Villaroman. He agreed that the current laws are too harsh on certain offenders, especially teenagers caught up in the game. But one thing threw me off about the good doctor: he supports Duterte's campaign.

'The president was clear in his mandate that he wants to go after drug pushers, and rescue or save the drug addicts. He doesn't even call them drug addicts, but drug victims,' Villaroman said. 'Now we're in the spotlight, we can set up clinics in even the furthest points of the archipelago.'

On the one hand that's understandable: since it's a government-run clinic, the doc doesn't want to roast his boss while his patients are getting more stuff. But the words 'rescue' and 'save' don't tend to crop up often in Duterte's speeches.

'If you know of any addicts, go ahead and kill them yourself, as getting their parents to do it would be too painful,' the president told slum-dwellers in Manila shortly after being sworn in, before hinting that people should start making coffins.

'I assure you, you won't go bankrupt. If your business slows, I will tell the police, "Do it faster to help the people earn money."'

Classic Duterte. The funny thing is that in other areas he's kind of progressive. He supports gay rights and has shut down mines that were polluting the rivers. The economy's doing well, and people are better off. Hell, if it wasn't for the whole death squad thing I might actually like the guy.

Then again, check out what this progressive had to say to his cops: 'Your duty requires you to overcome the resistance of the person you are arresting . . . You are free to kill the idiots; that is my order to you.

'Do your duty, and if in the process you kill a thousand persons because you were doing your duty, I will protect you.'

Even if he was chatting shit, many officers took it to heart – it was open season on junkies.

On 15 August 2016, Cherwen Polo got together with three drinking buddies and one of his neighbours to celebrate his thirty-ninth birthday. Cherwen had been a small-time dealer, but when he heard about the killings he jumped ship and found another job. By 11 p.m. that night he had passed out drunk while his wife Kathrina was making baby food upstairs, when there was a knock at their door. Cherwen's friend Blink got up to answer.

'There's nothing – please don't,' he stammered, before being blasted by a hail of gunshots. Heavy footsteps thundered up the stairs as uniformed cops told Kathrina to get out.

'Why? This is my house,' she said.

'You know what will happen; get out,' came the reply as Kathrina grabbed her three children and stepped out into the pouring rain.

Blink lay by the door, his head blown to pieces. Two more gunshots rang from the house as the family stood in the downpour.

Only one of Cherwen's friends, Harold, survived and he is now in hiding. The officers behind the birthday massacre were members of the Davao Boys, a team of hard-hitting cops from Duterte's hometown reassigned to the capital, bringing the DDS mentality with them. The officers claimed Cherwen opened fire on them as they were making a bust-buy. But as Kathrina later found out, an autopsy showed that Cherwen had been shot through the head, heart and forearm in the right corner of the upstairs bedroom. He'd been murdered in his sleep.

Even being arrested, handcuffed and jailed won't be enough to spare you. Harrah Kazuo agreed to come out of hiding and meet me by a fountain in downtown Manila. The first thing I noticed about Harrah was that she was a super-small lady, her head barely reaching above my waist. But what she lacked in size, she more than made up for in bravery.

On the night of 8 July 2016, right after Duterte's inauguration, police raided her home and arrested her husband, Jaybee Bertes, and his father Renato. As they searched the house, they molested Jaybee's two-year-old daughter, pulling down her underwear to check her anus for drugs. When Harrah came to the station house the next day, Jaybee and Renato had both been beaten so badly they could hardly walk. Harrah had left to check on their daughter when she got a message that both Jaybee and Renato were dead.

The cops claimed that the pair were shot as they tried grabbing an officer's gun, but who does that in a police station? Autopsies also showed that their arms and fingers were broken and swollen, making it impossible for them to have tied their belts, let alone made moves like Chow Yun-Fat. The police even tormented the family at their wake.

'They rode around in masked helmets, going round and round our house on bikes,' Harrah said. 'Almost every day the police were there. Once, I came out at midnight and screamed, "Are you not content? You killed my husband and his father already!" And they just smiled because they knew I couldn't do anything.'

The two cops responsible, Alipio Balo and Michael Tomas, were eventually indicted for murder, but they went on the run and haven't been heard from since. Harrah went on national television, being one of the first victims to speak out against the drug war. Together with her daughter, she's since had to enter a witness protection programme run by the CHR and has to change her address every few weeks.

But despite attracting enough attention for a Senate hearing, the case wasn't enough to put a clamp on the killings. Just a few months later, dirty narcs kidnapped a Korean businessman named Jee Ick-joo for ransom and strangled him to death in the halls of the PNP headquarters itself. When the scandal threatened to break relations with South Korea, Duterte was furious, briefly suspending the anti-drug campaign before ordering that the PNP's drug squad be disbanded. He then personally reprimanded 400 corrupt cops on the grounds of the presidential palace, threatening to send them away to fight Abu Sayyaf, and bring in the army to Manila as the police were too corrupt. Send dirty cops to fight an actual war, then bring in soldiers to be murder cops – it's foolproof. But after the Santos case and the Jee murder, the pressure was on and responsibility for the drugs war was reassigned to the more professional PDEA (Philippine Drug Enforcement Agency). In a weird coincidence, the murders stopped. At least for a while.

When the cops wanna whack someone, they usually plant drugs or weapons to make it look like they went down fighting. They don't leave bodies wrapped in plastic. So who else is behind the wave of killings?

The first suspects are the crime syndicates, chief among them the Chinese. While now (severe repression aside) China is communist in name only, everything is still so tightly controlled that the only way to get ahead is by greasing the palms of Party bureaucrats. In 2013, police and paramilitary troops raided the village of Boshe in Guangdong province, near Hong Kong, whose meth labs produced a third of the country's ice. The entire operation was run by a Party Secretary named Cai Dongjia, who used his political connections to buy chemicals, partnering with the Hong Kong triads to move his product overseas. Knockoff Hello Kitty bags aren't the only thing Made in China.

The Chinese, along with their local partners, may be using extra-judicial killings as a cover to liquidate informants and/or the competition.

People are also using the drug war to settle personal scores. Such was the case with Reynaldo Baa, who got six bullets in his back from motorbike-riding assailants – the typical MO for drug-related killings.

'My husband wasn't involved in drugs, but he had a guarantor who lent him money. They argued thirty minutes before the incident happened,' Reynaldo's wife Lucelyn told me. 'And two weeks before, he had another fight about money.'

'From our data, only 11 per cent of deaths are drug-related,' said Dionardo Carlos. 'Somebody in a love triangle could make it look like a vigilante killing so that no one will investigate their case. But the picture they try to put in foreign media is that all killings are drug-related. If you don't know the real score on the ground, you would think all killings are EJK.'

Love triangles? Well cuck-a-doodle-doo. Even if jealous house-wives are responsible for 89 per cent of the murder rate, Duterte's still enabled them to cover their tracks.

And then there's the vigilantes. Had they really been roused by the president's stirring rhetoric, or was there something else? I was about to find out.

'And now we go to Montalban. It's a bad place, lots of drug addicts,' our driver complained, comparing our hectic timetable to his old, comfy job in the film industry. It was already midnight when we pulled up to a neighbourhood bar on the outskirts of Manila, where the friendly female owner hurried me to an upstairs bedroom. The man was already waiting for us, stood in the middle of the room in his black jacket and balaclava. It was too late to back out now.

'At twenty-one I killed my first man in a fight,' he said in Tagalog, sitting down opposite me, 'then I killed another man with a knife. I got used to killing. I'm forty-seven years old now, so I've been doing this for twenty-six years. When I was twenty-eight I got my first gun, a .357 Magnum, and started doing jobs for my boss.' I scanned the room and I realised he had sat down between me and the door as karaoke music blared in the background. The song was 'My Way', by Frank Sinatra.

'First the boss will call me and I gather the team. We study the target for a few days or weeks, their movements. If it's an easy job, I'll do it myself, or sometimes there'll be two of us on a motorcycle. We work as a team – sometimes I'm the shooter, but sometimes I'm the driver or the spotter. But we have to make sure there aren't any police in the area or we have to postpone it. We always carry three clips, just in case.'

Reaching into his backpack, he pulled out a handgun. As he lifted the strap I was, for a brief moment, staring down the end of the barrel. He quickly lowered the piece and produced three loaded clips, which he laid down on the table. Just then, I clocked the bullet hanging off his backpack's zipper.

'We have to make sure of our target; if not, our boss gets mad. The payment depends: if it's a small-time pusher it's 15,000 pesos, but if it's a big fish it's 150,000. For example, last year there was the boss of a big syndicate, but the area was already packed [with dealers] so we told him to go away. But the man wouldn't leave, so the boss had him killed. Another time, a woman was not remitting the money, so the boss ordered her dead.

'Before, we only killed every four to six months. When there's no job, I sell utensils like plates, spoons, forks. And if we have a target that's hard to find, I disguise myself as a seller in that village. But now, since 2016, we have a job almost every week. Sometimes there's not enough time to scope out the target, so we just ride up and shoot.'

So this homicidal cutlery salesman gives some criminals a pass if they don't forget to pay. But who is his boss?

'Our boss is an army general, military, so we are protected because those we kill are social outcasts and criminals. I've been to prison three times for killing and stabbing, but our lawyers always get us out.'

Makes sense. In many cases, these 'vigilante killings' are little more than cover for a racketeering operation. When Duterte came to office, such killings became sanctioned in the name of cleaning up the streets, and the brass started calling in their debts. Using hitmen also gives them plausible deniability. If one of them gets caught, they can blame it on the Chinese drug gangs cleaning house.

'In my career I've probably killed thirty-two people. I have four kids, and I'll stop doing this job when my sons get out of high school and become successful. It's OK to quit, but we can never speak out. Our boss doesn't like traitors.'

The man hadn't revealed any specific details, but the danger is real. After his revelations, Arturo Lascañas, the repentant DDS chief, had to flee the Philippines in fear of his life.

I tried to get some cool shots, but our hitman's not much of a poser – just stood there like a schoolboy waiting for his prom date – so I shook his hand and made my way down. Since I was a white boy in a karaoke bar, the owner wanted me to sing a song. I warned her that my singing sounds like a kitten being drowned, but she insisted, so I chose 'My Way' by Frank Sinatra. It just felt right.

Every time there's a political debate on the Internet, it's only a matter of time before somebody's compared to Hitler: Putin is like Hitler! Trump is like Hitler! Charlie the cat is like Hitler!

Now, I don't usually like making the Hitler analogy. It's called Godwin's law and shows a lack of historical knowledge. The Nazis weren't the only bad guys in history. What about the Mongols, huh? They were pretty mean! But Duterte saved us the trouble at a speech in Davao.

'Hitler massacred 3 million [sic] Jews. Now, there are 3 million drug addicts. I would be happy to slaughter them. If Germany had Hitler, the Philippines would have ...' and the president pointed to himself.

This meta-Godwin may have stunned the world, but to anyone paying attention it was already crystal-clear: this was a genocide.

In his seminal work *The Destruction of the European Jews*, Holocaust researcher Raul Hilberg identified a series of steps that ultimately led to the murder of 6 million Jews. While the Holocaust was unique in many ways (its horrifying scale, for one), we can see the same patterns repeating again and again throughout human history; in Armenia, Cambodia, Rwanda ...

First, a group of people no one cares about is singled out as the cause of society's ills. As Duterte makes clear, for Hitler it was the Jews. For him, it's the drug addicts. They're subject to name-calling. In Rwanda, this was the point at which the Tutsis started being called 'cockroaches'. Duterte's rhetoric has similarly classed addicts as subhuman. Their property might be taken away and then they themselves might be taken away, either to prisons or internment camps or forced to leave their homes. This isn't limited to the Philippines either: one sheriff in Arizona proudly used to call his jail for drug convicts his very own 'concentration camp'.

The final step is extermination, where we do away with all pretences and just kill them. While no one took it as far as Duterte before, he wasn't the first. Since the retirementof Khun Sa, the Golden Triangle's opium king, in 1996, Burmese rebels have switched from tending their poppy fields to brewing up *yaba*, or 'crazy medicine', a party pill popular with clubbers in Thailand and Bangladesh that contains a mixture of methamphetamine and caffeine, as if the meth on its own isn't enough to keep you awake for the next three days. In 2003, Thailand slaughtered over 2,500 of its own citizens in just three months under President Thaksin Shinawatra's campaign against this new drug. It later turned out that most victims had nothing to do with *yaba* in the first place; the killing frenzy was mainly for settling scores.

True, drug users don't have an identity like the Jews, Tutsis or Armenians, but genocides don't necessarily have to target a specific ethnic or religious group. Look at the Khmer Rouge, the Soviet Union under Stalin or the Dirty War in Argentina. In the words of David Simon, crime reporter and co-creator of *The Wire*: 'The drug war is a Holocaust in slow motion.'

Yet if you tell a Filipino who supports Duterte that what he's doing is insane, they'll probably tell you that you don't understand the drug problem in the Philippines. Drastic times call for drastic measures. It's not nice, they'll say, but it has to be done.

'What works for you might not work for us, and what works for us might not work for you,' said PNP spokesman Dionardo Carlos. 'Let's try this: we'll bring kilos of *shabu* to the Netherlands, bring it to Portugal, and we'll see how these users will act in society.'

The spokesman has a point. Meth causes aggression and paranoia. The public's enthusiasm to be rid of it is hard to overestimate. One survey conducted in October 2017 showed that over three-quarters of Filipinos were scared that masked vigilantes would gun them down in the street – but nearly 90 per cent of them thought these vigilantes were a good thing, even when it's their families being slaughtered. On 14 August 2017, Ignacio Yutero, an occasional *shabu* user, and three of his friends were shot dead by masked gunmen in a raid over the corrugated roofs of their slum. But Jenny Yutero, Ignacio's wife, still supports the anti-drug campaign.

'It's good, but only if they are sure of their target; I think they screwed up, because there have been innocent targets, and they should give them a chance or else the mother is left alone looking after everything,' she said, seemingly rationalising her husband's death as a misstep in an otherwise worthy cause.

Have three-quarters of Filipinos lost the plot? Not really. It's easy for us in the West, with our social safety nets and mountains of gold, to look upon the Philippines as a barbaric Third World hell-hole where life is cheap. But walking through the slums – or even more upscale neighbourhoods like Malate – you encounter extreme poverty: families living in shacks, little girls selling themselves for something to eat. Throwing powerful stimulants in the mix is a recipe for disaster. You can see why the long-suffering Filipinos are desperate for someone, *anyone*, who can bring them change.

But as usual, lies, misinformation and exaggeration are used to take us to war. Duterte claimed that there were over 3 million addicts (out of a population of over 100 million), but data from the Office of the President's Dangerous Drugs Board survey in 2015 showed there were, at most, 1.8 million drug users, only a third of whom had used in the past year ('addicts') – and less than half used *shabu*. The rest mainly smoked grass. The Philippines' drug problem is actually milder than Australia's.

And yet the PNP considers druggies its top priority, even ahead of *actual* criminals.

'If the suspect's a known robber, we're not going to be knocking on the door, but if he's robbing to sustain a habit, we consider him a drug personality and put him on the list. If he's just a robber, we don't visit him,' Carlos told me.

So does mass repression even work? Duterte might think he's taking a leaf from Mao's book, but even after decades of his *Death*

Wish antics, between 2010 and 2015 Davao City still reported the highest rates of rape and murder in the Philippines.

And then there are those who deny EJKs take place at all, or that Duterte's responsible for them. Which of these sounds more plausible: that hundreds of foreign journalists, Filipino reporters, eyewitnesses, human rights groups and international organisations are all lying, or that the guy who boasted about feeding 100,000 criminals to the fish is actually killing people? What's more, if the body count isn't as high as is claimed, he's not lived up to his campaign promises.

There's one more similarity to Hitler that Duterte might not have intended. Like the German dictator, Duterte himself is a drug addict. In December 2016, the president admitted to using fentanyl (an artificial opioid fifty times stronger than heroin) to help him cope with back pain after a motorbike accident. Rodrigo 'snort coke, get smoked' Duterte, who'd declared war on drug addicts in his country, described the high as being 'on cloud nine'. They say that the things we hate most about others are those that we hate most about ourselves.

Before we close this chapter, I wanna leave you with one more story. A short drive from Jomar Libo-on's house lies another slum. There, right by the makeshift basketball court, lies a tumbledown shack where a man lives with his five kids. And I don't just mean a shitty-looking house, I mean an actual shack with some metal sheets and a few planks stuck together. His wife got caught up in a massive raid on a drug-dealing area, apparently in the wrong place at the wrong time, just after she'd given birth to their son, a baby boy. While she was in jail, she couldn't work or breastfeed the boy, and the father couldn't afford to buy enough food on his own. The baby starved to death.

33

Cocaine *Cariocas*

2019 started with a bang. If you're looking for a party on New Year's Eve, you could do worse than Rio de Janeiro. As the crowd watched the night sky light up with a cascade of fireworks over Copacabana, little bands of street kids ran around stealing their wallets. Mine stayed safely in my pocket, but as the clock struck midnight I got a text saying four hundred dollars had been withdrawn from my bank card . . . in Minnesota. I still got jacked.

A few days later, over 2,000 km away in the state of Ceará in the northeast (Brazil is *huuuuge*), there was quite another kind of excitement – looting and rioting as local hoodlums went on the warpath, torching buses, government buildings and police stations. At one point they blew up a phone tower, sending twelve cities back to the Dark Age. The army had to be sent in.

It was a collaboration between two of Brazil's biggest criminal organisations, the PCC and Red Command, feat. the new kids on the block, North Family. Just a few years before, they'd been at each other's throats. On New Year's Day 2017, members of the North Family attacked the PCC at the COMPAJ prison complex in Manaus, northwest Brazil. Over seventeen hours fifty-six prisoners were killed, several of their heads thrown over the prison walls. More mayhem followed: a week later, thirty-three people were killed at another prison riot in Roraima state, northern Brazil. But in 2019 they put all that aside to send a message to Brazil's newly-elected far-right president, Jair Bolsonaro.

Bolsonaro's a clown who'd somehow made it through the stench of Brazil's graft-ridden politics; an ex-army captain who thinks it's totally normal to tweet hardcore porn to his 3 million-plus followers. But many people voted for him (even in the slums, or favelas), because they were tired of the corruption of the ruling party (although other parties were just as bad). Bolsonaro said he'd give the police carte blanche to use lethal force on drug traffickers, modelling his law-and-order policies on cop thriller *Elite Squad 2*, like a sexy Latino Duterte ('Do you have a problem? Well, have you tried shooting it?'). Like Duterte, Bolsonaro's also been accused of ties to death squads, specifically militias of former and off-duty cops running Mafia-style protection rackets. The militias chase out drug traffickers from a favela, then start 'taxing' the local residents. In Ceará, the traffickers tried to send Bolsonaro a warning.

Like America, Brazil's war on drugs is inextricably linked to race and class. In 1830, Rio de Janeiro became the first place in the world to ban marijuana, on the grounds that it was making their black African slaves lazy as hell. Slavery itself wasn't abolished in Brazil until 1888.

Nowadays Brazil's in love with the coco, and being next to all three major coca-producing nations (Bolivia, Colombia and Peru) has helped create the second-biggest market for blow after the United States. While powder cocaine's popular among the affluent middle class, the situation's got so out of control among the more marginalised sections of society that whole neighbourhoods known as *Cracolândia* or 'Crackland' have sprung up across Rio, São Paulo and elsewhere.

In theory, personal drug use is depenalised, so you won't get locked up for smoking a zoot. In practice, what counts as 'personal' is fairly arbitrary. Owing to stereotypes that most slum-dwellers are thieves, drug dealers and gangbangers, this means that, as always, the rich get off with a warning while the poor get bent over and fisted by the long arm of the law. Over a quarter of inmates in Brazil, which has the highest number of prisoners worldwide after the US and China, are doing time for drugs charges. And so thousands of young men and women enter the system into the welcoming arms of the country's largest crime syndicate – the First Command of the Capital (*Primeiro Comando da Capital*, or PCC) – which draws its ranks from the cells of Brazil's hellish penal system.

I first met Hugo in HMP Isis when he was serving ten years for armed robbery (a .357 Magnum), importing cocaine, and selling cocaine, ketamine and mephedrone. If there's a law against something, he's probably done it. At the tender age of twenty, he'd already spent over a quarter of his young life behind bars; the first time was for killing a man.

'In Brazil, every day there is a murder inside jail,' he'd later tell me on the outside.

At one point we heard that his brother (who was the one sending him the coke and was imprisoned at the time somewhere near Rio) attempted a jailbreak with about a dozen others. Some of them got away, but his brother ended up being shot five times. He survived, but spent the next couple of months under armed guard at the hospital.

'Isis is cool. The only thing that's the same is that we're all in jail, so we can't be with our families,' Hugo told me, 'but apart from that, it's completely different. Unlike in the UK, we ain't got nothing to do; we don't go to school or workshops, we just stay in the cell. And every day the officers punch us and kick us.'

Brazil's prisons are notoriously overcrowded and inmates are left with zero privacy, meaning diseases spread fast.

'Brazilian jail is not clean,' Hugo explained. 'We ain't got no bed to sleep in, or there's only four beds but in the cell there's fuckin' twenty-four people and shit. You ain't got space for nothing.'

The PCC was ostensibly set up to fight for prisoners' rights after police massacred 111 inmates at a prison riot in 1992. The PCC boys don't fool around: back in 2006 they'd laid siege to the city of São Paulo, killing dozens of people in the bloodiest terrorist attack Brazil has ever seen. Over the course of five days in May, gang members rampaged through the streets, shooting cops, bombing buildings and torching buses, while their comrades ran riot in prisons across the state. The reason? Authorities tried to move a group of shot-callers to another facility.

From behind bars the PCC controls cocaine dealing across the nation, but first the coke has to make its way across the jungles of the Amazon, a territory controlled by the North Family. The North Family is a relatively new player on the scene (established 2006), but its massacre of the PCC prisoners in COMPAJ was at the behest of another cartel: Red Command (*Comando Vermelho*, or CV), based out of the favelas of Rio de Janeiro.

'We have two seasons here in Rio. One season is summer and one is hell, and right now we're in hell,' said one of my friends as he wiped the sweat from his brow.

Rio de Janeiro is probably the greenest city I've ever been in. Maybe not green as in eco-friendly, but literally half the city is forest and jungle with random mountains popping up everywhere. This is in the middle of Rio! You go to one neighbourhood, then there's a mountain with jungles and monkeys, and then there's another neighbourhood.

But the Marvellous City has an unfortunate reputation for crime that belies its golden beaches, beautiful women, stunning scenery and carefree *carioca* vibe.

This reputation is not entirely undeserved. Ever since the cocaine boom in the 1980s, fighting between and within the city's three major crime families – Red Command, Amigos dos Amigos and Third Command – as well as corrupt police militias, has contributed to Brazil having one of the worst homicide rates on the planet. One in every ten murder victims in the world is Brazilian, and around half of those cases are gang-related. Sometimes this has blown up into an all-out war, with police helicopters getting shot down for straying into the wrong hood.

I'm always amused when rabblerouser columnists and politicians talk about 'no-go zones' as if they know what they're on about. It gets funnier when they go on about Sweden. *Sweden.* The land of moose and meatballs where, apparently, all hell has broken loose. The term 'no-go zone' was originally coined by a journalist in 2014 when police reports identified scores of 'vulnerable areas' where gang rule, unemployment and Islamic radicalism run high. It's true, there are problems – tit-for-tat shootings in Malmö, Sweden's Chicago, and a gang war in Gothenburg where Serbian and Somali gangsters tossed hand grenades and set off car bombs. These are compounded by Sweden's weirdly puritanical drug laws,* drawing a clearer line between 'us' and 'them' (blond-haired, blue-eyed Aryan god-men named Sven, and dark-skinned fellas called Arif and Abdul). So there are problems, yes, but it's a bit of a stretch to say there are parts of Sweden, an industrialised, First World country with a generous welfare system, where the government has lost control. Statistically, the home of Ikea remains one of the safest countries on Earth. However, it's a different story when it comes to Brazil.

'It's a place where the gangs can take control because the state is incompetent,' said Paolo Storani, a veteran of Rio's elite BOPE unit. 'They let people live there without basic conditions, and without the state another kind of power can take control.'

Among middle-class Brazilians, the favelas have a reputation akin to the seventh circle of hell. Outsiders wandering in can look forward

---

* Although drug usage is very low, at the same time, overdose rates are extremely high (thirty times higher, in fact, than in Portugal). So there's less druggies, but more of them are dying. Seems like a shitty trade-off.

to being raped and robbed. Everyone knows the story of Tim Lopes, the Globo reporter who was dismembered with a samurai sword and set on fire after being taken for a spy. But having already been stabbed, crossed rebel territory and barbecued by El Chapo's house, I fancied my chances . . .

Together with a lady friend I caught the subway down to Rocinha, Rio's largest favela, where we waited for our guide while downing half a bottle of *cachaça* (Brazilian rum). Even though Rocinha is (by far) the best-known and safest favela, as a gringo who doesn't speak Portuguese its best to come with someone who actually knows the area.

It's night-time. Our guide arrives and we hitch a ride on a motor-bike taxi up the hill through the winding streets of the ghetto. While there's lively nightlife and music booming out of bars, it's not the kind of party we're after. At the top of the hill, we disembark and walk left through a narrow, winding concrete alleyway, going deeper into the favela. Most of what you see here was built by the community: favelas are essentially squats populated by migrants from the impoverished northeast of Brazil and descendants of slaves. Over 100,000 live here, and that's just officially.

The full blast of the pumping beats and the strong smell of weed hit us as we turn the corner onto a crowded street. There must be at least a thousand people here; humid, sweaty bodies bumping and grinding around a platform where two MCs stand next to a massive sound system. Pulsating lights beam over the crowd as girls dance in short shorts and bikini tops, shaking their posteriors. The energy has the same vibe as a rave.

Then, suddenly: rat-a-tat-tat! Machinegun fire crackles through the air. Two mofos in flip-flops walk by, waving assault rifles; one of them has a rounded clip like a 1920s gangster. They look barely old enough to drive, but they're not threatening anyone: this is Red

Command territory, and these boys are security. That's just how it is at these things: you could be walking along and suddenly boom, a fourteen-year-old kid's firing a machinegun into the air.

Like the PCC, Red Command has its origins in prison. The cartel formed from an alliance between bank robbers and left-wing militants thrown in together during the 1964 to 1985 military dictatorship. The guerrillas mixed with the common criminals, teaching them how to plan and execute raids with military precision, as well as their revolutionary ideology (which has since all but disappeared). In the mid-1990s, splinter factions broke off to form Third Command, known for its pseudo-evangelical fanaticism (they won't sell crack) and Amigos dos Amigos (ADA, or 'Friends of Friends'). Along with the militias, they exercise a near-total control of Rio's worst neighbourhoods.

The gang hosts these parties, or funk balls (*baile funk*) every weekend. Funk is a style of *carioca* music blending US-style hip-hop with tropical beats that make you wanna jiggle your booty. Like American hip-hop, funk talks about the struggles of growing up in the ghetto, although most of it's about shagging and having a good time.

And then, in the corner, a courtyard. I couldn't believe my fuckin' eyes: a teenage boy in a baseball cap manning a market stall of cocaine. Little vials of white powder neatly arranged by price and quality on a wooden desk, as if they were a selection of cheeses. The best stuff costs fifty reais (about £10) a gram.

Situated between three of the city's most upmarket neighbourhoods in the touristic South Zone, Rocinha is Rio's most strategic favela for the drug trade. This used to be an ADA neighbourhood under the stewardship of king-of-the-hill Antônio Francisco Bonfim Lopes, aka 'Nem' of the Amigos dos Amigos gang. Nem maintained his own brand of law and order and under his reign, theft, rape and robbery were not tolerated, which drew in more well-to-do cocaine aficionados. The playboys from the South Zone felt safe picking up there. In its heyday, ADA racked in $26m a year from Rocinha alone.

But since Nem got locked up in 2011, Red Command moved in, consolidating its hold as Rio's premier crime group.

Not everyone shares my enthusiasm for teenage boys waving military-grade assault rifles, and with all the heavy-duty firepower making my girlfriend nervous, we soon had to leave.

No-go zones? Bitch, please.

Earlier that day we passed the heavily armed, black-clad officers of the UPP (*Unidade de Polícia Pacificadora*, or Police Pacification Unit). In the run-up to the Olympics, paramilitary units like BOPE and UPP were mobilised en masse to effectively mount an invasion of the favelas to flush out the resident drug cartels. That's easier said than done, since walking through the favela is like wandering through a maze. With their tight little alleys and tall, vertical houses piled on top of each other, these concrete labyrinths are perfect for urban warfare.

But once a favela's been 'pacified' a permanent police presence can move in and the area is, at least officially, back under government control. In one such raid on a drug lord's mansion in a CV-controlled neighbourhood in 2010, officers found a swimming pool, a sauna, 10 tonnes of weed, a cache of assault rifles, a missile … and a small, hand-painted mural of Justin Bieber.*

Has Rocinha been pacified? If Saturday night was anything to go by, has it fuck. However, since the area's been declared 'safe', the locals have appreciated the extra infrastructure and investment that pacification brought to the hood. After pretending for decades they didn't exist, the government's finally started paying attention to the favelas. But while the gangs might have been bad, the locals told me, the cops are even worse.

---

* I imagine the old man thirty years from now, breaking it down for some young whippersnapper in the prison yard: 'Back in my day we had Justin Bieber and Katy Perry; now that was REAL music.'

'The drug dealers at least, they come from the community, so they respect the community,' they told me. 'They [the police] don't come from here so they don't care. They just do their jobs and go home.'

They call them the *caveiras* ('skulls'). I was in Barra Tijuca, in the west of the city, to meet BOPE veteran Paolo Storani. On the same level as the SAS or the Navy SEALS, BOPE are the elite of Rio's police force – when ordinary cops are too scared of going in the gang-ridden favelas, these are the guys they send in.

'People have the wrong idea about the skull, and after the movies people wanna change it because it's about death,' Paolo said, flexing his arm like Popeye so I could get a good view of his tattoo: a dagger going through a skull. 'But the knife in the skull is not about bringing death, but about overcoming death. People can think what they want, but that's the original meaning.'

He's bald, middle-aged and to my surprise speaks a little English, although I still need my girl to translate the juicier parts. His apartment's pretty neat, with a huge, panoramic, Japanese-style painting of Sugar Loaf on the living-room wall and a smaller, caricature version of his family in the corner. Paolo's since retired from the Force to be a motivational speaker, teaching suits how to go Martin Riggs on business meetings. He's done well for himself, and it shows – Barra Tijuca is the polar opposite of Rocinha; a posh, upper-class neighbourhood with its own beach and gated communities. If anything happened, the cops would be here in minutes.

'I didn't come from a police family – my father was a truck driver and my mother a hair stylist,' he said as we sat down round his table, 'but I wanted independence from them so I joined the army. I liked this military life, the discipline. Then I worked in the Military Police for seventeen years, the last five years of which I spent in BOPE. I know my career was a success because I came top of all my classes.'

After retiring from the police, Paolo became a teacher and also served as a consultant for the movie *Elite Squad* (if *City of God* is the tropical version of *Goodfellas*, *Elite Squad* is *Dirty Harry*). In the movie, the training was very harsh – beatings, humiliation, eating off the ground, sleeping rough, marching through swamp. If it was supervised by Mr Storani, the scenes must have been accurate.

'In Brazil there's a very famous teacher, Paulo Freire, who told people you can't oppress the student so they don't oppress other people. This is a great idea for the first years of school, but we have not prepared people to face reality this way. And in BOPE, we prepare people for the reality: in Rio, where the bandits have guns that we only see in warzones. How can you stop the violence if you're not prepared for this?'

Like I said, BOPE are who get sent in when someone needs to feel the pimp hand of the law. Paolo's taken part in many operations against drug traffickers and to clear out the slums. Before going into an operation, the team access the area, scouring over maps and intelligence reports; say their prayers and ask the Lord to guide them; and prepare themselves mentally for what the day may bring.

In 1997, his team got a call that someone had been kidnapped in a favela near Copacabana. When they got to the crew's stash house, they found a teenage girl drugged and raped.

'When we got the head bandit for an explanation, he said she was always there, buying drugs this way. We found her cell phone, which in '97 was very expensive in Brazil, so her parents had money. My boy was four years old at the time and my wife pregnant with a little girl, so I thought about my family. I put myself in their place. She was probably sixteen years old.'

Paolo is a nice guy. With his wife, he's setting up a centre to teach music and dance to kids from the slums. But the authorities' response to Brazil's crime wave has been brutal in a way that makes the problems behind #BlackLivesMatter look like a mild spot of bother. In 2018, police killed 1,444 people in Rio alone, mostly young, black and poor. Of course, drastic times call for drastic measures: the officers patrolling Rio often find themselves in a lot more danger than, say, those at the Shrewsbury Flower Show. Over 3,000 officers have been killed in the line of duty since 1994, a higher casualty rate than American soldiers in WWII. But many of their killings have been Filipino-style EJKs: in July 2013, protests broke out after UPP police kidnapped, tortured and murdered an innocent local bricklayer in Rocinha. I knew how Norm Stamper, a self-professed liberal who wanted Donald Trump impeached, felt on the matter. But Paolo told me he's a (reluctant) supporter of Bolsonaro, so I was curious to hear his thoughts on police violence.

'I love this question. Is it because society is very peaceful? The society is very violent, and the police is a reflection of this. The best way to keep poor people under control is to use the violent police, and they forget that the poor people deserve protection in the same way,' he said.

Like America, Brazil's police has a legacy of suppressing troublesome poor and minorities. In 1993, police officers murdered eight homeless children sleeping outside the Candelária church in central Rio – surveys found many people actually approved of the killing in the name of cleaning up the streets. The youngest was eleven years old.

'Police work in complex, ambiguous situations where you have to make decisions and react in a place where things can change very fast,' he continued. 'Most of the time, they make the right decision, but when they are wrong, innocent people die. It's like a doctor in the emergency room making a decision to save someone's life, except there you're not dodging bullets.'

Brazil is a society of extremes: rich and poor; black and white; Rocinha and Barra Tijuca. Because it's split into extremes, people take extreme positions. There's a popular saying, *bandido bom é*

bandido morto ('the only good bandit is a dead bandit'), and the new president, Jair Bolsonaro, exemplifies this saying. As with Duterte, you understand why people feel this way, but people want to solve complex problems with simple solutions. In 1997, Paolo was commanding an operation in the favela when he received information about a stash house next to the mountain. When they got there they discovered some sort of cave, but instead of drugs or guns they found a pregnant mum with three kids, and a little fire for making soup.

'The smell was terrible,' said Paolo. 'There were a lot of rats. I said sorry to the mother and took my team. Nobody said anything because of what they saw. What will these kids be in the future if they live this way?!'

What indeed. It's a vicious circle. So long as you have such huge gaps in society, you're gonna have no-go zones and gun-toting teenagers, and calls to kill them all. But while Brazil's new president wants to shoot drug dealers on sight, its mother country, Portugal, is trying something very different . . .

Part 8

A Better Tomorrow

34

Old World, New Rules

If you're ever in Lisbon, spend an afternoon strolling along the banks of the Tagus River. There you'll find museums; restaurants; the Padrão dos Descobrimentos, a giant monument to Magellan's Age of Discovery (the Portuguese are proud of their seafaring heritage); and the Belém Tower, rising from the water to guard the city from pirates and invaders. And then there's the April 25th Bridge. Standing tall over the estuary, its reddish-orange hue more than resembles San Francisco's Golden Gate Bridge. Built in 1966, it was originally named Salazar Bridge after Portugal's fascist dictator, António Salazar. If that name sounds familiar, it's because J.K. Rowling took it for the evil wizarding house of Salazar Slytherin.

From 1933 to 1974, Salazar's regime kept Portugal a closed and tightly surveilled society. There were few tourists, it was nearly impossible to travel abroad, and you needed a licence to own cigarette lighters. The secret police, which had informers everywhere, made sure dissidents were never heard from again. At the same time, the dictatorship was embroiled in very expensive, and unpopular, colonial wars in Angola and Mozambique, which claimed the lives of many young men.

But on 25 April 1974, a group of military officers went rogue and toppled the regime in a revolution. Tanks rolled through the cobbled streets of Lisbon, cheered on by joyous crowds, among them twenty-year-old medical student, João Goulão. João Goulão (pronounced *Zhu-au Gu-lau* – yeah, I struggled with this too) is now a bespectacled, middle-aged man who runs the Portuguese Health Ministry's drugs agency, SICAD. The day before we met in his office that spring morning it was his birthday, and his phone was constantly buzzing from old patients ringing to say hello.

'I was living at my sister's house at the time, and her husband was an officer who took part in the revolution. That morning, I went out on the street and took part in the popular movement to support the troops,' João told me, reclining in his chair. 'It was an explosion. The popular support for the revolution was crazy.'

Women ran up to the soldiers and, begging them not to kill, slipped flowers down their gun barrels. It was a fairly bloodless coup: the secret police only shot dead four people before surrendering. But after the euphoria was over, Portugal faced the arduous task of building its society back up again. And with freedom came a new set of problems.

'Suddenly we had the possibility of travelling abroad, and we had visitors from other countries. Then we had the decolonisation process, and a million people returned from Africa and the colonies where drug use, at least cannabis, was more tolerated. That was something new that came with freedom, and people wanted to try it,' Dr Goulão explained. 'Drug use spread very fast in our country and we were completely unprepared. We did not know the differences between certain drugs and, since we were completely naïve, we shifted from one to the other.'

By the 1980s, Portugal was in the grip of a heroin crisis, with around one in every hundred people addicted to smack. Lisbon neighbourhoods like Casal Ventoso degenerated into open-air drug markets, with hordes of zombie-like *drogados* (junkies) shuffling through trash-littered streets that looked like *The Wire* meets *Resident Evil*. When they wandered out of these enclaves, they committed petty crime to pay for their habit. By 1999, Portugal had the highest level of AIDS infections in Western Europe.

This led to the usual panic about drug users, of course, but it was clear that the normal approach – round 'em up and lock 'em up – wasn't working. Something new had to be done. João was a doctor working in the field of drug addiction when, in 1997, he was invited to sit on a commission reviewing the country's narcotics policy. João and his colleagues, which included judges and lawyers, realised there was a difference between casual users, who might do a line of cocaine on the weekend, and those shooting up in Casal Ventoso. The casual users didn't need any help.* So they recommended that drug use stop being a reason to call the police, and instead be something to see your doctor about. In conservative, Catholic Portugal, that was a ballsy thing to suggest.

'The communists and the socialists, they supported it, but the right wing believed the hard-line approach was the best way to deal with it. They believed the United Nations would be against us, and that Portugal will become the centre for drugs around the world,' João said. 'People would be coming here in planes to use drugs, our children will use drugs . . .'

But in 2001, the socialist government of Prime Minister António Guterres announced the decriminalisation of *all* drugs, including crack and heroin.

Police stopped chasing drug addicts. They just stopped. True, you can't just sit down and light a crack pipe in front of a school in broad daylight, but other than that, unless you're doing something stupid the chances are you won't get caught. In the slim chance you get searched for weapons and they find a few grams of illegal intoxicants in your pocket, you're hauled before a 'dissuasion committee', not a judge. If this panel, consisting of a doctor, a lawyer and a social worker, decides you don't have a problem, you're made aware of the

---

* Addiction isn't an inevitable consequence of using drugs, just as putting on 100 pounds, sitting down on your sofa and accidently crushing your chihuahua isn't an inevitable consequence of eating cake.

risks and are free to go. If not, hell, you're usually free to go anyway, but you can get some help and advice or some free treatment at the rehab clinic. That's it.

So what happened? Has Portugal turned into a post-apocalyptic no man's land, where ordinary people live in fear of the crazed, bug-eyed doper fiends?

Actually, no. Coercive, bullying strategies like those deployed around the world have a low success rate because the hardcore addict, who's probably had a fucked-up life beforehand, isn't given space to breathe and sort out their life. How can you put any faith in a system that's always trying to lock you up? But since drugs have been decriminalised in Portugal and everything has come out into the open, addicts, no longer fearing arrest or stigmatisation, are encouraged to come forward and get the help they desperately need. As a result, since 2001 the number of hardcore addicts fell from 7.6 out of a thousand people to 6.8; that of injecting drug users has halved; and the level of ODs is the lowest in Europe. The number of new HIV infections plummeted from a record high of 907 in 2000 to just 267 in 2008. Meanwhile, the number of casual drug users has grown only slightly, from 3.4 to 3.7 per cent of the population. Not all of this was down to decriminalisation, as we shall see, but it was a good start.

'What I can say is that decriminalisation did not make things more difficult, the opposite in fact,' said Dr Goulão. 'The law helped lower the stigma and create more tolerance and understanding of addiction as a disease with some dignity, and that people who suffer from this disease have the same right to be treated. You can talk about it anywhere; with family, in school, and you will not lose your job. That, I think, is the main achievement of the policy.'

This open-mindedness came from the fact that Portugal's drug problem was so severe that, unlike other countries, they couldn't afford to racialise it.

'It spread among all social groups, the middle classes and the upper classes, which I think changed the approach,' said Goulão. 'It wasn't like Brazil where you can say, "Those guys, they are the problem; it is a problem of the favela." It's different when you have a middle-class housewife telling her priest, "My boy is not a criminal, he needs help." This creates a mindset of compassion that doesn't exist with the poorest, most marginalised people. There was almost not a single family that wasn't affected by drug use.'

Other countries followed suit. The Czech Republic, where drugs poured into hard-partying Prague after the fall of communism, decriminalised in 2010. Now you can carry two grams of meth in your pocket without fear of arrest.

I had to find out more about how Portugal's drug policy works, so after wishing Dr Goulão a belated *parabéns* I went across town to see Nuno Capaz, a sociologist who sits on the dissuasion committee. We sat down in one of those rooms where someone unlucky enough to get caught ends up before Nuno and his colleagues.

'We decriminalised in 2001 but I stress this, and it is an important thing, this is not the same thing as legalising or regulating,' he said. 'It's just as hard for me to find illegal substances as it was before, except now there are no criminal penalties.'

Drug possession is an 'administrative' offence in Portugal, meaning you could theoretically get fined for it by the health board but it's like a parking fine or a speeding ticket – no one goes to jail. Unless you're dealing, at no point do you get a criminal record, and in fact employers even get a tax break for taking on recovering addicts.

'When someone gets caught by the police, they are notified to come here. If they decide not to show up, we can decide without them, but we prefer the person to be here. Then we have an interview to determine whether they're a recreational drug user or an addict, and see if they have any other problems. For first-time recreational users, the law clearly states we should not apply any sanctions. Usually the person's only problem is that their substance is illegal, and they got caught buying it.'

This sounds a little weird, like a judge letting a bank robber off the hook because they forgot to wear a mask. But that's how it works here. The Portuguese system recognises that people will use drugs, some will cope better than others, and has found a way to live with it.

'The main issue around drugs is whether you have enough money to pay for them or not. For example, Keith Richards of the Rolling Stones has been a heroin addict for fifty years, but you don't hear anyone saying "Keith Richards is a drug addict, lock him up!" He goes on holidays to the south of France; he can get a blood transfusion, so he cleans up pretty easy; and he takes some safety measures like he doesn't shoot up straight in his vein. That's why alcohol is so widespread and accepted. It's cheap, it's easily available, I can cross the street and get a shot of whiskey and for the next few hours I'll be OK. You can be an alcoholic for ten to fifteen years and no one would notice.

'We don't make a distinction between heavy and light substances. It's not about which drugs are heavy or light; it's about how you use them. For example, if I do cocaine twice a year, on New Year's Day and on my birthday, and you smoke ten joints a day . . . whose drug use is heavier?'

Because everyone is so different, there's no point telling anyone what they're doing is right or wrong. Instead, Nuno and his team see themselves more as doctors.

'If you go to the doctor and he says you should eat less salt, he knows once you leave his office you'll still put salt on your food, but he hopes with the information he gave you about what salt does to your body, you'll be more careful. That's what we do.

'If you're an addict and you tell me you need treatment, I can set you up at a clinic that very day. If I was a judge, I wouldn't be able to do that. I'd have to sign it, the clinic would have to approve it, and I can't send it by fax; it has to be registered mail. That might take days and the addict will not stop using drugs. Whereas I work for the Ministry of Health, and I probably know the guy on the other end of the line. And our healthcare system is free for all. Even if you relapse ten times and you wanna go back into treatment, we will pay for it.'

So far, so good. But there's one major snag. The dissuasion committees might not be hitting the right demographic.

'Usually, we mostly get first-time offenders. Most of the people we see here are under twenty-five-years-old,' Nuno admitted. 'My opinion is they still live with their parents, so if they wanna do drugs they have to go outside. I'm forty one years old. If I want to smoke a joint, I'll just open my window. If you have your own place, you're probably old enough to know the risks, but if you're fifteen years old, you've dropped out of school, your parents are getting divorced or you're getting abused, you can benefit from such treatment. That's why it's better for us to get a hold of these wayward kids than forty year old guys who smoke pot because they like it.'

But therein lies the problem. One of the reasons for Portugal's drop in addiction since 2001, as well as the end of the US crack epidemic in the mid-1990s, was the 'little brother' effect – youngsters saw their parents or older siblings fucked up on crack or heroin and decided they wouldn't go the same way. So Portugal's worst drug problem centres around a group of ageing smackheads who've been shooting up since the 1990s – an audience the dissuasion committees fail to reach.

'They just don't go,' said Adriana Curado, the project co-ordinator for IN-Mouraria, a drop-in centre for addicts in the old Moorish neighbourhood of Mouraria. 'It's mostly young people getting caught smoking cannabis. With our clients it's not a good strategy, because they just don't show up. And then what happens? Nothing.'

In the Middle Ages when Portugal gained its independence, Mouraria became a ghetto for the remaining Muslim population of the city. Since then it's been a multicultural melting pot famed for its hidden Chinese restaurants, as well as being the birthplace of Lisbon's iconic *Fado* music. It was also, until recently, one of the city's poorest neighbourhoods, but gentrification is pricing out many of its older inhabitants.

'Our clients are mostly men over forty, usually homeless, without a job and many health problems,' Adriana said. 'Middle-class people are being affected too, but the temptation is to clean out the city centre from these people nobody wants. Now it's almost impossible to find affordable housing. Some years ago, they could find a room; now, they are being pushed out of the city.'

I looked around. A few people sat on the sofas playing cards, mostly older-looking. Leaflets and posters plastered the walls, and a volunteer, a cute Spanish girl, went around handing out sandwiches. Around fifty to sixty people each day drop into the centre that acts as a community hub for the local addicts, where they can organise themselves, discuss their problems and catch up on the latest junkie gossip. Here they can hang out; have some coffee and browse the Internet; book doctors' appointments; and get help with immigration or housing paperwork.

'I would say every measure that reduces prohibition is a good measure,' Adriana said of decriminalisation. 'I think they did the right thing seventeen years ago, but they need to do more. We've managed to reduce the stigma, but it still exists. They need to regulate the drug market – every drug, or at least the classic drugs.'

Casal Ventoso sure looks different today. Getting off the train at Alcantra you walk into a dizzying graffiti display of the city, famous faces and psychedelic patterns, before stepping outside and finding yourself next to the April 25th Bridge. A little way up the road lies a brightly coloured pink housing project. It's not yet gentrified like Mouraria, but it's not the apocalyptic scenes of the 1990s either. There on the first floor lies the CRESCER headquarters.

'I started working in this area, Casal Ventoso, in 1998,' psychologist Américo Nave told me. 'I knew people were losing their hands and legs, and they were dying in the street from overdoses, and there were no programmes to help them. So me and the three other people working with me set up CRESCER in 2001 and we put out a call for outreach teams.'

Portugal wasn't the first country to decriminalise drugs: Costa Rica did it all the way back in 1988. But the reason the Portuguese drug policy was so successful was that it was backed up by harm reduction and generous social programmes. Harm reduction is the principle that people will do drugs. You cannot force them into rehab, and even if you do, there's no guarantee they will stay clean. That's why, instead of coercing them into clinics, sometimes the best you can hope for is that they keep doing what they're doing now, except a little safer. You do this by reducing the risk of HIV/AIDS, overdoses and other health problems, by handing out condoms, needles and wet wipes, or by offering help and advice. Of course, haters are gonna say that this only enables junkies to wallow in their vice, but then again, if the threat of dying isn't enough to stop them, what is? Harm reduction doesn't seek to stop drug use, only to minimise the damage it causes.

In 2001, the Portuguese government poured money into treatment. But after the global banking crisis of 2009, a lot of the funding dried up, and NGOs like CRESCER and IN-Mouraria were left to pick up the slack.

But it's not enough to hand out a few wet wipes and call it a day. Society still spits on *drogados*, and CRESCER tries to provide them with some dignity.

'Some of the people are in a homeless situation, so we help give them a house,' Américo said. 'It's a communal house where we pay for the rent, the water and the light. When these people start work or having money, they pay us 30 per cent. But if they don't have money, it's not a problem for us.

'It's important to create jobs for these people, so we're opening a restaurant. Only problem drug users work in this restaurant, from five to eight. It can be difficult for them to work eight hours a day, but for three hours they work very well.'

CRESCER's clean, swanky office with dozens of people sat behind computer screens stands in stark contrast to Andrey Rylkov's skeleton crew packed in their tiny Moscow hovel. But I wasn't gonna learn much hanging around sipping tea and eating digestive biscuits. Américo said I should go with one of his outreach teams.

I went round the back and hopped into a van with two cheerful ladies, Inês and Andreia. Sporting a pair of fluorescent vests, the girls made their rounds of the junkies' usual hangout spots, starting with a hillside squat outside town. We pulled up in the van and walked through a field of tall grass where a ramshackle shack awaited us. Out came Antonio. A tanned, middle-aged man with a cross tattooed on his arm, Antonio took the supplies to hand out among his friends.

'The police? No problem. They came here two times and both times they were looking for someone. They don't bother us,' he said, lighting up a cigarette.

There's something about this shack that's strangely romantic, like a sad version of a childhood castle. Antonio doesn't sleep there, but if someone needs to crash for a few days he lets them. After he lets me try on a pair of hilarious novelty glasses, we bid farewell to the squat and make our way to our next stop.

'So the police are fairly chill with all this being out in the open, then?' I asked.

'With us, they don't give us any problems, but with the clients . . .' Andreia replied. 'Once, I was in a neighbourhood nearby. There was an abandoned swimming pool, and users used to consume in the building. We used to go there every day to talk to the users, change the material and so on.'

'And once we got there to find it was walled up, so we could see outside but the people couldn't see us. The users let us in, but then they saw the cops walking outside and told us to shut up. We all sat there in silence, really, really quietly. The police passed so close they could almost hear me breathing. In that moment, I really felt in their shoes,' she laughed.

On my last day in Lisbon, I got word that a pro-marijuana rally was going down. As the number of people dying from marijuana over-doses had reached the same dizzying heights as Minotaur attacks, a group of so-called ganja goblins were gonna march for their right to spend all day shooting up reefers and watching *Rick and Morty*.

So that Saturday afternoon I made my way down to the park where the march's route began. It was a small crowd at first, less than a hundred people holding up banners and signs, but more joined in as we made our way through the streets. It was mostly the exact sort of crowd you'd expect at such a rally – lots of white boys with dread-locks – although there were a couple of middle-aged women in busi-ness suits as well.

'Legal, legal, like the beer!' they chanted.

The five-o stood nearby, in clear view. The surreal sight of a mass of stoners lighting up with a police escort made me think: if this was Russia, we'd all be battered with clubs and thrown into vans by now.

'They can arrest us, but then they'd have to arrest all of us, and they simply don't have resources for that,' said one of those degener-ate drug addicts. 'That's why we're here: to show them we can smoke.'

This is what happens when stoners get organised. But it's one thing not to get handcuffed over smoking a joint. These folks were marching for *legalisation*.

35

Free the Weed!

On 21 October 2015, retired kingpin Rick Ross was driving along the 101 Freeway through northern California when he got pulled over by a patrol car. In the trunk officers found a bag with $100,000 in cash. This densely forested part of California is known as the Emerald Triangle for its vast plantations of marijuana, and Ross was dragged to the local sheriff's office. Was the ex-crack lord back to his old ways? Not quite.

27 April. King's Day. The streets and canals of Amsterdam turned into one big party with music blaring out of every house as strangers in orange hats kept feeding me ecstasy left and right. After a heavy night of partying, I needed to clear my head and taking an afternoon stroll past the famous canals, one building in particular caught my eye – Coffeeshop Rusland ('Russia'), complete with an upstairs Putin Lounge for discerning smokers. In all my years dealing, I'd never actually visited Amsterdam – the world's pot paradise where you can take drugs and bang hookers like nobody's business. Yet here I was in the name of 'research'. Just around the corner lay the Hash, Marijuana & Hemp museum and the seedy red-light district, where one of the window girls let me use her charger when I needed an Uber. So this is what freedom feels like, I thought.

"Hey dude, can you roll this for me, please?" I asked the Latino budtender after acquiring 5 grams of Moroccan hash.

I know, I know, a drug dealer who doesn't know how to roll, but I'm a purely social smoker.

It turns out Coffeeshop Rusland is the oldest such establishment still open in Amsterdam. Back in the 1970s, the Dutch decided it was better to steer kids away from the dealers peddling crack and smack and let them buy and smoke pot at designated coffeeshops instead. The decision was also rooted in the great Dutch tradition of compromise, and the various Christian parties need to look hip and down with the kids. After Mellow Yellow, Rusland was the first coffeeshop to get a licence back in 1975.

In principle, it's a good thing – you can smoke freely and not worry about getting stitched up by some hardnosed Dutch police-man, and it's been a godsend to Amsterdam's tourism industry (come on, as if you went there to see the Anne Frank museum). But there's a catch: marijuana's not actually legal in the Netherlands, it's only decriminalised, so the supply side of these coffeeshops is still run by unsavoury characters like Surinamese and Moroccan gangs, and native Dutch criminals known as *penose*. Plus, locals are not too happy with the throngs of stoned-out Brits and Frenchmen invading their towns and villages each year.

So elsewhere in Europe they've taken another approach. A few months later, I was in Barcelona for a mate's wedding.

'Hey man, you must be Niko,' said José, pulling up on his motorcycle.

I'd only met José on WhatsApp a few days earlier, but as soon as he hit me with the dirty jokes, I knew he was on the level. José parked up his ride and we got buzzed through a small door, where I whipped out my passport, filled out a form and the hottie behind the counter gave me a card. I was now a proud member of the Barcelona Ganja Smokers' Association.

Through the corridor was a massive lounge. The wall was deco-rated with an enormous canvas of a tropical rainforest, while a calendar showed any upcoming events planned by the club (on Friday night there was a screening of *Back to the Future*). Huge flat-screen TVs were mounted on the walls, a group of lads sat sunk into the comfy sofas playing first-person shooters, and there was even an English-language class going on in the corner. There were pool tables, poker tournaments and, best of all, sexy tattooed budtenders to serve you the finest jazz cabbage Barça has to offer.

This is all thanks to a loophole in Spanish law. In the mid-1990s, the smoky backroom of a Barcelona comic bookstore called Makoki was the site of such radical debates as whether Batman could beat Wolverine and how you could legally smoke pot. One of the nerds had an idea: the Spanish constitution is very tolerant of what goes on behind closed doors, and freedom of association gives citizens the right to set up private clubs. Since what goes on at these clubs is treated the same as if you were in your own home, they could get around Spain's drug laws and smoke freely. The nerds sent a letter asking for clarification from the government and got an ambiguous enough reply to go ahead with the project, and so the Ramón Santos Association for Cannabis Studies (ARSEC) was born.

The police frowned on these studious endeavours and the club got raided a lot in those early days. But in 1999, the government of Andalucía, in the south of Spain, ruled it was OK for people to form these clubs, so long as the premises are open only to ganja-smoking deviants and not the general public. The number of clubs grew dramatically, from only forty in the northern region of Catalonia in 2011, to over five hundred by 2016. Barcelona is home to more than four hundred of these clubs, over half of those in the entire country. These are private members' clubs and you have to be sponsored by an existing member to get in, so that keeps away the hordes of red-eyed ninjas that have overrun Amsterdam. However, on Barcelona's main street of Las Ramblas you can find scores of promoters offering to take you to a 'coffeeshop'. These touts get around the law by being the local guy who sponsors tourists. Some of these guys can be sketchy, but luckily I got José's contact from a very good friend.

The crowd here was mostly young and middle-aged, fairly ordinary-looking, like the kind you'd see in a bar. Guys sitting with their dates, listening to chillout jazz in the lounge. You couldn't even smell weed because of the ventilation. It just seemed so ... normal, the way it ought to be.

In 2017, the Catalan government formally legalised the cannabis clubs, meaning that, in Barcelona at least, everything they're doing is now fully within the law. But remember, once you step outside, it's a different story. Marijuana's not strictly speaking legal, only tolerated in private. Conservatives keep trying to shut the clubs down, and while growing a few plants at home is OK, walking around with three kilos in your pocket is not recommended unless you wanna try Spanish prison food.

I put my joint out on the ashtray, said goodbye to José and stumbled outside. All that lounging around had left a massive hole in my stomach.

For decades, cannabis was either completely outlawed or existed in a legal limbo in places like Barcelona or the 'Dam. Gradually, it started being allowed for medical reasons – as well as soothing aches and pains, cannabis is also very effective at treating epilepsy and multiple sclerosis. Places like California began allowing doctors to prescribe medicinal marijuana for literally the most minor ailments. Suddenly, there were a lot of dreadlocked nineteen-year-old surfer dudes complaining about their chronic back pain.

From there, the next logical step was to legalise *recreational* marijuana – just to get high. For that, we must look to the United States. Yes, the United States, the country that started this whole mess. The first state was Washington, up in the rainy north-west. In 2011, campaigners had drawn up Initiative 502, a referendum that would have legalised ganja for adults twenty-one and over. And joining the activists on their campaign trail was our old friend, ex-cop Norm Stamper.

'I spent most of my time in hostile territory like eastern Washington, with a lot of farms and conservative interests,' Norm explained. 'I got in a couple of pitched battles, but they were surprisingly receptive to the argument. One question I ask when I'm talking to a group of officers is, "When was the last time you fought someone under the influence of alcohol?" Every hand goes up. "Now when was the last time you had to fight someone under the influence of marijuana?" They literally come up with goose eggs; they come up with nothing.'

Listen, grass never killed anyone. You'd need to smoke something like 15,000 joints in 20 minutes for a fatal overdose,* but you'll probably just knock yourself out and wake up a few hours later with an immense craving for chocolate-chip cookies. In fact, scientific studies have shown that alcohol and tobacco are actually *more* dangerous than many banned substances, including cannabis, ecstasy and magic mushrooms. A report published in the highly respected medical journal *The Lancet* assessed and ranked the levels of harm caused by different drugs, both for society and for the users themselves. In both criteria, leagues ahead of anything else including crack, heroin and crystal meth, came alcohol. Even if we account for the fact that *way* more people use alcohol and tobacco, a lot of these drugs (like weed, or ecstasy) are just a lot less deadly, period.

So I can get drunk, get in my car, run over some mum and her baby on the way home, then beat my wife, but while it's fine going for drinks after work with your boss, if you offer them a spliff you better make *damn* sure they are cool.

Why did alcohol prohibition only last a decade, but the war on drugs more than a century? Well, most of us have had a drink, so we know it won't make us fly into a blind rage. Whereas other things, like cannabis or opium, were the domain of the lower classes and *Untermensch*.

---

* Challenge accepted.

As Norm says, every day we take a step away from *Reefer Madness*. We used to believe all sorts of bullshit on marijuana. For example, the gateway drug theory, the idea that having one puff of a zoot will lead to intravenously taking heroin and a Pete Doherty-type meltdown. There's nothing in the chemical properties of THC (the active component of marijuana) that makes you seek out other highs. If even half of the people I sold weed to developed a coke habit, I'd be cruising the Bahamas right now and not tormenting my editor with shitty jokes. Well, either that or still in jail. The fact that most people who snort coke have smoked weed is an extremely tenuous argument, like claiming that Disney's *Mulan* is a gateway to Japanese tentacle porn. Hey, I'm not gonna sit here and judge you about where childhood cartoons and a fascination with Asian culture take you on a lonely night.

On 6 November 2012, Initiative 502 passed with a majority of 56 per cent. That same day in Colorado, voters passed Amendment 64. The Rocky Mountain *South Park* stoners led a more mischievous campaign. Mason Tvert, head of the campaign group SAFER (Safer Alternative for Enjoyable Recreation), famously challenged Denver mayor John Hickenlooper to a Wild West-style showdown: Hickenlooper, who owned a brewery, would drink beer, and Tvert would smoke joints, and whichever one of them died first would lose. Hickenlooper turned him down. To get voters ready for Amendment 64, Mason and his group hung up billboards with bikini babes reading 'Marijuana: no hangovers, no violence, no carbs!'

They won the ballot with 55 per cent. Seventy-six years after local man Samuel Caldwell got four years under the Marihuana Act, Colorado became the second state in the US to fully legalise cannabis. Even Hickenlooper had to concede. 'It seems like the people that were smoking before are mainly the people that are smoking now,' the now-governor told Reuters in 2014, noting that legalisation hasn't caused a surge in stoners (there's been a few kids getting poisoned from eating brownies, but there's an easy solution to this:

parents, don't let your kids eat brownies).

It has, however, brought a boom to their economy, a Green Rush you could say, creating thousands of new jobs and generating hundreds of millions in taxes. By 2018 the cannabis industry in Colorado alone was worth over a *billion* dollars, yielding $200 million in taxes. In the UK, still under prohibition, it's estimated the illegal cannabis market is worth at least £2.6 billion. Imagine if all that money went towards fixing potholes or running hospitals or finding a new excuse to bomb the Middle East.

After that, it was a domino effect. Once the wave started, it was unstoppable. State after state, pot prohibition fell: Maine, Alaska, Michigan, Massachusetts, Oregon, Nevada, Vermont, Washington DC. On New Year's Day 2018, California, that bastion of liberalism and the world's fifth-largest economy, finally allowed marijuana whether you have chronic back pain or not. Shortly afterwards, San Francisco District Attorney George Gascón announced he was throwing out thousands of cannabis convictions.

'Long ago we lost our ability to distinguish the dangerous from the nuisance, and it has broken our pocket books, the fabric of our communities, and we are no safer for it,' Gascón said in a statement. 'This example underscores the true promise of legalisation – providing new hope for those whose lives were derailed by a costly, broken and racially discriminatory system.'

Those who've had their lives shattered over the world's most dangerous plant could now go before a judge and have their record fixed. Not that that gives back the years they've suffered because of it.

Let's go back to Rick Ross for a second. Let's be real here – he *was* buying weed, trying to cash in on the legal marijuana business. In 2015 weed wasn't fully legal in Cali *yet*, but there were a lot of dispensaries catering to those with ... ahem, 'medical conditions'.

'It wasn't completely legal, but let's call it a grey area,' Ross said.

'But they absolutely racially profiled me – I was the only black man on that freeway and they pulled me over. Back then, when we talked to people in black dispensaries we'd tell them they're the first ones getting raided. But I'm kind of glad they did it now because it's made me eligible for the Social Equity program they have here, which helps people from certain zipcodes or criminal backgrounds get licences for marijuana.'

While weed arrests are down, those *still* getting nicked are mostly black and brown.

Also, let's not forget that this is still in defiance of federal law, which remains staunchly prohibitionist. While Obama wasn't the greatest president, he definitely set the mood – would legalisation have been possible without a president who admitted to smoking pot and openly questioned the justice system? Donald Trump, while a massive douche on other fronts, to his credit stayed silent on the marijuana issue and even fired the one guy on his team who was against it, Attorney General Jeff Sessions. But until weed gets recognised on the *federal* level, the battle's not over.

'Is everyone having a good time right now? Make some noise!' the MC announced excitedly to cheers from a smiling crowd, grinning from ear to ear.

It was 16 October 2018. The Mod Club in downtown Toronto. In the middle of the hall, a giant, green cannabis bud hung from the ceiling like an upside-down Christmas tree. As the seconds neared midnight, the band onstage reached its crescendo, confetti rained down on the crowd to flashing lights and the bud dropped. The end of an era. Prohibition was over.

Because of local smoking laws, everyone hurried outside. They weren't scared of the cops. As of 17 October, Canada had become the biggest and most important nation on the world stage (politically speaking) to free the weed. Demand was so high that, by 18 October, the country almost ran out on the first day, with one shop in Newfoundland running dry at exactly 4.20 p.m.

The Canadians weren't the first to legalise on a national level. Instead, the mantle went to the little nation of Uruguay. José 'Pepe' Mujica wasn't your typical president – he's an ex-guerrilla who's been shot six times, lived in a tiny shack rather than a presidential palace, gave 90 per cent of his income to help single mothers and small businesses, and had a three-legged dog called Manuela. So that's probably why it was under his leadership that the tiny South American country made history in 2013 by making the buying, selling and smoking of Mary Jane a lawful activity. It took a while, but sales finally began in summer 2017, albeit with some conditions: advertising was banned, it's tricky to get a licence, and to buy you must register on a pothead database to avoid drawing in druggies like Amsterdam.

But whereas Uruguay is a small nation, sandwiched between Brazil and Argentina, which most people confuse with Paraguay, when Canada does something, people sit up and notice. Like Amsterdam, Canada's long been world famous for its high-quality nugs like BC Bud, grown in the woods of British Columbia. With its vast acres of coniferous forest wilderness, the Great White North is a place where you could grow thousands of pounds of high-potency chronic and not worry too much about neighbours complaining about the smell. And just like Canadian whiskey during Prohibition, a good deal of the weed makes its way south, smuggled across Native reservations that straddle both sides of the border. Canadians have always been less uptight than their southern cousins anyway, so what's the deal aboot a bit of pot, eh?

Different parts of Canada legalised differently. In Alberta you can head to a dispensary, whereas in Ontario and Nova Scotia you can only buy from government-run stores or online. Since the law came in, some people have complained it's actually harder to get weed now that the government runs everything. Some First Nations (as Native Americans are called here) operate their own ganja shops outside the law.

Canuck Prime Minister and photogenic liberal poster boy Justin Trudeau said the move was for two reasons. The first was to protect the kids. I mean, I never sold to no young 'uns, but I never had to check ID either . . . can you imagine if I did?

'Hello, I'm a dodgy guy you've just met and I would like to verify your full name and date of birth while we conduct illegal activity.'

Yes, kids can still get hold of booze, but as the movie *Superbad* shows us, they usually have to go on wacky adventures with fake ID, creepy adults, period blood and other shenanigans to do so.

The second reason for the move was to drive criminals out of business. Why would you buy bud from a sketchy cokehead who'll stab your sister when you can get it from a dispensary? In Canada, those kinda deals usually involve the Hell's Angels. A fearsome biker gang from Oakland, California, the Angels rode their Harleys all the way up north and started 'patching over' local biker clubs, absorbing them as local chapters and letting them cash in on their reputation.

The other major player in Canada's drug trade is the Mafia. Unlike the American Mafia, the Canadian Mafia is still going strong. The Rizzuto crime family reigned supreme over the Montreal under-world for over forty years, until 2004, when its godfather, Sicilian-born Vito Rizzuto, was sent to prison for his role in the murder of three New York mobsters in 1981, shown in the movie *Donnie Brasco*. While he was in jail, his family began to fall apart – his son Nick was gunned down in broad daylight, while his dad was shot dead by a sniper as he sat down for a family dinner. In 2012, Rizzuto was released and began plotting his revenge. Bodies began dropping across Canada, Mexico and Sicily. Rizzuto died (ironically) of natu-ral causes in 2013, but the gang war rages on as Calabrian mafiosi move in on his territory.

But one man who wasn't happy about the so-called legalisation of cannabis is Blair Longley, president of the Canadian Marijuana Party.

'It's Pot Prohibition 2.0, based on Reefer Madness 2.0,' he told me on the phone from his home in Montreal. 'They're still treating pot like plutonium. You could say we were sorta successful, but the devil is in the detail. If you look at the overall situation in some areas, cannabis is more criminalised than before. It's being legalised in the worst possible way.'

Over the course of our forty-five-minute-long conversation (before I got cut off for using up my allowance), I quickly surmised that Blair was not only a cannabis crusader but a radical anti-capital-ist. Blair began his political career in the 1980s under the Rhinoceros Party led by Cornelius the First, an ill-tempered, four-hoofed states-man from Quebec's Granby Zoo. The Rhinoceros Party campaigned for, among other things, repealing the law of gravity and improving higher education by building taller schools. Longley then joined the Marijuana Party shortly after its founding in 2000, and became the leader in 2004. Marijuana is a one-issue party, meaning that though candidates are free to express any other positions, what brings them together is love for da 'erb. They've never won a seat in parliament, but use their position to campaign for the cause.

In Blair's view, the legalisation is a sham, which rather than bank-rupting the Maple Leaf Mafia, screws over small growers in favour of international banking cabals and big corporations.

'All the talking points of the Trudeau Liberal government, all their bullshit about it being dangerous for young people, and organised crime and how bad they are, the media repeats these lies,' he contin-ued. 'Legalisation's not really changing anything that matters. They kind of lost control of cannabis with millions of people growing and selling and smoking, so they legalised it in a way to recapture control.'

Before the government laid down the law, there were already hundreds of little unofficial coffeeshops and dispensaries operating semi-openly. Most of these were mom-'n'-pop operations, not hairy bikers or guido wiseguys auditioning for *The Sopranos*. But by raising the spectre of these bogeymen selling drugs to *our kids*, the authorities made an excuse to squeeze out the little guy.

'The government is the biggest form of organised crime, dominated by the best gangsters, the international bankers. It's always been there, it never went away. Every industry you look at, it's the same. Now you have a small group of wealthy people controlling everything. The privatisation of profits is more important than anything else, and that's given them every excuse to build a fascist police state.'

I was slightly taken aback by Longley's rant. Surely anything that ends prohibition is a good thing? But the corporations are moving in, and that's a problem. Mere months before legalisation, one of Canada's biggest weed companies, Canopy Growth, received a $4 billion investment from Constellation Group, the American owners of Corona beer, propelling it to the top of the cannabis league. I mean, we always knew this was gonna happen – money begets money – but we don't wanna repeat our mistakes with alcohol and tobacco. For decades, Big Tobacco actually paid Hollywood to have their stars light up on the silver screen, kinda how Converse paid Will Smith to wear their 'vintage' All Stars in *I, Robot*, except instead of just having him strut around in a pair of sneakers they also gave the Fresh Prince cancer. Then, when the evidence started piling up, the tobacco lobby denied or downplayed the risks, saying the evidence wasn't conclusive. In 2015, smoking was responsible for over one in ten of all deaths worldwide.

Still, it's a step up that the fate of the world's favourite plant is decided in boardroom meetings rather than by paramilitary death squads.

Other countries are following suit. As of the time of writing, courts in Mexico, Georgia and South Africa have legalised marijuana use, although they haven't taken the plunge to sales.

Many of the same arguments for pot can apply to other drugs. If more people pop Molly when they go out instead of having a drink, maybe that's a plus. Annoying and repetitive conversation aside, clubbers on ecstasy are a much easier, and friendlier, crowd to deal with than drinkers – ask any bouncer. Plus, I'm a grown, adult man. Who is anyone to tell me what I can and can't do with my own body? *SCREW YOU, MOM!* If I want to pop a pill, then spend the next four hours listening to shitty house music on repeat while rubbing my hands together and have my eyes looking like I've been living in a cave, I will, fascists!!!!

Of course, that's not an argument that's gonna sway the soccer moms. But there's other reasons too. Some drugs might actually be *good* for you. Psychedelics like LSD, magic mushrooms and ayahuasca may be useful for treating alcoholism and depression because they break down your existing thought patterns and let you think outside your traditional boundaries. Remember my trip to the Amazon?

MDMA, meanwhile, has all the key ingredients to be successful in treating PTSD: fast acting, non-addictive, non-toxic, it's impossible to feel bad on it and it brings doctor and patient closer together . . . just like Shulgin did back in the day. One study even showed an 83 per cent success rate for traumatised patients, with no serious side-effects.

But before we get too carried away, there's already stuff out there that's gone through the licensing bodies, passed the safety tests and still killed more people than 'Nam. And it's all legit.

36

The Panic in Needle Park

The Mexicans were not only transporters, they were producers. Opium poppy was first brought over to Sinaloa by Chinese immigrants in the nineteenth century. Now, the resin ends up with guys like Pedro, a 'cook' in a small village outside Culiacán. Pedro's a friend of Baldo's from his weed-growing days, so when me and Miguel went to his village, Baldo wanted to come with us.

Pedro greeted us outside his house in a huge sombrero that made him look like a washed-up mariachi. We had a few beers and went round his back garden where he had the equipment all set up – a couple of buckets and a makeshift stove.

'Ten kilos of poppy makes one kilo of heroin,' he explained. 'I charge $1,500 for one kilo. No, I'm not doing too badly; the only problem is I spend a lot. On a good week, I can make 400 kilos.'

To make heroin, Pedro boiled the raw opium over a stove and poured in a bottle of acetic anhydride, stirring the mixture till it turned from a brown sludge to a kind of cranberry juice. Then he took the bucket off the stove and began stirring it with a knife until it formed a solid paste. This is morphine, which will be purified with more anhydride to make some premium Mexican brown. He showed us the process while his little children ran around the garden – it's normal for them. Has he ever been caught? No, like Steven Seagal, he's just the cook. But after a few drinks, Pedro told me he doesn't want his sons to get into the family business.

'I struggle with my son, for him not to be like me. I make a lot of money but I have to hide all the time. You have to be something: an engineer, a lawyer, whatever you want, but not this. I have to lie all the time. When people ask me what I do, I say I'm in agriculture, I have a field. My whole life is a lie; I don't want that for my kids.'

Baldo was about twelve beers in by this point, so it was time to go home. On the way back in the car, he composed for me my own narcocorrido:

'I'm going to sing a ballad, one born from the heart / I'll talk of Miguel, of his brother Baldomar, and I'll sing too of Nicolas / He doesn't get in tangles, he'll always toe the line / He'll always respect the rules, never take it too far . . .'

In the 1980s, smack was going out of fashion. Heroin was something poor people did in the seventies, doctors hesitated to give patients morphine, even for crippling pain, and the Mafia was losing out. It would take another, better-connected class of businessmen to rebrand this seedy image, and in 1996, Purdue Pharmaceuticals unleashed OxyContin, the latest opioid-based painkiller, on the world.

From the mid-1990s, Big Pharma in the US caused the opioid crisis in two major ways. First, they lied about the addictive potential of the drugs they were peddling. Purdue's sales team claimed that OxyContin, which has similar withdrawal symptoms to heroin, was less addictive than morphine. Doctors, who got such perks as free holidays courtesy of America's capitalist healthcare industry, didn't ask too many questions.

Second, they overproduced painkillers like OxyContin and sent them to places like Florida, where they knew they would leak to the black market through dealers and pill mills (rogue pharmacies). Florida had no regulations about how much doctors could prescribe and to whom, leading certain patients to stock up on more pills than they could swallow and selling them on to their friends. Meanwhile, once-powerful industries like coal and steel were crumbling across the Rust Belt of the Midwest. It was these areas that formed the voter base for Donald Trump's 2016 campaign, and the customer base for the latest narcotics bonanza. Once again, the Sunshine State became the nation's hub for drug trafficking. The interstate highway from America's wang became known as the Oxy Express.

The Feds caught on in the 2010s and ordered doctors to start cutting off their patients' prescriptions, but then there was another problem: the painkillers were gone but patients were still hooked, so now where were they gonna go? To the dealers, of course.

'Ten years ago, marijuana was our main thing,' Hector, the Sinaloa Cartel operative, told me. 'But since the gringos legalised weed, there's no point to us growing it any more. What they want from us now is poppy.'

The gradual legalisation of weed was eating away at the Mexican cartel's profits, but after seeing the gringos downing Oxy pills like there was no tomorrow, they upped their production on the poppy fields, flooding the US with cheap black tar heroin (remember, in America healthcare ain't free, so paying for heroin is a lot cheaper than prescriptions or alternative therapy in many cases). The price of heroin dropped from $200,000 to $50,000 for a kilo of pure Mexican brown. Pill-popping Oxy-heads were not used to this level of purity and started ODing.

So, the gateway drug theory is bullshit when it comes to cannabis, but with prescription pills, it might just be onto something. u/alexonheroin is a member of the r/opiates subreddit, an online community for skag fiends to share their experiences and warn each other about bad batches. I don't know who she is or what she looks like, but after I got cleared by the moderators, she was one of the first to respond to my call for stories about the opioid crisis.

'Outwardly, I'm a typical twenty-something living in a south-eastern city; I've held down a few different jobs, one being at a school for several years. I am married. I don't have a degree, but I attended college for six years, and that should count for something . . . right?' she wrote. 'Anyway, for the last year and a half, I've been a heroin addict.'

'Like many people on this train, I was first prescribed Lortab for menstrual cramps and endometriosis pain,' she continued. 'I began taking them every day regardless of my pain level, because, well, opiates are awesome haha. Then, it was Opana because a friend of mine had access to 100 a month. They were 10 mg instant-release kind, and I would do half a pill every night (up the nose) because taking any more would have me throwing up all night. Eventually, though, the Opana started to fuck with my sinuses. I couldn't breathe through my nose at all for months. So I decided enough was enough, and I made the switch to heroin to see if it would be easier on my nose. And it was! And it's so much more mellow than Opana – I can take heroin and do whatever daily activity I need to get done.

'But therein lies the problem. Heroin is insidious and it is charming and deceptive and all the things you've heard. Not because once you do it, you're hooked, but because it pulls the wool over your eyes, you think, hey, this shit isn't as crazy as the movies make it sound, I'm not out sucking dick for a bag, in fact, my life has IMPROVED because I'm happier, more productive. And then shit hits the fan, and you realise what being dopesick means, what it truly fucking means. It's hell. So I do my very best to avoid that feeling. Luckily, I make enough money to afford to buy in bulk, so it's only occasionally that I find myself without. Every addict abhors that day though, and it's always looming on the horizon.'

While OxyContin and the like may be deadly, at least with prescription meds you know what you're getting. Mexican cartel heroin is of an unknown quality and may be cut with fentanyl (an artificial opioid fifty times stronger than heroin). Fentanyl can be made in a lab (so no need for brightly coloured, Fed-magnet poppy fields) and since it's so potent you don't need as much to smuggle across. It was this fatal ingredient that killed Prince and Lil Peep. By 2016, over 60,000 Americans were dying of overdoses each year, more than in the entire Vietnam War. Another Reddit user, spacetimeismygang, lost three friends to the opioid crisis.

'The first friend of mine to go was Nick,' he told me. 'I remember reading my friend's post on Facebook about how Nick had just passed, and my heart sank to the fucking ground and all I hoped was that it was some kind of cruel joke. He had overdosed in a hotel room while my friend Christian's sister (Nick's girlfriend) was running out to get some food. He was completely dead when she got back, face down in the hotel room. They tried everything they could do to revive him. His funeral really broke me up.'

Just a year later, Ian, another one of spacetime's friends, was dead, having killed himself with an overdose of heroin. But it was the last friend to go that was the real kick in the nuts.

'My last friend to go, Christian, actually had an infected heart valve, endocarditis I think, at age 23 from using needles for heroin. He suffered many strokes because the infection broke off and went to his brain. At the time he thought it was the flu so he didn't get in the hospital for a while. He was on life support in the ICU in downtown Atlanta for weeks. The doctor told his mom that Christian was the sickest man in Atlanta. Eventually they gave him open heart surgery (they had to stop his fricking heart and run his blood through a machine during it – scary!!!). And he actually survived it, so now he had a pig heart valve. Unfortunately he never really treated the problem that led him there. A year and a half later he died with a needle still in his arm. I got to hang out with him a week before he passed at least. We went out and got dope … he was definitely my best friend.'

As the opioid crisis grabbed the media spotlight, tough-on-drugs rhetoric, which had taken a nap in the Obama years, awoke with a vengeance. While the Obama administration told prosecutors to go easy on low-level offenders, Trump reversed that order. Mandatory minimums are back: in 2016 then-Indiana-governor-now-Vice-President Mike Pence reinstated laws requiring a ten-year stretch for heroin and meth dealers if they'd been caught once before. Several states passed laws charging people with homicide if they supplied the drugs leading to someone's death. This might put some dealers off mixing fentanyl in their product, but then again, it might not (after all, the percentage of those ODing is relatively low), and it will definitely put off addicts from calling ambulances for their dying friends. Donald Trump even floated the idea of capital punishment at one point.

'We're wasting our time if we don't get tough with drug dealers,' the Donald told a crowd in New Hampshire, 'and that toughness includes the death penalty.'

Interestingly, despite the rhetoric amping up on dealers, we're not seeing the same level of racism as we did before, because this time, like Alex, more victims are either white or middle class. Plenty of Trump-supporting politicians, like governor Chris Christie of New Jersey, have come out and said that opioid addicts need support, not punishment. This could be because, as upwardly mobile white Americans, these politicians find it easier to show more compassion to these addicts than to a black man in the ghetto or a redneck in a trailer park. Unfair, clearly – where was this sympathy for 'crack babies' and their mothers in the 1980s? – but it's good that white America's finally waking up.

In 2007, Purdue Pharmaceuticals was found guilty of criminally 'misbranding' OxyContin and lying to doctors, and was fined $600 million. A few senior executives got slapped with community service, but no one went to jail. At the same time, Purdue and other compa-nies used their powerful lobby in Congress to pass laws such as the 2016 Ensuring Patient Access and Effective Drug Enforcement Act, which made it harder to seize suspiciously large orders of painkillers. Big Pharma spent $102 million lobbying Congress, making hefty contributions to the twenty-three politicians who pushed through the bill.

Legitimate, licensed corporations acting like the Mafia and a death toll approaching warzone proportions, all while drugs are being 'regulated' . . . surely that means the buck stops with Mary Jane?

While lots of people got hooked through the pharma industry, they're only a tiny percentage of those who take prescribed painkillers. As with other drugs, the number of those actually addicted to them is low. But the number of people who take opioids for their pain is high, and they shouldn't be treated like criminals. Yet when doctors suspect you're becoming addicted, they cut off your prescription or face being stripped of their licence, and THAT'S when people turn to crime and heroin, meaning this is still a black-market problem.

But whichever way you put it, corporate greed caused the opioid crisis, and as long as someone can squeeze some money out of it, this unethical behaviour – bribing congressmen, coddling the black market – will continue. So how do you take profit out of the equation?

In the late 1980s and early 90s, Switzerland was facing a heroin crisis. The police, struggling to keep a lid on the problem, announced they'd stop patrolling Zürich's Platzspitz Park. The idea was to give druggies an area where they could do their thing and not bother everyday people, but the *laissez-faire* approach turned into a free-for-all as up to 20,000 junkies from all over Europe descended upon the park, turning it into a needle-strewn wasteland. Crime exploded as the addicts robbed and stole to pay for their next fix, while rival crews from Turkey, Lebanon and Yugoslavia routinely clashed over a piece of prime real estate. Emergency services were overwhelmed with overdoses, which happened almost every night, and by 1992, know-ing the situation had got out of control, the authorities finally said 'Fuck it' and closed Needle Park. The junkies simply moved some-where else.

In 1994, the Swiss tried something different. They started hand-ing out free, clean heroin in clinics under medical supervision. At first, everyone was like 'Woo, free gear!' But then the public started to see the benefits. To pay for their fix, addicts had to rob passers-by or sell their bodies to dirty old men. Or they'd start dealing them-selves, and then they'd have an active interest in getting others hooked on their wares, who in turn let others get addicted, and so on, like a pyramid scheme. But there's no need for any of that if it's all free.

Having heroin delivered through strictly controlled, government-run clinics takes the shit out of the black market and away from unscrupulous execs. It's not ideal, but not being preoccupied with where the next hit is coming from gives addicts a chance to lead normal lives, have jobs, raise a family, and so on. Having a safe place to inject also means no one's overdosed at those clinics, and there are no ugly needles scattered around for children to pick up.

But why should hard-working taxpayers pay for these crusties to get high? First, these people are sick. Why shouldn't someone who's messed up their body with drugs be entitled to the same rights and healthcare as a skier who breaks their leg going down the mountain, or a couch potato who spends too much time on Netflix and not enough staving off heart disease? Second, it's all very well to be outraged at freeloaders, but this is the problem as it stands, so you can either grit your teeth and deal with it or keep getting your TV stolen.

If the United States carpet-bombed every square inch of the Sierra Madre tomorrow, that still wouldn't solve the opioid crisis. The poppy fields would just spring up somewhere else. Maybe if you stopped all wars, ended all corruption, and brought the Third World up to the level of Switzerland . . . but that's a lot of ifs.

In the Philippines, the police were very keen on showing me how much dope they'd seized. Again, it's a measure of how well they're doing. If they haven't already disappeared from the police evidence locker, the drugs are usually incinerated (often causing an ecological disaster as clouds of smoke waft through the nearby hills, leaving local wildlife dozing around, licking out Nutella jars and listening to Bob Marley).

In 2017, Colombia made its biggest-ever drug bust – 12 tonnes of uncut blow. It brings a tear to my eye, all that cocaine that will never be snorted, but it's a drop in the ocean compared to how much of the white stuff has left the country already. To the cartels, that 12 tonnes is probably worth less than 10 per cent of what it goes for on the street. It's like a mosquito bite on an elephant's ass.

'All of the large seizures you see in the newspapers on a regular basis are a complete con,' said Neil Woods, the undercover policeman. 'It's a photo-op. It's complete propaganda. They say, "Look at the work we're doing", but without the context it's meaningless. In some countries it's estimated less than 1 per cent of heroin is seized annually, so claiming these seizures as a success is ludicrous. To put it into context, most high-street shops write off 5 per cent as losses through shoplifting or food waste or something like that.'

There's little evidence that bigger seizures or stricter punishments make drugs significantly more expensive for the average Joe. In 1993, a gram of charlie cost around £80 in the UK; in 2010 the same gram cost half as much. But-but-but, what about countries like Singapore, you ask? They've got no drug problems because they hang smugglers there (it also helps being small, fabulously rich and surrounded by the sea).

Part of that is their conservative culture, meaning there's not much drug-taking there anyway, but that's not because of the laws.

But Singapore's clean-living image is a façade. There's no reliable stats on drug abuse in Singapore, but it has one of the highest imprisonment rates in Asia, with around 80 per cent of prisoners there for drugs – and that's just the ones who got caught. Someone, somewhere is getting high.

This never-ending cat-and-mouse game is very expensive. If America put aside what it spends on filling up jails and sending Black Hawks and weedkiller to Colombia, it could easily give each addict the help and support they need. If you're worried about how much it would cost to keep paying for these druggies on the taxpayer's dime, I've got a newsflash for you . . . we're spending fuckloads of money already! How much has America spent running investigations, securing the border, feeding the prisoners and sending aid to places like Mexico and Colombia? Billions and billions of dollars. Meanwhile, how much does Portugal, a relatively poor country by European standards, spend fighting drugs? Around $10 per person, per year. Guess who has the bigger drug problem.

But it's all totally worth it, the argument goes, to stop yuppies snorting lines whilst listening to power ballads. Even if the drug war had racist origins, that's not why it's being fought *now*. The government has the right to protect people from themselves (hence the rules about seatbelts and motorbike helmets) and it also has a duty to prevent society from sliding into the hellish, *Purge*-style nightmare that would go down if everyone was hopped-up on speed. But is this really true?

First, drug users might be lazy, bad parents and look like extras from *The Walking Dead*, but none of those are crimes. Second, just because something's there doesn't mean everyone's gonna do it. Between 1880 and 1902, when there were no laws about who could buy or sell heroin and cocaine in America, pharmacists reported addiction rates of between 0.8 and 2.5 out of every thousand people. Obviously, now we're living in an age where #CocaineOverdoseChallenge can go viral, but the option to partake was there and no one took it. Drug use going up and down has little to do with law and everything to do with culture: the 1960s were all about herbal remedies and LSD, cocaine epitomized the greedy 80s excess and now millennials are rediscovering the joy of opiates.

So what are our options here? No one who's directly affected is happy with the status quo (except, ironically, drug dealers and anti-drug crusaders, who'd otherwise be out of a job). Well, we could pull a Duterte and just fuckin' kill everyone, but I'm not sure a Third World quasi-dictator who compares himself to Hitler is really someone we should be taking notes from. We could *decriminalise* drugs, like in Portugal, and stop arresting users while going after the evil, baby-raping dealers. But that's a half measure – as long as someone wants to buy them, someone's going to sell them. Supply and demand, baby. Since those selling them often (but not always) come from economically disadvantaged communities, we've created a situation where we keep arresting people from those communities, perpetrating the cycle of crime, racism and despair. Plus, as with Jack and Torin, there's no way of knowing *what* they're selling: a bag of coke doesn't come with the label 'may contain nuts'.

So where does that leave us? Well, some people say we should legalise drugs.

'Then, while we're at it, why not legalise burglary?' I hear you shout. 'Hell, why not legalise all crimes? Rape, bank robbery . . . of course, if bank robberies were legal there'd be a massive reduction in heists! Why not legalise *murder*?'

Whoa, pump the brakes there, pal. You're comparing a crime that harms other people to a crime that only really harms yourself. Plus, there's only so many burglars: in a town of a 10,000 people, how many will there be? Two? Five? You can probably halve the burglary rate by just arresting one guy. How many people snorting coke? Hundreds, and they're not gonna stop just because you caught their mate in the parking lot with a gram in his pocket. Arresting me probably disrupted the drug supply at Queen Mary by about five minutes.

Let's be honest. You picked up this book, got to this page and thought: 'OK, here we go – I was caught dealing drugs, drugs are fun, drugs should be legal – that's his argument? Well, colour me surprised . . .' But drugs are banned for a reason: they fuck you up. Whether or not drinking's as bad is beside the point. But indulge me for a moment. Let's say we threw in the towel: how would legalisation even work? Surely I'm not saying we sell crack in Waitrose next to the frozen-fish aisle?

One way could be the New Zealand experiment. New Zealand is simply too damn far for any South American coke baron to smuggle into. Instead, Kiwis smoke meth cranked out by tattooed gang members who are cooking it up in their backyard or smoke weed grown deep in the hobbit hills. Their isolation has also led New Zealanders to find more creative ways to get high. Benzylpiperazine (BZP), once a de-worming pill for cows, became a popular legal alternative to speed in the early 2000s and was sold with no restrictions whatsoever until 2008, when it was suddenly banned (even though a quarter of Kiwis had tried it, and no one had actually died). Once that happened, it opened the floodgates for dozens of wannabe-Walter Whites to have a go at producing their own legal highs, which could be quite a bit deadlier. New compounds were appearing faster than lawmakers could find them, so in 2013, the New Zealand government threw up its arms and said, all right, we'll let you have your fun as long as you can prove that it's safe. The 2013 Psychoactive Substances Act mandated that all new head-tripping highs have to go through rigorous health-and-safety testing, you need a licence to sell them and sales to under-eighteens are illegal.

Could it be, for the first time, that substances would be banned or un-banned because of scientific evidence, and not moral panic, racist paranoia, or because America said so? Well, it was a good idea, but it was scuttled, funnily enough, not by worried mums but animal rights activists. You see, every product, as mentioned, has to go through health-and-safety testing, and the only way to do that is with rats and monkeys. A year later, the government banned animal testing.

Even though New Zealand's experiment has been put on hold, the idea behind it is noble: we have an honest, fact-based discussion about which drugs are harmful and in what way. The benchmark could be alcohol.

But still, who'd want to be the first to legalise ecstasy or coke? In 2015, Ireland, through a loophole in its law, accidentally legalised ecstasy for a day and no one died. It's doubtful this scenario will repeat, but perhaps you could test it on a smaller scale first before unleashing it on society . . . maybe at a festival? Of course, then you'd have to do some preliminary surveys, like how many people would have taken Es anyway. And you'd also have the problem that once it becomes public knowledge, the novelty factor might be too much for staff to cope with.

Ganja should be fully legalised and sold at coffeeshops, private clubs and dispensaries. There's no reason this plant should be why anyone's in handcuffs. Milder stuff, such as coca tea (which is almost completely harmless), should be sold in any shop, as it already is in South America.

Heroin should be handed out in free clinics, while opium, being less addictive, could be sold at licensed establishments, as was the case in Hong Kong until 1943, when the Americans forced the British to close shop. The city's substantial dope-fiend population soon switched to heroin. That's right, the opium dens are coming back, baby!

But if smack's available on prescription, where would newbies get their first dose? I'll admit, the first time I heard this question it threw me off, before I realised it's completely pointless. Lex Luthor? Pablo Escobar's ghost? Who cares? The point is that no system – not prescription, not prohibition and not legalisation – is gonna work out perfectly, but at least this way we'll be prepared when wraps of heroin appear in people's pockets.

Cocaine would be best sold in a pharmacy, where druggies can be lectured on what they're buying – taking a lot of the 'cool' factor away from getting it from some guy named Niko. It would be rationed, of course, so you won't be able just to hoard mountains of coke for a White Christmas. There's no need to legalise crack or crystal meth, but we can *decriminalise* it (like they do in Portugal), while legal coke and ecstasy will take most of their market share anyway.

Having said that, use *will* rise.* In a way, Prohibition actually worked: judging by the number of hospital admissions for liver cirrhosis and alcohol poisoning in the 1920s, drinking went down somewhere between 10 and 40 per cent. But even if *use* goes up, the *harm* from everything will go down. No more drinking toxic, illegal hooch from the bathtub like in the good ol' days. Imagine if, say, McDonald's moved on the ecstasy market, putting a whole new spin on the term 'Happy Meal'. Big corporations might be exploitative, unethical pieces-of-shit, but if someone dies on their pills, they'd get bad publicity, fined, boycotted, their stock would plummet and they'd get sued to high heaven. If the government fucks up, there's a paper trail and you can vote their ass out. Bad publicity isn't really a problem for the Gambino crime family.

So how are you gonna keep it from the kids? One way is you take that money you've been spending on bombing Afghan opium fields (literally billions of dollars) and put it into fighting the root causes of addiction – people's miserable lives. Sport is very effective. In the mid-2000s, Iceland set up more after-school sports and music programmes to get kids more active. As result, the number of fifteen- and sixteen-year-olds who got hammered in any given month fell from 42 per cent in 1998 to just 5 per cent by 2016. Similar numbers for smoking

---

* Although, it's gonna *seem* like a lot more because people are doing it more openly.

cigarettes and cannabis. They were getting high on life. At the same time, invest in poor communities. Make kids see there are better options other than gangs and drugs. The US helped Europe rebuild after WWII but there is no Marshal Plan for the US ghetto. Help people make good choices, don't punish them for making bad ones.

What else are people afraid of? That people will start turning up to work high, causing the collapse of civilisation as we know it? Well, I dunno . . . do people normally come in to work drunk?

At the end of every war, the troops left alive go back to their families. So what will happen to the soldiers of dopeworld? Will they get to come home?

Obviously, not every dealer's gonna go straight and become a hack author. But people don't commit crimes just because. They're not animals whose instinct is simply to break the law. That's stupid. They do it because they want something, and they think they won't get caught.

Will some of the more psychotic types move to other crimes? Sure. A couple of years ago my friend's Mexican cousin got kidnapped by the cartels. As the war makes drug profits less reliable, they've branched out into oil theft and kidnapping. They eventually let him go, but gave him nothing but Frosties to eat the whole time. Now he hates Frosties.

But not everyone has the balls to kidnap someone or pull off a heist. It's a totally different class of criminal, just like a desk jockey and a fireman are both honest jobs but you won't send a bunch of screaming secretaries to put out an inferno. Other crimes are a lot riskier and attract far more attention . . . and since cops won't be looking to bust druggies any more, the others will be a lot easier to catch. Remove the motive, remove the opportunity and you remove the crime.

There'll still be smuggling – remember my Lynx-covered ciga-rettes adventure? As long as the price difference between, say,

Amsterdam and Albuquerque ecstasy makes it worthwhile, contra-
banding will continue. But even though the cigarette racket is worth
tens of millions of pounds, it's still a tiny portion of the tobacco
industry – even if half of dopeworld stays in criminal hands, that's
better than what we have now. As it stands, the system forces anyone
who numbs their face with rocket fuel to make a donation to the
Sinaloa Cartel.

It's one thing to put the Mafia out of business, but what about
those poor peasants from Mexico to Afghanistan? They've got nothing else to turn to – poppy's the only thing that feeds families in
those hills. One way is to keep using their land for growing the same
crops legally and brand local delicacies such as Moroccan hash – just
as real champagne *must* be from the Champagne region in France –
so farmers don't go under. If I could buy Fair Trade Cocaine where
the profits go directly to struggling Peruvian farmers, I would!

That's already happened in Turkey and Bolivia. In 1988, the US
forced Bolivia to adopt the hated Law 1008. All coca outside the
Yungas province had to be eradicated and thousands of penniless
farmers were thrown into jail or had their crops destroyed, leaving
them with nothing. But under its indigenous President Evo Morales,
the former president of a coca-growers' union himself, in 2008 it
kicked out the DEA and effectively legalised coca production, setting
each farmer a quota, which is used for everything from tea, biscuits
and even toothpaste. There are no more angry peasant uprisings or
scheming generals plotting cocaine coups.

Turkey, meanwhile, used to be a major source of opium, supplying
the Corsicans and the Pizza Connection, but caved under US pressure to outlaw cultivation in the early 1970s. Poppy farmers, the
backbone of the Turkish economy, didn't take kindly to this, so in
1974 the ban was reversed, but opium growing was strictly regulated
so as only to feed the needs of legit pharma companies.

Stopping the war against drugs also means cutting other kinds of crime. In 2001, Commander Brian Paddick of the Metropolitan Police ordered his officers on the beat in Brixton to stop arresting smokers for cannabis. With their time freed up from chasing teenage stoners on the playground, the effect was phenomenal. Burglaries fell by 18 per cent while the number of muggings almost halved. But after a year, the scheme was shut down after claims that Paddick was letting the drug trade go unabated.

In February 2017, detectives in the sleepy Wiltshire countryside made a startling discovery. Just outside the village of Chilmark lay an abandoned Cold War bunker where officials planned to go and hide in case of nuclear armageddon. There, behind five-inch-thick metal blast doors and spread out over room after room lay a thick canopy of greenery as far as the eye could see, and three teenage boys from Vietnam. They'd been tricked or kidnapped from the streets of Hanoi, taken to the UK, then trapped in the bunker with no fresh air or sunlight, forced to tend the multi-million-pound crop until they'd paid off their captors.

'On social media people are asking: "Why are police taking action on cannabis? It's harmless." I think perhaps people don't appreciate that these are the conditions people are working in, that people are being trafficked, and that this is what it takes to get that product on to the streets,' said Paul Franklin from the Wiltshire police.

Because, Detective Franklin, weed farms are illegal. You don't see the line manager of Innocent Smoothies being involved in some kind of macabre human trafficking ring, do you? Sometimes you can't see the forest for the trees.

Epilogue

The night before I went to jail I'd put on *25th Hour* with Edward Norton, about a drug dealer's last night of freedom before he's sent to the pen: next to *Malcolm X* and *BlackKklansman*, it's one of Spike Lee's best. I didn't know how to cap off this book so back at my parent's house I put it on again, hoping to take things full circle, when my mum walked in.

'Instead of watching your film you could have called your parents. You knew you were going away but you told us nothing, only thinking about yourself!'

I elected not to tell them for two reasons. Firstly, this was my mess and I didn't want to drag them into it. Secondly, I thought there might be a chance, however remote, that I might not go to jail after all and do community service or some bullshit, so this whole episode could stay hush-hush.

Truth be told, if you hadn't already gathered from my stalker antics earlier, my whole encounter with the justice system sent me into a tailspin. I came up with a ridiculous plan for when I did go down. Rita, the better half of my stalker–stalkee relationship, was Indian and agreed to play along with meeting my mum and pretending to be my fiancée with whom I'd eloped to escape from her family, who wanted to give her away in exchange for a herd of goats or whatever. We'd hide out, bin Laden-style, somewhere in

387

Asia, where I'd occasionally send postcards through my mate in Thailand.

Unsurprisingly, my cunning ploy to convince my parents I was off to live in the wildlands of Cambodia didn't work (perhaps because that's not how arranged marriages actually work) but I still couldn't face up to telling them their little boy, who liked playing with LEGO and wanted to be Batman, was now locked away with rapists and murderers. It was selfish, but when something like this is happening to you it's hard to think of anyone else.

People always ask me, what did my parents think of me going to jail? Well, they weren't exactly over the moon. My mum deals with stress by going out and buying a bunch of things she doesn't need. It was hard for her. My dad was more understanding ('Why don't they catch some real criminals?' he'd say as we watched a show about cops busting growhouses) but still, disappointed.

Still, that's in the past now. I've tried to take what's happened to me and turn it into something positive. I want to make a difference, and it's given me an excuse to travel the world. They're proud of me now. Well, I hope they are.

God himself couldn't stop Adam and Eve eating the forbidden fruit. Remember when we drowned women for being witches because we didn't like the cut of their jib? Me neither. Hopefully, one day we'll look back on this era and think, goddamn, we were stupid.

In the East, Duterte's drug war is picking up steam. The Indonesian and Bangladeshi police have adopted a shoot-to-kill policy, while Sri Lanka's reinstating the death penalty. Meanwhile, the Chinese Dragon is rising up to be the world's third superpower, after the Russian Bear and the American Eagle. Like the US, China's been flexing its muscles over its sphere of influence, Southeast Asia, building fake islands to claim ownership over the South China Sea. And just like Uncle Sam, China's dispatched special forces to prowl the jungle for drug lords in the Golden Triangle.

Luckily, while the drug war heats up in the East, it's been simmering down in the West – Canada, Uruguay, Portugal, the US. People are realising we've got this system that poisons kids, destroys families, drives wars, creates terrorists and splits our society. Want to help defeat the Taliban? Legalise drugs. Want to keep it away from your kids? Legalise drugs.

So why hasn't it happened yet? Well, first there's the matter of perspective. Most politicians wouldn't know drug culture if they came home and saw it doing lines off their wife's tits. They might have dabbled in a few party powders, but they've never really had to face the consequences, so they have trouble seeing things from a junkie's perspective. A junkie doesn't care about going to jail. A junkie just wants his next fix.

Second, it's very risky politically. Ever since Richard Nixon, politicians have found that being tough on drugs and tough on crime gets them more votes than sitting behind the polling booths handing out free lollipops. Anything else and they might as well tie their career to an anvil and push it off a bridge.*

Listen, I've worked in the media, so I know how sensationalism works. What if every week, the *Daily Mail* wrote about someone dying from lung cancer? They won't, because no one gives a shit. Everyone knows smoking kills. It's boring. But ecstasy is something new, it's sexy. People will read stories about ecstasy because it's something that threatens YOUR KIDS. Then politicians react and ban this sick filth. It's a cycle of outrage.

Anslinger's spirit lives on, as lawmakers are so scared of not being seen to be taking a moral stand by their electorate that when

---

* There are exceptions of course: Pepe Mujica; Evo Morales; Justin Trudeau; António Guterres of Portugal who became the Secretary-General of the United Nations; Ruth Dreifuss of Switzerland; and Barack Obama, whose presidency saw Black Lives Matter and the legalisation of marijuana.

someone comes to them with objective, scientific evidence they'll stick their fingers in their ears and sing 'la-la-la, I'm not listening!' And that's something very easy for politicians to get behind, because otherwise they'd have to get behind a mic and say something like, 'Hey guys, remember how we threw a bunch of you in prison, tore apart your families, destroyed your job prospects and spent a whole bunch of money? Yeah, well, about that . . .'

So what can you do? Well, there's what David Simon of *The Wire* says, which is if you find yourself on jury duty at a drug trial, any drug trial, say 'not guilty' – that should throw a spanner in the works. If you're a cop, use your discretion. Stop writing off users as worthless skagheads. Write to your local politician/MP/representative. Vote.

And then there's, as Norm Stamper says: 'Organise, mobilise, agitate. As a supposedly free and democratic society, it is the answer. We've seen it with the civil rights movement.'

As absurd as that sounds, holding a Martin Luther King-style protest so you can get loopy – why not? The war on drugs is one of the greatest civil rights issues today. And it's not like it hasn't been done before.

One of the biggest dangers of taking drugs alone is that, if you OD, there's no one to help you. In the 1990s, a group of addicts calling themselves VANDU – the Vancouver Area Network of Drug Users – in Vancouver's heroin-infested Downtown Eastside got together and mounted junkie patrols, searching for OD victims through the back alleys. When parents complained about needles on the school playground, they cleared them up. Then in the city's Oppenheimer Park they planted a thousand wooden crosses, each one standing for one of their dead friends. It looked as solemn and grave as a First World War memorial. People stopped to take it all in. VANDU wouldn't be ignored.

The authorities tried to assuage the group's leader, a homeless poet named Bud Osborn, by putting him on the city's health board. It's easy to dismiss someone as a worthless junkie until they're staring you in the face. Bud used his position to lobby for safe injection rooms, where they could inject in peace with medical supervision in case anything goes wrong. That's right, the smackheads had an official representative. Even the city's right-wing mayor got onboard, and in 2003, Vancouver opened its first safe injection site. Ten years later, the Downtown Eastside's life expectancy had gone up by a decade. The junkies won.

OK but that's Canada, and everyone knows Canada's full of wussy liberal crybabies. What about somewhere like Georgia, the birthplace of Stalin? Like Russia, Georgia too had a zero-tolerance policy. In May 2018, armed police raided two legendary Tbilisi nightclubs, Bassiani and Café Gallery, searching everyone inside, only to arrest eight people *outside* the club. Thousands showed up to fight for their right to party. Braving the attacks of ultranationalists, who denounced them as a bunch of sluts, queers and druggies, the young clubbers held a weekend-long electro-dance party in the streets until eventually the interior minister showed up to apologise and offered to sit down with the protesters to discuss a new drugs policy. Two months later, the country's Constitutional Court struck off marijuana use as a crime (although it weirdly didn't allow possession, so if you see a policeman coming, you'd better spark up).

As for me, I didn't get into drugs for any greater cause other than making money and looking cool. I wasn't running a charity, 'Coke for the Poor', or nothing like that. In a way, I consider myself lucky – I'm white, I have a Master's degree, which helps fill that year-long gap on my CV I spent 'exploring the Himalayas', and my parents looked after me when I got out. I can't say the same for everyone else. And I guess if it all hadn't happened, I wouldn't have written this book.

I think back to my old crew. One of them's a lawyer now and

another does risk assessment for an insurance firm. But how many more people must be deprived of their freedom before we realise our mistake? How many more mothers must cry themselves to sleep every night? How many more addicts must remain stuck in a never-ending cycle of hopelessness and despair?

It's not enough just to end the drug war. There's got to be apologies, restitutions (for non-violent offenders, of course). Anyone who's sitting in jail now, they should let them all out. Today. Total amnesty. And as for Duterte – Rodrigo 'I love to get fucked up on fentanyl and kill homeless people' Duterte – that fucker needs to be in The Hague.

One day, prohibition will come to an end. It has to. And on that day, I'll take a leaf from Freeway Ricky Ross. I'm gonna open my own weed shop. But first I'm gonna track down the name of the judge who sent me down so I can name the shop in his honour, something like Lord Justice Bancroft's Ganja Emporium. I just hope he'll live long enough to see the day.

End Credits

Firstly I'd like to big-up everyone who took time out of their busy schedules to be interviewed for the book, and everyone who either set things up or helped me in my travels: Edoardo Zaffuto, Stefano Tringali and the rest of the Addiopizzo team, as well as Leonardo, Margarita and Riccardo Giaccobe, in Sicily; Alexander Van Hirtum in Amsterdam; Sherbien Dacalanio, Alma Enriquez, Joel Bolito, Marina Kosareva and the Jesus of Nazareth parish in Manila; Miguel Ángel Vega and Ulises Escamilla Haro in Mexico; Dean Armstrong, Sebastián Flórez Gaviria and Margarita Valdiviesos in Colombia; Silvia A and Obi-Wan in Rio; Anya Sarang, Vyacheslav Matyushkin, the Andrey Rylkov Foundation and Kristina Dudkovskaya in Moscow; Golib Bakhtulchamolov, Zaidula Faragis, and Maram and Hakim Azizmamadov at NGO Volunteer in Pamir; Dave and Luke of Newman Tours in Shanghai; Ian Hadfield, Valentina Gorbacheva, Melissa Lynne Stangl, Tamara Garriga and Wiler Noriega Rodrígues of Pulse Tours, and Elvis Sanga and Samuel Aymamendoza of Loki Tours, in Peru; Rouzbeh M; Haze Palmer; Elsa Maia at SICAD, Adriana Curado at IN-Mouraria and Mariana Teixeira Santos at CRESCER in Lisbon; Patricia Gerber at Locked Up, South Africa; the beautiful people of Iran; Nick Paddle, Chris Sentongo, Mohammed Goess, Nicky Foteinopoulou, Stathis Aposporis and of course Rick Wright in London; and Jane Slater and Danny Kushlick at Transform.

Shout-out to Marlon Cameron, Georgi Georgiev, Ivo Benatov, Chris Reid, Bryce Goertzen and Mike Harker for checking my drafts; Thiago Nunes Correa for helping with the proposal; Dahlia Beckles for some interesting suggestions; and Gabriel Krauze and Seth Ferranti for encouraging me to write.

Hats off to everyone who supported me in jail: Christ Murray, Katherine Vassallo, Sacha N, Keeren F, Shakirah Chowdhury, Alex Vissaridis, Julian Richardson, Giannis Mavrakis, Ginger G, Evgeny Dimchenko, Adellion Abrar, Barnaby, David Saunders, Dasha Khassenova, Mike 'Wallace' Barnett, Jazz C, Rory O'Gorman, Chon, Ali, Mike Walsh, Cal, Maggie, Liam Keelan, Edward Stanford-Davis, Rich M, Asha S, Tahmina Adan and Professor Smele.

I appreciate Steve from InTheKnowTraveller.com and Matt Stabile of TheExpeditioner.com letting me re-use parts of my old articles.

Cheers to my agents, John Ash and Patrick Walsh, my editor, Huw Armstrong, my copyeditor Nick Fawcett and the rest of the team at Hodder.

Finally, I'd like to thank my parents for putting up with me all this time and helping finance a hefty part of this project, and little Rigsby for moral support.

If I've forgotten anyone, may the Man Upstairs have mercy on my soul.

Sources

General

Abel, E.L., 2013. *Marihuana: the first twelve thousand years.* Springer Science & Business Media.

Alexander, M., 2012. *The New Jim Crow.* The New Press.

Arsovska, J., 2015. *Decoding Albanian organized crime: Culture, politics, and globalization.* Univ of California Press.

Baum, D., 2016. *Legalize it all.* Harper's Magazine.

Bewley-Taylor, D., Blickman, T. and Jelsma, M., 2014. *The rise and decline of cannabis prohibition. The history of cannabis in the UN drug control system and options for reform.* Swansea: Research Institute for Arts and Humanities.

Brandt, A.M., 2007. *The cigarette century: the rise, fall, and deadly persistence of the product that defined America.* Basic Books (AZ).

Booth, M., 2013. *Opium: a history.* St. Martin's Griffin.

Dickie, J., 2014. *Blood Brotherhoods: A History of Italy's Three Mafias.* Hachette UK.

Dickie, J., 2005. *Cosa Nostra: A History of the Sicilian Mafia.* St. Martin's Press.

DuVernay, A., 2016. *13th. A Netflix Original Documentary.* Sherman Oaks, CA: *Kandoo Films.*

Gingeras, R., 2014. *Heroin, organized crime, and the making of modern Turkey.* OUP Oxford.

Glenny, M., 2009. *McMafia: Seriously organised crime.* Random House.

Gosch, M. and Hammer, R., 2013. *The Last Testament of Lucky Luciano: The Mafia Story in His Own Words.* Enigma Books.

Grass. (1999). [DVD] Directed by R. Mann. Canada: Unapix Home Entertainment.

Grillo, I., 2012. *El Narco: inside Mexico's criminal insurgency.* Bloomsbury Publishing USA.

Grillo, I., 2016. *Gangster warlords: Drug dollars, killing fields, and the new politics of Latin America.* Bloomsbury Publishing.

Hari, J., 2015. *Chasing the scream: The first and last days of the war on drugs.* Bloomsbury Publishing USA.

Horvitz, L.A. and Catherwood, C., 2014. *Encyclopedia of war crimes and genocide.* Infobase Publishing.

The House I Live In. (2012). [film] Directed by E. Jarecki. United States.

Kamienski, L., 2016. *Shooting up: a short history of drugs and war.* Oxford University Press.

Marks, H., 1997. *Mr Nice.* Random House.

McCoy, A.W., Read, C.B. and Adams, L.P., 1972. *The politics of heroin in Southeast Asia.*

McGirr, L., 2015. *The war on alcohol: Prohibition and the rise of the American state.* WW Norton & Company.

Nutt, D., 2012. *Drugs without the hot air.* Cambridge: UIT Cambridge.

Phillips, R., 2014. *Alcohol: a history.* UNC Press Books.

Power, M., 2014. *Drugs 2.0: The web revolution that's changing how the world gets high.* Portobello Books.

Raab, S., 2016. *Five Families: The Rise, Decline, and Resurgence of America's Most Powerful Mafia Empires.* Macmillan.

Ross, R. and Scott, C. (2014). *Freeway Rick Ross.* Createspace Independent Pub.

Streatfeild, D., 2003. *Cocaine: an unauthorized biography.* Macmillan.

Santino, U. and La Fiura, G., 1993. *Behind Drugs.* Edizioni Gruppo Abel.

The Union: The Business Behind Getting High. (2007). [film] Directed by B. Harvey. Canada: Netflix.

United Nations Office on Drugs and Crime. *Statistics and Data.* https://dataunodc.un.org/

United Nations Office on Drugs and Crime, 2017. *World drug report 2017.* United Nations Publications.

Wainwright, T., 2016. *Narconomics: How to run a drug cartel.* PublicAffairs.

Winslow, D. (2016). *El Chapo and the Secret History of the Heroin Crisis.* Esquire. Available at: https://www.esquire.com/news-politics/a46918/heroin-mexico-el-chapo-cartels-don-winslow/

A Brief History of Molly

Reynolds, S., 2013. *Energy flash: A journey through rave music and dance culture.* Faber & Faber.

LDN

Jenkins, S. (2018). *Resist the calls for 'solutions' to London's murder surge.* the Guardian. Available at: https://www.theguardian.com/commentisfree/2018/apr/06/solutions-london-murder-surge-new-york-crackdown.

McKenna, K. (2017). *Glasgow's dark legacy returns as gangland feuds erupt in public killings.* [online] the Guardian. Available at: https://www.theguardian.com/uk-news/2017/jul/22/glasgow-gangland-feuds-erupt-in-public-killings.

Summers, C. 2013. *What lies behind murderous Turkish gang feud?* https://www.bbc.co.uk/news/uk-21592288

Townsend, M. 2019. *Kings of cocaine: how the Albanian mafia seized control of the UK drugs trade.* https://www.theguardian.com/world/2019/jan/13/kings-of-cocaine-albanian-mafia-uk-drugs-crime

Townsend, M. 2015. *Heroin trade continues to claim lives as UK drug gangs compete for power.* https://www.theguardian.com/society/2015/dec/20/heroin-gangs-london-wood-green-shooting

Williams, P. 2016. *Three AK-47 assault rifles used in Regency Hotel attack seized by gardai*. https://www.independent.ie/irish-news/three-ak47-assault-rifles-used-in-regency-hotel-attack-seized-by-gardai-34527790.html

Williams, P. 2017. *Under the gun: Paul Williams on the Hutch-Kinahan feud, one year on from the Regency shootings*. https://www.independent.ie/irish-news/crime/under-the-gun-paul-williams-on-the-hutchkinahan-feud-one-year-on-from-the-regency-shootings-35401806.html

Vasić, M., 2005. *Atentat na Zorana Đinđića*. Politika.

CrIsis

Al-Juzi, A. 2016. *Some of the Everyday Stuff You Have in Your Home That's Illegal from Today*. https://www.vice.com/en_uk/article/jm9aa4/psychoactive-substances-act-list-of-banned-stuff

Bird, S. 2018. *Inside Britain's prisons where inmates are addicted to spice – and 999 calls are made every 40 minutes*. https://www.telegraph.co.uk/news/2018/09/01/inside-britains-prisons-inmates-addicted-spice-999-calls-made/

Child, B. 2014. *The force of law: Prisoner claims persecution for Star Wars faith*. https://www.theguardian.com/film/2014/apr/17/prisoner-persecution-star-wars-jedi

Crossley, L. 2014. *The farce is strong with this one: Inmate complains that prison 'bigots' are preventing him from practising his JEDI religion*. https://www.dailymail.co.uk/news/article-2609706/Jedi-inmate-unable-use-force-prison-bosses-refuse-recognise-Star-Wars-based-religious-beliefs.html

Laville, S., Taylor, M. and Haddou, L., 2014. *Inmate suicide figures expose human toll of prison crisis*. The Guardian.

HM Inspectorate of Prisons, 2015. *HM Chief Inspector of Prisons for England and Wales Annual Report 2013-14*.

Inside Time. 2014. *Never mind the Jedi, here's the Sith Lord*. https://insidetime.org/never-mind-the-jedi-heres-the-sith-lord/

Inside Time. 2014. *Return of the Jedi*. https://insidetime.org/return-of-the-jedi/

Sullivan, D. 2017. *Caught In The Act*. http://volteface.me/features/psa-act/

Wilding, M. 2017. *The Story of Spice, the Street Drug That's Not Going Away*. https://www.vice.com/en_uk/article/z4je55/the-story-of-spice-the-street-drug-thats-not-going-away

A Trip Through the Ages

Thelwell, E. 2014. *Why do people take ayahuasca?*. https://www.bbc.co.uk/news/magazine-27203322

Yi-Mak, K. and Harrison, L., 2001. *Globalisation, cultural change and the modern drug epidemics: the case of Hong Kong*. Health, Risk & Society, 3(1), pp.39–57.

Shanghaied

Dikötter, F., Laamann, L.P. and Xun, Z., 2004. *Narcotic culture: a history of drugs in China*. C. Hurst & Co. Publishers.

Dirks, E. 2018. *China Is Treating Muslims Like Drug Addicts*. http://foreignpolicy.com/2018/10/03/china-is-treating-muslims-like-drug-addicts/

Lovell, J., 2015. *The Opium War: Drugs, Dreams, and the Making of Modern China.* The Overlook Press.

Zhao, C. 2017. *Chinese Drug Dealers Are Being Sentenced To Death in Sports Stadiums and Public Squares.* https://www.newsweek.com/china-criminals-sentenced-death-sports-stadium-thousands-spectators-750983

Dry Season

Blum, D. 2010. *The Chemist's War.* https://slate.com/technology/2010/02/the-little-told-story-of-how-the-u-s-government-poisoned-alcohol-during-prohibition.html

Gill, V. 2015. *Chimpanzees found to drink alcoholic plant sap in wild.* https://www.bbc.co.uk/news/science-environment-33050939

Johnson, S., 2008. *The Ghost Map: A Street, an Epidemic and the Hidden Power of Urban Networks.* Penguin UK.

MacDonald, A., 2011. *Al Capone and His Gang.* Scholastic

Phillips, S. 2016. *The Bootlegger Who Took Down the KKK.* https://www.riverfronttimes.com/stlouis/the-bootlegger-who-took-down-the-kkk/Content?oid=3065612

Time. *Top 10 Prohibition Tales.* http://content.time.com/time/specials/packages/article/0,28804,1864521_1864524_1864537,00.html

Vallee, B.L., 1998. *Alcohol in the western world.* Scientific American, 278(6), pp.80–85.

Keep Off the Grass

Curry, A. 2015. *Gold Artifacts Tell Tale of Drug-Fueled Rituals and 'Bastard Wars'.* https://news.nationalgeographic.com/2015/05/150522-scythians-marijuana-bastard-wars-kurgan-archaeology/

Chemical Warfare

Brasor, P. 2017. *Once a drug user in Japan, always an outcast.* https://www.japantimes.co.jp/news/2017/07/01/national/media-national/drug-user-japan-always-outcast/

Greenfield, R., 2006. *Timothy Leary: a biography.* Houghton Mifflin Harcourt.

Ito, M. 2014. *Dealing with addiction: Japan's drug problem.* https://www.japantimes.co.jp/life/2014/08/23/lifestyle/dealing-addiction-japans-drug-problem/

Kaplan, D.E., 1996. *The cult at the end of the world: The terrifying story of the Aum doomsday cult, from the subways of Tokyo to the nuclear arsenals of Russia.* Crown Pub.

Kaplan, D.E. and Dubro, A., 2012. *Yakuza: Japan's criminal underworld.* Univ of California Press.

Ohler, N., 2016. *Blitzed: Drugs in Nazi Germany.* Penguin UK.

Marks, J., 1979. *The search for the 'Manchurian candidate': The CIA and mind control.* New York: Times Books.

Mitchell, J. 2014. *Cannabis: the healing of the nation.* https://www.japantimes.co.jp/life/2014/04/19/lifestyle/cannabis-the-healing-of-the-nation/

Summers, C. 2000. *Australia's most lethal export.* http://news.bbc.co.uk/1/hi/entertainment/1037417.stm

Hail Satan

Jenkins, S. (2002). *At last, a way out of our drugs shame.* Evening Standard. Available at: https://www.standard.co.uk/news/at-last-a-way-out-of-our-drugs-shame-6310746.html
Woodstock. (1970). [DVD] Directed by M. Wadleigh. Warner Bros.

Havana Nights

Cannell, D., 2006. *638 Ways to Kill Castro.* Silver River and Channel 4.
Von Tunzelmann, A., 2011. *Red Heat: Conspiracy, Murder, and the Cold War in the Caribbean.* Random House Digital, Inc.

The Pizza Connection

BBC News. 2017. *Sicily fire crew 'caused fires for cash'.* https://www.bbc.co.uk/news/world-europe-40848289
Reguly, E. 2007. *The killing the Vatican would rather forget.* https://www.theglobeandmail.com/news/world/the-killing-the-vatican-would-rather-forget/article20398234/
The Telegraph. 2015. *Licio Gelli, financier – obituary.* https://www.telegraph.co.uk/news/obituaries/12054716/Licio-Gelli-financier-obituary.html

Corleone

Pantaleone, W. 2018. *In historic ruling, court says Italian state negotiated with mafia.* https://www.reuters.com/article/us-italy-mafia-idUSKBN1HR2JJ
BBC News. 2017. *Archbishop in Sicily bans mafia from being godfathers.* https://www.bbc.co.uk/news/world-europe-39313674

New Blood

Khandaker, T. 2015. *The Notorious Black Axe Has Put Down Roots in Canada.* https://news.vice.com/en_us/article/vb835b/the-notorious-black-axe-has-put-down-roots-in-canada
Latza Nadeau, B., 2018. *Roadmap to Hell: Sex, Drugs and Guns on the Mafia Coast.* Oneworld Publications.
Perry, A., 2018. *The Good Mothers: The True Story of the Women Who Took On the World's Most Powerful Mafia.* HarperCollins.
Reski, P., 2013. *The Honored Society: A Portrait of Italy's Most Powerful Mafia.* Nation Books.
Saviano, R., 2012. *Gomorrah: Italy's Other Mafia.* Pan Macmillan.

The Three Musketeers

Griffin, S.P., 2003. *Philadelphia's Black Mafia: A Social and Political History.* Springer Science & Business Media.
Lehr, D. and O'Neill, G., 2012. *Black Mass: Whitey Bulger, the FBI, and a Devil's Deal.* Hachette UK.

Ready Rock

Bogazianos, D.A., 2012. *5 Grams: Crack Cocaine, Rap Music, and the War on Drugs.* NYU Press.

Biggie and Tupac. (2002). [DVD] Directed by N. Broomfield. FilmFour/Lafayette Films.

Cocaine Cowboys, 2006. [DVD] Directed by B. Corben. Magnolia Pictures.

English, T.J., 2018. *The Corporation: The Rise and Fall of America's Cuban Mafia.* Bonnier Publishing Ltd.

Levitt, S.D. and Venkatesh, S.A., 2000. *An economic analysis of a drug-selling gang's finances.* The quarterly journal of economics, 115(3), pp.755–789.

MacDonell, A. 2003. *In Too Deep.* https://www.laweekly.com/news/in-too-deep -2137087

Reed, T. and Hoye, S. 2015. *Former crack baby: 'It's another stigma, another box to put me in'.* http://america.aljazeera.com/watch/shows/america-tonight/articles/2015/3/10/ crack-baby-myth.html

Sager, M. 2013. *Say Hello to Rick Ross.* https://www.esquire.com/news-politics/a25818/ rick-ross-drug-dealer-interview-1013/

Incarceration Nation

McCarthy, N. 2016. *Homicides In Chicago Eclipse US Death Toll In Afghanistan And Iraq.* https://www.forbes.com/sites/niallmccarthy/2016/09/08/homicides-in-chicago-eclipse-u-s-death-toll-in-afghanistan-and-iraq-infographic/

#BlackLivesMatter

Basra, R. and Neumann, P.R., 2016. *Criminal pasts, terrorist futures: European jihadists and the new crime-terror nexus.* Perspectives on Terrorism, 10(6).

Friedersdorf, C. 2017. *A Police Killing Without a Hint of Racism.* https://www.theatlantic.com/politics/archive/2017/12/a-police-killing-without-a-hint-of-racism/546983 /

Fyfe, D. 2018. *How Sierra and a Disgraced Cop Made the Most Reactionary Game of the 90s.* [Online]. [21 March 2019]. Available from: https://waypoint.vice.com/en_us/article /a3n8ea/how-sierra-and-a-disgraced-cop-made-the-most-reactionary-game-of-the-90s

Goyette, J. 2017. *'Never been about race': black activists on how Minneapolis reacted to Damond shooting.* https://www.theguardian.com/us-news/2017/jul/22/black-activists-minneapolis-race-reacted-justine-damond-shooting

Hill, M.L., 2017. *Nobody: Casualties of America's war on the vulnerable, from Ferguson to Flint and beyond.* Simon and Schuster.

Lartey, J. and Swaine, J. 2017. *Philando Castile shooting: officer said he felt in danger after smelling pot in car.* https://www.theguardian.com/us-news/2017/jun/20/philando-castile-shooting-marijuana-car-dashcam-footage

Lowery, W., 2017. *They Can't Kill Us All: The Story of Black Lives Matter.* Penguin UK.

Mac Donald, H., 2017. *The war on cops: How the new attack on law and order makes everyone less safe.* Encounter Books.

Misra, T. 2017. *The Othered Paris.* https://www.citylab.com/equity/2017/11/the-othered -paris/543597/

Nix, J., Campbell, B.A., Byers, E.H. and Alpert, G.P., 2017. *A bird's eye view of civilians killed by police in 2015: Further evidence of implicit bias.* Criminology & Public Policy, 16(1), pp.309–340.

Smith, M. 2016. *Philando Castile's Last Night: Tacos and Laughs, Then a Drive.* https://www.nytimes.com/2016/07/13/us/philando-castile-minnesota-police-shooting.html

Zaleski, E. 2017. *Alleged French Police Rape of a Man Could Set the Country on Fire.* https://www.thedailybeast.com/alleged-french-police-rape-of-a-man-could-set-the-country-on-fire

Planes, Chains and Automobiles

Atkin, C. 2015. *Police seize two tonnes of 'black cocaine' bound for Mexico.* https://www.independent.co.uk/news/world/americas/police-seize-two-tonnes-of-black-cocaine-bound-for-mexico-10491258.html

BBC News. 2017. *Cocaine suitcase: 'Drug mule' arrested in Shanghai.* https://www.bbc.co.uk/news/world-asia-china-40186508

BBC News. 2011. *Colombia police catch drug-smuggling pigeon.* https://www.bbc.co.uk/news/world-latin-america-12220886

BBC News. 2017. *Medieval-style drugs catapult found on US–Mexico border.* https://www.bbc.co.uk/news/world-us-canada-38986804

Bell, D. 2007. *Jail for man who smuggled cocaine hidden in doors.* https://www.theguardian.com/uk/2007/feb/24/drugsandalcohol.drugstrade

Burillo-Putze, G., Becker, L.T., Rodríguez, M.G., Torres, J.S. and Nogué, S., 2012. *Liquid cocaine body packers.* Clinical Toxicology, 50(6), pp.522–524.

Davison, P. 1998. *Global alert for undetectable black cocaine.* https://www.independent.co.uk/news/global-alert-for-undetectable-black-cocaine-1196670.html

Edgar, J. 2014. *Drugs in rugs: heroin worth £5 million found woven into carpets.* https://www.telegraph.co.uk/news/uknews/crime/10889639/Drugs-in-rugs-heroin-worth-5-million-found-woven-into-carpets.html

Emmott, R. 2008. *Mexico drug smugglers make Jesus statue of cocaine.* https://www.reuters.com/article/us-mexico-drugs-idUSN3031343320080530

Farrell, J. 2017. *Police shoot carrier pigeon dead as it flies drugs into jail in 'backpack'.* https://www.independent.co.uk/news/world/americas/police-shoot-pigeon-dead-drugs-cannabis-santa-rosa-la-pampa-argentina-a7926301.html

Franklin, J. 2006. *Pinochet 'sold cocaine to Europe and US'.* https://www.theguardian.com/world/2006/jul/11/chile.drugstrade

Goodman, A. 2009. *Smuggler with broken leg wears cocaine cast.* http://edition.cnn.com/2009/CRIME/03/06/spain.leg.cast/

Marks, P. 2006. *Gangs turn cocaine into clear plastic products.* https://www.newscientist.com/article/dn8998-gangs-turn-cocaine-into-clear-plastic-products/

Newbery, C. 2018. *An Embassy, 850 Pounds of Cocaine and Now 6 Arrests.* https://www.nytimes.com/2018/02/22/world/americas/argentina-russia-cocaine.html

Operation Odessa. (2018). [film] Directed by T. Russell. Showtime.

Parker, A. and Zapiro, 2011. *50 People who stuffed up South Africa.* Two Dogs.

Skelton, R. 2010. *Drug hub Guinea-Bissau awaits first prisons.* //www.bbc.co.uk/news/world-africa-10611635

Smoltczyk, A., 2013. *Africa's cocaine hub: Guinea-Bissau a drug traffickers' dream.* Spiegel Online.

Veitch, H. 2015. *Obituary: Andrew Chan, 1984–2015.* https://www.smh.com.au/national/obituary-andrew-chan-19842015-20150428-1muvpu.html

Vulliamy, E. and Ferrett, G., 2008. *How a tiny West African country became the world's first Narco State.* The Guardian.

Young, R., 2016. *Marching Powder.* Pan Macmillan.

Plata o plomo

Alsema, A. 2018. *Is Medellin on the brink of another war?* https://colombiareports.com/is-medellin-at-the-brink-of-another-war/

Bowden, M., 2009. *Killing Pablo.* Atlantic Books Ltd.

Brodzinsky, S. 2016. *'The horrible night has ceased': Colombia peace deal resounds in Farc's heartland.* https://www.theguardian.com/world/2016/sep/27/colombia-farc-peace-deal-resounds-homeland-uribe

Buder, E. 2018. *Killing With Impunity, Every Three Days.* https://www.theatlantic.com/video/index/561194/colombia-social-leaders/

Centro Nacional de Memoria Histórica. c.2018. *Observatorio de Memoria y Conflicto.* http://centrodememoriahistorica.gov.co/observatorio/

Escobar, R., 2012. *Escobar: The Inside Story of Pablo Escobar, the World's Most Powerful Criminal.* Hachette UK.

'Sins of my father', Los pecados de mi padre. 2010. Directed by N. Entel. HBO.

Gettleman, J. and Bleasdale, M., 2013. *The price of precious.* National Geographic.

Kremer, W. 2014. *Pablo Escobar's hippos: A growing problem.* https://www.bbc.co.uk/news/magazine-27905743

Kryt, J. 2017. *Colombian Security Forces 'Massacre' Coca Farmers Under Pressure From Trump.* https://www.thedailybeast.com/colombian-security-forces-massacre-coca-farmers-under-pressure-from-trump

Kryt, J. 2018. *The Mexican Cartels Are Becoming a Hemispheric Threat – With Trump's Help.* https://www.thedailybeast.com/the-mexican-cartels-are-becoming-a-hemispheric-threatwith-trumps-help

McDermott, J. 2016. *Colombia Elites and Organized Crime: 'Don Berna'.* https://www.insightcrime.org/investigations/colombia-elites-and-organized-crime-don-berna/

McFarland Sanchez-Moreno, M. (2018). *There Are No Dead Here: A Story of Murder and Denial in Colombia.* New York: Avalon Publishing Group.

Palomo, A. 2018. *La Escombrera: una fosa común en Medellín clave para el futuro de Colombia.* https://www.elconfidencial.com/mundo/2018-05-23/escombrera-fosa-comun-medellin-colombia_1566616/

Plumptre, A.J., Nixon, S., Critchlow, R., Vieilledent, G., Kirkby, A., Williamson, E.A., Hall, J. and Kujirakwinja, D., 2015. *Status of Grauer's gorilla and chimpanzees in eastern Democratic Republic of Congo: historical and current distribution and abundance.*

Sontag, D., 2016. *The Secret History of Colombia's Paramilitaries and the US War on Drugs.* The New York Times.

Steade, S. 2017. *Manuel Noriega: Call of Duty, the invasion playlist and his preteen pen pal.* https://www.mercurynews.com/2017/05/30/manuel-noriega-call-of-duty-the-invasion-playlist-and-his-preteen-pen-pal/

Vulliamy, E., 2013. *Medellín, Colombia: reinventing the world's most dangerous city.* The Guardian.

The Boys from Sinaloa

Beith, M., 2010. *The last narco: Inside the hunt for El Chapo, the world's most wanted drug lord*. Open Road & Grove/Atlantic.

Cartel Land. (2015). [film] Directed by M. Heineman. The Orchard.

Connolly, K. 2010. *US border violence: Myth or reality?* https://www.bbc.co.uk/news/world-us-canada-10779151

Devereaux, R. 2016. *After an Uprising in Mexico, the Return of the Narco Warlords*. https://theintercept.com/2016/06/29/after-uprising-in-mexico-return-of-narco-warlords/

Newton, M., 2006. *The encyclopedia of serial killers*. Infobase Publishing.

Trump, D., 2015. *Presidential announcement speech*. Address at New York City, New York.

Secretariado Ejecutivo del Sistema Nacional de Seguridad Pública (2019). *Víctimas de Delitos del Fuero Común 2018*.

The Wall

Barnes, T., Elias, R. and Walsh, P., 2016. *Cocky: The Rise And Fall of Curtis Warren, Britain's Biggest Drugs Baron*. Milo Books Ltd.

Cooper, B. 2008. *Never Get Busted: Understanding Police Drug Dogs*. https://www.cannabisculture.com/content/2008/08/22/never-get-busted-understanding-police-drug-dogs/

Etellekt Consultores: *Informe de violencia política en México julio-agosto 2018*. Ciudad de México

European Monitoring Centre for Drugs and Drug Addiction, 2016. *EU drug markets report: In-depth analysis*. Office of the European Union.

Moor, K. 2015. *World's biggest ecstasy bust: How a Google search foiled Aussie tomato tin mafia's drug plots*. https://www.heraldsun.com.au/news/national/worlds-biggest-ecstasy-bust-how-a-google-search-foiled-aussie-tomato-tin-mafias-drug-plots/news-story/0dboce6a9d6d61706420b975484ba7ea

Hernández, A., 2018. *A Massacre in Mexico: The True Story Behind the Missing 43*. Verso Trade.

Parmeter, J.E., Murray, D.W., Hannum, D.W., Sandia National Laboratories and United States of America, 2000. *Guide for the Selection of Drug Detectors for Law Enforcement Applications, NIJ Guide 601-00*. National Institute of Justice, Law Enforcement and Corrections Standards and Testing Program.

Dinner at El Chapo's

Beith, M. and Hootsen, J. 2017. *El Chapo Is Going Down How Many Drug Lords, Assassins, Politicians and Policemen Will He Take with Him?*. https://www.newsweek.com/2017/10/27/el-chapo-drug-lords-assassins-politicians-policemen-687773.html

Breslow, J.M. 2015. *The Staggering Death Toll of Mexico's Drug War*. https://www.pbs.org/wgbh/frontline/article/the-staggering-death-toll-of-mexicos-drug-war/

Grigoradis, V. and Cuddehe, M. 2011. *An American Drug Lord in Acapulco*. Rolling Stone.

Hamilton, K. 2019. *The 10 wildest moments and stories from El Chapo's trial*. https://

news.vice.com/en_us/article/vbweqj/the-10-most-insane-moments-and-stories-from-el-chapos-trial

Keefe, P.R., 2014. *The Hunt for El Chapo*. The New Yorker.

Lakhani, N., 2016. *Violent deaths in El Salvador spiked 70% in 2015, figures reveal*. The Guardian.

Mackey, D. 2017. *The Election Fraud in Honduras Follows Decades of Corruption Funded By the US War on Drugs*. https://theintercept.com/2017/12/23/honduras-election-fraud-drugs-jose-orlando-hernandez/

Martínez, J.B. 2018. *Entregan enseres y colchones a damnificados, presuntamente a nombre de 'El Chapo'*. http://www.eluniversal.com.mx/estados/entregan-enseres-y-colchones-damnificados-presuntamente-nombre-de-el-chapo

Penn, S., 2016. *El Chapo speaks*. Rolling Stone.

Sahagun, R.Z. 2011. *De frente y de perfil*. https://www.informador.mx/Mexico/De-frente-y-de-perfil-20110430-0172.html

Thompson, G. 2017. *How The US Triggered A Massacre In Mexico*. https://www.propublica.org/article/allende-zetas-cartel-massacre-and-the-us-dea/

Torres, A. 2018. *'Thank you El Chapo!' Villagers affected by a tropical depression shower the jailed drug kingpin with love after receiving a donation of mattresses and electric stoves attributed to the cartel boss*. https://www.dailymail.co.uk/news/article-6320771/Thank-Chapo-Guzman-Villagers-affected-tropical-depression-thank-jailed-cartel-leader.html

Shottingham

Doward, J., 2007. *Brutal ganglord who fell victim to his own drugs*. The Observer.

Huffington Post UK. 2012. *Nottingham's Notorious Gang Leader Colin Gunn Campaigns About 'Incorrect Cost Of Stamps'*. https://www.huffingtonpost.co.uk/2012/10/04/nottingham-gang-leader-colin-gunn-stamps-_n_1939441.html

Woods, N. and Rafaeli, J.S., 2016. *Good cop, bad war*. Random House.

Nisha

Davidson, K., 1999. *Carl Sagan: a life*. New York: Wiley.

Friedman, R., 2017. *What cookies and meth have in common*. The New York Times.

Hart, C., 2013. *High price. A neuroscientist's journey of self-discovery that challenges everything you know about drugs and society*. New York: HarpenCollins.

Hendricks, P.S., Crawford, M.S., Cropsey, K.L., Copes, H., Sweat, N.W., Walsh, Z. and Pavela, G., 2018. *The relationships of classic psychedelic use with criminal behavior in the United States adult population*. Journal of psychopharmacology, 32(1), pp.37–48.

Isaacson, W., 2011. *Steve Jobs*. New York: Simon and Schuster.

Obama, B., 2007. *Dreams from my father: A story of race and inheritance*. Canongate Books.

Jack and Torin

Buchanan, D. 2015. *Leah Betts died 20 years ago and we still can't be honest about drugs*. [Online]. [21 March 2019]. Available from: https://www.telegraph.co.uk/women/life/leah-betts-died-20-years-ago-we-still-cant-be-honest-about-drugs/

Codrea-Rado, A. 2018. *The UK's radical club drug safety experiment is working – and now it's going high-tech*. https://www.wired.co.uk/article/drug-testing-safety-uk-festivals

Fishwick, B. 2017. *Portsmouth drug dealer who used the dark web to sell thousands of ecstasy tablets is jailed for 16 years.* https://www.portsmouth.co.uk/news/crime/portsmouth-drug-dealer-who-used-the-dark-web-to-sell-thousands-of-ecstasy-tablets-is-jailed-for-16-years-1-8298129

Measham, F.C., 2018. *Drug safety testing, disposals and dealing in an English field: Exploring the operational and behavioural outcomes of the UK's first onsite 'drug checking' service.* International Journal of Drug Policy.

Nutt, D., 2015. *The Superman pill deaths are the result of our illogical drugs policy.* The Guardian.

RT. 2017. *UK festival offers to test partygoers' drugs for safe use.* https://www.rt.com/uk/397972-uk-festival-drug-testing-loop/

Treasure Hunting

Aboriginals Protection and Restriction of the Sale of Opium Act 1897.

BBC News. 2017. *Silk Road: Google search unmasked Dread Pirate Roberts.* [Online]. [21 March 2019]. Available from: https://www.bbc.co.uk/news/av/magazine-40977474/silk-road-google-search-unmasked-dread-pirate-roberts

Bearman, J. and Hanuka, T., 2015. *The Rise and Fall of Silk Road.* Wired Magazine.

Interfax. 2017. *Почти треть всех заключенных в РФ отбывают наказание за наркотики* https://www.interfax.ru/russia/579131

Комсомольская правда. 2005. *Москвичи рискуют провалиться во времени* https://www.kp.ru/daily/23537.5/41637/

Jeong, S. 2015. *DEA Agent Who Faked a Murder and Took Bitcoins from Silk Road Explains Himself.* https://motherboard.vice.com/en_us/article/8q845p/dea-agent-who-faked-a-murder-and-took-bitcoins-from-silk-road-explains-himself

Mozhayev, A. 2012. *Under the capital's streets: a guide to ancient Moscow.* https://www.opendemocracy.net/en/odr/under-capitals-streets-guide-to-ancient-moscow/

Petruccelli, D. 2016. *Vienna's War on Drugs: Refugee Crises and the Recriminalization of Narcotics.* http://www.iwm.at/transit-online/viennas-war-on-drugs-refugee-crises-and-the-recriminalization-of-narcotics/

Phillips, M. 2015. *Russia is quite literally drinking itself to death.* https://qz.com/403307/russia-is-quite-literally-drinking-itself-to-death/

Smart, E. 2015. *Unsealed Transcript Shows How Judge Justified Ross Ulbricht's Life Sentence.* https://cointelegraph.com/news/unsealed-transcript-shows-how-judge-justified-ross-ulbrichts-life-sentence

TASS. 2017. *МВД сообщило о ликвидации крупнейшего интернет-магазина наркотиков* https://tass.ru/proisshestviya/4572560

Шарафиев, И. 2017. *Нужно подкинуть – подкинут, нужно подставить – подставят Как в России сажают за употребление наркотиков и почему это не работает.* [Online]. [21 March 2019]. Available from: https://meduza.io/feature/2017/07/18/nuzhno-podkinut-podkinut-nuzhno-podstavit-podstavyat

Just Say *Nyet!*

Dawisha, K., 2015. *Putin's kleptocracy: who owns Russia?* Simon and Schuster.

De Danieli, F., 2013. *Counter-narcotics policies in Tajikistan and their impact on state building.* In *The Transformation of Tajikistan* (pp.157–174). Routledge.

Galeotti, M., 2018. *Vory: Russia's Super Mafia*. Yale University Press.

Greitens, S.C., 2014. *Illicit: North Korea's Evolving Operations to Earn Hard Currency*. Committee for Human Rights in North Korea.

Harding, L. and Hopkins, N. (2017). *How 'dirty money' from Russia flooded into the UK – and where it went*. Available at: https://www.theguardian.com/world/2017/mar/20/how-dirty-money-from-russia-flooded-into-the-uk-and-where-it-went

Interfax.ru. (2012). *Пациентку Ройзмана держали в наручниках*. https://www.interfax.ru/russia/276947.

Ivanov, A., 2014. *Eburg*. AST.

Klebnikov, P., 1996. *Godfather of the Kremlin*. Forbes

Kramer, A.E., 2017. *Chechen authorities arresting and killing gay men, Russian paper says*. The New York Times.

Комиссарова, А. (2017). *«Весь город наш!»*. Lenta.ru. Available at: https://lenta.ru/articles/2017/12/17/opg.

Lantreev, E. (2016). *Why Russia's Heroin Addicts Are Going Through Hell*. Gizmodo. Available at: https://gizmodo.com/why-russias-heroin-addicts-are-going-through-hell-1787892724.

Лейва, М. (2015). *Соратник Ройзмана из «Города без наркотиков» осужден на 4,5 года*. РБК. Available at: https://www.rbc.ru/society/09/04/2015/55267ec39a7947de3029b546.

Лушина, В. (2015). *Суд вынес приговор по громкому делу семьи Полухиных*. KP.RU – сайт «Комсомольской правды». Available at: https://www.msk.kp.ru/daily/26403/3278750/.

Luhn, A. (2016). *Why did Russia shut down its version of the DEA?* VICE News. Available at: https://news.vice.com/en_us/article/wjaak9/vladimir-putin-shut-down-russian-version-of-the-dea-fskn.

MacWilliam, I. (2005). *Pamirs adapt to life without Russia*. BBC News. Available at: http://news.bbc.co.uk/1/hi/world/asia-pacific/4284083.stm.

Markowitz, L.P. and Peshkova, V., 2016. *Anti-immigrant mobilization in Russia's regions: local movements and framing processes*. Post-Soviet Affairs, 32(3), pp.272-298.

Meduza.io. (2016). *Депутат убил пенсионерку ради квартиры Бывший соратник Евгения Ройзмана осужден на 16 лет колонии*. Available at: https://meduza.io/feature/2016/03/03/deputat-ubil-pensionerku-radi-kvartiry.

Mirovalev, M. (2015). *Life-destroying 'spice' drug engulfs Russia*. Aljazeera.com. Available at: https://www.aljazeera.com/indepth/features/2015/02/life-destroying-spice-drug-engulfs-russia-150219080536897.html.

Национальный Антинаркотический Союз. (n.d.). *Существуют ли безвредные наркотики? – Национальный Антинаркотический Союз*. Available at: https://nasrf.ru/articles/narkomaniya/sushhestvuyut-li-bezvrednye-narkotiki/.

Oakford, S. (2016). *How Russia Became the New Global Leader in the War on Drugs*. VICE News. https://news.vice.com/en_us/article/bjk3b4/how-russia-became-the-new-global-leader-in-the-war-on-drugs-ungass.

Orth, M. (2008). *Afghanistan's Deadly Habit*. Vanity Fair. https://www.vanityfair.com/news/2002/03/afghanistan200203?verso=true.

В. Панюшкин, 2014. *Ройзман: Уральский Робин Гуд*, Москва: Альпина Паблишер

Rotella, S. (2017). *Gangsters of the Mediterranean*. The Atlantic. https://www.theatlantic.com/international/archive/2017/11/russian-mob-mallorca-spain/545504/.

Родионова, А. and Брусникин, А. (2017). *Ройзман прошел через фильтр либералов.* Gazeta.Ru. https://www.gazeta.ru/politics/2017/06/21_a_10731677.shtml.

Ройзман Е. В., 2014. *Город без наркотиков.* Москва: Центрполиграф

Рождественский, И. (2018). *Чеченский транзит: как в республике с помощью пыток борются с наркоманами.* Republic.ru. https://republic.ru/posts/88870.

Recuero, M. (2018). *La Audiencia Nacional absuelve a las 17 personas del 'caso Troika' juzgadas por colaborar con la mafia rusa.* ELMUNDO. https://www.elmundo.es/espana/2018/10/18/5bc85a27e2704e4f8f8b46f3.html.

Sarang, A. (2012). *Interview with a man who just got out of the "City without Drugs" center.* Andrey Rylkov Foundation. http://en.rylkov-fond.org/blog/voices-from-russia/cwd-interview-2012/.

https://www.vice.com/sv/article/dpw8yy/kyrgyzstan-is-the-latest-victim-of-the-global-heroin-trade

Stephenson, S., 2015. *Gangs of Russia: from the streets to the corridors of power.* Cornell University Press.

Светова, З. (2016). *«Не знаком я с Путиным Владимиром Владимировичем».* [online] Openrussia.org. https://openrussia.org/media/704544/.

Thieves by Law. (2010). [film] Directed by A. Gentelev. Israel: Arte

Tyler, P. (2000). *Russian Vigilantes Fight Drug Dealers.* The New York Times. https://www.nytimes.com/2000/03/04/world/russian-vigilantes-fight-drug-dealers.html.

WikiLeaks. (2010). *SPAIN DETAILS ITS STRATEGY TO COMBAT THE RUSSIAN MAFIA.* [online] Available at: https://wikileaks.org/plusd/cables/10MADRID154_a.html. https://openrussia.org/media/704544/

The Golden Crescent

Armanios, F. and Ergene, B.A., 2018. *Halal Food: a History.* Oxford University Press.

Aikins, M., 2014. *Afghanistan: The Making of a Narco State.* Rolling Stone

Axworthy, M., 2013. *Revolutionary Iran: a history of the Islamic republic.* Oxford University Press.

BBC News. (2017). *Iran's drug addicts 'double in six years'.* https://www.bbc.co.uk/news/world-middle-east-40397727.

BBC News. (2014). *Iran Happy dancers given 91 lashes.* https://www.bbc.co.uk/news/world-middle-east-29272732.

Gharib, M. (2017). *They Dreamed Of Being Doctors. Now They Help Syrians With The Same Dream.* NPR. https://www.npr.org/sections/goatsandsoda/2017/07/05/532140694/medical-school-via-mobile-phone-for-some-syrians-it-s-a-growing-option?t=1553208242754.

Ghiabi, M., Maarefand, M., Bahari, H. and Alavi, Z., 2018. *Islam and cannabis: Legalisation and religious debate in Iran.* International Journal of Drug Policy, 56, pp.121-127.

Hafezi, P. (2014). *FEATURE-Moonshine is just a phone call away in Islamic Iran.* [online] Reuters. Available at: https://www.reuters.com/article/iran-alcohol/feature-moonshine-is-just-a-phone-call-away-in-islamic-iran-idUSL5N0LF1GK20140326.

InSight Crime. (2018). *Drug Trafficking Within the Venezuelan Regime: The 'Cartel of the Suns'.* https://www.insightcrime.org/investigations/drug-trafficking-venezuelan-regime-cartel-of-the-sun/.

Iran Human Rights. (2016). *Iran: Every single man in a village executed for drug offenses.* https://iranhr.net/en/articles/2456/.

Isaacs, M. (2016). *Smoking Opium in the Islamic Republic of Iran.* World Policy. https://worldpolicy.org/2016/09/15/smoking-opium-in-the-islamic-republic-of-iran/.

Khayyam, O. and Herron-Allen, E., 1898. *The Ruba'iyat of Omar Khayyām: Being a Facsimile of the Manuscript in the Bodleian Library at Oxford, with a Transcript Into Modern Persian Characters, Translated, with and Introd. and Notes, and a Bibliography, and Some Sidelights Upon Edward Fitzgerald's Poem.* LC Page.

Matthee, R.P., 2005. *The pursuit of pleasure: Drugs and stimulants in Iranian history, 1500-1900.* Princeton University Press.

McCoy, A. (2018). *How the heroin trade explains the US-UK failure in Afghanistan.* [online] the Guardian. Available at: https://www.theguardian.com/news/2018/jan/09/how-the-heroin-trade-explains-the-us-uk-failure-in-afghanistan.

Meyer, J. (2017). *The secret backstory of how Obama let Hezbollah off the hook.* POLITICO. https://www.politico.com/interactives/2017/obama-hezbollah-drug-trafficking-investigation/.

Namazi, M. (2014). *Iran's Alcoholics: Anonymous, Neglected & Stigmatized.* IranWire | مهرخانه. https://iranwire.com/en/features/524.

Nawa, F., 2011. *Opium Nation: Child Brides, Drug Lords, and One Woman's Journey Through Afghanistan.* Harper Perennial.

Nikpour, G., 2018. *Drugs and Drug Policy in the Islamic Republic of Iran.* Middle East Brief, (119), pp.1-8.

Risen, J. (2010). *Propping Up a Drug Lord, Then Arresting Him.* The New York Times. https://www.nytimes.com/2010/12/12/world/asia/12drugs.html.

Shah, S. (2011). *Snake country.* The Economist. https://www.economist.com/asia/2011/10/01/snake-country.

Killers and Karaoke

ABS-CBN News. (2017). *Duterte on Fentanyl use: Felt like cloud nine.* https://news.abs-cbn.com/news/02/10/17/duterte-on-fentanyl-use-felt-like-cloud-nine.

Aldama, Z. (2018). *How Rodrigo Duterte's war on drugs has become a war on the poor.* South China Morning Post. Available at: https://www.scmp.com/magazines/post-magazine/long-reads/article/2129538/how-philippines-war-drugs-has-become-war-poor.

Aljazeera.com. (2016). *Rodrigo Duterte: Shoot a drug dealer, get a medal.* https://www.aljazeera.com/news/2016/06/rodrigo-duterte-shoot-drug-dealer-medal-160605140900213.html.

Baldwin, C. and Marshall, A. (2017). *How a secretive police squad racked up kills in Duterte's drug war.* Reuters. https://www.reuters.com/investigates/special-report/philippines-drugs-squad/.

Berehulak, D. (2016). *'They Are Slaughtering Us Like Animals'.* The New York Times. https://www.nytimes.com/interactive/2016/12/07/world/asia/rodrigo-duterte-philippines-drugs-killings.html.

Bouckaert, P. and Human Rights Watch (Organization), 2017. *License to Kill: Philippine Police Killings in Duterte's" War on Drugs".* Human Rights Watch.

Buan, L. (2018). *Policemen guilty in Kian delos Santos killing.* Rappler. https://www.rappler.com/nation/217770-caloocan-policemen-convicted-murder-kian-delos-santos-killing.

Conde, C. (2009). *The Making of a Massacre in the Philippines.* The New York Times. https://www.nytimes.com/2009/12/11/world/asia/11iht-massacre.html.

Dallaire, R., 2009. *Shake hands with the devil: The failure of humanity in Rwanda.* Vintage Canada.

Hatton, C. (2015). *The Ketamine Connection – BBC News.* BBC News. https://www.bbc.co.uk/news/resources/idt-bc7d54e7-88f6-4026-9faa-2a36d3359bb0.

Human Rights Watch. (2018). *World Report 2018: Rights Trends in Philippines.* https://www.hrw.org/world-report/2018/country-chapters/philippines.

Inside the Gangsters Code – with Lou Ferrante: The Commandos. (2013). [DVD] Directed by P. Berczeller. United States: Discovery Channel.

Lamb, K. (2017). *Thousands dead: the Philippine president, the death squad allegations and a brutal drugs war.* the Guardian. https://www.theguardian.com/world/2017/apr/02/philippines-president-duterte-drugs-war-death-squads.

Lema, K. (2017). *Philippines' Duterte says police can kill 'idiots' who resist arrest.* Reuters. https://uk.reuters.com/article/uk-philippines-drugs/philippines-duterte-says-police-can-kill-idiots-who-resist-arrest-idUKKCN1B80D7.

ABS-CBN News. (2016). *MAP, CHARTS: The Death Toll of the War on Drugs.* https://news.abs-cbn.com/specials/map-charts-the-death-toll-of-the-war-on-drugs.

Miller, J. (2018). *Duterte Harry.* Brunswick, Victoria: Scribe Publications.

Murray, S. (2017). *Rodrigo Duterte stands accused of mass murder. So why do most Filipinos still love him?.* VICE News. https://news.vice.com/en_ca/article/434mm3/rodrigo-duterte-stands-accused-of-mass-murder-but-most-filipinos-still-love-him.

Narra, R. (2019). *Real Numbers PH: 5,104 drug suspects killed in Duterte's ongoing war on drugs.* The Manila Times Online. https://www.manilatimes.net/real-numbers-ph-5104-drug-suspects-killed-in-dutertes-ongoing-war-on-drugs/501924/.

Paddock, R.C., 2017. *Becoming Duterte: The Making of a Philippine Strongman.* The New York Times

Pulse Asia Research Inc. (2017). *September 2017 Nationwide Survey on the Campaign Against Illegal Drugs.* http://www.pulseasia.ph/september-2017-nationwide-survey-on-the-campaign-against-illegal-drugs/.

Simangan, D., 2018. *Is the Philippine "War on Drugs" an Act of Genocide?.* Journal of Genocide Research, 20(1), pp.68-89.

Talabong, R. (2017). *Except for killings, all crimes drop in Duterte's 1st year.* Rappler. https://www.rappler.com/nation/178494-crimes-killings-pnp-statistics-duterte-first-year.

The Guardian. (2016). *Philippines president Rodrigo Duterte urges people to kill drug addicts.* https://www.theguardian.com/world/2016/jul/01/philippines-president-rodrigo-duterte-urges-people-to-kill-drug-addicts.

Villamor, F. (2018). *Second Philippine Senator Who Defied Duterte Is Arrested.* The New York Times. https://www.nytimes.com/2018/09/25/world/asia/philippines-antonio-trillanes-duterte.html.

Cocaine *Cariocas*

Alves, L. (2017). *Brazil Has World's Third Largest Prison Population* The Rio Times. https://riotimesonline.com/brazil-news/rio-politics/brazil-has-worlds-third-largest-prison-population/.

Berntsson, J. (2016). *Gängkrigets oskyldiga offer i Göteborg.* Expressen.se. https://www.expressen.se/gt/gangkrigets-oskyldiga-offer-i-goteborg/.

Biller, D. (2018). *License-to-Kill Policing to Get a Trial Run in Rio de Janeiro*. Bloomberg. com. https://www.bloomberg.com/news/articles/2018-12-22/license-to-kill-policing-to-get-a-trial-run-in-rio-de-janeiro.

Bus 174. (2002). [DVD] Directed by J Padilha. Metrodome Distribution Limited.

Dalby, C. (2019). *Ceará Gang Truce Shows Brazil Government Could Be Common Enemy*. InSight Crime. https://www.insightcrime.org/news/brief/gang-truce-brazil-common-enemy/.

D'Agostino, R. (2015). *Com Lei de Drogas, presos por tráfico passam de 31 mil para 138 mil no país*. Globo. http://g1.globo.com/politica/noticia/2015/06/com-lei-de-drogas-presos-por-trafico-passam-de-31-mil-para-138-mil-no-pais.html.

Duffy, N. (2019). *Brazil's anti-gay President Jair Bolsonaro tweets golden shower video*. PinkNews. https://www.pinknews.co.uk/2019/03/07/brazil-anti-gay-president-jair-bolsonaro-tweets-golden-shower-video/.

Glenny, M., 2015. *Nemesis: One man and the battle for Rio*. House of Anansi.

Gudmundson, P. (2014). *55 "no go"-zoner i Sverige | SvD*. SvD.se. Available at: https://www.svd.se/55-no-go-zoner-i-sverige.

Hari, J. (n.d.). *The Myth Of The Place Where The War On Drugs Worked – Volteface*. Volteface. http://volteface.me/features/myth-place-war-drugs-worked/.

Human Rights Watch. (2018). *Brazil: Police Killings at Record High in Rio*. https://www.hrw.org/news/2018/12/19/brazil-police-killings-record-high-rio.

Human Rights Watch. 2015. *The state let evil take over: The prison crisis in the Brazilian state of Pernambuco*. New York: Human Rights Watch.

Kaiser, A. (2019). *'It's complete chaos': Brazilian state overwhelmed by rash of gang violence*. [online] the Guardian. Available at: https://www.theguardian.com/world/2019/jan/09/brazil-ceara-violence-fortaleza-gangs-bolsonaro

Langewiesche, W. (2008). *City of Fear*. Vanity Fair. https://www.vanityfair.com/news/2007/04/langewiesche200704?verso=true.

Londoño, E. and Andreoni, M. (2018). *'We'll Dig Graves': Brazil's New Leaders Vow to Kill Criminals*. The New York Times. https://www.nytimes.com/2018/11/01/world/americas/bolsonaro-police-kill-criminals.html.

Olliveira, C. and Eiras, Y. (2018). *Death of a Rio Cartel*. The Intercept. https://projects.theintercept.com/death-of-a-rio-cartel/.

PMERJ, 2017. *A Guerra Urbana não declarada no RJ e seus efeitos na PMERJ*

Scrutton, A. and von Hildebrand, E. (2015). *In a port city, grenade attacks shatter Swedish sense of safety*. Reuters. https://uk.reuters.com/article/uk-sweden-grenades-idUKKCN0QE09F20150809.

The Local. (2017). *So . . . are they no-go zones? What you need to know about Sweden's vulnerable areas*. https://www.thelocal.se/20170621/no-go-zones-what-you-need-to-know-about-swedens-vulnerable-aeas.

Old World, New Rules

Ferreira, S. (2017). *Portugal's radical drugs policy is working. Why hasn't the world copied it?*. the Guardian. https://www.theguardian.com/news/2017/dec/05/portugals-radical-drugs-policy-is-working-why-hasnt-the-world-copied-it.

Kristof, N., 2017. *How to win a war on drugs*. New York Times

Scheuermann, C. (2013). *Czeched Out: The Losers of Prague's Drug Liberalization – SPIEGEL ONLINE – International*. SPIEGEL http://www.spiegel.de/international

/europe/the-winners-and-losers-of-drug-liberalization-in-the-czech-republic-a-888618.html.

Tierney, A. (2017). *The Costa Rica Model: Why Decriminalization of Drug Use Sometimes Isn't Enough.* Vice. https://www.vice.com/en_ca/article/kbjvax/the-costa-rica-model-why-decriminalization-of-drug-use-sometimes-isnt-enough.

Free the Weed!

Bluestein, A. 2019. *How Canopy Growth became the Jolly Green Giant of cannabis.* Available from: https://www.fastcompany.com/90285740/how-canopy-growth-became-the-jolly-green-giant-of-cannabis

CBC News. 2018. *Weed supply low and NL stores running out, but pot plants can't grow any faster.* Available from: https://www.cbc.ca/news/canada/newfoundland-labrador/marijuana-shortage-newfoundland-labrador-1.4867441

CBC Radio. 2015. *Outside Looking In: Small Parties.* https://www.cbc.ca/radio/rewind/outside-looking-in-small-parties-1.3257368

Chafin, C. 2017. *Pot's Not Legal in Canada Yet – So Why Are Dispensaries Selling it?.* https://www.rollingstone.com/culture/culture-features/pots-not-legal-in-canada-yet-so-why-are-dispensaries-selling-it-128930/

Child, K. 2018. *The highest court has spoken: You are allowed to smoke – and grow – dagga at home.* https://www.timeslive.co.za/news/south-africa/2018-09-18-ban-on-private-use-of-dagga-at-home-is-ruled-unconstitutional/

Cooper, J. (2018). *California now world's 5th largest economy, surpassing UK.* USA Today. https://eu.usatoday.com/story/news/nation-now/2018/05/05/california-now-worlds-5th-largest-economy-beating-out-uk/583508002/.

Daly, M. (2017). *We Asked an Expert About Catalonia's Ground-Breaking New Weed Law.* [online] VICE. Available at: https://www.vice.com/amp/en_uk/article/qvpknx/we-asked-an-expert-about-catalonias-ground-breaking-new-weed-law.

Meissner, D. 2017. *Trudeau: Legalizing pot will take money from gangs.* https://www.ctvnews.ca/politics/trudeau-legalizing-pot-will-take-money-from-gangs-1.3308700

Feuer, A, 2014. *The Rise and Fall of the Biggest Pot Dealer in New York City History.* The New York Times

Graf, C. 2018. *How First Nations Are Dealing With Thriving, but Illegal, Cannabis Stores.* https://www.vice.com/en_ca/article/kzv54m/how-first-nations-are-dealing-with-thriving-but-illegal-cannabis-stores

Grund, J.P. and Breeksema, J., 2013. *Coffee shops and compromise: separated illicit drug markets in the Netherlands.* Open Society Foundation.

Hassan, A. (2018). *Michigan just voted to legalize weed. Here's where else in the world it's legal.* Quartz. https://qz.com/1453960/where-is-weed-legal-in-the-us-and-the-world/.

James, T. (2016). *The Failed Promise of Legal Pot.* The Atlantic. https://www.theatlantic.com/politics/archive/2016/05/legal-pot-and-the-black-market/481506/.

Kenning, C. (2018). *San Francisco to dismiss thousands of pot convictions.* [online] Reuters. Available at: https://www.reuters.com/article/us-san-francisco-marijuana/san-francisco-to-dismiss-thousands-of-pot-convictions-idUSKBN1FL3IT

Londoño, E., 2017. *Uruguay's Marijuana Law Turns Pharmacists Into Dealers.* The New York Times.

McDonell-Parry, A. 2018. *Did Mexico Just Legalize Pot?.* https://www.rollingstone.com/culture/culture-news/mexico-marijuana-legal-decriminalize-pot-weed-751030/

McGreevy, P. (2018). *A 'monumental moment' for fully legal marijuana in California*. LA Times. https://www.latimes.com/politics/la-pol-ca-pot-recreational-sales-20180101-story.html

Mithoefer, M.C., Wagner, M.T., Mithoefer, A.T., Jerome, L. and Doblin, R., 2011. *The safety and efficacy of±3, 4-methylenedioxymethamphetamine-assisted psychotherapy in subjects with chronic, treatment-resistant posttraumatic stress disorder: the first randomized controlled pilot study*. Journal of Psychopharmacology, 25(4), pp.439-452.

Peritz, I. 2007. *After years of near-extinction, the whacky Rhino party is back*. https://www.theglobeandmail.com/news/national/after-years-of-near-extinction-the-whacky-rhino-party-is-back/article18142763/

Politzer, M. (2016). *Barcelona's Pot Boom and Bust*. Reason.com. Available at: https://reason.com/archives/2016/02/18/barcelonas-pot-boom-and-bust

Pot By Province. https://potbyprovince.ca/

Reuters. (2014). *Legal weed no a-pot-calypse: Colorado governor*. https://www.reuters.com/video/2014/07/01/legal-weed-no-a-pot-calypse-colorado-gov?videoId=316630458

Romero, D. 2015. *Do Cops Think Ex-Crack King "Freeway" Ricky Ross Is a New Prince of Pot?*. https://www.laweekly.com/news/do-cops-think-ex-crack-king-freeway-ricky-ross-is-a-new-prince-of-pot-6214877

Rubino, J. (2018). *Colorado cracks a billion in annual marijuana sales in record time, generating $200M in tax revenue*. The Denver Post. https://www.denverpost.com/2018/10/18/colorado-cracks-billion-marijuana-sales-record/.

Schneider, S., 2017. *Canadian Organized Crime*. Canadian Scholars.

Snowdon, C., 2018. *Estimating the Size and Potential of the UK Cannabis Market*. Institute of Economic Affairs

Tremlett, G. (2019). *José Mujica: is this the world's most radical president?*. the Guardian. https://www.theguardian.com/world/2014/sep/18/-sp-is-this-worlds-most-radical-president-uruguay-jose-mujica

Uitermark, J., 2004. *The origins and future of the Dutch approach towards drugs*. Journal of Drug Issues, 34(3), pp.511-532.

YouTube. (2018). *Torontonians mark the legalization of cannabis*. https://www.youtube.com/watch?v=3Qs-bV7fuuo

The Panic in Needle Park

Adda, J., McConnell, B. and Rasul, I., 2014. *Crime and the depenalization of cannabis possession: Evidence from a policing experiment*. Journal of Political Economy, 122(5), pp.1130-1202.

Bean, P., 2014. *Drugs and crime*. Routledge.

Cheong, D. 2016. *'Drug situation is under control Why should we legalise drugs?': K Shanmugam*. https://www.straitstimes.com/singapore/drug-situation-is-under-control-why-should-we-legalise-drugs

Clifton, J. 2017. *How Colombia's Biggest Ever Cocaine Bust Will Affect the Coke Supply Worldwide*. https://www.vice.com/en_uk/article/evbqn7/how-colombias-biggest-ever-cocaine-bust-will-affect-the-coke-supply-worldwide

Cohen, R., 1992. *Amid Growing Crime, Zurich Closes a Park it Reserved for Drug Addicts*. The New York Times

Courtwright, D.T., 2009. *Dark paradise*. Harvard University Press.

Drug Policy Alliance, 2017. *An Overdose Death Is Not Murder: Why Drug-Induced Homicide Laws Are Counterproductive and Inhumane.*

Gentleman, A. 2017. *Huge cannabis farm 'was staffed by trafficked Vietnamese teenagers'.* https://www.theguardian.com/uk-news/2017/feb/24/huge-cannabis-farm-staffed-trafficked-vietnamese-teenagers

Gentleman, A. 2017. *Trafficked and enslaved: the teenagers tending UK cannabis farms.* https://www.theguardian.com/society/2017/mar/25/trafficked-enslaved-teenagers-tending-uk-cannabis-farms-vietnamese

Glazek, C., 2017. *The secretive family making billions from the Opioid Crisis.* Esquire

Higham, S. and Bernstein, L., 2017. *The drug industry's triumph over the DEA.* The Washington Post.

Katz, J., 2017. *Drug deaths in America are rising faster than ever.* The New York Times

Korte, G. 2018. *Trump pushes death penalty for drug dealers: 'It's not about being nice anymore'.* https://www.usatoday.com/story/news/politics/2018/03/19/trump-pushes-death-penalty-drug-dealers-new-hampshire-opioid-speech/438975002/

Lines, R. 2018. *Trump take note – why Singapore's claim that the death penalty works for drug offences is fake news.* http://theconversation.com/trump-take-note-why-singapores-claim-that-the-death-penalty-works-for-drug-offences-is-fake-news-92305

Lopez, G. 2017. *The new war on drugs.* https://www.vox.com/policy-and-politics/2017/9/5/16135848/drug-war-opioid-epidemic

Lopez, G. 2017. *When a drug epidemic's victims are white.* https://www.vox.com/identities/2017/4/4/15098746/opioid-heroin-epidemic-race

New, M., 1997. *Switzerland unwrapped: exposing the myths.* IB Tauris.

Pollack, H.A. and Reuter, P., 2014. *Does tougher enforcement make drugs more expensive?.* Addiction, 109(12), pp.1959-1966.

Quinones, S., 2015. *Dreamland: The true tale of America's opiate epidemic.* Bloomsbury Publishing USA.

Rolles, S. and McClure, C., 2009. *After the war on drugs: blueprint for regulation.* Transform Drug Policy Foundation.

Szalavitz, M. 2016. *Opioid Addiction Is a Huge Problem, but Pain Prescriptions Are Not the Cause.* https://blogs.scientificamerican.com/mind-guest-blog/opioid-addiction-is-a-huge-problem-but-pain-prescriptions-are-not-the-cause/

Transform Drug Policy Foundation, 2014. *Debating Drugs: How to Make the Case for Legal Regulation.*

United Nations Office on Drugs and Crime. *Cocaine and heroin prices.* https://www.unodc.org/unodc/secured/wdr/Cocaine_Heroin_Prices.pdf

Young, E. 2017. *Iceland knows how to stop teen substance abuse but the rest of the world isn't listening.* https://mosaicscience.com/story/iceland-prevent-teen-substance-abuse/

Epilogue

Антидзе, А. 2019. *Без палева.* https://lenta.ru/articles/2019/01/20/legalais/

Bergman, D. 2018. *Are Bangladesh activists being killed amid the war on drugs?.* https://www.aljazeera.com/indepth/features/bangladesh-activists-killed-war-drugs-180810083219446.html

Bram, B. 2018. *How techno became the sound of protest in Georgia.* https://www.dazeddigital.com/music/article/41340/1/inside-bassiani-tbilisi-georgia-techno-protests

Burns, E., Lehane, D., Pelecanos, G., Price, R. and Simon, D., 2008. *The Wire's War on the Drug War.* Time.

Cook, E. 2018. *Beware Indonesia's Quiet Drug War.* Available from: https://thediplomat. com/2018/01/beware-indonesias-quiet-drug-war/

Howe, J. 2013. *Murder on the Mekong.* https://magazine.atavist.com/ murderonthemekong

Lomsadze, G. 2018. *Georgia Protests: Nightlife against Nationalists.* https://eurasianet. org/georgia-protests-nightlife-against-nationalists

Mitra, P. 2019. *Sri Lanka, narcotics laws and death penalty: Another war on drugs?.* https: //qrius.com/sri-lanka-narcotics-laws-and-death-penalty-another-war-on-drugs/